Jack of Jumps

Jack of Jumps

DAVID SEABROOK

Granta Books
London

Granta Publications, 2/3 Hanover Yard, Noel Road, London N1 8BE

First published in Great Britain by Granta Books 2006

A CIP catalogue record for this book
is available from the British Library.

1 3 5 7 9 10 8 6 4 2

ISBN-13: 978-1-86207-770-6
ISBN-10: 1-86207-770-3

Typeset by M Rules
Printed and bound in Great Britain by
William Clowes Limited, Beccles, Suffolk

Contents

For David Foulser and Anthony Frewin

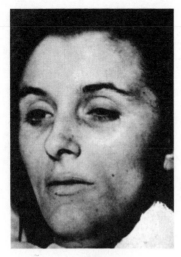

1959
ELIZABETH FIGG
Also known as
Ann Phillips

1963
GWYNNETH REES
Also known as
Tina Smart

1964
HELENE BARTHELEMY
Also known as
Helen Paul and 'Teddy'

1964
MARY FLEMING

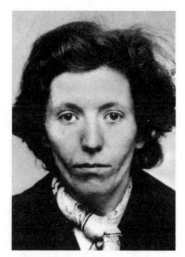

1964
HANNAH TAILFORD
Also known as
Terry Lynch

1964
IRENE LOCKWOOD
Also known as
Sandra Russell

1964
FRANCES BROWN
Also known as
Margaret McGowan

1965
BRIDGET 'BRIDIE'
O'HARA

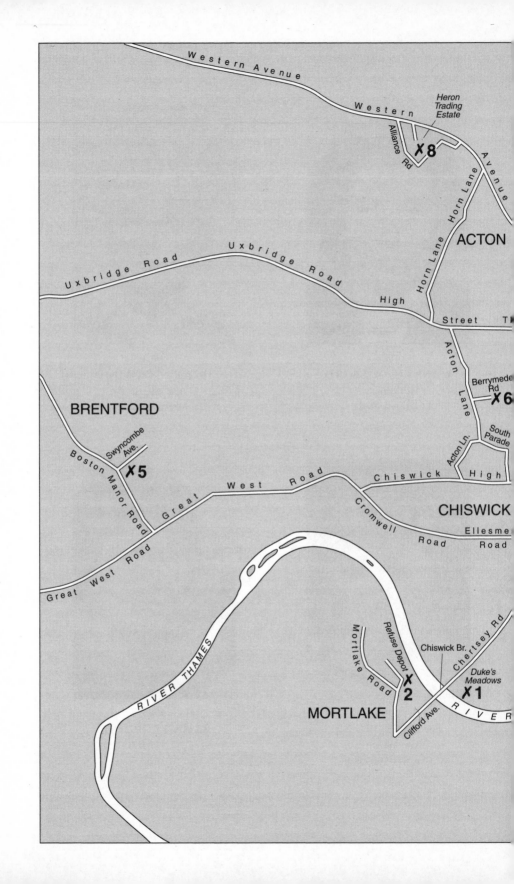

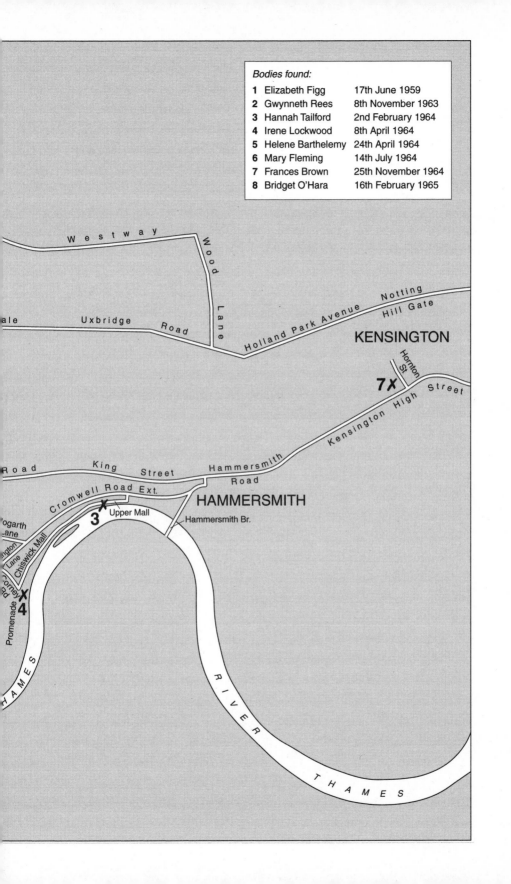

Bodies found:

1 Elizabeth Figg   17th June 1959
2 Gwynneth Rees   8th November 1963
3 Hannah Tailford   2nd February 1964
4 Irene Lockwood   8th April 1964
5 Helene Barthelemy   24th April 1964
6 Mary Fleming   14th July 1964
7 Frances Brown   25th November 1964
8 Bridget O'Hara   16th February 1965

Groundwork

Good health . . .

I drain my glass.

One more in the Ship, I suppose, looking through a leaky window at sheets of rain on the river. Standing in my coat and scarf in this empty pub.

A lone rower struggles into view. I see imitation oil lamps, near – graspable, reflected just above him.

Here comes the barman.

It's only shandy I'm drinking, nothing exciting. As soon as the rain stops I'm off. But while I'm here I can't help wondering when exactly the Ship picks up. Evenings? Weekends? Boat Race day?

On the far side of the river, close by Chiswick Bridge, stands the finishing post; on this side a warning: 'This area is liable to sudden flooding. Parked vehicles are liable to be partially submerged.'

I try to imagine hampers and cheers.

Poplars line the opposite bank, and beyond them it's Duke's Meadows.

Back in the Fifties, under cover of darkness – *real* darkness – Duke's Meadows was the ideal spot for couples eager to test their car springs. You could drive down there any evening and catch them at it like rabbits in your headlights: listen hard and you could hear the whole beastly business.

And yet even in the dark there were certain things which certain girls said no to, so now and again some men would splash out on a lady of the night.

Duke's Meadows.

They called it 'Gobblers Gulch'.

For some reason, probably a shortage of staff at Chiswick police station, no uniform officer was posted to the beat covering Duke's Meadows on the night of 16/17 June 1959. Instead this area was covered by F Division team police car F4, which contained PC Mills (driver), PC Sparke (radio operator) and PC Baker (acting team sergeant).

'At approximately 12.30am,' Baker recalled, '. . . I patrolled the road running through Riverside Lands, Chiswick W4. There were a number of vehicles stationary in the area, as is usual. Nothing unusual occurred and we left the area at 12.45am approximately.'

At 5.10am the police car was making a second patrol along the road beside the river bank when PC Mills noticed a pair of bare legs sticking out from behind a small willow tree. He stopped the car and got out.

The tree stood about halfway between the road and the river bank at a point 200 yards west of Barnes Bridge. Beneath it, on rough grass, lay the body of a young woman, her feet towards the river.

Her eyes and mouth were open, as was her dark blue and white striped dress, revealing her breasts and some scratches on her throat. ('She was quite cold and obviously dead. I . . . immediately suspected foul play.') She was lying on her back with her head turned slightly to the right, her right foot crossed over her left, her left hand extended and her right hand slightly bent over her hip. The dress was torn horizontally at the waist (there were loopholes for a belt but no belt was present) and was up just over her knees, exposing a white cotton slip. She wore no paint, no jewellery, no shoes.

Who was she?

PC Sparke radioed for the duty officer and a few minutes later Inspector Edwards arrived and examined the body. He arranged for immediate assistance, and within the hour the riverside land between Chiswick Bridge and Barnes Bridge was sealed off. At 7am a temporary shelter made of corrugated-iron sheeting was erected around the body.

At 7.30am pathologist Dr Donald Teare turned up to make his preliminary examination. He noted the marks on her throat, suggestive of manual strangulation, and the beginnings of rigor mortis in her arms and legs. The atmospheric temperature was 65°F and the vaginal temperature was 90°F, indicating that she had been dead for several hours. Teare later estimated that she had died some time between midnight and 2am.

At 8.15am Detective Sergeant McMacken took three photographs of her lying in the grass. And then, while CID and uniform officers began to search the vicinity (which yielded two cigarette ends, a used condom and no surprises) her body was conveyed to Acton mortuary, where, at 9.45am, Teare performed the post-mortem.

She measured 5′–5′ ½″ and weighed 8½ stone. Her feet were dirty and there were small scattered abrasions on her legs. A small patch of lipstick on her upper lip was the only indication that she used cosmetics. Her stomach contained approximately four ounces of undigested food in which peas and fatty material were distinguishable. Her stomach also contained an active gastric ulcer just under 1″ in diameter but this did not affect her general health.

A series of abrasions covered an area 1½″ wide and 1¼″ long on the front of the throat and appeared to have been caused by the victim's fingernails as she struggled with her attacker. But that's as straightforward as it gets; there were other abrasions on her body and we can only speculate – as the pathologist did not – about what might have caused them

There was a single abrasion, ⅜″ long by a maximum of ⅛″ wide, on the inner aspect of the right collarbone which may have been caused by a ring: an ill-fitting ring, perhaps, such as might belong to a newlywed man. In the lower part of this area there were two abrasions, each ¼″ long, running vertically and ⅜″ apart, just to the right of the midline, and to the left of the midline were two less obvious abrasions ¼″ long and ½″ apart, running obliquely. Immediately above this area was an area of blushing of the skin. (Teare believed this was caused by pressure.) The upper part of this area contained an abrasion ½″ long, running horizontally ½″ to the left of the midline, and an abrasion ¼″ long, running horizontally immediately to the right of the midline. Might these three pairs of abrasions have been caused by a single pair of cufflinks?

Was she with this person?

Why was she with this person?

Who was she?

Nobody knew. There was nothing on her body by which she could be identified and her fingerprints weren't on file at Scotland Yard.

A message went out to all stations:

Dead body of woman found on bank of Thames at Chiswick at 5am today, 17.6.59. Age about 25, height 5ft 2 inches, slim build, hair dark brown, eyes light brown, teeth discoloured, tooth on left upper jaw recently extracted, two teeth on right side upper jaw missing. Small circular scar below knee on each leg. Faint scar on right knee.

Dressed in summer dress, black and white narrow stripes, white underskirt, no shoes. Please have missing persons register searched to identify.

They didn't get her height right, or the stripes on her dress. Still, some quibbles are more important than others.

According to the constables who discovered her body, she was lying in the grass beneath the willow tree, yet Arthur Phillips, a detective constable present at the scene later that morning, remembers differently.

'I'd swear on a stack of Bibles . . . she was sitting against the tree, looking out over the river, quite relaxed. It was just as if she was sitting down having a rest there. If it had been later on in the morning you'd have probably walked by there and said, "Oh, she's sunbathing" or something. She looked so natural. A plain sort of girl, you know. Not beautiful or anything. Working-class girl.'

Against the tree? But according to —

'Someone had put her there. She was sitting against the tree, quite peaceful, looking across at that pub, the Ship, and the brewery.'

Someone had put her there . . . But who? The crew of F4?

'No. I'm telling you there's no way they would have moved that body. They wouldn't have *dared*. I knew Mills — and Sparke. Little ginger-haired fellow. I didn't know Baker.'

Who then? Donald Teare?

'Teare would have been the only person with the authority to move the body. Those pathologists were a law unto themselves, you know.'

But why would he move her?

'You know, I've been racking my brains . . . there's something bloody funny here. I can see her now . . . she was my first murder. That's why I remember her.'

That afternoon he and DS McMacken visited Acton mortuary. McMacken was to take a fourth photograph of the woman for circulation to the London press with a view to establishing her identity. 'And I had to get her ready. A hell of a job I had. I was trying everything I could to get her eyes to stay open.'

Eventually, her eyes propped open with pieces of matchstick, she was ready to face the world.

'Two days after Elizabeth Figg was found, this couple turned up at Chiswick police station and asked to see the body. It was late at night and I had to go and fetch the keys to Acton mortuary and drive them there – me and Jim Mitchell, who was the detective superintendent in charge of the case. A very dour Scotsman, but a lovely man, always very calm. "Gentleman Jim", we used to call him.

'We got there about midnight. There weren't any lights on and I couldn't find the light switch at first (there were no windows, you know).

'Anyway, I'd told the mortuary keeper to leave her in the bottom drawer. But when I got there there was somebody else in the bottom drawer, and in the second drawer there was somebody else, and I found her in the third one up, the top one. And I didn't know what to bloody do. I didn't know how to get her out.'

In the room was a trolley. When the trolley was wound up to the required height the drawer could be slid out.

'But I never knew that. I never knew you could do that with the trolley. So I thought, "I'm going to have to lift her out myself." Jim Mitchell was waiting outside the door with this couple, and so I shouted out to him, "Chief! Do you think you could come in here and give us a hand?" But he said, "No, you're all right, Taff. I'm just taking a statement from this couple." He wouldn't come. He didn't like dead bodies, see.'

The detective constable eventually managed to lift her out of the drawer onto the trolley. For modesty's sake he took out his pocket handkerchief and draped it, like a fig leaf, over her genitals. ('I threw it away afterwards, mind.')

Elsie King (née Mort) and her husband, George, now entered the room. Mrs King identified the body as that of her daughter Elizabeth;

after which they all trooped out and left her lying there on the trolley.

'And in the morning the mortuary keeper rang me and gave me a roasting for leaving the body out. And I gave him a roasting back. I said, "I told you to leave her at the bottom so I could get her." And then he explained about how I should have wound the trolley up and I said, "Oh, I didn't realize that." He said, "Well, don't bloody do it again – and leave my bodies alone." They're very proud people, mortuary keepers. They bloody well are.

'And on top of everything I didn't get back home till three or four in the morning. When I told my wife what I'd been doing she said, "Don't come near me – and get that suit cleaned."'

Elizabeth Figg was born in Bebington, Cheshire, on 24 March 1938, the second daughter of James Figg, a commercial traveller, and his wife, Elsie. The family lived together in Bromborough, Cheshire, until February 1941, when James Figg joined the RAF. In the autumn he was posted to Canada to complete his training as a ferry pilot, and did not return home until June 1942. Upon discovering that Elsie had been unfaithful in his absence, he instigated divorce proceedings and almost immediately returned to Canada. Elsie Figg left Cheshire for Crewe, but her daughters Patricia (who was born in 1936) and Elizabeth remained in the area, moving in with James's mother in Bebington.

In July 1943 James Figg returned to England, where he continued his career as a pilot. However, in November he spent several months in hospital following a crash, and was subsequently grounded. He went to live with his mother and his children and applied for a posting nearby. In March 1946 he was demobilized. He was now divorced, and in November he remarried – just in time. A daughter, Pamela, was born in December.

The following year Patricia and Elizabeth joined their father and his new wife, Florence, in Rhyl, North Wales, where they had rented a house. In December 1948 another daughter, Susan, was born, and according to Florence Figg all was well until 1950, when her husband received a legacy from an aunt. He and his adolescent daughters left her and went to live with another woman.

'Six weeks later he contacted me and asked if he could return to live with me. By this time I had my own two children, and for their sake I agreed that he could return.'

He did so, bringing Patricia and Elizabeth – who was known to the family as 'Bobby' – with him. But in 1953 the family was evicted from the house in Rhyl and James Figg received a conviction for assaulting a county court bailiff.

He didn't like Bobby much, either.

'As Bobby grew older she began to stand up to her father, and trouble developed between them frequently, and they began to hate each other. Her father had no time for her at all and used to tell her that she was a filthy slut, just like her mother, and at other times he would say the most disgusting things to her and use filthy language. Every time there was any trouble he would tell Bobby to leave home.'

Home was now back in Cheshire and in the summer of 1954 she left it to work at the Belvedere Hotel in Colwyn Bay. Here she began a relationship with a young motor mechanic, Thomas Jones. (He remembered her as immature 'but of a very generous nature'.)

Did she remain at Colwyn Bay after the season ended? Her movements for the rest of that year and part of the next are unknown. However, in August 1955 she visited her mother, having traced her to an address in south-west London. They hadn't seen each other since 1944 and Elsie Figg was now Elsie King, wife of George King, a heating engineer. Elizabeth stayed with them and worked as an assistant selling groceries and provisions at a shop in Wilcox Road.

But she and her mother soon began to row, and at Christmas Elsie told Elizabeth to get out. She moved in with a friend, Patricia Lee, on New Year's Eve.

In May 1956 she left London for Cheshire, where she stayed with Florence, Figgless once more (another windfall, another woman) and bringing up Pamela and Susan on her own. A week later she was back at the Belvedere, and that summer, for whatever reason, the relationship with Thomas Jones ended and another affair began to blossom. Theresa Lee, a waitress who worked with Figg that summer, recalled talk of marriage to a man named Sidney Carruthers, whom Figg had met when living in Cheshire.

At the end of October, the season over, Elizabeth Figg stayed with Theresa Lee at her flat in Liverpool, yet after about six weeks she announced that she was returning to London. She told her friend that she had received a letter from a man who had offered to look after her and find her a job as a cashier, and Lee borrowed £5 for her to help her on her way.

Figg's potential benefactor was Sidney Carruthers. On a visit to her stepmother she explained that he'd just come out of prison and wanted her to join him in London.

Well, he sent the fare but that seems to have been the extent of his assistance. Carruthers soon disappeared (possibly from public view) and Figg fell back on a window cleaner named George Harvey.

Harvey had first met her earlier in the year when she was living with Patricia Lee and her mother in a block of flats off Wandsworth Road. Lee's mother was the mother-in-law of his friend George Cooper, and Cooper agreed to play matchmaker, with the result that Harvey and Figg went out together, usually to the cinema, for about two months, and corresponded after she left London. According to Patricia Lee, Harvey seemed very fond of the girl 'but I don't think she wanted him'.

Still, money, any man's money, spends, and when Figg returned to London towards the end of 1956 George Harvey made life easy for a while. He arranged for her to live with George Cooper and his wife, Jean, at their house in Lambeth. He resumed his doomed courtship and began to take her out to the pictures again in the evenings. What else did he do? 'When she came back from Liverpool she was run down and I used to give Georgie some money each week for her keep.' But he was no mug. 'I realized she was not making any effort to work and I stopped paying for her keep. Although I still used to go round to Georgie's place whilst Betty was still there, we sort of drifted apart and I did not take her out any more.'

Betty was beginning to push her luck. She got a job as a cleaner at the American Embassy in Grosvenor Square yet continued to live at the Coopers' address without paying. Moreover she told a work colleague, Frances Phillips, that George Cooper had made advances to her. But Frances Phillips was Jean Cooper's sister and suddenly it was time to move on.

Her next known address is 18 Alderbert Terrace, where, in April 1957, she rented a room from a Trinidadian landlord, Camelo Francois, yet left after about ten days. She was out of work again and before she left she asked Francois whether he wanted any cleaning done. 'I told her she could come back each Saturday morning and clean my hallway for me, and I would pay her 7/ 6d for this.' But she took the money without doing the job and when he found out he sacked her.

She was now living with Phyllis Brown, her husband and their six children at Corfe House, a block of council flats in Dorset Road, SW8. Brown, who lived at No. 46, had a slight acquaintance with Figg through Frances Phillips at No. 54, and took her in for 25s per week. As a lodger she was quiet and well behaved ('All the time she was with me she hardly went out but would sit indoors nearly every night reading') and the only difficulty lay in extracting the rent from her. Yet this time when she was told to leave she didn't have to move very far, thanks to Kathleen Donlon at No. 52.

A deal was struck whereby no money changed hands. 'Betty did not go out to work whilst she was with me and she stayed at home looking after my baby whilst I was engaged on night work.' She was good with children but the arrangement didn't last. Donlon claimed that she left of her own accord, but Figg told her next landlady, Frances Phillips, that she'd been locked out.

Phillips had left Corfe House and was now living at 18 Ariel Court, Opal Street. Figg joined her there in the early summer of 1958 and continued her rent-free existence by acting as babysitter to the three children.

Phillips found her a needy creature, always looking for sympathy. 'I am sure she thought she was suffering from some illness, and when she had small pains she always made a lot of it and imagined she was seriously ill.' Yet like the paranoiac with flesh-and-blood enemies, Elizabeth Figg was a hypochondriac with genuine complaints such as boils on her legs and problems with her eyes (double vision, according to her mother) and teeth. (The problems with her teeth persisted to the end of her life. On 11 June 1959 she visited the Royal Dental Hospital in Leicester Square and had two extractions.)

However, she appeared more settled, and 1958 passed peacefully enough. There were no changes of address, no boyfriends on the scene – although George Harvey was hanging around again, and having the same luck as before: 'She was not too keen on him, saying he was not her type.'

But after Christmas she found her type, and in a long letter dated 19 March 1959 she told Florence Figg her news:

> I dont know how you are going to feel about my news. But be straight with me & let me know O.K. Well some time ago I decided to go to the Dental Hosp. in Leister Square. On my way at the tube station I knocked a chap down the esculator & we got talking & made a date etc. But first let me tell you he is coloured. He is from Trinidad a pro-boxer & in the money. He is a very nice chap clean & smart & all that I was only taking him for a mug a first & then I got to like him a lot mind you Im being talked about by my mates family etc . . . You see Flo the real trouble is my mate (where I am now) Has started on regular night work & that means I have the kids all day long and 6 nights a week. Well I left Mrs Donlon for that reason I can feel myself getting very miserable etc. I reacen it is too much. I would walk out and go to Fen only I wouldnt feel secure just living with him like that. Only Id never want as he gets hundreds of £ each time he wins a fight . . .

Did you hear that, George Harvey? You can watch the double feature on your own from now on.

And as for −

> By the way Syd got done for stabbing a bloke. He found out I was going out with him whilst he was inside. (Syd was only out a week). His case comes up MAY 28 they say hell get 7 years. Well I wrote and told him I was finished. But all the same remember the date & look in the L' Echo.

The *Liverpool Echo* neglected to report the trial − but so what? Sid was history.

Fen was the future.

And everybody else could say what they liked.

Some time in April 1959 Elizabeth Figg left 18 Ariel Court − only it wasn't quite as straightforward as that. Frances Phillips remembered the tale.

'On the particular night she had been out and got back in the early hours of the morning and said she could not get in. This was not so, because the key to the flat door had been left just inside the toilet window and Betty knew where to find it. Betty left me a note through the letter box saying she was going to sit in the lift for a time and then go elsewhere.'

But where?

In a letter of 4 May headed 'Dont worry if you dont get a letter for months' she told Florence Figg

not to write to me anymore at this address. Wait until you receive a letter from me . . . I am sorry this is scribble only I am writting this at Fen's flat & we have a few friends up here & a party just warming up . . . Also Fen has a constract for 6 months tour of the continent & we will be going soon but the exact date has not be fixed yet. We are going to see his manegar on Tues all being O.K.

In a spare moment Fen arranged, through his Trinidadian friend Barton Boyce, for Figg (who seems to have been staying at an address in Camden Town) to rent a furnished room at 97 Duncombe Road, Archway.

There were no kids to look after.

The rent was £2 8s per week.

Cash money.

Yes, Elizabeth Figg had finally entered the real world.

She was a prostitute now and Fenwick Joseph 'Baby' Ward was her ponce.

Figg was a street-girl. She worked Bayswater Road, and also Holland Park, which is where, in March 1959, she met a young East Ender, a plain fat girl named Pauline Mills, who, at the age of nineteen, had thirty-three convictions for soliciting.

Mills became friendly with Figg, whom she knew as Ann Phillips (Frances's middle name), and a couple of months later accepted her invitation to share the room, and the rent, at Duncombe Road. 'After we lived together we both went soliciting in the Haringey district. I had never been there before. We usually went to Haringey before midnight and to Holland Park Avenue afterwards. We never took clients back home.'

The only visitors to their first-floor room were Ward and his West Indian friend and fellow boxer Raymond Reefer, who was Mills's boyfriend/ponce. Barton Boyce was resident on the ground floor and could keep a watchful eye in their absence.

On the afternoon of Tuesday 16 June both women were in bed in their room when Ward and Reefer arrived shortly after 3pm. Ward handed Figg a box containing a summer dress he'd had made for her; the pattern was blue and white stripes and there was a white under-skirt attached. Figg went to the bathroom to put it on.

When she returned she complained of pains in her chest, so Ward sent her out to see a doctor. She came home about an hour later and, without mentioning where she'd been, said that the queue was too long.

Ward asked her to go out with him.

Mills asked where they were going.

'I knew that she was going soliciting. Baby said, "You won't see her because she is going out on her own." Out of Baby's hearing Ann told me she was going to Haringey and then Holland Park and I said I would see her.'

Ward wanted Figg to work alone, for when she and Mills went out together they wasted time, larked about; and in his view his woman should be earning at least £6 per night. However, before he escorted her off the premises it was arranged that all four should meet back there at 4am. ('We sometimes made this arrangement and would go out to a cafe or a club.')

According to Mills, Figg was wearing her new dress, and beneath it a bra with foam padding and a pair of loose-legged white nylon knickers. She wore no make-up, no jewellery and no stockings. On her feet were a pair of imitation leather shoes – originally white yet dyed black three days previously – with steel-tipped stiletto heels.

She was carrying a small white imitation leather or plastic envelope bag shaped like a purse. This bag contained a Goya compact with the top off and the puff missing; a small maroon autograph book; a bunch of keys on a ring; and probably condoms, in a blue and white box.

Peter Turner, the proprietor of the Rainbow Cafe in Elthorne Road, adjacent to Duncombe Road, recalled that at about 4.45pm on 16 June 1959 a black man, 'about one of the biggest built men I have seen', entered, accompanied by a white woman wearing a blue and white striped dress which looked brand new. She ordered sausages, chips and peas, and he ordered apricots and ice cream, and they washed down their food with two small bottles of Tizer. Turner noticed that they hardly spoke to each other; the man was humming songs all the time. 'They stopped in the cafe until about 5.15pm to 5.25pm. Before they went the coloured man paid me with a £5 note. The bill would have come to 3/ 10d.' Flash. 'When I gave him his change I said, "Thank you very much" and "Goodnight", but he just took his change and didn't say a word.'

The Rainbow sounds like a nice place, doesn't it? All colours served there, cheap filling fare, courtesy and civility. . .

And yet Peter Turner's words are just a little bit unsettling. According to him, the couple entered the cafe at about 4.45pm and stayed for thirty to forty minutes; they couldn't have stayed much later because he closed at 6pm prompt every day. Pauline Mills stated that Ward and Reefer entered the bedroom at about 3pm and Ward and Figg left the room – and presumably the house – just before 5pm.

But Reefer stated that he was already present at the address when Ward turned up, and Ward claimed that he arrived at about 6pm and left with Figg at about 7.50pm. (Figg's landlord, Roger Craig, a middle-aged Ghanaian accountancy student, saw Figg leave the house *alone* between 7pm and 7.30pm, in which case Ward was either waiting outside for her or he was best not mentioned.) He stated that upon leaving the cafe they visited a nearby pub, where he had a lager and Figg had a tomato juice. He then accompanied her to the bus stop near her home, as she intended to visit the seamstress at Stamford Hill to have another dress made.

Ward's story does not correspond with the times put forward by Turner; some two hours remain unaccounted for. She was next seen alighting from a trolley bus at Stamford Hill between 8.30pm and 9pm. Byron Gilchrist, a West Indian boxer who lived at the same address as Ward, got off at this stop and spoke to her briefly. She told him that she was going to Durley Road to see Mrs Simmons about a dress and that she was a little bit late. She had a pain in her chest, she said, and every time she breathed it stifled her.

According to Eileen Simmons, Figg arrived at 6 Durley Road at 8.30pm. She had previously visited her in the company of Ward to be measured for the dress she was now wearing; Ward had bought the

Thursday, June 18, 1959

THE STAR

No 22,895 ** 2½d

CLOSING CITY PRICES

LATE NIGHT

MURDERED GIRL: YARD ISSUE PICTURE

The Queen flies off: Plane is diverted

The Queen and the Duke of Edinburgh waving goodbye as they left London Airport this afternoon to begin their 45-day tour of Canada. Owing to bad weather at Torbay, Newfoundland, which was their intended destination, the Comet was re-routed to the U.S. air base Argentia, 80 miles away. BOAC said a decision would be taken in mid-Atlantic whether the aircraft would land there or touch down at Seven Islands, Quebec Province.
Story: Page Ten. Queen Mother and Princess Margaret's Farewell: pictures Pages Ten and Eleven.

Do you know this Miss X?

ON THE RIGHT YOU SEE MISS X, THE GIRL FOUND STRANGLED BY THE THAMES TOWPATH AT CHISWICK.

Tonight, 36 hours after she was found, the riddle of her name is still unsolved.

So Scotland Yard have issued her picture—and this appeal: Do you know her?

Anyone who does is asked to get in touch with the Yard or the nearest police station.

The photograph is being sent to police stations all over Britain.

Hunt held up

If this move fails to solve the riddle of the girl's identity, the Yard will send despatch a diagram of her mouth, showing dental treatment she had received.

"The work of finding the killer cannot begin until police knew who the girl was.

Reports of missing women aged between 25 and 30 have been pouring into Chiswick police station, the murder headquarters.

About ten people have been taken to Acton mortuary but have failed to identify the dead girl.

Detectives are almost certain that the girl was murdered in

CONTINUED ON PAGE TWO

Bardot married —today

BRIGITTE BARDOT and Jacques Charrier were married today at Louveciennes, near Paris. For a week they had been giving "Yes" and "No" replies to rumours they had already married in secret.

Brigitte, who wore a pink dress with a deep plunging neckline, wept when photographers broke in the door of the Town Hall and forced their way to the wedding room.

The bride and groom had done everything possible to throw reporters off the scent. Until last night they were on holiday at St Tropez, on the Riviera.

But rumours of the marriage leaked out just in time for a small crowd, mainly of villagers, to gather at the Town Hall.

Charrier was the actress's leading man in the film Babette Goes to War.

Both are 23. It was her second marriage and his first.

Mabel takes over

Wilfred Pickles has been taken ill and is in a London nursing home. His wife, Mabel, takes over his part in a radio show tonight.

SUNNY

Forecast tread 6 am tomorrow until midnight: Wind E.rth. Dry with sunny periods. Average temperature. Outlook: Probably dry.

Lights on 9 39

TV & radio—page 17

What did Billy Graham see? ask MPs

Star Reporter

BILLY GRAHAM, the American evangelist, was criticised in the Commons this evening for his remarks about behaviour in London parks.

Mr Marcus Lipton (Lab, Brixton) asked the Home Secretary what complaints he had received.

Mr Butler said he received complaints from time to time about the behaviour of prostitutes in Hyde Park.

Everything possible was being done to deal with them and he hoped the police would be able to act more effectively when the new Street Offences Bill becomes law.

Complaints about the behaviour of the public generally were a matter for the Minister of Works.

Mr Butler replied that in the past three months there had been 528 prosecutions for soliciting and indecent and insulting behaviour in Hyde Park alone.

Mr Lipton: But is the Home Secretary aware that according to Mr Billy Graham and others —(Labour shouts: "Who is Billy Graham")—sexual intercourse in the parks takes place in daylight in full view of passers-by?

'A blot'

"If this is going on is there not a duty for the Home Secretary to deal with this blot on the fair name of London?" he asked.

"Why don't they use their influence about what goes on in the U.S.?"

Mr Butler: I admire the patriotism of your observations.

INDIA 144 FOR 4

INDIA
P R Roy c Evans b Statham	15
N J Contractor not out	64
P R Umrigar b Statham	1
V L Manjrekar lbw b Trueman	12
G S Gherpade lbw b Greenhough	41
Extras	11
Total (4 wkts)	**144**

FALL OF WICKETS: 1—32, 2—48, 3—81, 4—144.

TO BAT: A C Kripal-Singh, M L Jaisimha, R G Joshi, Surendra Nath, S P Gupte, N S Desai.

ENGLAND: C A Milton, K Taylor, M C Cowdrey, P B H May, K F Barrington, M J Horton, T G Evans, F S Trueman, J B Statham, A S Nute, T Greenhough.

L. N. BAILEY'S REPORT ON PAGE 15.

material and paid 25s for labour. On this second occasion the black seamstress told her that she would make another dress from a piece of material she had and that 'it was to be a gift from me to her'.

Figg mentioned stomach pains (which were probably caused by her ulcer). She chose a fashion from a book and left at about 9.30pm with the intention of catching a trolley bus to Commercial Road. She was going 'Aldgate way'.

Aldgate way? Well, that wasn't unusual. Both Mills and Figg liked to while away the hours in all-night cafes in the East End. Handy pick-up points, perhaps, although the girls never put themselves out: their attitude to work was nothing if not relaxed.

So did Elizabeth Figg make any money that night? Did she graft?

She didn't return to 97 Duncombe Road. Pauline Mills was alone in the bedroom the following morning when Ward and Reefer entered shortly after 4am. Ward asked where Betty was. She didn't know, hadn't seen her. Ward said nothing and went downstairs to Barton Boyce's room while Reefer explained.

They'd picked up two Scottish girls in a snack bar in Euston, and these girls were waiting outside in a car driven by Baby's friend Ken. Reefer told her that one was for Baby and one was for Ken. Mills wanted to go and have a look but he wouldn't let her.

The two men were soon on the move again. ('I think that Baby only came there to see whether Ann was there and to get some money from her if possible.') Mills went to bed and slept until about midday, when 'I vaguely remember waking up momentarily and seeing Baby looking into the room from the door.'

She didn't see him again until the following afternoon. Reefer had telephoned her to tell her to stay put and at about 4pm the two boxers arrived at the house in a taxi. They entered her bedroom and showed her a copy of the *Star* newspaper: its front page featured a photograph of an unidentified girl found murdered at Duke's Meadows. Mills – who was wondering where Figg was and had toured Bayswater Road and Holland Park Avenue several times the previous evening in a friend's car – recognized the photograph immediately.

'I said that it was Ann and Baby said, "Do you want to get involved in this?" I said, "There is nothing else I can do." He asked me not to tell the police that he had been poncing on her and that he had not been at Duncombe Road since Sunday. He asked me not to mention him to police but just to say that she had a boyfriend. I must have looked at him queerly because he said, "I never murdered her. You know that, don't you, but a coloured man has got no chance in this country."'

As soon as Ward and Reefer had left Pauline Mills telephoned the police. At 9.45pm that day, Thursday 18 June, at Acton mortuary she identified the body of the woman she knew as Ann Phillips. (Figg's mother, Elsie King, made her identification the following day.)

Meanwhile, Baby was a worried man. Individuals express their grief in different ways, and Ward chose to run around London reminding friends and acquaintances, men such as 'Ken' and 'Pick' and 'Red Box', where he was and what he was doing on the night of 16 June. He was anxious, edgy, not himself at all.

But he needn't have fretted, for it wasn't very long before somebody far more attractive came crawling out of the undergrowth.

This man was a builder and decorator. He often picked up prostitutes and on the night of 16 June he did business with Elizabeth Figg. Unfortunately for him, he was the last person known to have seen her alive.

At 11.45pm on 16 June Ernest Patrick Forrest drove his 1939 black Morris Ten along Endymion Road, parallel with Finsbury Park, and pulled up alongside a young woman standing on the pavement. She stuck her head in the car to discuss business and then at his invitation she got in beside him and supplied expert directions to some garages at the rear of Mount View Road, Hornsey. A quiet spot. 'No one came near the garages whilst we were there.'

A price of 30s was agreed and she opened a purse-like handbag and took out a condom from a small square cardboard box. She told him that she bought them in the East End because they were cheaper there.

He undid the buttons on the front of her blue and white summer dress and she undid the straps of her stiffened bra. They had intercourse on the back seat. Her breasts were of average size, her hair was cut short ('Eva Bartok style') and her knees were bony. 'To enable me to have sexual intercourse she did not remove her knickers but pushed them to one side.' Half an hour later he was driving her to Holland Park.

He was driving her to Holland Park because during their

negotiations they'd made an arrangement. He asked her to spend the night with him and she said she had to be at Holland Park at 2am (but didn't say why). He asked her how she would get there and she said she would probably get a cab from the Archway. ('She said that usually she went back to the Archway from Holland Park in a cab and that she gave the cab driver a wank or whatever he wanted in payment for the fare.') It was then agreed that after intercourse he would take her to Holland Park and pick her up there later, when she would spend the rest of the night with him for £4.

She didn't tell him her name but she told him other things. She said that she had worked in Park Lane the previous week and hadn't earned a penny. She said that the dress she was wearing had been altered for her by a dressmaker for 25s and that she hadn't paid her. She said that she had got pregnant and had then found out the man was married. She said that she was sharing a room with another girl at 57 Duncombe Road. This girl was a business girl, and she was at home looking after the little boy who was ill.

On the way to Holland Park he asked her if she wanted a cup of tea. She said no, but they stopped and had a milk each from the machine in Brecknock Road. When he dropped her off by Holland Park tube station he looked at his watch and saw that it was exactly 1.10am.

'I said to her how long would she be and she said about a couple of hours. I said, "What time then?" and she said, "Half past three," and I said, "All right, I will meet you here then."'

Upon leaving her, he drove down Bayswater Road and stopped at a mobile coffee stall near Marble Arch. He ate hamburgers and drank tea and chatted to the proprietor, who was complaining that he'd been charged with obstruction.

Half an hour later he drove off along Oxford Street to Tottenham Court Road, then down Charing Cross Road, Leicester Square, Piccadilly, Park Lane and back to Marble Arch, by which time it was about 3am. He returned to the coffee stall, now on the corner of Bayswater Road, and had another hamburger and a cup of tea. He drove along to Holland Park Avenue and pulled up at their meeting point at about 3.10am. 'She was not there and I walked out to the junction of Lansdowne Road and Holland Park Avenue to see if I could see her but I could not.' Presently two police officers approached him and asked him what he was doing, and he told them he was having a smoke. They took down particulars of his car insurance before telling him to switch his lights on and finish his cigarette and clear off.

He waited for her until 3.45am and then turned right into Holland Park Avenue and stopped at a garage for petrol. As he was leaving the garage a prostitute in a white pleated skirt waved to him, and he stopped and spoke to her. She told him the heel had come off her shoe and asked him for a lift to Elgin Crescent. During the journey he described to her the prostitute who had stood him up, but she said she hadn't seen her. He dropped her off and drove straight home to 62 Springdale Road, Stoke Newington, arriving at approximately 5am. At around midday he paid a visit to 57 Duncombe Road but an old woman lived there and he didn't find the girl.

I said, 'What time then?' and she said, 'Half past three.' By half past three Elizabeth Figg was almost certainly dead; if she left Forrest at 1.10am she probably died within the hour. But even if she'd still been in business it's unlikely that she would have showed; a previous all-nighter had robbed her. Besides, she had made an arrangement to meet the others at 4am. So it's safe to assume she just wanted a lift to Holland Park.

And even if she had turned up to meet him where could they have gone? Forrest rented a furnished room from a resident landlord who allowed no female visitors. So where? 'It was not discussed where we would spend this time but I assumed it would be her place.' Duncombe Road? With Ward and Reefer poncing around? Not to mention Pauline Mills in the next bed looking after the little boy who was ill ha ha. Dream on.

According to Mills, Figg sometimes mentioned that she had a child at home as part of her patter to extract more money from punters. But it didn't work with Ernie. He was keeping his hand on his ha'penny for later.

So what kind of a suspect did the handyman make?

Ernest Forrest was thirty-four years old, self-employed. He had juvenile convictions which included shopbreaking and receiving stolen goods but he was respectable now, with a respectable girlfriend whom he visited from 5.30pm to 11pm each evening, after which time he'd drive around looking for whores.

And on Tuesday 16 June he picked up the wrong girl on the wrong night . . .

But at least he wasn't in the wrong place. Shortly before 3am on Wednesday 17 June, following a refreshment break, PC Nash left Notting Hill police station, accompanied by PC Dalton, who was learning beats. From 10pm to 6am Nash was posted on 3 Beat, part of which covered Holland Park Avenue. 'At that time in the morning it was quite clear, and we could see a man standing on the corner of Lansdowne Road and Holland Park Avenue. There wasn't anybody else about.'

They decided to speak to him, yet on their approach he turned and walked round the corner into Lansdowne Road. They followed, and saw a man sitting alone at the wheel of a black Morris saloon parked without lights just back from the junction. Nash asked him what he was doing there and he said that he was just having a smoke. He was told to switch his lights on as his car was only about five yards from the junction. When asked to produce his licence he said he hadn't any papers with him. He eventually produced an insurance certificate for the car.

Nash told him local residents complained about prostitutes and men loitering in the neighbourhood and advised him to move on. 'His attitude changed then and he was more cooperative. He apologized for hanging about and said he didn't realize he was doing anything wrong. He told me he was a builder and had just finished doing a job, and was just riding around . . . He said he would finish his cigarette and go.' He was presently observed to drive out of Lansdowne Road and down Holland Park Avenue.

PC Nash spoke to this man at 3.20am and he gave his name as Ernest Forrest.

So that night he was in one of the places he said he was, at the time he stated. Other parts of his statement could also be corroborated. The prostitute with the broken shoe – a 'pretty rough' type, he recalled, with a Scottish accent – was eventually traced and confirmed his account, and Mrs Simpson, the elderly woman at 57 Duncombe Road, did indeed open her door to a man who asked if a girl aged about twenty lived there. The crucial period, however, was the hour between 1am and 2am, when Elizabeth Figg most likely met her death, and during this time Forrest's only witness was the coffee stall proprietor. This man, it transpired, loathed the police and in an attempt to side with Forrest against them claimed an acquaintance which the builder denied, and which rendered his identification worthless.

And yet Forrest himself couldn't have been more helpful. He came forward voluntarily three days after the discovery of the body. (He was Catholic, he said, and had consulted a priest before acting.) He answered all of Detective Superintendent Mitchell's questions – no, he'd never visited Duke's Meadows, no, her dress wasn't torn – and made both his rented room and his Morris Ten available for examination.

There was an extensive urine stain on the underslip of Figg's dress, sufficient to indicate an emptying of the bladder. The garment also showed some poorly defined patches of reddish staining; possibly a dye stuff transferred through moisture, although the amount present was insufficient to allow for confirmation of this. The rear upholstery of Forrest's car, on which he and Figg allegedly had intercourse, was red, as was part of the lining of the interior. In an attempt to discover whether the dye from the upholstery – admittedly a different shade to that found on the slip – was transferable an experiment was conducted with strong urine, without success.

There's a woman in a flat in Earls Court who – look, she's calmed down these days, grandmother and all that – but once upon a time she was – *you know*, she was –

'In the winter of 1958/9, for about three months, I was working on the streets. I was twenty. I had a baby to feed. Where I worked . . . we called ourselves the Curzon Street girls. We thought we were a cut above the Bayswater Road women, and we charged more. It was £3 for a short time, a quickie. They charged £2.

'Anyway, one night I got into a taxi with this customer and we drove off, I don't remember where. Quite far out, off my usual beat. I wouldn't go far normally because of the time factor, but he was the last one for the night. Dark hair, well built.'

On they drove. She imagined they were heading for a room somewhere, in a hotel or a flat.

They weren't.

'I don't know where we ended up. It was waste ground, that's all

I know, because I remember following him and worrying all the time about my heels.'

He undid the padlock on the doors of a massive warehouse and they went inside.

'It was just filled with junk. I saw a big armchair right at the end, so I went and sat down and took my knickers off while he began to get undressed.'

He wanted her to take her top off.

She wanted £2 extra.

'They knew this: all the men knew this. It was a way of bumping the money up. You'd get your £3 and then mention it afterwards.'

But he wouldn't pay.

'So I said, "I'm not taking it off then." Well, by this time he was naked and he dashed across to where I was sitting and put one hand on each arm of the chair. He was literally frothing at the mouth. He said, "I'm going to fucking *kill you!*" He pointed to a calendar on the wall. It was one of these larger-than-life nude calendars and there were long pins stuck through the woman's body. He said, "See that? That's what's going to happen to you."'

She looked over at the calendar and nearby she saw a fireplace, with an axe resting alongside.

'And this man's naked and frothing at the mouth and it's going all over my new pink woollen jumper that I'd bought. I thought, "I'm not wearing this again. I'm getting rid of this." I looked up at him and I was absolutely terrified. But I knew if I screamed he'd kill me. So instead of screaming I said, "Now, what's upset *you?*" He said, "I *hate* women." I said, "Well, I *hate* men," and then he began to calm down.'

He stood naked before her in that derelict warehouse and talked about himself. He was married, he said, with two children, when he'd met a girl in a dancehall and had intercourse with her. She was under-age and he went to prison for three years.

'He told me he'd lost everything – wife, kids, everything. He started to froth again . . . and he had these staring bulging eyes. They looked like they had a layer of cellophane across them: they were like robot's eyes.'

Upon his release he raped a woman and went back inside for seven more years. Now he was out. He felt he'd been wronged and as if to prove it he showed her his hands. 'They were black and gritty, they looked like they were covered in some sort of dye. He said they'd got like that in prison and it wouldn't come off.' He used to have a job illustrating calendars, but who would employ him now?

In return for hearing his story she told him her own, about how she came from a well-to-do family, how she ran away and ended up at an approved school. 'I talked to him as if we were in the same boat. I said, "Look at the injustice done to *me*."'

At which point he appeared to get confused and asked her if she had a boyfriend. He said, 'We're quite alike, you and me. Why don't you be my girlfriend?'

She said yes, and suddenly he pulled himself together and told her he was sorry, that he hoped he hadn't frightened her.

He went off and telephoned for a taxi for her. When the car arrived he stayed behind at the warehouse. She got the impression he was living there.

Before she left they made a date.

'I got in the car and the taxi driver saw me shaking. He wanted to call the police but I said no.

'Now that happened in February 1959. In June I was in prison when I saw the photograph of the girl in the paper. And I thought about it for days, agonizing. In the end I went and talked to the governor, and two officers came down to interview me. I told them what I knew.

'Now I didn't want to help the police at all. It was just that I saw that photo and I thought, "It's him. He's done it. He's finally done it."'

Maybe.

In the early hours of the Saturday before her death Elizabeth Figg, along with Pauline Mills, Barton Boyce, Raymond Reefer and two other black men, was driven to the Blue Parrot club, Harrow Road, in a cream Zephyr convertible by Ken, who'd borrowed his landlord's car. Here Figg picked up Ernest 'Small Boy' Grizette, a twenty-year-old Trinidadian factory worker. He went back with her to her room at Duncombe Road and stayed there all day. When Baby came round at 7.30pm that evening he found Small Boy keeping the bed warm while Figg went out to buy cigarettes. He was not best pleased, and Pauline Mills caught a glimpse of what it was that made this young boxer a man to watch.

'Baby went out of the room and as Ann came up the stairs to our room . . . he hit her several blows to the back of the neck with his hand. He asked Ann what Small Boy was doing there but I cannot remember whether she said anything. When they came into the room I saw Baby twist Ann's arm. I told him not to do this and pulled Ann away. Baby told me that he would not hit Ann with his fist because a punch would kill her.'

Pauline Mills, our eyes and ears. Where would we be without Pauline Mills? And she saw something else, earlier that day, before the trouble started.

'I saw Ann having sexual intercourse "backwards" with Small Boy. Ann had all her clothes off. Later that day I jokingly accused Ann of having sexual intercourse with Small Boy up her back passage but she said it was a normal sexual act.'

No doubt it was, although at this time buggery may have had its attractions. Earlier in the year, it seems, she found herself pregnant (pregnant by Baby?). However, on 4 May her stepmother received a letter in which Figg mentioned that she had had a 'miss'. That was one problem solved, yet she was also probably diseased courtesy of Ward, who told her that there was something wrong with him and advised her to visit a hospital. On 26 May at St Mary's Hospital, Paddington, she had a test for venereal disease; she was asked to return on 28 May but failed to do so. The test was inconclusive yet the pathologist noted a bead of pus extruding from her cervix; this pus, which contained a few non-fresh sperm, would appear to confirm suspicions.

But would Figg have consented to any form of anal penetration? The question is worth asking, because when Donald Teare made his preliminary examination under the willow tree he turned her body over and saw traces of partially dried blood around the anus. Teare's post-mortem report stated that the blood had come from injuries to the anterior aspect of the anus and rectum. Such injuries, he judged, were more likely to have been caused by a fingernail than a penis, although he admitted at the inquest that they could have been caused in a variety of ways.

So Chiswick police were looking for a man with blood on his hand.

All summer long they searched for him.

All over town.

Holland Park Avenue, Finsbury Park, Endymion Road, Mount View Road . . . They conducted house-to-house enquiries and kept observations. They interviewed taxi drivers and scores of prostitutes. They issued a duplicated circular, together with a copy of the dead woman's photograph, to both uniform and CID officers, with instructions to show these to any likely person encountered in the course of their duties. They scrutinized the crime books at stations covering the Finsbury Park, Holland Park and Chiswick areas to see if Forrest, Figg or any other likely person had come to the attention of the police on the night of 16/17 June. They made a check on cars stolen, or otherwise suspect, at the time in question, including cars listed by uniform officers in Notting Hill sub-division between 10pm and 1am on 2–6 June during an observation on kerb crawlers.

But you know how it is, sometimes . . .

Nothing.

And they found no clue at the scene. Thames police scoured the river bed and council employees assisted in a search of the surrounding area with its tennis courts, playing fields and allotments. The nearest building, about 500 yards from the scene, was the Ibis Club, the sports club of the employees of the Prudential Assurance Company. On Tuesday 16 June the club was shut by 11pm and the resident steward and his wife saw or heard nothing unusual during the night.

An enormous effort was made to recover Figg's missing property, her underwear, handbag and shoes. At the inquest, held on 13 August at Ealing Coroner's Court, Detective Superintendent Mitchell said, 'The description of the clothing and handbag has been sent to every police force in Great Britain, but no trace has been found.' The absence of these items suggested to him that the murder was committed elsewhere, probably in a car, as it was her habit to solicit men in cars. 'It could have been that she kicked off her shoes, that she removed her own garments, and that her clothing and handbag were in the back of the car and remained in the car after the body was taken to where it was found.'

'Suggesting it was someone in the car who she had solicited?' asked coroner Harold Broadridge.

'That had occurred to me,' Mitchell replied.

He was right to be cautious. It's impossible to reconstruct with

any certainty the sequence of events which led to Figg's death.
Having removed her dress in readiness for intercourse, she may have
been reclothed, minus bra and knickers, after death. Her attacker –
if it was her attacker – may have inserted a finger – if it was a
finger – into her anus during strangulation as her sphincter opened
and closed repeatedly. Her bladder may have emptied at the
moment of death as her muscles relaxed or she may have wet herself
earlier through fear.

In what condition was she driven to Duke's Meadows? Dead or
alive? Prostitutes working the streets of west London were often
reluctant to make the time-consuming journey to Duke's Meadows
for fear of robbery and/or violence. On the other hand, if a punter
paid well, perhaps promised a return lift . . .

Was Figg plucked at that spot? No one seems to have seen or heard
anything unusual that night, but what qualified as unusual at Duke's
Meadows? The area was in darkness; a woman's scream might, at the
right moment, have encouraged the others.

There was no apparent motive for the murder (robbery seemed
unlikely) and the police had no real suspect. Apart from Ernie
Forrest – who wasn't charged, as no evidence could be found against
him – all they had were a few time-wasting tip-offs: anonymous,
probably malicious. Par for the course.

Elizabeth Figg was buried at Chiswick New Cemetery on 5
September 1959, the sixth interment in a common grave. None of
her family attended her funeral (her sister Patricia had emigrated to
Canada in 1958). 'It was just me and the undertakers,' recalled a
detective inspector who worked on the investigation. 'The vicar
thanked me for coming. I felt sorry for her really, you know. She was
only twenty-one. It's bad to lose your life at that age. You haven't
really seen much life, have you?'

Figg's body was discovered in the early morning of Wednesday 17
June. At about 11.30pm on Monday 15 June a seventeen-year-old
model was attacked less than a mile from where the body was found.
Anne Lewingdon, also a brunette, was walking home from Turnham
Green tube station because she couldn't get a taxi. 'I hoped to pick
one up in Chiswick High Road.' But a quarter of a mile from her
home in Ranelagh Gardens a fair-haired man in his twenties sprang at
her and tried to strangle her. He forced her, struggling, to the ground.

He kicked her in the stomach and tore at her blouse and punched her in the face. He said, 'Come on, darling, relax.' They struggled for ten minutes. 'But although I thought he was going to kill me, I didn't give up the fight. As I collapsed on the ground he must have thought he had killed me and ran away.'

Chiswick police didn't connect this incident with the murder of Elizabeth Figg.

Why not?

'We just didn't connect it,' recalled the detective inspector.

According to Lewingdon, the would-be strangler had staring eyes.

'Well, they've all got staring eyes, haven't they? That's because they're excited, or wanking, I expect.'

I found her in the third one up, the top one. And I didn't know what to bloody do . . .

Cover her thighs – prop her eyelids open – she died young.

She died before she could be stamped out.

For Figg lived in the days of the forty-bob fine, the days when convictions for soliciting were mere inconveniences. They were the good old days, and they ended at midnight on Saturday 15 August 1959, when the new Street Offences Act became law. The act, which followed certain recommendations set out in the Wolfenden Report of 1957, made it an offence for a prostitute either to loiter or to solicit in a street or public place for the purpose of prostitution. (The word 'street' now covered passages, doorways and entrances of buildings.) The maximum penalties were a fine of £10 for a first offence, £25 for a second offence and £25 and/or three months' imprisonment for a third or subsequent conviction.

National news.

Serious news.

Of course, any woman doing respectable business could easily afford the increased fines. Prison, on the other hand, meant no business at all.

The first London prostitutes to be imprisoned under the new act were Ann Doyle, aged twenty-four, of Kensington and Sally Curry, twenty, of Camden Town. On 17 October they appeared at West London Magistrates' Court, where they pleaded guilty to being common prostitutes, loitering in Kensington Road for the purpose of prostitution, and admitted three previous convictions apiece. Doyle broke down in the dock and pleaded with the magistrate, Eric Guest, for one more chance, but he told them that they knew the risk they were running and that they could not defy Parliament: 'Though I hate it, I must say six weeks.' (Eric Guest was a notoriously stern magistrate, capable of instilling fear in police and prostitutes alike; he alternated at the court with a brother of Boris Karloff.)

On 6 November 1959, three months after the act came into force, a reporter for the *Daily Express* took a nocturnal walk around the West End with Sir John Wolfenden. Wolfenden briefly reiterated the main aims of the act which, he said, was never meant to abolish prostitution. '"We had two objects. First, to promote public order and decency. The streets really were rather objectionable. Second, to protect from exploitation those who ought to be protected – that is, young people."' They then set off.

Their walk began in Mayfair, along streets formerly thronged with prostitutes yet which were now deserted 'except for an occasional policeman'. The story was almost the same in Shepherd Market; here they were solicited, yet only once. All clear in Soho and so back to Mayfair, then on to Hyde Park, where the two strollers saw 'nothing in the shadows but trees', and down Bayswater Road towards Notting Hill. 'There used to be scores of prostitutes all along that route. Now there was none.'

All gone.

Clean streets at last.

At last streets clean enough for tourists to visit.

Congratulations all round.

But wait a minute. What about those unclean women? What happened to them? Where did they go?

Harold Macmillan's Conservative government won a second general election and returned to dominate the House of Commons with a majority of more than 100. David Niven won an Oscar for his role in the film version of Terence Rattigan's *Separate Tables*. Liberace won his libel case against the gossip columnist William 'Cassandra' Connor – who called him a 'deadly, winking, sniggering, snuggling, chromium-plated, scent-impregnated, luminous, quivering, giggling, fruit-flavoured, mincing, ice-covered heap of mother love' – and collected £8,000 damages. (At the Chiswick Empire he told his audience, 'It has been said many, many times, ladies and gentlemen, that British justice is the finest in the world. I am absolutely convinced of it now.')

1959 at a glance. And on 16 June the *Evening Standard* reported:

> Seamus McGrath, the 36-year-old Dublin trainer, achieved a personal triumph on the opening day of this year's Royal Ascot meeting here at Ascot this afternoon. He won the first two races of the fixture, the Queen Ann Stakes, with Lucky Guy, owned by his brother, Joseph McGrath, jnr., and the Gold Vase with Vivi Tarquin, which belongs to his father, Mr Joseph McGrath.

Lucky Guy.

Unlucky Baby.

Laid out 25s of his hard-earned money on a dress that got worn once, torn at the waist and ended up stinking of piss.

Yes, he backed the wrong whore that night.

The fat mare romped home.

At 10pm on 16 June Pauline Mills left 97 Duncombe Road and travelled by tube to Notting Hill Gate, where she accepted a lift from a stranger to Holland Park Avenue. 'As soon as I got out of the car a taxi drew up and a man in it asked me whether I would spend the night with him.' It was midnight, he was drunk, and the taxi driver knew where to take them: the Winchester Hotel, King's Cross. The man paid £2 for the room and gave Mills £7. Later, at about 2am, she left him asleep in the hotel. She got a lift in a newspaper van to Old Street and then walked to a cafe in Brick Lane. At 3.30am she got another lift and arrived home half an hour later, and then Baby turned up, wanting his wages, asking, 'Where's Betty?'

Poor Baby.

Talking sometimes helps.

Do you want to get involved in this?

Too late, Baby, too late.

A coloured man has got no chance in this country.

But what chance has any man got?

What chance have I got, eh? Fat? Slim? Non-existent?

As I sip my bitter shandy and watch the rain attack the river I wonder where in hell this business will end, and why it is there's only me here, as usual, to wish me well.

1
Going Down

Mortlake.

Mortlake, where Edward Kelly, assistant to Elizabethan occultist Dr John Dee, was set upon by 'three or four spiritual creatures like labouring men, having spades in their hands and their hair hanging about their ears'; Mortlake, where Dr Stephen Ward, sacrificial victim of the Profumo affair, was incinerated; Mortlake, where nine mourners attended the cremation of that burnt-out old tart Charles Hawtrey.

Mortlake.

Mortlake?

Mortlake.

What you say is what you get.

Barnes Borough Council Household Refuse Disposal Plant, Townmead Road, occupied an unfenced space behind Mortlake Crematorium, some forty yards from the Thames towpath. The public had access to the site and exercised this freedom. Fly-tippers came and went. Children, courting couples played their games there. Across the river, less than a mile away, was Duke's Meadows.

In June 1962 the refuse plant's incinerator was replaced by a transfer station. While building was taking place refuse was deposited in a large pit dug at the side of the existing plant from where it was loaded onto lorries. When building was completed the pit was filled with rubble and clinker from the surrounding land. It was roughly on the edge of this filled-in pit where three council labourers made a discovery.

At 1.30pm on Friday 8 November 1963 Edward Kimpton, foreman, Peter Taffurelli, lorry driver, and Patrick Dineen, mechanical shovel driver, visited the plant to collect ash. Having loaded one lorry, they crossed the site to where the finer ash was situated – close to, if not over, the refuse pit – and at about 2pm Dineen was operating his digger when he noticed what appeared to be a dead animal.

'I was driving over it and I didn't take a lot of notice, although I did notice a horrible smell. I changed course and turned right, I put my shovel into the muck and lifted it up and I saw two legs hanging out of the shovel. There was a stocking on one of them and I stopped my machine and shouted to the foreman, "There is a body there!"'

Kimpton telephoned Richmond police station and the scene was immediately attended by Detective Superintendent Frederick Chadburn and other officers. The body, which hung suspended by its right arm, was in an advanced stage of decomposition: the internal organs had disappeared. The action of Dineen's digger had wrenched the torso from the skull, which, with the upper cervical vertebrae attached, was lying several feet away, still embedded in the ground. The body was unclothed save for a beige nylon stocking rolled down to the right ankle.

At 3.45pm the pathologist Dr Arthur Mant arrived and examined the body and its surroundings. The body was then wrapped in a plastic sheet and, together with the skull and the surrounding soil and ash, transported to Kingston mortuary where, at 10.30am the following day, Mant performed the post-mortem.

Calculation of height from the long bones was 5' 3". The pelvis, skull and long bones were all female, and study of the epiphyses and X-ray examination of the pelvis, ribs and skull put the age at between twenty and twenty-five years.

The upper thoracic spine had been rotated and disarticulated by the action of the digger. All connective tissue had putrefied and there were deep grooves on the right arm, owing to the ridging of the grab. The brain was missing, and the skin was missing from the upper back, the face and the perineum. Some remnants of bowel and stomach were recognizable but the other viscera had putrefied. However, the right lower leg was not decomposed, and decomposition of the left leg was only moderately advanced. The size of the feet indicated a 4½ shoe.

The body showed no fractures or bone deformations. Four teeth were missing from the skull; others were badly decayed and showed no evidence of dental treatment. The long dark brown hair attached to the skull was interlaced with grass and plant life. It was at first thought that these had grown through the hair after burial but a scientific officer who attended the examination established that the entanglement had occurred when the digger removed the body from the ash.

Mant speculated that death had occurred between four and eight weeks previously. It was impossible for him to be more specific for it was impossible to ascertain how deeply the body had been buried. She had been buried on her side, and the fact that her legs were less rotten than her head and trunk indicated that she had been buried head uppermost, probably about six inches below the surface of the soil. (Judging by the temperature of the clinker – 42°F twelve inches down, 50°F twenty-four inches down – as taken by a forensic officer, her feet were buried approximately two feet below the surface.) At the spot where the skull was found, the careful sifting of several tons of ash had uncovered three teeth and a hyoid, the U-shaped bone that supports the tongue. The right horn of the hyoid was missing. Had the break occurred during strangulation? Unfortunately this was impossible to prove, as the remainder of the larynx could not be found.

Detective Superintendent Chadburn was in charge of the investigation – but what precisely was he investigating? Misadventure? Murder? Something in between?

Open to suggestions, he paid a visit to Guy's Hospital, where the dead woman's skeleton had been transported and where Arthur Mant lectured in forensic medicine. Mant, whose report had concluded simply that the cause of death was unascertainable, had since conferred with his colleague Professor Warwick, an anatomy specialist at the hospital, and now told Chadburn that the hyoid bone had been broken at the time of, or possibly shortly after, death; that it was 95 per cent certain that the woman, a European, had been strangled. However, as the body was probably buried with the head close to the surface, this bone might have been broken after death by some external means such as the impact of a heavy object immediately above the throat – a foot perhaps, stamping down the soil. (Or maybe even that digger.) In short he didn't know how she died.

All right. So how did she live? Who was she? Aside from the three teeth and the hyoid bone and a second beige nylon stocking, nothing of any significance was found at the scene and the police still had no clue to her identity.

A search was made and particulars obtained of 144 girls reported missing to the various police forces in the United Kingdom and Eire. All stations in the Metropolitan Police District were notified and particulars obtained from their missing persons registers of girls of a similar description. Meanwhile, the discovery of the body was well publicized on the radio and in the national press. Hundreds of people contacted Richmond, where the investigation was based, and their local police stations, concerned lest a relative, who seemed to have vanished off the face of the earth, was lying low beneath a pile of ash. There were girls missing from home, it emerged, who had not previously been reported to police; and others who had long since ceased to keep in touch with their families and whose whereabouts were unknown. In all, particulars of 483 girls were received. Eighty-five were traced, and of the remainder 258 were eliminated by virtue of height, age or dental history. Which meant that 140 were left outstanding on Saturday 23 November, the day Frederick Chadburn got the news.

The decomposition of the woman's flesh had extended to her hands and fingers; however, the left hand was almost intact and was removed, frozen and X-rayed. A small area of skin on the left thumb and middle joint of the forefinger was forwarded for examination and had now produced a fingerprint – on file.

Gwynneth Rees.

She was twenty-two and she had thirteen convictions, twelve for soliciting and one for theft, to her name – her other name.

Tina Smart.

She was a street-girl, a prostitute, and Chadburn knew what that meant – happy times ahead chasing ponces, punters, uncaged beasts of every stripe, any one of whom might have closed her legs for good . . .

And so began the investigation proper, in the course of which Chadburn and his men discovered that, although Gwynneth Rees's body had been left to rot in an isolated spot in west London, hers was essentially an East End story; of the traditional sort, in which everybody takes care of their own.

Gwynneth Rees was born on 6 August 1941 in Barry, Glamorgan, the daughter of Gwilym Rees, a labourer, and his wife, Amelia. At the age of five she began attendance at a local girls' school, where she remained until the age of fifteen, becoming a prefect during her final year. Upon leaving school she went to work as a machinist at a lingerie factory in Barry, and she was in this job in September 1957 when her mother died suddenly of a blood clot to the brain.

After Gwynneth, Amelia Rees had given birth to three more daughters, Margaret in 1943, Hilary in 1946 and Julie in 1950. Gwynneth's brother David, aged twenty-one, and sister Joan, twenty-four, had both married and moved out, and by the time her mother died she was the eldest child living at home. Her father, who was working as a painter at Barry docks, wanted her to stay at home and look after the girls but she refused to give up her job; and whenever she had to babysit her sisters she resented it. She preferred to go out with her friends, her boyfriends, most of whom were from the nearby RAF camp in St Athens.

One Saturday night in the autumn of 1957 she didn't come home and her father reported her to Barry police as a missing person. The following Monday they informed him that officers had found her alone in a cafe in Swansea; she was now at Swansea police station, awaiting collection.

'I asked Gwynneth why she had left home and she said she had been too late to come home Saturday night and had found her way to Swansea. She said she had slept in a car on some waste ground at Swansea.'

About a fortnight later she went missing again, and again her father notified the police, who found her some twenty miles away at Bridgend. He then contacted the local probation officer, who agreed to speak to her. She told him that rather than stay at home looking after her younger sisters, she would prefer to go and live with her older married sister, Joan, in Canvey Island, Essex.

Joan Oxley agreed to receive her and Gwilym Rees eventually agreed to let her go, and that autumn she left home. She found work in Canvey Island and began to settle down.

In March 1958 Joan suspected Gwynneth was pregnant and questioned her. No, she said, she wasn't. The following month she announced that she was going back to Wales. 'This was after we had had a few arguments about her staying out late at night.'

She returned to live with an aunt, Emily James, in Barry and got a job at a rope factory in Cardiff. 'She went out about twice a week, but she had to be in by 9.30pm.' She behaved herself while at her aunt's, but she didn't stay there long. In June Joan Oxley received a letter from the welfare officer at the rope factory, stating that Gwynneth Rees was pregnant and wished to return to Canvey Island to live with her. Joan agreed to have her back and she returned in July. The following month Kim Rees was born.

Who was the father? Gwynneth Rees named a local labourer whom she'd been seeing prior to her departure for Wales, yet no attempt was made to contact this man, who recalled that she was 'an easy type of girl and would allow anyone to have intercourse with her'. (It was not until some two years later that the alleged father heard the news, having met the mother by chance outside the labour exchange at Canvey Island. 'I didn't dispute the fact . . .' Although he might have done if she'd asked him for money.)

She wanted to have the baby adopted and so her sister made the necessary arrangements through an adoption society. However, she later changed her mind and Joan reluctantly agreed to look after Kim while Gwynneth went out to work, first at a shoe factory in Rayleigh and then at a shoe factory in Tilbury.

Once again she began to stay out late at night. Worse, she began to bring men home. Joan Oxley had words with her, for all the good it did.

'One Saturday in February 1959, at about 3am, I heard my sister coming in, and getting up to find out why she was late I found her in company with a man, whose name I don't know. Gwynneth asked me if this fellow could stay the night but I refused, and she said if he couldn't stay she wouldn't and she left the house with this fellow.'

She returned at 11am, but only to collect her clothes. She left, 'leaving the baby with me, as we had previously decided to bring it up as our own'. It was understood that she was returning to Wales.

But at noon on 5 March, when WPS Rawlings and WPC Hartgen stopped and questioned her, she was in Backchurch Lane, Stepney, apparently soliciting. She gave her name as Tina Smart and her address as 1 Batty Street, Stepney. Who was she living with? Her friend Pat and two Maltese, Carlo and Michael.

As Maltese men in London at that time had acquired an almost legendary reputation for poncing, this was not a good answer. The officers took her to Leman Street police station and questioned her further. Here she admitted her true name, explaining that she had changed it because she didn't want the same name as her father, whom she detested. When she was young her father would hit both her and her mother; and so at the age of fourteen she ran away from home, but later returned. Her father's treatment of her prompted an attempt at suicide when her mother died. She seemed obsessed with her hatred of him.

She told the officers that until recently she had been living with her sister Joan on Canvey Island but had left because Canvey was too quiet for her. She would be starting work as a machinist in Stepney the following Monday. The police let her go, back onto the streets.

Gwynneth Rees and her father were briefly reunited that autumn when she turned up unannounced at the family home in Barry. She told him that she was now living in the Paddington area, and that she had got into a fight and ended up in court. The court had recommended that she return home, and so here she was.

In a hopeful mood, Gwilym asked her to stay at home and look after the house and the children.

'She stayed for one and a half days. The local assistance people gave her 30s and after lunch that day she went and I have never seen her since.'

Gwyn and Gwilym.

Did he beat her? Was it true, as she claimed in later years, that he was a drunkard and that he was always trying to get into bed with her? Her brother David recalled that 'Gwynneth and my father never got on well together, even when she was six,' and her sister Joan stated that 'Gwynneth has had a very bad home life.' So there may have been substance to at least some of these allegations, always bearing in mind the fact that Gwynneth Rees was a chronic liar.

Anyway, from this point onwards the only relative with whom she maintained regular contact was Joan Oxley. She visited her every few weeks. Sometimes she stayed for just an hour or two, sometimes for a night or a weekend. She often arrived by car, and it was a different car on each occasion. She never introduced the drivers, although Joan picked up a few names: Norman, Alan, Bob, Barry, Micky – and Jimmy, the only man whom Joan allowed to sleep with Gwynneth under her roof. ('I only allowed this because I understood they were getting married.')

So how was she managing? Was she putting bread in her mouth? What else was she putting in her mouth? She didn't seem to want to talk much about life in London.

But don't worry. Big sister had big ears.

'During our conversations little things came out, such as the parties she had been to and the fact she slept during the day and went out
at night. I knew she wasn't working and I had a good idea how she was
getting a living.'

Our Gwynneth.

She had the same oval face, the same brown eyes, the same strawberry birthmark on the back of her head.

But she now had a different name.

Goodbye, Gwynneth.

Hello, Tina.

Tina Smart.

Why? Why 'Smart'? What did it signify? Neatness? Canniness?
Cockiness? Pain?

During her London years she stayed at twenty-eight known addresses,
one of which was a two-room flat at 18 Oban Street, Poplar. This was
occupied by a prostitute named Peggy James, a Welsh woman who
had known Rees when Rees was living in Barry but had lost touch
with her when she moved to London. But then in 1959 Rees came to
London and began soliciting in the East End, and they met up again.

When Gwynneth Rees turned up at her friend's address on 26
November 1962 she had just been released from Holloway prison.
(She appears to have served three months, the maximum sentence for
soliciting.) And there was more good news – she was pregnant.

Actually it was old news. She'd mentioned the fact to Peggy James
prior to her imprisonment and had also disclosed the identity of the
father: Micky Calvey.

Rees met Michael Calvey, a twenty-year-old stevedore, in January
1962. They lived together for about four months, first in a block of
flats at the Elephant and Castle and then at the Regina Hotel, King's
Cross, where they booked in as Mr and Mrs Carr. In May Rees was
sentenced to one month's imprisonment for soliciting and Calvey
moved back in with his mother.

After her release, Rees did not contact him straight away. She
stayed with Peggy James at 18 Oban Street for about two weeks
before moving to a flat in Hoxton to stay with Elizabeth Norris, a per-
oxided prostitute known as 'Betty the Bottle'. On 27 December Rees

gave birth to a boy, Peter, at the City of London Maternity Hospital, and was discharged with her child on 5 January 1963. Peggy James collected her and the three of them returned to Oban Street.

A few weeks later Rees telephoned Calvey at his mother's address and invited him round to the flat.

Peggy James recalled a mood of optimism in the wake of his visit. 'Gwynneth told me later he denied he was the father, but after looking at the child he admitted it was his and agreed to pay her £4 a week.' He gave her £6 to buy a cot and promised to return that weekend with some money for baby clothes.

On his next visit he asked to speak to her alone and they went outside to his car. Ten minutes later she returned smiling. She told James that he had given her £10 and asked her to go back to him. He wanted to settle down, and he wanted to take care of her first child, Kim, as well as Peter. If he could find a flat he would marry her.

A new year. A new beginning?

Four days later she went out for the evening. Peggy James agreed to babysit but wanted her home by 11.30pm. In fact she returned much earlier, and she was in tears.

'I asked her what was wrong and she told me Micky Calvey had got knocked for stealing cases out of London Bridge railway station, and I never saw the man again.'

Career to consider, baby to care for . . . it can add up to a bit of a juggling act for a working single parent, yet Gwynneth Rees resolved the difficulty by taking Peter with her on the night shift. She went out with him in all weathers, including snow.

And then she didn't. She stayed inside the flat for two whole weeks. One night Peggy James opened the front door to find what she described as a 'mob' outside. There were three men on the doorstep plus two in one car and four in another. Their leader, about 6' 1", mousy hair, mid-twenties, asked her if Tina was living there because he wanted to see her. 'I told him that she didn't live with me and the big fellow told me I was a fucking liar.' But James threatened to call the police and everybody went away.

They returned later that night and this time one of the other tenants opened the front door and let them in. When Peggy James refused to open the door to her flat they forced it open and the leader asked again for Tina. 'I told them she was not living with me, but the big fellow called me a liar and said that the baby in the room was hers.' However, they eventually left and Rees emerged terrified from the kitchen where she had been hiding. 'She told me she had had a message from the prison to say that she had to go there to see Micky, and she had better go as he was in trouble, but she had ignored this message and that is why the mob had come.'

The following night James left the baby with a friend and she and Rees went out for a meal at a Jewish cafe in the East End. While they were eating, the gang leader appeared and asked Rees outside. She came back in tears and had just finished telling James that the gang were going to beat her with a chopper when she was pulled out of the cafe. James followed and saw the leader brandishing a chopper, 'making as if to strike Tina with it', and demanding money on Micky Calvey's behalf. 'Tina was petrified and replied the only money she had was for baby milk.' James came between them and told him that Tina had just had a baby and that he had better shove off, which he did.

Two days later, following a row with her friend, Rees disappeared for three days, leaving the baby behind. She came back covered in blood and complained that the gang had assaulted her.

What was it all about? Detective Superintendent Chadburn believed that this gang were trying to raise money for Calvey's defence and that the leader, from James's description, was one George Kitchener Dixon, a friend of Calvey and his brother Terence.

Dixon, a ship repairer, told police that he had first met Rees when she was living with Calvey. Later, when Calvey was in prison, he would sometimes meet her by chance in the cafes around Aldgate. He knew she was a prostitute but he never discussed – or did – business with her and, furthermore, 'I was always on friendly terms with Tina and at no time have I ever threatened or slapped her.'

George Dixon was an associate of the Kray twins, and Rees had mentioned to James that the twins were members of the gang. Interesting. An interview with these two local businessmen might prove fruitful.

But the twins had no wish to be interviewed, and there followed many unsuccessful attempts to gain an audience, until finally:

27 January 1964.

At 3pm Detective Inspector Buckley and Detective Sergeant Wheeler arrive at the offices of Sampson & Co., solicitors.

Both Mr Sampson and his clients are present. Mr Sampson understands that police wish to see his clients about a matter of a girl who was found dead at Richmond. 'They assure me they know nothing about it and are perfectly innocent. I understand you want to ask them some questions?'

'Yes, we would like to,' replies Detective Inspector Buckley. He holds out a photograph of the dead girl towards Reginald Kray, who avoids looking at it and looks instead at Mr Sampson.

Mr Sampson says, 'They have asked my advice and I have instructed them not to answer *any* questions about this matter.'

'Then this interview is pointless. Knowing this, I should have thought you could have told us this and avoided a waste of time.'

'You asked to see them and there they are.'

There they are. We're not doing very well here, are we? Come on, let's change the scenery. Let's change the year.

7 January 1969.

In No. 1 court at the Old Bailey the trial opens for the murders of George Cornell, Jack McVitie and Frank Mitchell. Ten men stand in the dock accused of involvement in one or other of these crimes. They are Ronald Kray, John Barrie, Ronald Bender, Reginald Kray, Charles Kray, Anthony Barry, Christopher Lambrianou, Frederick Foreman, Anthony Lambrianou and – Cornelius Whitehead.

The one at the end. The tenth man. As an accessory to the murder of Jack McVitie he will receive seven years' imprisonment. Not a sentence to be sniffed at, no, but nevertheless this man's name will go unremembered by generations of Kray fans, and he will stand ultimately as a mere footnote in the history of the Firm.

But his name meant something once to Gwynneth Rees.

Go and whisper his name to her scattered remains.

See her pull herself together and run.

'. . . and so Ronnie and Reggie drove their prospective biographer to a pub in the East End, and showed him upstairs to his room. Ronnie said, "There you are. Get writing. And if you want any local colour try the pub downstairs – it's full of fucking niggers."'

Brian McConnell, veteran press man, leans back chuckling, almost, but not quite, spilling his recently replenished glass of red, and grips our table's edge as if at sea.

What a talker: for the last hour or two or more I've sat listening, all ears, in this dingy candlelit cellar, listening to Brian put story after story to bed. He shows no signs of letting up either. Dabbing briskly in the vicinity of his spectacles with a square of white handkerchief, he abandons the Kray twins and turns his attention to Esther Rantzen's late husband, the television producer Desmond Wilcox.

'I was asked if I'd appear on *This Is Your Life* . . . to talk about what a great fellow he was. I was given a choice of three anecdotes. To relate.' Brian sips his wine and sighs. 'Well, I knew the man, and I told them, "Two of these aren't true." They said, "What are you talking about?" I said, "The third one's true, the one where Wilcox surprises a cat burglar."' He spreads his hands wide in disbelief. 'This man burgled cats.'

I shake my head and Brian continues. 'Anyway, I said, "I don't mind telling that story because that actually happened." But they said, "We don't want you to tell that story, Brian." "Well, you can forget it then."' He drains his glass triumphantly. 'So there we are. Anyway, speaking of TV producers –'

Brian breaks off to goggle at my untouched schooner; holding his bottle aloft, he tells me, 'It's too late now, you know, to seize the day. You and I must seize the year!'

He watches intently as I raise my glass.

We have seizure . . .

Hurry up Rees it's time

It was the evening following the incident outside the cafe when Peggy James came home to find a different group of men intimidating her lodger. 'One was a relation of Calvey, two friends of his and two other men, who I don't know.'

When this group had left, the two prostitutes rowed about Rees allowing strange men into the flat. James understood that these men had wanted her to hand her baby over to Calvey's mother but she refused.

Shortly afterwards she received her beating.

Hurry up Rees it's time

Time for Peter to meet his new mummy.

The arrangements had all been made. Back in Canvey, Joan Oxley, acting in accordance with her sister's wishes, had made enquiries and found a local woman willing to take care of the boy, but only on the condition that she could adopt him. Rees made no objection to this and in February 1963 she took Peter to Canvey Island and left him there. But she neglected to sign the adoption form. 'She made various excuses,' Joan Oxley recalled, 'such as she had mislaid the form etc. I formed the opinion that she, Gwynneth, was not interested in signing the form once she knew the baby had been taken care of.' Or perhaps signing an adoption form (as opposed to simply dumping a child on her sister) would have made it all just a bit too real.

Calvey had no further contact with the child. He told police that in April, shortly after his release from prison, he had met Rees by chance in Berner Street, an occasion on which she threatened to 'do' him for maintenance. 'I told her she was taking a liberty and she said to forget it and walked away.' He never saw her again.

No sooner had Rees delivered Peter to his new home than she began to look for one herself, as Peggy James had been evicted for subletting. In March 1963 Rees was frequenting the Nimbus Club in Upper Street, Islington, and here she met Alexander Harris, a bookmaker's assistant who soon set about solving the problem. He moved her in with his friend Elizabeth Chambers, a prostitute who occupied the top-floor flat at 12 Middleton Buildings in Islington High Street. Rees remained at the flat for about a month, during which time Harris and his friend James 'Joxy' Stone were frequent visitors. Harris told police, 'I used to go up there and poke whichever one was available. I wasn't poncing on either of them, neither was Joxy – he was thieving on his own at the time.'

Harris recalled that his brother Gerald also used the flat, as did Irish Frank, Scotch Jake, Scotch Steve ('I knew he was a screwsman'), Micky ('I think he was a poof') and Pedro Gonzalez, 'a Cuban spade', and his African friend. 'A lot of other spades used to go there, but I can't remember anything about them.'

It certainly sounds like a crowded month – and there was one more on the way. Gwynneth Rees, at it like a rarebit, was pregnant again.

Who was the father this time? Jake? Pedro? Steve the screwsman? No, none of that lot. They only came to play cards and listen to records and smoke the weed. It could have been Harris or Stone, of course, but fortunately for them she decided that the father was a bath moulder named Frederick Chapman.

Chapman was twenty-two years old and lived with his parents and elder brother in east London. He first met Gwynneth Rees just after Christmas 1962 when he had a short time and gave her £1. But he soon knew in his heart that he could give her so much more. He began to see her several times a week, picking her up in New Road in his black Ford Consul. Scruffy and unwashed was how most men remembered her, but her swain maintained she was always clean and smartly dressed. 'I found her a friendly person, well spoken and good company, and all my relatives who met her liked her.' They went to pubs together (Rees, teetotal, would drink bitter lemon). At the end of the night she would ask him to drop her off where he'd picked her up. He had no idea where she lived.

In May she told him she was pregnant and he accepted responsibility for the child without question. In fact he wanted her to give up her way of life and marry him. (They'd already enjoyed a trial run when they booked in for a night as Mr and Mrs Chapman at a hotel in King's Cross.) His elder brother William (who'd also had her) approved his choice and thought that marriage might 'settle him down a bit', stop him going with prostitutes.

Chapman proposed to Rees several times but each time 'she would only laugh and it was obvious she didn't want to get married'. Well, she'd heard that one before.

Anyway, why spoil a good thing, eh? They had fun together, so he settled for that. He was enjoying her services free of charge by this time. But he'd pay, eventually.

At the beginning of April Gwynneth Rees met another young man, Robert Woodford. He picked her up one night in Vincent's, a cafe in Stepney, and he spent the night with her at her new address. Thereafter he saw her several times, and they spent odd nights together at hotels in King's Cross. (Woodford, who was already married, didn't bother booking them in as husband and wife.)

'After about two weeks of seeing her she went on the missing list. I didn't see her for about four or five days. I thought she had gone off with someone else.'

But she resurfaced on 14 April, and complained to Woodford that a man had attacked her at the Islington flat. She said she was lying on the floor when he kicked her in the back. Woodford understood that he was a 'local boy from the Angel', not a client. 'If she knew who it was she didn't tell me.'

Later that evening Woodford met a friend, Michael Holland, and they discussed the assault on his girl. 'We had a few drinks and we decided to go over to the Angel and find the bloke who had done it.'

Woodford, Holland and another man, Joseph Davis, arrived in Islington in a borrowed Ford Zephyr at around 10.30pm. Their first stop was 12 Middleton Buildings, where Rees met them on the stairs and told them not to come in. They ignored her and entered the flat, but her flatmate Elizabeth Chambers got rid of them, explaining that they could see Tina later. They encountered a man on the way out; Rees said he knew the man who'd kicked her. During the altercation which followed Woodford punched him on the chin, and the three avengers set off to search the local cafes.

Their visit supplied Chambers with an excuse to tell Rees, who'd been stealing her food, to leave. And when Alexander Harris turned up she very nearly got a backhander, only Chambers intervened and caught it instead.

Harris and Chambers went out to a club. They returned around dawn to find that the door of the flat had been kicked in and that Rees had disappeared, leaving her clothes behind.

Robert Woodford hadn't found the attacker but he'd found a way to prevent further attacks: he allowed Rees to move in with him. (He was separated from his wife and lived with his parents in Commercial Road.) Everybody could relax now, or so he thought.

But in the early hours of 17 April Woodford and Holland were in Vincent's cafe, drunk, when a gang of men armed with choppers entered and began to cut them about the face and hands. 'We didn't stand a chance. I cannot remember much about it at all, it happened so quick. All I can remember was getting into a cab outside with Micky and asking to be taken to hospital . . . They said that had I not got to hospital I would have died.' The two men received approximately eighty stitches between them.

The identities of the perpetrators never came to light. Alexander

Harris and James 'Joxy' Stone, interviewed during the Rees inquiry, denied any involvement, yet Detective Superintendent Chadburn believed that these two, absent from their usual haunts that night, were the instigators. In which case the episode becomes even more intriguing, for why should a bruised jaw and a damaged door warrant a near-death experience? What kind of a liberty had Woodford and Holland taken? Was it diabolical? What was it Harris had said — 'I wasn't poncing on either of them, neither was Joxy . . .'

Of course not, that would be illegal. And it would mean that when they lost Rees they lost a meal ticket, which would . . . explain the attack, its severity.

Robert Woodford had one conviction for poncing yet denied taking any money from Rees. (He went no further, he said, than granting her permission to pay for their hotel rooms.) In truth he'd forgotten all about the manhunt over the Angel; mending slowly, mulling things over, he cast his mind back to a different night out.

'Some time in 1958 me and my mates, including Micky Holland, had been involved in a fight in the same club, with some Maltese blokes. We had got the worst of it and had left, but me and a few others went back and chucked a petrol bomb in there. One of the Malts was badly burned.'

Could it be that the gang had kept quiet for five years, planning this revenge attack?

No . . . *never* . . . Mind you . . .

Woodford didn't know what to think until Holland helped him out. He suggested that the assault had some connection with the Islington boys, and that the cause of all this misery was a certain Tina Smart.

His words made a kind of murky sense, although Woodford wasn't entirely convinced. 'Even so, I was concerned over the trouble Tina seemed to cause to everyone who associated with her, so I told her to go.'

Woodford recovered, found himself a straight girlfriend and a steady job driving lorries and began to lead a normal life. Retaliation? More stitches? Forget it.

But Michael Holland, who lived solely on the earnings of his prostitute girlfriend Teresa, had time to brood. He pestered Rees for the

names of the axemen and she promised to try to find out. In June he
was arrested for possession of an offensive weapon and went to prison
for three months. Even more time to brood.

At 2.20am on 28 June 1963 a woman was lifted onto a stretcher at
Leman Street police station and driven by ambulance to Poplar
Hospital. She was a prostitute and she had been haggling over the
price with a customer prior to getting in his car. He snatched her
handbag and when she tried to snatch it back he drove off, dragging
her along with him for a short time. She had sustained multiple
injuries.

This woman gave her name as Gwynneth Rees, yet told an ambulance attendant that she was also known as 'Tina Wales' or 'Tina
Rees'. She was treated in the casualty department for abrasions to her
legs and feet, and when these had been dressed she left the hospital
with instructions to return four days later. She failed to do so.

A month later Gwynneth Rees attended London Hospital,
Whitechapel, where she was found to be approximately twelve weeks
pregnant and suffering from a venereal disease. An appointment was
made for her to reattend the hospital but she didn't keep it, and she
didn't stop working either.

She was an earner.

'Speaking of TV producers –'

Were we? When? Half-searching for a clock, I gaze around me, at
all the stumps of candles jammed into wine bottles, at the faded newspapers ('Thatcher Resigns', 'Crystal Palace burned to ground in an
hour') framed and mounted on damp peeling walls. Two men at a
neighbouring table are discussing *ITMA*. Here in Gordon's wine bar
off the Strand, chosen for its proximity to my station, Charing
Cross – which is beginning to seem rather a long way away . . .

'– a chap took me out to lunch a couple of weeks ago. Said he was
planning a film about the murders and wanted to get a few things
straight.' A nod to me. 'I mentioned that someone else was interested
as well. Do you know what he said? "The more the merrier!"' Brian
shrugs. 'I ended up lending him my copy of the book. I don't suppose
I shall see it again.'

The book in question is *Found Naked and Dead: The facts behind the*

Thames-side murders by Brian McConnell. Pushing aside the empties, I produce my own copy and begin to read aloud.

'You do learn quickly,' said one of the other girls and that was promise enough. Little Betty learned it all in the Bayswater Road, beneath the luxurious arch of trees provided by the generous ratepayers of Westminster, as if for the protection of the negotiators below. Here, the heart of whoredom, in a tight tapering skirt, her five-feet-two inches perched perilously on exaggerated high heels, she found her first stud and had much reason to remember it. He came full of beer from a rugby game in a Ford Popular full of rust, and mounted the pavement in his eagerness.

'Elizabeth Figg!' says Brian brightly.
Encouraged by this, I turn the page and read him some more.

'That's what happens when you talk about money. I have some, and I suppose you now want to know how much?'
    'How much are you going to give me?' she corrected.
    'How much do you normally charge?'
    'Do you have a fiver?'
    'No. How much then?'
    'How much do you think I'm worth?'
    'A quid,' he grinned.
    'Five.'
    'Two.'
    'Three.'
    'Three, no more.'
    She giggled and slid her hand between his legs. 'I hope you can wait until we get there.'

My second sliver delivered, I place the book on the table and we both stare at it in silence. I tilt my head, admiring the cover photography, the slender nude decorating the undergrowth from which the letters of the title are formed. Taking advantage of the lull, I ask Brian about something that's been puzzling me.

    'How do you know . . . that Figg's first customer, first *ever* customer, was a rugby player?'

Silence.

'And how do you know . . . what they said?'

Brian continues to gaze downwards. He blows his nose extravagantly. 'Oh, you put yourself about a bit, talk to a few of their friends, you get the general picture . . .'

Rees left Woodford's address in late April. Details of her movements over the following three months are vague but towards the end of July she moved in with another prostitute, Evelyn Day, at an address in east London.

One night the two of them were in Vincent's, soliciting, when the Welsh one went outside and met – guess who?

'Tina went outside and came back shortly afterwards and asked me whether I wanted to go for a ride. I went with Tina and we met Whitehead . . . and went for a drive in Connie's grey motor car. It had a busted light on the front.'

Connie Whitehead.

Friends reunited.

Cornelius John Whitehead – twenty-six, slim, fair-haired, blue-eyed, persuasive – was an East End docker living in Stepney. He had convictions for theft and assaulting a police officer.

He was also an experienced ponce.

He had ponced on Rees for several months leading up to April 1963, when he apparently lost interest. (He was a friend of Michael Holland and had lent Holland his Ford Zephyr on the night of 14 April. He had no contact with Robert Woodford, yet when Woodford began his association with Rees he asked her to ask his blessing. Whitehead replied by blacking her eye.) That spring he was introduced to a young unemployed woman, Rita Darvill, in a pub in Smithfield, and offered to take her to a club up west which had a vacancy for a waitress. He said he knew a girl who worked there, who called herself 'Ruth Ellis': she'd show her the ropes.

'I thought he meant a big, well-known club, where there was a genuine vacancy for a waitress.'

No. He installed Rita Darvill in the Desire Club, a clip joint off Dean Street, Soho, and she began work as a hostess. (The punter, having paid his £1 2s 6d entrance fee, was permitted to sit at a table and ply her with soft drinks, thinking they contained alcohol. She received 5s commission per 15s glass; and her job was to keep the glasses coming.) Whitehall would meet her after work, take half of her earnings, drive her back to her parents' house.

But Whitehead had a wife and two young children to provide for and Rita Darvill was a poor earner. Why not welcome Gwynneth Rees back into the fold (with the folding)? When Rees and Day mentioned they were looking for fresh accommodation he said he would see what he could do.

He enlisted the help of an acquaintance, a club tout named William Frost, and secured a room for them at 39 Clanricarde Gardens, Bayswater. William Frost lived with 'Ruth Ellis' at No. 21, so he could keep an eye on them. Everything was in place.

'It seemed to be understood by Tina that Connie would be poncing off her,' Evelyn Day recalled. 'I had a feeling that Eddie would be poncing off me and I wondered when it would start.'

Whitehead's friend Edward King was also married, yet unemployed. Well, King was by no means the sharpest shiv in the drawer, but Whitehead found him useful: he did as he was told.

Just like these two.

Each afternoon their new boyfriends would pick them up at Clanricarde Gardens and drive them to the East End in one of Whitehead's cars, the blue Ford Zephyr convertible or the grey Austin A40 saloon. They would be dropped off in Middlesex Street at 5.30pm and the grafting would begin, with Rees heading for Commercial Road and Day concentrating on the Cavell Street area. At midnight Day would rejoin her in Commercial Road, meeting her outside the Hole in the Wall, a groceries and provisions store where Rees bought her condoms (as had Elizabeth Figg). Day would then telephone King at a gambling club in Cannon Street and he and Whitehead would drive over and pick them up.

'Tina would give Connie some money which she had earned by hustling that evening. I would do the same with Eddie. Some nights I would give Eddie £8 or £10; on others it would be as little as £3. Eddie would never complain and sometimes he gave me money back, according to what I wanted.'

Eddie, yes, but not Connie. If Rees wanted to keep any of her money she had to hide it before Whitehead showed up. She would sometimes return alone to the East End to continue working, arriving home as late as 4am.

Nevertheless she seemed happy with the arrangement: unhappy, though, with the address. In her first week at Clanricarde Gardens she told Whitehead that she'd been cautioned for soliciting in Bayswater and he agreed with her that it was already time to move on. One afternoon he drove to Battersea to look at a basement flat to let – ladies only – and explained to the Spanish landlady that he required it for his sister and her friend. She supplied a second bed and the girls moved into 27 Warriner Gardens that evening, and thereafter it was business as usual. Only this time they were under observation.

Francisca Salleras had never been a landlady before. 'I had no idea how one should carry out the business of letting rooms, so I decided to use a notebook to record details of my tenants.' On 10 August she noted their reluctance to reveal their names and places of work. The following morning she observed the departure of two men, one of whom was the brother, via the basement entrance; they had apparently spent the night with the sister and her friend. ('They said it would not happen again.') She wrote down the registration number of the Ford Zephyr in which the men collected them in the afternoons. ('I never heard the girls come home in the evenings.') She recorded numerous details yet she failed to find out precisely what was going on.

But any day now Whitehead's wife might find out what was going on, for back in Stepney people had begun to talk about his association with Rees. One day in late August he told her she wouldn't be seeing him for a week.

They had a row.

She disappeared.

Perhaps that's the wrong word. Evelyn Day still saw her working her patch but she wouldn't return to Battersea ('Each time she promised to return, but she didn't'), and no one seemed to know where she was staying.

Whitehead, furious, trawled Aldgate. He'd threatened her with a beating if she ever ran away from him, but of course he had to find her before he could hit her and . . . and that Rita Darvill was playing him up as well. She was such a lousy earner at the Desire that he'd taken her out for the day and introduced her to Micky Holland's girlfriend Teresa Burke and afterwards, 'He said to me, "You know she is a prostitute. Would you work with her?" I said, "You would have to kill me first." Then he said, "Well, think about it", and then he left.'

These bitches . . .

Christ, what would they do if they ever met a real bastard?

18 Oban Street.

Memories:

Peter Rees (gone for ever).

George Dixon (but not of Dock Green).

Hurry up police it's time

In August she turned up at 18 Oban Street. Peggy James didn't live here any more, of course, but Rees spoke to one of the other tenants, Elizabeth Speakman. In fact Speakman had received a visit from her the previous month, following the incident of the snatched handbag, and had expressed shock at her bruised legs and black eyes. This time Rees was intact but terrified. She told her former neighbour that she had run away from a man 'and as she had been away from him for a short time he would definitely kill her'.

Speakman remarked that she appeared to be putting on weight and she confessed that she was roughly three months pregnant. ('She wasn't very pleased about being pregnant.') Rees's condition no doubt influenced Speakman – who was aware that the girl was soliciting – in her decision to offer shelter. Rees stayed for two nights. She left saying she was going to visit a friend in Poplar and would return the following day for dinner. 'Tina never kept the dinner appointment and I have not seen her since.'

This was the point at which Hatt reared his head.

Victor Hatt, who, at the age of twenty-three, had already served two prison sentences for poncing and should have known better than to take on Tiny Tina. After all, he was in Vincent's having a cup of tea when Woodford and Holland were attacked with axes, and he understood she was to blame.

He should have known better but he was out of work and short of money and – well, he couldn't resist her.

Victor Hatt and his friend Sidney Saunders met Gwynneth Rees in Farmer's Cafe one night and shortly afterwards drove her in

Saunders's van to what would be her last known address: 4 Hague Street Buildings, Bethnal Green. Saunders, a brewery worker, had recently rented the flat as a home for him and his wife after her release from prison. Hatt had a key and divided his time between living at the flat and living with his parents, while Saunders spent most nights at his pregnant girlfriend's address in Cable Street.

And so, en route to Cable Street, Saunders dropped Hatt and Rees off at the flat in Bethnal Green. Hatt had squared matters with his friend in advance: Rees would stay for a couple of days and part of the money he collected from her would pay for the groceries and rent.

'When he said a couple of days I knew that he meant a longer time.'

The weeks that followed may well have represented the calmest period in Rees's adult life. She could work the streets secure in the knowledge that she had a man, maybe two men, to protect her if the going got rough (and, unbeknown to them, she continued seeing Frederick Chapman). She had Hatt's key and came and went as she pleased; she cooked for them.

But back to business. 'She would earn about £6 or £7 per night. I would take it from her and then give her 30s for food and accessories and 50s for what she wanted. She was quite happy with this.'

As well she might be, for it was 80s more than Connie Whitehead ever gave her. But where did the money go?

Well, she certainly wasn't spending it on haute couture. Hatt, in an attempt to 'smarten her up a bit', gave her one of a dozen blue wool suits he'd acquired from a street trader friend. (She wouldn't wear it, and after she disappeared he gave it to a woman who worked in a clip joint on Rupert Street.)

Yes, Hatt treated Rees with consideration. He wasn't a ponce with a conscience, he was a ponce with a brain. He may have slapped her on one occasion 'for being saucy' but he never punched her; he was, in the words of his friend, 'too cunning for that'. He didn't want her running away from *him*.

When she came home early one Saturday night and explained that she'd been arrested for soliciting Hatt gave her £10 to cover her fine; and on 24 August Saunders gave her a lift to Thames Magistrates' Court for her final public appearance. She received a conditional discharge and returned Hatt's money.

It was around this time that Rees announced her intention of visiting

Barry again. On 19 October her sister Margaret was marrying Glynn
Davies, an RAF mechanic, at the parish church. Margaret had chosen
Kim, Rees's daughter, now aged five, to be her bridesmaid and she
wanted Gwynneth to attend as well, to be there in person, not just in
spirit.

Rees mentioned to Hatt that she had a child, but neglected to mention that she had two, or that she was now pregnant again. ('She
didn't show any signs that she was. Her stomach was rather flabby and
I thought that she had just had one.')

Yet she revealed her condition to Sidney Saunders, and when he
asked her who the father was she merely shrugged and smiled ('I
don't think she knew'). On another occasion he asked her what she
intended to do about the baby. She said she was going to get some pills
from a girl she knew.

'She was normally grafting with this girl Brenda,' recalled Victor Hatt.
'She was about twenty-five years old, she was short and plump. She
looks half-caste . . .' This was Brenda Meah, a former tenant of 18
Oban Street who was forced to leave at the same time as Gwynneth
Rees and Peggy James. Rees liked Meah a lot, trusted her to a degree.
She told her she was living with Hatt: she didn't say where.

At 11pm on 10 September Rees and Meah were sitting in the
Quatas Cafe in Rampart Street when Edward King came in, and from
the street outside the voice of Cornelius Whitehead asked, 'Who's in
there?' Upon hearing King's reply, 'The face', Rees gave Meah her
purse for safekeeping and instructed her, if they became separated, to
leave it at the Hole in the Wall.

Whitehead, Michael Holland and Evelyn Day now entered. They
bought drinks and sat with King at a nearby table. Whitehead made a
pointed remark about slags. The proprietor, Ann Bari, told him to
take his foot off a chair and he told her to go and fuck herself. When
her assistant Andrew Cunningham went over to remonstrate with him
Whitehead picked up a glass and threw orangeade in his face. He then
dragged Rees out of the cafe while the others remained inside.
(Holland apologized for his friend's behaviour and handed over 5s to
cover the dry-cleaning bill.) Presently Whitehead re-entered the cafe
alone and the other three left with him.

Outside the hood was up on the Ford Zephyr convertible. Rees was in the back and Whitehead and Holland got in either side of her. Day sat in the front with King the driver and they set off.

Almost as soon as the engine had started Whitehead began punching Rees repeatedly in the face, demanding to know where she was living and with whom. On her other side sat Holland, who, like Whitehead and King, had been drinking prior to entering the cafe. But drunk or sober, every time he saw this creature he felt the axes fall. According to Day, he now had two fingers paralysed yet he valiantly joined in the assault, punching Rees again and again in an attempt to beat out of her the names of his attackers.

She told him she didn't know their names. She was crying and asking the two men to leave her alone; at one point she shouted, 'Mind my baby!' (Rees had previously denied being pregnant when quizzed by Whitehead.)

But the blows kept on coming, and there were threats of something worse. Whitehead declared that they would throw her in the river. Holland, who had nicknamed Rees 'Soapy', said that was a good idea because she needed a wash. When Day told them not to be stupid, Holland threatened to throw her in as well.

Anyway, they were making progress. Rees had spilled the name of Freddie Chapman, whom she said was her boyfriend.

The car stopped twice on its journey to Battersea. The first stop occurred when Rees directed them to Carr Street and pointed out Chapman's black Ford Consul, parked outside his parents' address. King pulled up round the corner, and Whitehead and Holland went and smashed the front and rear windows. (Holland took over the driving when they returned. Day, who was now with Rees in the back of the Zephyr, noticed that Whitehead had a handkerchief wrapped around one of his hands.)

The second stop was at a stall on Battersea Bridge, where they bought some pies. That's right, Gwynneth Rees was on her way back to Warriner Gardens, and the flat she thought she'd escaped from. She and Day were dropped off some time after midnight.

'Tina was not hurt badly at all,' Michael Holland remembered. 'She was grand the next day.'

On the contrary, she looked as if she'd just gone a couple of rounds with Freddie Mills. When she walked into the Quatas Cafe in the morning, Andrew Cunningham was shocked by her appearance.

'Her face was very swollen, her eyes were black, her nose was bent. I've never seen a face so bad in my life.' When he asked her who was responsible she replied, 'Guess who? You saw me go.' To Ann Bari she said, 'I was locked in all night. It was my own fault, I asked for it.'

Shortly afterwards Whitehead spotted her in Cannon Street and drove her back to Warriner Gardens, ordering her to stay put. But she left the flat an hour later and turned up at midnight at 4 Hague Street Buildings, where Victor Hatt bathed her face and put her to bed. (In keeping with his enlightened approach to poncing, he allowed her two nights off.) After learning her story he announced impressively that he would be going over to see Whitehead 'to sort him out'.

But he soon thought better of it, and decided against taking any action whatsoever. And so Gwynneth Rees, in the short time remaining to her, walked the streets in fear.

Whitehead and Holland told police investigating Rees's death that they had smashed the front and rear windows of Frederick Chapman's Consul. However, the two nearside windows were also broken (house bricks were found inside the car) and the cost of the damage amounted to £60. Chapman never drove this car again; the Consul was towed to a yard in Crystal Palace Road and there returned to the repossession agent who had sold it to him.

Although Chapman was seeing Rees less frequently now, he had taken her out on the night of 10 September. He wondered dimly whether the damage to his car might have something to do with someone she knew.

Two nights later he was out on his motorcycle when he spotted her standing on the corner of New Road and decided to discreetly sound her out.

'I told her a motor had been smashed up round my place, but I didn't say it was mine. The reason for saying this was that I hoped someone would say something about it and I might be able to find out who was responsible.'

But this, their final meeting, proved unremarkable. Rees, it seemed, had no revelations to offer him. They chatted for twenty minutes or so, then the wonderer went on his way.

Another man who made the mistake of showing Rees affection was Albert Martin, a factory worker in his early thirties. They frequented the same cafes, and he often bought meals for her. He fancied her, and he didn't like to see her accepting lifts from men in cars. 'I used to say to her, "Why don't you pack this up?" but she never answered.'

Albert Martin. He was a mug, there to be used, and on three occasions in August she used him, puny though he was, as her protector. He escorted her back to Bethnal Green late at night, accompanying her as far as Vallance Road. She would then say goodnight, take off her shoes and run along an alley in the direction of Hague Street Buildings. 'She seemed scared of someone. She told me never to mention that I had taken her to Vallance Road.'

One night in late September Albert Martin, having visited a drinking club in the West End, was walking along Artillery Lane when a black car, 'like a Hillman', pulled up beside him. Four men, 'on the short side', got out and jumped him, punching him to the ground. A deep husky voice said, 'Don't see Tina – this is a warning.' The men then picked him up and put him into a taxi, instructing the driver to drop him off at Cannon Street Road. 'They must have paid the driver, because when we got there I got out and the cab drove off.'

Had they bashed the right man? Who did they think he was? Whitehead? Holland? Chapman? Hatt? And who did the deep husky voice belong to? A new ponce on the scene? An old one restaking his claim?

And much of Madness, and more of Sin, and Tina the soul of the plot . . .

'The next day was Sunday and I stayed in bed as my chest and back hurt.'

Tales of Misery and Intimidation. Stories that accumulate steadily, impressively, like birds in a tree in the desert.

Stories of a girl you used to know.

Dirty, scruffy, malnourished, she ran on Senior Service and purple hearts.

She met you and let you, received you and deceived you (look you). She was the hair of all dogs, she was the griefs of the ages, she was the fear of the dark (mark you, mark you) at the end of your working day . . .

Tiny Tina.

You didn't have to try too hard to hate her.
But did you – any of you – kill her?
Or what?

I never wear a watch (I get nauseous) and I don't know the time right now. But I know that the *ITMA* men have disappeared and that an office crowd is beginning to gather in Gordon's; seats are at a premium and several newcomers hover nearby, awaiting developments at our table.

Brian is explaining to me why the book before us has remained out of print for nearly thirty years.

'Of course back in the Seventies the business was still fresh in people's minds – but who cares about it now? Mention it to anyone under fifty, they won't know what you're talking about. Anyway, I had a word with my publisher a few years ago, to no avail. They said, "Brian, take a walk along Charing Cross Road. You'll find one-eyed killers, one-armed killers, one-legged killers . . ."'

'What about security guards?'

'What?'

'Your final chapter. The killer turns out to be a security guard who eventually commits suicide to avoid arrest.'

'Yes . . .'

'Now you refer to him simply as "Big John", but I was wondering, since it all happened such a long time ago, if –'

'He must never be named!' Brian brings his wine glass down on the table like a gavel and I stare at him, shocked. 'At least, not while members of his immediate family remain alive. They must be shielded from the knowledge of his guilt.'

'But *was* he guilty? I was reading an account by another journalist, and he suggests the killer was a policeman.'

'Oh, that old chestnut.' Brian relaxes, shakes his head. 'Who served up that one?'

'Owen Summers.'

He smiles. 'Good old Owen. Dead now, of course. Nearly all the old gang are dead. Norman Lucas (he was a rogue) . . . John Ponder . . . Peter Earle . . . all gone. Speaking of which . . .' Brian shrugs on his jacket, pats the pockets and eventually, with an air of concentration, stands up. 'I hope you've got everything you want. We can always repeat the experience, if necessary.' At the foot of the stairs he pauses. 'John du Rose. Threw a police cordon around the *whole* of west London. Imagine that.'

'Did you ever go and talk to him about the case?'

'*I* didn't. But I knew a man who did. He went down to East Anglia, where du Rose was living out his last days. He found him at a football match, watching Norwich play Wogga-Wogga.'

'What did he say?'

'He didn't say much at all. Side of the mouth job. Barely spoke to him.'

It was the early hours of Sunday 29 September 1963. In the Commercial Cafe in Commercial Road Gwynneth Rees and Brenda Meah sat drinking tea and chatting to Peggy James and John Gale, a young man known to these women as 'Carol'. After a while Rees and Meah left the others and went outside on business. Afterwards they visited Farmer's Cafe. Here Rees spoke to three Welsh lorry drivers, and they asked her to go with them to their caravan at Shoreditch. 'Tina asked me to go with her. I refused, saying it was madness to go with three men.' So Rees put them off, telling them she would see them later.

The two friends returned to the Commercial and rejoined Peggy James and Carol. James and Rees were invited to Brenda Meah's flat for dinner that evening. 'I told Tina and Mrs James not to let me down as I didn't want to get dinner if neither of them were going to turn up, and they both promised to come along.'

But it was just as Meah feared: neither woman materialized. Peggy James later explained that she had been too busy looking for some-where to live. So what was Gwynneth Rees's excuse?

At about 4am that Sunday Rees and Meah finished work and walked together along Commercial Road with the intention of getting a taxi home. They had reached the junction of New Road and Commercial Road when a car drove past.

This car . . . it was two-tone, possibly a Consul, possibly a Zodiac, possibly a Zephyr. ('I can't remember if it was a saloon or not.') The driver stopped in New Road, facing north towards Whitechapel. 'Tina said, "He's all right, I know him," and asked me if she should ask him to give me a lift as well, but I said not to bother.'

Rees ran up to the car, calling out to her friend that she would see her later that day. She got in and the car drove off. 'I didn't see the driver but I think he was young.'

Gwynneth Rees was wearing a black and white speckled coat with patch pockets and a large collar; a white woollen jumper with a red and blue zigzag pattern; a tight black skirt; tan-coloured nylon stockings; and navy-blue high-heeled shoes, well worn.

According to Brenda Meah, the last person known to have seen her in one piece.

It couldn't have been Chapman's Consul. Was it Whitehead's Zephyr?

On 24 November, the day following the identification of Gwynneth Rees's remains, Cornelius Whitehead was brought to Richmond police station, where he was detained for the next two days. He admitted knowing the dead woman and confessed to assaulting her on the night of 10 September, although he denied poncing on her. ('She could never have earned sufficient to make it worthwhile.') He saw her for the last time in Cannon Street three days after the assault, but didn't speak to her. He had never driven either of his cars to a rubbish dump at Mortlake ('In fact, I don't know where Mortlake is') and, furthermore, 'Tina has never been on the floor of my Zephyr convertible car or in the back of the vehicle.'

Whitehead's address was searched and his clothes and vehicles seized and submitted for forensic examination. In addition to driving his own cars, Whitehead regularly borrowed his father Alfred's maroon and grey Ford Classic saloon, which was also seized and examined.

Human bloodstains discovered in both pockets of a sheepskin jacket and in the right trouser pocket and left sleeve of a brown suit were of the blood group O, M; those on the right sleeve were of Group O; and those on the front of the suit jacket were of group O, M N. O is the commonest of the blood groups; Rees was blood group O, yet the condition of her body had prohibited a finer classification.

Whitehead was now interrogated further. He told police, 'Any blood found on my clothing may have come from fights I have had . . . It may also have been as a result of the punching I gave Tina in the back of my Zephyr convertible.'

The back seat and rear mat of the Zephyr gave reactions to human blood; the effect was as if they had been washed after staining. The assault on Rees was one possible explanation here, but what explanation could there possibly be for the human bloodstains discovered in the seams of the back seat of his father's car?

Well . . .

'It might have been from my father's dog when he cut his paw. It might have come from Tina when I gave her one of her whackings, or might have come from Eve Day, from her thing when she came on. I know she used to bleed.'

Whackings . . . Whitehead now admitted that he had assaulted her on at least four occasions prior to 10 September. And his wrath wasn't restricted to Rees. Rita Darvill had told police that one night in September he'd dragged her out of the Desire Club in a drunken rage and punched her in the face (more blood). She was terrified of him.

As was Patricia Harrison, an eighteen-year-old prostitute who moved into the basement flat in Battersea during Rees's first absence. After a couple of weeks she too fled, leaving most of her clothes behind in her eagerness to escape his attentions. But he found her in a cafe, forced her into a car (the Classic?) and drove her to the canal at Wapping. He wanted £20 by Friday or he'd throw her in.

Rees, Darvill, Harrison . . . It sounded great, sweeter than Shakespeare, but it wasn't enough. A blood sample obtained from him proved to be group OM, so negating the value of the bloodstains found on his clothing, and the quantity of blood discovered inside the Ford Classic was insufficient to allow for grouping. No evidence could be found that connected Cornelius Whitehead with the death of Gwynneth Rees.

Whitehead's associates Edward King and Michael Holland were also interrogated. Neither man owned a vehicle, but their addresses were searched and their clothing forensically examined. Holland admitted taking part in the assault on Rees on 10 September, after which date he saw her several times soliciting with Meah in the East End but didn't speak to her.

'I did not kill Tina. I have never been to Mortlake or Richmond until I was brought here by police. I have used Connie's motors, that is, his A40 and his Anglia when he had it, but I have never been over this way in either of them.'

Holland had seven convictions, including one for causing grievous bodily harm with intent. He also had a landlord who waxed mournful at the mention of his name. 'He is a violent man, more so in drink . . . He is a boy who lives by violence, it seems to have a fatal attraction for him.' Before he battened on Teresa Burke he was living with a woman known as 'Scouse Maria'. 'Maria was about 4' 9", like a dwarf . . . I used to hear her screaming when Micky used to hit her . . . I stopped him trying to throttle her one night. I took her to Hammersmith Hospital, she couldn't speak.' Final thoughts? 'My personal opinion is that one day, especially under the influence of drink, he will go too far. I have told him that many times.'

But once again it was all in the promise, for no evidence could be found which connected Holland – or King – with Rees's death. Indeed, her days and nights had come to revolve around *avoiding* Whitehead and Holland and, by association, King, so she was hardly likely to run towards a vehicle with any of those faces at the wheel. The witness Brenda Meah may not have remembered much but she insisted that the car she saw did not belong to Whitehead or Chapman.

So who did it belong to? Was it borrowed? Stolen? Had it been sold on, or otherwise disposed of at any time during the previous two months? Who was the driver?

Well, unfortunately Gwynneth Rees had enjoyed a far more extensive male acquaintance than would prove traceable. A happier question might be: where was the young driver supposed to be driving her?

Home.

Home. Of course. Mr Hatt, Mr Saunders, step this way.

At 1pm on Saturday 28 September Victor Hatt set off from 4 Hague Street Buildings with the voice of Gwynneth Rees ringing in his ears, complaining that he left her on her own all day.

But that afternoon Hatt had important business to attend to. He was on his way to a gambling club at the back of a barber's shop in Old Montague Street where he had arranged to sell a suit length (which he admitted to police was stolen) to a Robert 'Teddy' Evans. When he arrived Evans, an Antiguan who helped to run the spieler, was not there. He waited and waited until eventually, at 5pm, he left the club and visited his parents' house in Bow; here he washed and changed into his best clothes before returning to Old Montague Street.

He met Sidney Saunders in the street and reminded him that they had arranged to see Count Basie and his orchestra at the Astoria Theatre, Finsbury Park, that evening. ('I had forgotten all about this.') Saunders drove them both back to Hague Street Buildings in his van. However, he entered the flat without Hatt.

'He said that he wouldn't come up to the flat because if Tina saw him in his new suit she would think he was going with another bird. He stayed downstairs and I went upstairs to see if Tina was there. I was to tell her that I had not seen Vicki [Hatt], but that she was to go out to graft all the same and that Vicki would probably be back later.'

By now it was about 7pm; Rees had already left. He looked inside the cold oven and saw that she'd cooked a meal for her absent friends. He rejoined Hatt downstairs.

Count Basie was appearing at the Astoria for one night only and gave two performances, the second of which began at 9.10pm. They arrived in the van at about 8.15pm and met Robert Evans coming out of a pub. Evans and George Kuss, his Jamaican business partner, had also turned up to see the show. Sala McGregor, another Jamaican and a student at the card school, joined the group and they all entered the theatre.

The first half was good, but the second half went with an extra swing.

They'd visited an off-licence during the interval, with the result that Hatt sat swigging from a bottle of vodka while the others shared two halves of cherry brandy. As they left the theatre he was sick; he went to sleep in the van, which was now heading for Teddy Evans's address in Stoke Newington. More drinks, and then a cafe in Dalston.

Chicken and chips, and then Soho. Ronnie Scott's was full but they got into the Flamingo Club and finished up at the Roaring Twenties in Carnaby Street. McGregor stayed behind when the others left at 3am.

Sidney Saunders dropped off Evans and Kuss at or near their homes and drove back to his flat with Hatt asleep in the seat beside him. They arrived at Hague Street Buildings between 3.30 and 4am, and here Hatt emerged from the van for the first time since leaving the theatre. Before setting off for his girlfriend's address in Cable Street, Saunders helped Hatt up into the flat, undressed him and put him to bed.

'I can remember being sick, being bundled into the van, and the next thing I remember is waking up at Sid's flat. It was Sunday morning. Tina was not in the flat.'

He thought at first she'd been arrested. A few days later he found a note, possibly an old note, which read, 'Thanks for coming home like you promised. The dinner's burned . . . Tina'. ('There was something else on it but I cannot remember what.') He destroyed it out of fear that it might incriminate him as her ponce.

Ponce with no tart, no less. Where the hell was she? He asked around; no one seemed to know. Sidney Saunders thought that she might have gone to Wales to her sister's wedding, but pretty soon Victor Hatt feared the worst. The end had come. Fed up with being left on her own, she'd run away to live with another man and so . . . no more great nights out, no more money.

She'd taken his flat key with her, but she'd left some of her clothes behind in the wardrobe, hanging beside clothes which belonged to Saunders's wife (and a few other women who'd lived there).

The flat was searched and nine items of women's clothing were found, of which four – a white jumper with a red and blue diamond pattern, a black skirt, a waist slip and a roll-on belt – were identified by Brenda Meah as similar to items worn by Gwynneth Rees. (The identification cast doubt on Meah's reliability as a witness, for the jumper and skirt were most likely the ones she claimed Rees was wearing at the time of her disappearance.)

Hatt and Saunders were interrogated over a period of two days. Hatt's story was corroborated by Saunders, and Saunders's story was corroborated by Evans, Kuss and McGregor. The police understood that neither Hatt nor Saunders had ever visited Mortlake. Hatt had no vehicle of his own but sometimes borrowed his friend's pale blue Commer Cob van, which was duly seized and examined, without result. The two men were released but were ordered to report weekly at Leman Street police station (as were Whitehead, Holland and King).

What of the three Welsh lorry drivers? Well, three were found who, when loading in east London, slept in a caravan parked in the yard of Thomas Griffith Ltd, a general haulage company based in Shoreditch. None of the men was Welsh; however, each admitted having intercourse with Rees in the caravan one night earlier in the year. This episode occurred probably in August or September; they couldn't agree on a day although Friday, Saturday and Sunday were out of the question as they went home at weekends. Two of the men agreed that all three had met her in Farmer's Cafe and driven her to the caravan some time around midnight, but the third man claimed that he had gone to bed earlier with flu. 'I went to sleep and some time after I was awakened by Harry and Donald, who had Tina with them. We had sexual intercourse with her and I fell asleep again.' She was driven back to Commercial Road between 12.30am and 2.30am and walked off in the direction of Farmer's Cafe.

A director of Thomas Griffith Ltd stated that London drivers who used their yard never loaded at weekends, and that the last weekend in September was no exception.

So the night in question now appeared to be out of the question. Perhaps the gang bang had taken place on another, more ordinary night.

Christmas was coming. The inquiry was now several weeks old, and all Frederick Chadburn had to show for it was a few grubby ponces and a frighteningly sketchy account of the dead woman's final movements.

If only brasses kept diaries, eh?

If only corpses could talk . . .

But this was no time for morbid thoughts.

The situation was about to change.

There were bigger better things waiting –

There were smaller formless things lurking –

Just around the corner.

Just around the bend.

At 10.30pm on 24 September 1963 WPC Suttle and WPC Humberston had stopped a young woman in Commercial Road as she appeared to be soliciting. WPC Suttle asked her who she was and the woman replied, 'You know me. I'm Tina Smart.' Of course they knew her, only she seemed to have lost weight. Or had she put weight on? Suttle said to her, 'You look pregnant, Tina.' 'Yes, I think I am.' She had been to hospital that day, she told them, and she'd had it confirmed.

'Yes, I think I am,' sounds like a bit of an understatement, as we know that by this date she was approximately five months gone. But a lot had happened since she broke the news to Frederick Chapman back in May. She'd been dragged along by a car, she'd been savagely assaulted by Whitehead and Holland . . . She'd grown anxious because she could feel no movement inside her. But now she knew the baby was still alive.

Brenda Meah understood that she wanted to kill it.

'She said she didn't want the baby and said she was going to get a syringe and hot water and carbolic soap and try and get rid of the baby. I asked her who was going to do this and she said no one and that she was going to do it herself. I told her not to be silly . . .'

Yes, a bit of harmless drama no doubt helped to while away some of the long hours in the all-night cafes, ensuring that the mother-to-be/not-to-be remained the centre of attention.

Promise me, Tina.

Don't do it, Tina.

Of course she'd done it before.

On 6 June 1960 Gwynneth Rees was admitted to St Andrew's Hospital, Bow; she was suffering from the effects of an attempted abortion and aborted while there. (She told the hospital authorities that she had manually interfered with herself.) She was discharged on 11 July, but returned on 17 July with heavy menstrual bleeding and was finally discharged five days later.

On 2 October 1961 she was admitted to Charing Cross Hospital; she was suffering from salpingitis, an infection of the Fallopian tubes which, according to the hospital authorities, might have been the result of an abortion. She was discharged on 11 October.

These were the years before abortion law reform, and the law relating to the operation was ambiguous. Any attempt to induce abortion was a felony, punishable by imprisonment if it was done unlawfully – that is, with the sole aim of ending an unwanted pregnancy. But the operation was deemed to be lawful if performed in good faith, with the aim of preserving the life or health of the woman. A test case was the trial of the eminent surgeon Aleck Bourne at the Old Bailey in 1938. Bourne had aborted a fourteen-year-old girl who was pregnant as the result of rape; he was charged under the Offences against the Person Act of 1861 with unlawfully procuring the abortion of the girl, and subsequently acquitted.

Summing up, the judge declared that if a doctor 'is of opinion, on reasonable grounds and with adequate knowledge, that the probable consequence of the continuance of the pregnancy will be to make the woman a physical or mental wreck, the jury are quite entitled to take the view that the doctor who, in those circumstances and in that honest belief, operates, is operating for the purpose of preserving the life of the woman'.

Reasonable grounds . . . There was a loophole here, and by the Sixties it was being routinely exploited. Thousands of technically legal abortions were performed each year, most of them arranged in Harley Street by doctors who enlisted the help of a sympathetic psychiatrist or (preferably) two to assess the patient's level of distress (*'Suicidal despair' all right?*) Fees of between £100 and £200 were charged, and a busy surgeon might perform up to twenty abortions a day.

The professionals were a protected species but the amateurs . . . well, they were fair game, and very popular with the police.

Every copper wanted one for Christmas.

Gwynneth Rees talked about self-aborting yet she was now five months pregnant, and had botched the operation in the past. So did she decide, for safety's sake, to hire a stranger? Did somebody else make this arrangement for her? Was this how she died?

On 27 November police interviewed a prostitute named Jean Anderson, also known as 'Scabby Jean' and 'Jean the Beast', and she told them that on Friday 13 September she was playing the pinball machine in Farmer's Cafe when an acquaintance, Terry Dawson, entered, looking for Rees. He left a message with Anderson: Rees was to contact another prostitute, Brenda O'Neill, and she would get in touch with Billy, who frequented the Nucleus Club in Monmouth Street.

Anderson passed on the message later that day. 'I told her I knew Billy was an abortionist and asked her if she was thinking of getting rid of her baby and she told me she was. She said it was costing £25.'

Names, places, prices. Exciting news? Not really. There was something a bit depressing about Scabby Jean. She seemed too eager to talk, too addled to think; and soon an incident occurred which confirmed her reputation as an epic liar.

On 4 December she got into a customer's car in the area of

Commercial Road and told him, 'A pound with a rubber.' But protection wasn't necessary for he couldn't perform, and eventually they agreed to split the pound between them. Anderson departed and immediately pointed his car out to police as belonging to a man who claimed to be Rees's murderer.

Yes, they soon had the number of the Beast; and yet by 4 December events had taken an unexpected and rather heart-warming turn.

On 28 November, the day after the interview with Anderson, one George Hamerton telephoned New Scotland Yard and volunteered information regarding his knowledge of the deceased.

Hamerton was forty years old, lived in East Acton and owned two hot dog stalls, one situated at Brook Green, Hammersmith, which he operated himself, and the other at Western Avenue. He used a blue Bedford van to transport his goods and equipment and his hours of business were 10pm to 2am on Fridays, Saturdays and Sundays.

After work one night in spring of that year Hamerton and Terry Dawson, his employee at the Western Avenue stall, visited the Nimbus Club in Islington. It was Dawson's first visit and he was surprised to spot a face from the East End, a woman he knew well and introduced to his boss as Tina. This was the woman whose photograph Hamerton had seen in the newspaper.

Hamerton bumped into her in the club on several subsequent occasions, the last of which was in early August. They never talked about anything special, and he had no idea she was pregnant. Had she ever asked his advice about illegal operations of any sort? No. 'As I have said, Tina was not a friend of mine. She was a friend of Dawson's.'

Dawson again. He was clearly the man to speak to. But Dawson no longer worked for Hamerton and was proving difficult to find.

On 30 November they interviewed Patricia Bold, a prostitute who had known Rees as a casual acquaintance for the six months prior to her disappearance. However, for the final two months, following a fight over Bold's boyfriend, Bold refused to speak to her.

So what was there to talk about now?

Not much.

Unless, of course, she happened to have heard about a man who did –

'I have heard his name but I cannot remember it. He is always in the Nucleus Club and when you go into the club he always stands by the milk machine in the corner.'

Description?

'He is about thirty-four or thirty-five years old, about 5′ 11″ in height, very stocky build. He has reddish-ginger hair . . . He wears a brown suede jacket, it is nigger brown in colour and I think the jacket is real suede.'

Profession?

'He owns a Dormobile van, beige colour, and the two windows at the rear have no glass in them. He sells hot dogs in the West End, I don't know where . . .'

George Hamerton was brought to Richmond police station the same day, and he remained there until 2 December. He talked and talked: abortions poured from his lips.

About ten years ago he'd had a girlfriend, Mary, who was pregnant by another man. She wanted to get rid of the baby and he took her to see a woman in Clapham. 'I don't know who gave her the address and I can't remember where it was in Clapham.' Anyway, nothing happened. They went again a week later and again the treatment proved unsuccessful.

What was the treatment? 'She told me she had been syringed out with reddish-coloured liquid with disinfectant in it.' Well, that sounded easy enough; he suggested she buy a douche syringe and do the job herself.

But when Mary had no luck either it was obvious the solution, like the problem, lay in a man's touch.

He did it at her digs in Chiswick. She went down on one knee as in Clapham, so lowering the neck of her womb to meet the nozzle of the syringe. A washing-up bowl was placed immediately beneath her.

'I boiled some water, put it in a bowl, shredded some Lifebuoy household soap into the water and added some Dettol to the liquid. When the soap had melted I put some of the liquid in the syringe and squeezed it into her.'

He continued this process until he had used up all the liquid; his girlfriend appeared to feel no pain, and aborted within two days. Later in their relationship she became pregnant by him, and he repeated the experiment with similar success.

Seven years later George Hamerton, now married (but not to

Mary), was looking for a love nest, somewhere he and Valerie, his married girlfriend, could be alone together. He found a basement flat at 130 Albion Road, Stoke Newington. The lovers shared the rent and installed new furniture, a radio, a record player and a television set; they had intercourse there once or twice a week.

But Hamerton liked to enjoy the flat when Valerie wasn't around. 'Sometimes I have invited groups of people there for a small party. I mean mixed groups. Sometimes they stay the night but nothing resembling an orgy takes place.'

And then there were the prostitutes.

And then there was a pregnant prostitute, Anne, whom he met at the coffee stall at Marble Arch. She said she was three months gone and asked him if he knew of anybody who performed abortions. 'I told her I had done this sort of thing before and I was willing to try to do it to her.' A week later he drove Anne back to 130 Albion Road. He boiled a kettle, mixed his soap and Dettol, and prepared to spurt. 'Anne had had abortions before and she suggested that she lay on the floor with her legs up.' The operation was a success.

A few months later he aborted Carol, the girlfriend of a man who ran a wireless shop off the Portobello Road. Next came Jackie, who was brought to his hot dog stall at Hammersmith by a peanut vendor from Wembley. Norma, a black girl, was aborted in the presence of one of his employees (he came into the flat to count his money and fell asleep in the chair). And then Jackie got pregnant again . . .

'Apparently I became quite good at this. I suppose it was more by luck than judgement.'

Luck's the word here, isn't it? Any one of these women might have died. Hamerton was using non-sterilized equipment, equipment that attracted fresh bacteria with each successive operation. The potentially fatal effects of introducing these infective agents into the vagina, and possibly even the womb, were unlikely to be diminished by the presence of Dettol and melted Lifebuoy. Hamerton also ran the risk of inflicting internal injury, and if, say, the nozzle of the syringe pierced the wall of the vagina the possibility of infection would be greatly increased.

Stick it up me now, George . . .

He wasn't cheap either.

He was free, although he accepted donations. Norma gave £4;

Jackie gave £10, the second time. She didn't feel too bright afterwards. He wrapped her in a blanket and took her home in his van.

'I have not done any since . . . All I have made out of all this is £14.'

Hamerton's Bedford van and his private vehicle, a Canadian Ford Fairlane, were seized and examined without result. His home address and a rented garage at Acton Hill were searched, as was the flat at 130 Albion Road, scene of all the abortions from Anne onwards.

'There is a plastic bed in the flat which Valerie and I bought from the Ideal Home Exhibition. I have never used this when doing my abortions.'

Forensic examination revealed this bed to be lightly smeared with human blood, the quantity insufficient to allow for grouping. Hamerton attributed the blood to Valerie, who on one occasion 'became unwell' while in the flat, and added that there were also flecks of blood on the wallpaper near the bed. 'Valerie would use the syringe after her periods.' Valerie had no knowledge of any of the abortions, with the exception of the abortion he'd performed on her eighteen months ago. 'Valerie and Jackie were the only difficult ones. Still, all women are different.'

On 11 December George Hamerton was charged with aborting Jacqueline McMullen and later sentenced to two years' imprisonment.

This was doubtless gratifying for the detectives involved, yet it failed to advance the investigation into the death of Gwynneth Rees. Hamerton insisted that he had never been known as 'Billy'. He admitted frequenting the Nucleus Club but insisted that he never met Rees anywhere apart from the Nimbus Club, and never by arrangement. He knew Terry Dawson but did not know a Brenda O'Neill.

He knew Jean Anderson. 'She is noted for lying about anyone, so I've heard.'

But was she lying on this occasion? Richmond police turned over the Beast's statement in their minds as if it were the riddle of the Sphinx.

And while they were trying to puzzle that one out another problem presented itself in the shifting shape of Evelyn Day.

On or about 23 September Evelyn Day vacated 27a Warriner Gardens, leaving a plundered gas meter and a seething señora in her wake, and returned to the East End, moving into 32 Cavell Street three weeks later. She was first interviewed on 23 November in Holloway prison, where she was on remand awaiting sentence for soliciting and for possession of purple hearts. She spoke at some length about her life and associates, about Whitehead and Holland and their assault on Rees, but gave no indication that she knew who was responsible for her friend's death.

However, police learned that upon her release from prison on 5 December Day, discussing the subject of Rees's death with two neighbours in a cafe, had stated that she died while being aborted against her will; according to one listener, 'Eve said, "Tina was put unconscious and somebody tried to place an abortion on her but she came round halfway through and two geezers gave her a good hiding."'

On 18 December Day was interviewed at Richmond police station and she confirmed that Rees had indeed been aborted, 'at the end of September or the beginning of October'. She hadn't mentioned this before because she was frightened of the two geezers – Whitehead and Holland. They wanted to get rid of the baby and Day knew a woman, Emily, who performed abortions; she was short, fat, fortyish and Scottish and she lived in a house in Bacon Street, Bethnal Green. The three of them visited her one Friday afternoon, and it was arranged that Rees would be aborted at her address at midnight on the Saturday.

Whitehead, Holland, Rees and Day turned up in Whitehead's A40 at the appointed hour, and the three women entered Emily's bedroom. Rees was wearing a grey mohair coat with a wide collar, a white jumper with a red and blue diamond pattern ('She bought it from "Joe the Suitcase"') and a tight-fitting royal-blue skirt. She kept her jumper and skirt on but removed black knickers, tan stockings and a suspender belt before lying down upon a double bed.

'Then this woman put her hand inside her between her legs. She appeared to be twisting her hand inside her. Tina screamed and appeared to be in agony. A few minutes after this she began to bleed.'

The sight was so awful Day left the room and joined the two men, who were waiting outside the door. She told them the abortion had been performed, and Whitehead entered the bedroom while she and Holland went and sat in the car.

Ten minutes later Whitehead came outside and announced that

Rees was dead. Day became hysterical; she was told to keep her mouth shut. They drove her home, and on the way Whitehead mentioned something about burning clothes.

How much did the operation cost? Well, during the outward journey she saw a roll of notes fall out of Rees's pocket: £100, or so Day said. 'I did not see her pay the money to Emily but she could have done this whilst I was out of the room.'

Cash in hand, hand in gash – it was spellbinding stuff; even if this account of events didn't exactly correspond to the précis as provided in the cafe, even if the detail of the white jumper with a red and blue diamond pattern was almost certainly inaccurate. So what? Here, from the mouth of a well-placed associate, came a credible solution to the mystery of Gwynneth Rees's death. Evelyn Day's story carried convictions.

On 19 December detectives descended on 19 Bacon Street; Emily Lawson, a 46-year-old cleaner, was taken to Richmond police station and interrogated for four days. Her rooms were searched and examined for fingerprints and items of property were seized and forensically examined, but nothing came to light to connect her either with abortions in general or that of Gwynneth Rees in particular. However, Lawson confessed to having aborted three women, Sylvia Cadera, Sonia Menditta and Pauline Smith, at two separate premises, and on 22 December she was charged with these offences. But she'd never heard of a Tina Smart or even an Evelyn Day.

Good God, another prostitute had lied. But why? Did Evie hate Connie and Micky that much? Had Emily cleaned her out in the past?

No.

No; it was nothing like that.

It was to do with pleasing men.

'The reason I made this story up was because I thought if I told you that, you would let me go. I realized that when you checked up on it you would find out that I had lied.'

Questions . . . lies . . . questions . . .

'I don't want to stay in police custody and by telling this story I thought I would be released.'

Questions, questions . . . bouncing off the walls.

'The clothes I said Tina was wearing were clothes I had seen her wear at the Battersea address.'

Evelyn Day based the story of Gwynneth Rees's fatal abortion on what she'd heard of the abortion of Sylvia Cadera, who survived.

Cadera, a prostitute, was approximately three months pregnant (father unknown) when she began to seek an abortion. A gynaecologist had quoted her a price of 100 guineas for the operation. 'I said I could only afford forty and he said that wouldn't pay for the anaesthetist.' He told her to come back if she could lay her hands on the money.

Now, a prostitute's abortion was usually arranged by her ponce, but Sylvia Cadera's ponce, her Maltese husband, Victor, was currently in prison (for poncing) and, in view of the fact that the baby wasn't his, visiting time might have proved awkward. What was she going to do?

She went round to 38 Cavell Street to ask her friend Rosetta Cribben if she knew of anyone who performed abortions. Cribben suggested she speak to another tenant, Sandra Fairclough, who said that she knew a woman who lived off Brick Lane, and that it would cost £10 or £20. 'I told Sandra I would give her £5 if she would arrange it for me.'

On 11 October 1963 the abortion took place in Sandra Fairclough's room at 38 Cavell Street. Emily Lawson arrived at lunchtime and brought with her a leather bag containing an enema syringe, a bottle of Dettol and some Epsom salts tablets wrapped in paper.

The patient was frightened, so they all had a cup of tea. Afterwards Sandra Fairclough boiled the kettle again and Lawson unwrapped her tablets. (The salts would act as a purging agent, drawing the foetus through the neck of the womb.) She dissolved them in a bowl of hot water and added Dettol.

Sylvia Cadera removed her knickers, pulled her clothes up and sat on the edge of a couch. She held Fairclough's hand, turned her head away. Lawson's fingers explored her vagina; Lawson's syringe shot the liquid into her womb, flushing out a smelly brown discharge. The operation lasted about two minutes, and then she put her knickers back on and they all had another cup of tea. Cadera was told that she would miscarry later in the day.

At 7pm on 13 October she was visiting Rosetta Cribben when –

'Rosetta got a bucket for me and I sat on it and I bled into the bucket. The baby was only about four inches long and I couldn't tell its sex. Her two little children were in the room and started shouting, "Look, there's a baby!" and so I picked it up, put it in the baby's pot and flushed it down the toilet in the yard.

'I felt all right and then I went to bingo at the Odeon in Hackney Road.'

Cadera told police she paid £20 for the abortion (not including the £5 she never gave Sandra Fairclough), yet Lawson claimed she received nothing.

The abortion of fifteen-year-old Sonia Menditta in June 1962 was similarly unprofitable. Her father, Luigi, said he handed over 'eight to ten pounds' but Lawson remembered otherwise. According to her, Luigi and his wife, Myra, 'promised to come over to see me and give me a night out, but they never came'.

In September the Mendittas organized a second abortion at their home in Brockley. This time the patient was Myra's friend Pauline Smith. She arrived with between £70 and £100 in cash and a half-bottle of brandy, yet there was no drink in it for her saviour. 'I had no money for doing it . . . I never got anything.'

On 21 February 1964 Emily Lawson stood trial at the Old Bailey. She pleaded guilty to three charges of procuring an abortion and received three concurrent sentences of three years' imprisonment.

But she hadn't aborted Gwynneth Rees.

And she didn't know Billy.

So who did?

Police eventually traced Thomas ('Terry') Victor Dawson, an unemployed Scot, to 29 Artesian Road, W2, where he was living with a married woman and two prostitutes. Dawson recalled a one-night stand with the deceased, whom he knew as 'Trina', in 1961, and corroborated in general terms Hamerton's story of the encounter at the Nimbus Club. However, when questioned regarding his alleged appearance in Farmer's Cafe on 13 September 1963, he pointed out — correctly — that on that date he was in prison for driving while disqualified; he was released on 23 September. He knew Brenda O'Neill by her nickname 'Sexy' but had never spoken to her about abortions, and he had not seen Trina since he left prison. 'I never mentioned that Billy wanted to see her. I do not know the Billy in question.'

A session with Brenda O'Neill proved to be more rewarding. Sexy, it transpired, knew Billy. 'He is about forty-five, short, stocky, losing his hair, and has a yellow and white American car.' One night about three years ago she was in the Nucleus Club when he told her that if she ever got pregnant he would be able to help: as a matter of fact, any girl who needed help should come to him. 'He said it would be safe as houses.'

Indeed. And where might Billy be found?

The Nucleus Club, of course.

He owned it.

Not all of it, you understand. Billy had a partner, 'Taffy'.

In any case we're talking lease, not freehold. In 1961 William Hayward, a motorcycle fitter, and Albert 'Taffy' Bridgewater, his former employer, pooled their financial resources and paid £700 (cash) for the coffee bar at 9–11 Monmouth Street, WC1. The establishment's correct name was the Nucleus Coffee House, commonly known as the Nucleus Club. Opening hours were formerly 8pm to 6am, yet since June 1963 the club had remained open twenty-four hours a day.

Bridgewater was shown a photograph of Gwynneth Rees and recognized her face; but she was just a face, nothing more. 'I feel positive that I have seen her in the club in the past. The nearest I can get to it is that was many, many months ago.'

The Welshman also recognized photographs of Thomas Dawson and George Hamerton, both of whom used the club. A rumour had been circulating that Hamerton performed abortions; the source of the rumour was 'Andy Capp', 'a short man, about 5′ 6″, with a small beard, and he nicks gear out of cars'.

He wouldn't have felt out of place among the clientele. There was Jake, 'who seems to be a thief. He has part of his ear missing, but I don't know which one.' There was Eddie, who had a blue star tattooed on his forehead; 'He nicked 30s from our till so I don't suppose we shall see him again.' And there was 'a little slag, a flash boy, who I have only seen once since he was nearly strangled by Bill Hayward. It was a fight over the entrance fee into the club, which is 2s, and Holland refused to pay this amount and the fight followed.'

Not him, not Holland again. Fancy having to waste time on a toerag like Holland when you could be taking care of real business.

Meeting and greeting.

Circulating.

Arranging abortions.

William Hayward, thirty-nine, was a married man with three children. But in June 1956 he had two children and Joan, his wife, was expecting another one. He didn't want her to have it.

Hayward first met Betty Couzens when he took a pair of shoes into her husband's shoe repair shop in Battersea. Bridgewater, who was then employing Hayward at his motorcycle shop in Wandsworth, subsequently told him that this woman performed abortions. Arrangements were made and Couzens aborted his wife for £5.

Pretty soon Couzens was giving him money for supplying her with customers; so many, it seems, that he couldn't remember them all.

So who came to mind?

Well, in 1961, or thereabouts, a performer with Chipperfield's Circus came to see him. 'He was an Australian. He said that he had been sent to see me as I might know someone who did abortions.'

The circus was in Ilford; Couzens entered a caravan and Hayward waited outside. 'I understand the girl was coloured, but I never saw her.' On the journey home he received £4.

In June 1963 he arranged an abortion for an Irish girl named Eileen or Helen. 'I don't know where she lives, I think she hustles.' He took this girl to Couzens's house in Tooting; Couzens received £10, and paid Hayward £3 commission.

In November 1963 he promised to arrange an abortion for Helen, the girlfriend of his friend Jeff. The figure agreed was £10, and Hayward was soon on his way to his business partner's new address in Battersea. He brought glad tidings, but for once Couzens appeared reluctant to get involved. She said she could not possibly do it at her flat and asked if Jeff's girlfriend could find somewhere suitable.

No. No, she couldn't. In the end Hayward agreed to act as host. He picked up Jeff and Helen at Waterloo station one evening in his Pontiac saloon (*seized and examined*) and drove them to his current address, 62 Shore House, Willard Estate, SW18 (*searched*). Betty Couzens arrived shortly afterwards, yet for some reason she hadn't brought a syringe. Hayward got back in his car and drove her to

Clapham Junction, where she entered a block of flats, emerging presently with a small brown-paper parcel.

When they returned to the flat Betty Couzens went into the main bedroom with Helen, while Hayward joined his wife and his father in the front room. Jeff was there as well. 'They all knew why Helen and Jeff were there.'

On this occasion Hayward received £5 but a couple of days later Jeff called round to report that nothing had happened.

'I told my wife that Betty and Helen would have to come to our flat again.'

In the meantime Hayward's friend Dick approached him on behalf of his girlfriend. Couzens was due to reabort Helen at the flat one afternoon in the week, so Hayward booked this woman in as well.

Once again Betty Couzens did not come equipped. She arrived at his flat, borrowed £1 off him and went out and bought a douche syringe. Dick's girlfriend ('I don't know her name') arrived with a friend, Pat. It was Pat who wanted an abortion. ('I don't know Pat's surname and I don't know where she lives.') Helen arrived (also with a friend). The action took place in the bedroom, as before.

'I remember Pat and Helen went into the bedroom with Betty separately. Each of them was in the bedroom about five minutes and after having a cup of tea they left.'

He'd already received his commission for Helen; he now received £5 for Pat. The afternoon was a success, apart from two things.

'As far as I know, both Pat and Helen are still pregnant.'

How come?

Well, Pat and Helen weren't the only ones who had got into trouble.

In June 1963 Elizabeth Couzens, thirty-five, of 21a Thirsk Road, Battersea, was arrested and charged with conspiracy to procure an abortion. She pleaded guilty at the Old Bailey in October and was fined £20 and £10 for estreating bail or six months' imprisonment. She paid the fine.

She told police she was reluctant to perform another abortion. 'I said no several times but he insisted it was a good friend who was desperate.' For the sake of a quiet life she gave in to him, yet maintained that she douched Jeff's Helen with clear water only, in the hope that this would fail to achieve the desired effect.

But there was to be no peace. Hayward pestered her, his wife pestered her, and so in the end she visited their flat again and carried out the procedure as before, on Pat this time, as well as Helen. 'I did not intend that I should be responsible for either girl's aborting and knew they wouldn't.'

She did not recognize the name of Tina Smart or Gwynneth Rees and she did not recognize the woman in the photograph shown to her. She had never performed an abortion on this woman.

Neither had William Hayward. He was merely the go-between, he insisted; as regards the operation itself, 'The whole idea is revolting to me.' However, he had recognized Rees from the photograph shown on *Police 5*. Yes, Tina was a customer at the club, but so were a great many other prostitutes. (In fact he and Bridgewater had been summonsed to appear in court in the new year for harbouring prostitutes.) There was Sexy, Pandy, Half-caste Margie, Vicky Pender (until she got murdered), Scabby Jean ('covered with acne'), Susie Wong ('broad Scottish accent'), Sandra. He had no cause to remember Tina Smart: he never met her anywhere else.

On 10 April 1964 William Hayward, Joan Hayward and Elizabeth Couzens stood trial at the Old Bailey. All three were charged with procuring an abortion: Hayward with three counts, his wife with two counts and Couzens with five counts. (Hayward and Couzens each admitted four other offences of procuring an abortion which were taken into consideration.) Hayward and Couzens were sentenced to twelve and fifteen months' imprisonment respectively, and Joan Hayward was bound over on recognizance in the sum of £5 for three years.

Flushed out.

Hamerton, Lawson, Couzens.

Carted off and locked away. Forgotten.

Memories?

Douches.

Wonders.

Waters.

Tears.

The life so short, the craft so long to learn.

They found Billy but they couldn't find Joe.

A prostitute named Eileen Allen, also known as 'Cross-eyed

Eileen', told police that she last saw Rees in late September. 'I think it was Friday 20 September.' The two women were standing outside the Gloucester Arms in Commercial Road at about 11.30pm and Rees, who had two black eyes, was talking about the beating she'd received from Whitehead and Holland, and also about her plans to attend her sister's forthcoming wedding in Wales – an opportunity for her to escape from Whitehead. Also present was a man known as 'Joe', a lorry driver; he drove a blue Dodge lorry from Tiger Bay to the London docks twice weekly, carrying all types of loads. Joe had agreed to take Rees back to Wales in his lorry, provided he was able to unload on the Saturday morning. Otherwise, Rees said, she would have to travel alone by train. Joe remarked that if that turned out to be the case he would see her back in Wales.

It appeared unlikely that he had taken her, for the last time Eileen Allen saw Joe, on or about 17 November, he asked her if she'd seen Rees.

'He used to give her money when she had a period and couldn't go on the street.' Joe seemed very fond of Rees. He was a regular client of hers. He wished he could be her only client. 'He said once when I was present with Tina in Farmer's Cafe that he didn't like the thought of her being out on the street with other men when he had enough money to give to her.'

Joe was between thirty-five and forty years old, 5′ 8″, with dark hair and a broad build; he had a small scar or birthmark near his left ear. He wore a flat uniform-type peaked cap, a green boiler suit and boots with steel toecaps.

Seventy-five haulage firms were contacted for information regarding this man, and enquiries were also made all around the area of the London docks; posters featuring an identikit portrait and detailed description of Joe were widely distributed and prominently displayed. All police forces covering the main A40 route from London to South Wales were contacted, and requested to make enquiries at all transport cafes in their areas.

Police questioned nearly 400 lorry drivers but Joe wasn't among them and, as the rest of Eileen Allen's story was clearly wrong – Rees did not travel to Wales on 21 September – they kept in mind the possibility that Joe never existed.

The search was also on for Jock.

Susan Howitt James-Wong, the Scottish-Chinese prostitute known as 'Susie Wong', claimed to have seen Rees, whom she knew as 'Tina Dawson', on Saturday 12 October, thirteen days after the date of her suspected disappearance. Rees arrived at James-Wong's flat between 2pm and 3pm with a man whom she introduced as 'Jock', and the two of them accompanied James-Wong and her cousin Sandra, aged three, to Kewei's, a Chinese restaurant in Tottenham Court Road.

James-Wong felt that Rees was pointedly ignoring Jock throughout the meal. Jock himself never spoke at all. Afterwards they all went to see *El Cid* at the Odeon, Marble Arch. 'In the cinema Tina went to the toilets three times, and every time Tina went Jock followed and waited outside for her, and after each occasion they walked back to the seat together.'

The film ended at 11pm and Rees and Jock departed, walking off in the direction of Edgware Road. Before she left, Rees told James-Wong she would visit her the next day, Sunday. Jock remained silent. 'He appeared to be a very sly type of person.'

Jock was 6', very thin, with high cheekbones and dark greased hair brushed back 'DA style'. He smoked tipped cigarettes and on the third finger of his right hand he wore a heavy silver ring embossed with a sphinx.

An identikit portrait of Jock was prepared and shown to all customers of all establishments used by the deceased, without result. Moreover, none of the staff at Kewei's or the Odeon recalled seeing James-Wong or any of the people she mentioned, on that date or any other.

James-Wong was shown the identikit portrait of Joe and photographs of all Rees's close male associates but failed to make an identification. However, she identified a blue-green tweed skirt as part of a suit Rees was wearing on 12 October. This skirt had been handed to police by Jean Anderson, who claimed that Rees had left it at her address on 16 September, and so they concluded that James-Wong was either mistaken regarding the date she last saw Rees or deliberately lying.

Detective Constable Frost was interviewing a prostitute named Sheila Monger at Leman Street police station when he realized her overcoat looked familiar. He asked her where she got it.

'I swapped it for one of my coats with Betty Norris, who lives in Hoxton. This coat was Tina's.'

Gwynneth Rees, heavily pregnant with her second child, Peter, had stayed at Elizabeth Norris's flat the previous December. Her dark tweed overcoat was now too tight for her so she exchanged it for Norris's loose-fitting white mac. DC Frost recognized this overcoat because Rees was wearing it in the police photograph attached to her descriptive form.

August 1962.

Well, what do you know?

There she is.

All there: hair, nose, eyes, everything.

A hint of sauce about the mouth.

A pound a poke, and mind my baby.

6 August 1962.

Twenty-one today.

On 13 November 1963 an inquest into the death of Gwynneth Rees was opened at Kingston Coroner's Court. Formal evidence was given regarding the finding of the body and the hearing was then adjourned until 11 December, when it was further adjourned pending the result of police enquiries.

On 4 March 1964 a coroner's inquisition was held before the deputy coroner and jury at Kingston Coroner's Court. After hearing the evidence of various witnesses the jury found that the body was that of Gwynneth Rees alias Tina Smart and returned an open verdict, stating that the cause of death was not ascertainable.

On 11 March Gwynneth Rees was buried, at the request of Joan Oxley, in the grounds of St Katherine's Church, Canvey Island, her grave marked by an aluminium cross.

Tiny Tina, tiny terror of the earth, had certainly kept Frederick Chadburn and his men guessing throughout the winter months. They failed to establish what she was wearing at the time of her disappearance, and they failed to find the person she disappeared with, the young man who gave her a lift in his two-tone car. They found no evidence that she had been aborted, yet Chadburn, noting the rapid decomposition of the body, concluded that she probably died from septicaemia, caused by an abortion. She probably died while being aborted or very shortly afterwards and was then transported to the site at Mortlake and buried there.

That is the explanation that has been handed down to us. It's a bizarre explanation, for in both medical and practical terms it makes no sense at all.

Septicaemia is not necessarily an immediate consequence of an abortion. Blood poisoning may result from a wound in the cervix, uterus or vagina, but then again it may result from a wound of any description. (The rapid decomposition of the body may be explained by its burial, as darkness, warmth and moisture create ideal breeding conditions for germs.) Moreover, it would take several days for septicaemia to become systemic, by which time Rees, experiencing symptoms such as a high temperature, rapid pulse and heavy discharge, would surely have sought medical help, as she had done in the past for salpingitis and venereal disease.

Might she have died *during* an abortion? This is highly unlikely, unless, well, the abortionist punctured the wall of her vagina while inserting a knitting needle or some such implement, in which case she might possibly have died from shock. But what self-respecting back-street practitioner would use such methods? Even a clown like Hamerton knew that sort of thing was inadvisable. And if she didn't drop dead there and then, she was off the premises, and if she was off the premises, where was she?

Life becomes much simpler when we accept that Gwynneth Rees did not die as the result of an abortion.

She died as the result of being killed.

The first time Frederick Chapman had intercourse with Rees was as a customer. He told police that on this occasion and all subsequent occasions, other than in bed, she did not strip off but merely removed her knickers. (Another customer – coincidentally Chapman's brother – also recalled this practice of hers.) It seems likely therefore that if picked up by a punter for intercourse in his car Rees would have remained more or less fully clothed. There exists the possibility of financial inducement, of course, which may also explain why, if she was alive, she found herself being driven to Mortlake, far from her usual haunts. On the other hand, it's worth remembering that when last seen Rees had finished for the night: she was going home.

Gwynneth Rees was murdered – almost certainly strangled,

according to the pathologist – and probably stripped after death. The press took an initial interest in the case ('The Ashpit Jigsaw', 'Clue of the tattered nylon') but the discovery of a dead whore at Mortlake was presently eclipsed by news of a president's assassination in Dallas. And yet Fleet Street would have cause to recall her name soon enough, and to wonder whether Tiny Tina was the start of something big.

2

Don't Fall Backwards

Through the park . . . down the alley . . . turn right . . . stop.

DANGER

I hear you.

THIS IS A MULTI-HAZARD AREA.

I understand.

NO UNAUTHORISED ADMITTANCE.

ALL VISITORS MUST REPORT TO RECEPTION.

I don't think I'll bother. I think I'll just stand out here in the driz-zle and the dark; here, on the south side of Upper Mall, where I can stare down at the floating pontoons. There are two pontoons, now as then, each moored to the river wall.

Back then somewhere between sixty and seventy corpses were recovered from the river each year; that is, from the fifty-one miles crossing the metropolis. Nowadays the figure is lower, at least in rela-tion to suicides; thanks to the widespread use of mobile phones, the river police or the RNLI can sometimes arrive in time.

But the main facts haven't changed. Your life expectancy may be measured in minutes the moment you enter the Thames. The initial shock will close up your throat and prevent you from taking in air or screaming, and within a couple of minutes you'll be too numb to escape unaided. And here come the eddies, the whirlpools, the bridge abutments; there's no telling where you'll end up. Some years ago a couple leapt hand in hand off Westminster Bridge only to find them-selves drifting further and further apart . . .

Still, it's never too late to fall in love. It's never too early either, I remind myself, as I turn my gaze away from the Thames to the two young snugglers there on the bench behind me.

Have they walked here straight from school? They're wearing uni-forms, and bags slung round their waists which are clearly cramping their style but they won't disengage, no, not for one second (they won't even come up for air).

I study their faces for as long as I can bear it and then I look over their heads, and over the railings and beyond the floodlights at the rather grand building in the distance. Linden House, home to the London Corinthian Sailing Club for the past forty years.

A small scream rouses me, and I lower my gaze to where something – that's right, something's working free of its moorings. Now let's just see if –

Whoa . . . no, no way; not tonight.

Leave it, leave it.

Get off me.

Get off her.

Off.

All the same, I'd say that pretty soon now (tomorrow? next week?) it'll be access all areas. She'll be twirling his boxer shorts around her little finger, he'll be hurriedly unwrapping his fruit-flavoured protection . . .

Ripeness is all.

Yes.

I turn away, grip the rungs of the tide board.

I hear you.

The two of you.

You can't wait to take the world by the throat –- but you don't know a thing about this, do you . . .

At 1.15pm on Sunday 2 February 1964 two young Corinthians, Douglas and George Capon, were on the foreshore below the clubhouse, preparing a rescue dinghy for a race that afternoon when Douglas spotted an object lying nearby. Curious, he walked across and discovered the lifeless body of a woman lying face down on the foreshore, her head wedged beneath the second pontoon from the landing stage. She was lying on her right side, head facing upstream, feet pointing towards Hammersmith Bridge. Her head and shoulders were covered with driftwood (which included a discarded Christmas tree). She was naked save for a pair of nylon stockings which were bunched around her ankles and lower legs.

Douglas Capon waited by the body while his brother went into Linden House to telephone for the police. At approximately 1.30pm the crew of F1 area car attended the scene, followed by other officers and, at 2.30pm, the divisional surgeon, Joshua Stein. He was unable to examine the body adequately as found and so an inspector eased her out from beneath the pontoon and turned her over onto her back. 'I then saw that she had an item of clothing stuffed in her mouth.'

Stein could not see any obvious signs of injury, but noticed that her eyes appeared to be rather red. There was no rigidity present. Her hands were sodden and in a semi-closed position. The skin of her body was livid in parts and the abdomen was blue. The impression he gained was that she had been in the water for some days.

The body could not be photographed where found owing to the rising tide. Permission to move the body was granted by the Hammersmith coroner, Gavin Thurston, and at 3.30pm it was transported to Hammersmith mortuary, where three photographs were taken later that day. Nothing of evidential value was found at the scene.

At 6pm Donald Teare performed the post-mortem. The deceased was a sparely built but adequately nourished woman, 5' 2", with dark brown hair, brown eyes and a pair of knickers, on which human semen was present, partially stuffed inside her mouth. Gross stretch marks were seen on the abdomen. A scar on the front of the uterus represented an old Caesarean operation; an old surgical scar on the lower abdomen may have represented the same operation.

Her teeth were badly stained with nicotine and the following were present: left upper 1, 2, 3, 5, 7; right upper 1, 2, 3, 4, 5; left lower 1, 2, 3; right lower 1, 2, 3, 4, 6. She had many fillings, and caries were seen in the gum margins of the left upper and lower 2 and 3 and the right lower 3 and 4.

Her fingernails were bitten to the quick, and her body was covered with mud (yet the quantity, it seems, was insufficient for comparison with a sample taken from the scene). There was a 1½" post-mortem wound on the back of the right calf. (Teare made a subsequent examination of the tissue beneath the skin on the angles of the lower jaw and found ante-mortem bruising, which he considered could have been caused by fist blows. However, he was unable to determine at what period before death these injuries might have been caused.)

The stomach contained a fairly large undigested meal. The lungs showed the ballooning typical of death by drowning; a large quantity of fine froth and fluid was found in the air passages, and there was also some vomited material in the trachea. Teare gave the cause of death as drowning, and it was later established that the water found in the

lungs had not been treated for domestic use. The body was water-
logged, its condition consistent with immersion in water for between
two and seven days.

On 5 February Mrs Elsie Youngman, sister of the deceased, visited
the mortuary and formally identified the body. By that time the dead
woman's fingerprints had been taken and checked and her CRO file
drawn. They knew who she was, and they knew she was anybody's.

Hannah Tailford was born on 19 August 1933 in Heddon-on-the-
Wall, Northumberland, the second daughter of John Tailford, a coal
miner, and his wife, Elsie. (Hannah's sister, also called Elsie, was born
in 1923.)

At the age of fifteen Hannah was committed to an approved school
for three cases of theft and for being a person in need of care and protection, as her parents could no longer control her behaviour. 'She
used to stay out at night and go with men,' her sister recalled.

Hannah was released from Parkside approved school, Liverpool, in
October 1951 and returned home. In March 1952 she got a job as a
domestic servant, working for a Dr Nicholson in Ponteland. A month
later she left this job and left home as well, and moved in with an
Indian in South Shields.

She stole clothing from this man's house and was arrested at South
Shields docks. On 1 July 1952 she was convicted of theft at South
Shields Magistrates' Court and placed on probation for two years.
'We refused to have her home as my mother by this time was on the
verge of a nervous breakdown.' She was ordered to reside at St
Cuthbert's, an approved home in South Norwood, for twelve
months.

In January 1953 Hannah Tailford escaped from this home; in March
she was rearrested on warrant for breach of probation. On 27 April
she appeared at Croydon Magistrates' Court, where she was discharged absolutely for this breach, and told that her probation order
was to continue with a condition of residence at an approved home in
Addiscombe, Surrey. Three days later she absconded from this home
as well and a warrant was issued for her arrest.

She eventually resurfaced in February 1954, when she was arrested
on East Carriage Road, Hyde Park, for soliciting and fined 40s. She
was rearrested on the warrant for breach of probation and on 26

February at the Croydon quarter sessions was sentenced to borstal training.

In May she escaped from East Sutton Park borstal, and in August she was again arrested on East Carriage Road for soliciting, and returned to borstal training. She was released on licence in July 1956.

In September an order of recall to borstal training was issued by the prison commissioners. On 2 December Tailford was again arrested in Hyde Park for soliciting, this time in the name of Anne Lynch, and the following day she was fined 40s and returned to borstal training. She was released on second licence in July 1957.

In August a further order of recall was issued, with a direction that she was not to be arrested after 25 February 1958, when the period of supervision expired. This order was never executed.

In early 1959 Hannah Tailford placed a card in the window of a south London newsagent's. It read:

Young mother-to-be (25)
offers unborn baby for
sale to good home. Due
end of April.
Letters only to T.F. within

A few short lines, brimming with possibilities.

Would the baby be a boy? A girl? A piccaninny?

Was the advertiser expecting sealed bids? Or was a loving home more important?

Would there be any replies at all? Would the little bundle end up at the bottom of the Thames, wrapped in a copy of the *Sunday Pictorial*?

Or would the *Sunday Pictorial* come to the rescue?

On 19 April, beneath the headline 'She wanted to sell her baby', reporter James Cameron recounted his interview with 'Mrs Theresa Foster' at her lodgings in Filmer Road, Fulham. She told him, 'I know it is wicked and shameful of me, but I was forced to make this terrible offer to attract attention to my plight.' She had no savings, and no relatives to help her – her parents, she said, were dead.

'I met my husband, John, a merchant seaman, five years ago at a fairground in Manchester. We married eighteen months later. He seemed to like the idea of becoming a father. But when I told him the baby was on the way, it started a terrific row. Next day he left to join a ship. I haven't heard from him since and I don't know where he is . . . I cry at nights wondering what to do. Now that I know it's illegal I have withdrawn the advert. But my baby must have a good home. I shall be broken-hearted parting with it but I'm only doing my best.'

Mrs Foster has been in Fulham Hospital. She is going back to have her baby by Caesarean operation.

On 22 May Hannah Tailford gave birth to a son, David, at St Stephen's Hospital, Fulham. On 5 June, the date of her release, a married couple from Staffordshire met her by arrangement inside the hospital. They had read the newspaper article and contacted her with a view to adopting her baby. She now handed him over, signed their prepared agreement and received £20.

As this action contravened Section 50 of the Adoption Act 1958 the matter was reported for the information of the legal department of London County Council, but they decided not to institute criminal proceedings.

After all, at least she wasn't thieving.

In the summer of 1956, shortly after her release from borstal, Tailford had met a Scotsman who called himself 'Allan Lynch', and for the rest of her life they lived together at various addresses in south London, moving from one furnished room to the next and passing themselves off as man and wife. Little is known of Lynch's history. He was born William Ewing in Pennsylvania in 1932 and at some stage he acquired a criminal record.

In October 1959 Hannah Tailford and Allan Lynch moved to Newcastle. They stayed with her parents for a few weeks before renting rooms in the city. Details are few, but around this time Tailford found work as a domestic servant.

In January 1960 at Newcastle upon Tyne Magistrates' Court Tailford, in the name of Theresa Bell, was conditionally discharged for twelve months with 15s costs and ordered to pay £5 compensation for stealing money from her employer.

The couple returned to London shortly afterwards. They were

living at 75 Highbury New Park, Islington, when, on 9 April, Tailford stood trial at West London Magistrates' Court.

She had found a paper bag containing a chequebook and driving licence in a gutter in Fulham and forged a cheque in order to obtain groceries and cash together worth £3. She was sentenced to one month's imprisonment for stealing a chequebook and driving licence and three months' imprisonment for obtaining money by means of a forged cheque, the sentences to run concurrently.

A daughter, Linda, was born in April 1961, and a boy, Lawrence, was born in May the following year. Lawrence, like David, was adopted before leaving hospital. (All three children were registered in the name of Lynch, yet during police interrogation Lynch would later deny paternity of the two boys. He understood that she'd had a son before she met him. 'I don't know what became of this child.')

Following the birth of Lawrence the couple had a discussion and, according to Lynch, she got herself sterilized.

In 1963 Hannah Tailford was living at 36 Wickersley Road, Battersea. Every day for the past two years she had been leaving her baby daughter in the care of a local woman, Mrs Amy Higgs, dropping her off at noon and collecting her at 5pm. On her way home at lunchtime she would sometimes call in for a cup of tea with a neighbour, Jean Bishop. This woman knew her by her official alias of 'Mrs Terry Lynch', husband of 'Jock', who worked in a billiard hall in Wandsworth Road. Terry told her she was the manageress of a police canteen at Victoria. 'She used to talk about police inspectors who showed her photographs, and about canteen work in general. She used to go out to work about eleven o'clock at night.' She mentioned that she'd had four Caesarean births and was now sterilized. 'She also mentioned a man called "Tommy" but didn't tell me very much about him.'

'Tommy' was Thomas Trice, an elderly bachelor who had known Tailford since the late Fifties. They frequented the same cafe in Wilton Road, Victoria (Tony's, just past the Biograph cinema), and often used to pass the time of day. 'I knew she was a prostitute . . . I looked upon her as a person whom I could help.'

An opportunity to help her had presented itself in the winter of

1961. Trice, who was then sixty-seven, had just retired, and Tailford had recently moved into a flat in Lavender Hill. She told him that the man she was living with was in Brixton prison and asked if he would decorate the flat.

'The work took me about four evenings. I did the front room.' During the course of these visits he took several photographs of Tailford in the nude. These he regarded as payment for his services. He developed them himself and gave her a set.

Trice lost contact with her shortly afterwards. They did not meet again until 1963, when he bumped into her at Charing Cross Station. She and Lynch had been evicted in August and were now renting an unfurnished room at 40 Chestnut Road, West Norwood.

Trice visited her at this address on numerous occasions. 'It was about this time I realized what a slut she was.' It didn't put him off her, though. 'It was at Chestnut Road that the friendship between Terry and myself ripened.'

Who were her other friends?

Well, she was still leaving Linda with Amy Higgs, so she kept in touch with Jean Bishop in Battersea. She was also friendly with Juliana Bicknell, who lived downstairs at 40 Chestnut Road. She told Bicknell that she was married to Jock, 'and that she had six or seven children, and they were either all dead or died at birth'. Bicknell looked after Linda, the live one, while her mother went out at night 'very heavily made up'.

Bicknell met Tailford's young male friend Graham, also known as 'Carl'. He was about nineteen years old, 6', slim, pale and fair-haired. From October onwards he visited her every morning, and would stay for the rest of the day. Bicknell suspected he was unemployed. 'He did mention that he had a painting job for a couple of days, but didn't get paid for it . . .'

Hannah Tailford had another frequent visitor, a woman with a van. I speak of 'Auntie Gwen'.

Auntie Gwen?

Yes, that was one name for her.

Don't ask questions.

Don't look too close.

'Gwen was about fifty, 5' 8" or 9", well built, and I would say she had mannish features, with a large hooked nose, and the hair was short and pulled round the sides. This made me think at the time that it was a man dressed as a woman.'

Shortly before Christmas 1963, Thomas Trice recalled, Allan Lynch won about £60 on the horses. He gave Tailford £30, and she asked Trice to take her to a shop in Battersea. 'It was a shop where one could pay one shilling in the pound deposit and pay the rest in instalments.' He drove her there ('She bought shoes and clothing'); he drove her anywhere she wanted. He was one of her chauffeurs, and sometimes that meant driving Carl around as well, although he was always suspicious of him. Carl was 'vicious': 40 Chestnut Road was where he went for a sleep, but when he was awake Tailford said he had a terrible temper. 'I understand that he has struck Terry on occasions, but I have never seen any marks of violence on her.' (Tailford herself had a 'vile' temper and would 'lash out if she wasn't pleased with things'.) She gave Carl money and Trice suspected that he pimped for her or, failing that, was her ponce. (Or one of her ponces? Allan Lynch eventually got fed up with Carl and his visits and told Tailford to tell him to stay away.)

About a week after the big win the couple received notice to quit 40 Chestnut Road. Tailford told Trice that she had secured a flat at 37 Thurlby Road, West Norwood, and the senior citizen was duly pressed into service as removal man, only to discover that most of the furniture had been seized by the landlord in lieu of the outstanding rent. 'I gathered that she was hopelessly in debt.'

37 Thurlby Road consisted of three three-room flats. Robert Clark, a painter, occupied the ground-floor flat at the rear of the house with his wife and baby boy, and above them lived Alfred Eyles, a postman, with his wife and three children. Tailford and Linda moved into the top-floor flat on 11 January 1964 (Lynch joined them a day later). They arrived in a van driven by a woman who must have turned a few heads in her time.

'I would say that she was about fifty,' Theresa Eyles recalled, 'and she was heavily made up, she had a lot of that pancake mixture on. She had gingery dyed hair, she had heavy eyebrows, and they appeared to be pencil, the same colour as her hair. She had a large nose which seemed to be spread out all over her face . . .'

Sweet Gwendoline.

Imp among aunts!

Confirmed spinster!

Who could tame her?

Or her niece? For no sooner had Hannah Tailford moved into
Thurlby Road than she told Gwen she was about to get married, but
not to Jock (he'd turned her down). She was marrying a man in the
RAF – his name was Don or Dennis – and she was taking Linda with
her. They were going to buy a house for £4,000 just as soon as his
divorce came through. She would soon be meeting her future
mother-in-law, and she sought Gwen's advice on dress and etiquette.
'She was very keen to get married. I thought she wanted to break
away from the life she had been living.'

Tailford told a slightly different story to Jean Bishop when she visited her later that month. Aware, no doubt, that to her friend's
understanding she was already married, she stated simply that the
RAF man, whom she referred to as 'Del' ('She did say his surname,
but I can't remember it') *wanted* to marry her. Anyway, they were
going house-hunting in Putney. 'She told me that she had said she
would like to live at Battersea but Del had said no, as his wife lived in
Battersea with a coloured man.'

Del had a lot of money, she said. He had bought her a radiogram,
which was now at Tommy's, and he was going to buy a house. As well
as being in the RAF he was part-owner of a coffee stall at Shepherd's
Bush.

But there were other coffee stalls, and other men to meet at them.
At 6.30pm on Thursday 23 January Gwen picked her up at the flat by
arrangement and drove her to the coffee stall at Charing Cross
Embankment. Gwen parked the blue Thames van nearby and headed
for the public lavatories while Tailford walked across to the stall. She
got into conversation with a customer named William Sales.

'I said to her, "A nice friend you've got." She said to me, "It's not a
woman, it's a man." I laughed when she told me.'

Sales was a chauffeur. Sometimes he drove a Bentley and sometimes
he drove a Triumph Herald. That night he had the Bentley, and when
Tailford saw it parked on the Embankment she asked him if it was his.

'I told her it was and asked her why. She said she would like to go
for a ride in it as she had never been in a Bentley before. I said, "Yes,
all right."'

She left the two teas and slice of cake she'd ordered and got in. He asked her where she wanted to go and she replied, 'Anywhere,' so he drove her to Epping Forest. 'When we arrived at Epping Forest – I think it was a place called High Beech – we were in the front seat talking when she suggested having intercourse.' She suggested she strip naked but he told her to remove her knickers only and pull her skirt up. They had intercourse on the front seat 'after I had adjusted the back rests' and afterwards, although payment was not mentioned, he gave her a pound. 'I realized she was a prostitute by her behaviour in the car.'

Sales drove her back to the coffee stall, dropping her off at about 9.50pm. On the way back Tailford remarked that they were going up to Newcastle the following morning, her and the man she was living with.

On Friday 24 January Hannah Tailford visited Jean Bishop again. As on the previous occasion, she arrived at midday and stayed for most of the afternoon. She mentioned that she and Del were going to see *The Black and White Minstrel Show* on Saturday. She also mentioned that she was going to leave Jock, though Bishop didn't think she meant it.

On the other hand, she and Del appeared to have reached a new level of understanding.

'She told me she had told Del she was married and that he seemed shocked about it and said they would buy a house and live together. She said he knew about Linda.'

She left at about 4.30pm. She was wearing a blue coat with a large hem and a large blue woollen pixie hat with a long scarf attached. 'I didn't see her dress as she didn't take her coat off.'

Allan Lynch arrived home at 7pm to find Tailford playing with the baby. She cooked his dinner and later, at about 9pm, changed her clothes and went out. He told police she went out every night of the week except Wednesdays and returned home at about 5.30am. He understood she was working in a cafe in Southwark Bridge Road.

When she left 37 Thurlby Road she was wearing a flame-coloured frilly nylon blouse, a black cardigan and skirt, a dark blue winter coat and a light blue pixie hat, and black leather court shoes. She was wearing a wristwatch with a black leather strap and a plain gold wedding ring on her left hand. She was carrying a large black patent-leather

handbag containing £27 10s in notes and 8s in silver, a black leather
wallet, a small chipped mirror, a brown plastic purse, their only front
door key, a blue biro, two packets of Kleenex, a packet of Benson and
Hedges, and a blue Jack Swift bookmaker's diary. 'I know she had
these things in her handbag because just before she went out the baby
had tipped the contents on the floor and was playing with them.'

Lynch remained in the flat and watched television until closedown,
and then went to bed. On Saturday morning he rose at about 9am,
and a couple of hours later went downstairs and bought ten Richmond
off Theresa Eyles for 2s. Later that day he asked her if she had seen his
wife. According to her, he then said, 'The cow's left me with the kid.'

At this stage Lynch wasn't unduly concerned about Tailford's
absence. She'd left home before for brief periods and anyway, he'd finished work for the week so he was in a position to look after Linda.
On Sunday afternoon he made enquiries at pubs and cafes in the
Victoria area, to no avail.

By Monday he had become desperate. 'I couldn't go to work as I
had the baby to look after.' At 11am he deposited her with Jean Bishop
in Battersea. He returned at 5pm and said he had searched for Terry
around Victoria and Vauxhall without success. 'He said he ought to
have realized something was wrong because Terry kept asking Linda
if she would like a new mummy. He seemed very worried about Terry
because she would not have left the child.' He collected Linda, refusing Bishop's offer to keep her overnight, and the next day left her with
Amy Higgs. For some reason, possibly financial, Tailford had ended
the arrangement with Higgs shortly before Christmas, but she now
accepted Linda for an indefinite period.

On the evening of Tuesday 28 January Lynch made further
enquiries at pubs and clubs in the West End. He visited the coffee stall
at the Embankment, Charing Cross, and described the missing
woman to the night manager, Frederick George, who said, 'You mean
the girl who goes with Carl.' Carl worked part-time at the stall in the
evenings, and George gave Lynch his telephone number.

At 1am Lynch called in at the Nucleus Club in Monmouth Street
and played cards for the rest of the night with William Hayward, the
co-owner, James McIntyre, an employee, and Alexander McGrory, a
porter. During the game Lynch told McGrory that he had won about
£8 on the dogs that afternoon, but that Terry had bailed out on him,

taken the rent money and left him with the kid. 'He said to me, "If you see her, don't ask her any questions as to where she's been – just give her a dig." By that I understood he meant me to give her a thump.'

Several hours later Lynch had lost £16, leaving him with approximately 30s. The game hadn't mellowed him. When Hayward asked him what he was going to do if he found his wife Lynch replied that he would smack her round the face for leaving their child. 'He seemed more concerned in case she was with another man than anything else.'

At 8.40am Hayward and the others left the club and he gave them a lift to a bus stop in Whitehall. The three men took a bus to Victoria station, where they had a cup of coffee in the cafe and discussed Lynch's predicament further. McGrory learned that he had the telephone number of 'somebody he reckoned was knocking her off'. He seemed confident he could find her at this man's address, if only he knew it. By quoting the number McGrory obtained the address, 64 West Cromwell Road, SW5, from the operator and wrote it down for Lynch on a cigarette packet.

Carl couldn't help. He and Tailford had arranged to meet the previous Sunday at 11pm at the coffee stall at Charing Cross, but he didn't keep the appointment and he hadn't seen her since.

That night an acquaintance of Tailford's, a chestnut seller named Idris Bowen, drove Lynch around west London while he searched for her. He revisited the coffee stall at Charing Cross, where Carl gave him the address of Thomas Trice, who was living in Kent.

Lynch and Trice now met for the first time. According to the pensioner, Lynch was almost in tears. He said that his wife had left him, and Trice revealed that she was going to get married. 'I told Jock about Don or Dennis.' In the light of this information – or the fact that Tailford had disappeared with the rent – Lynch decided to leave 37 Thurlby Road. Trice drove him back to London and arranged to help him clear the flat.

At 9pm that day, Friday 31 January, Jean Bishop met Lynch in the street. He reported that he had been to Kent to see Gwen, and Gwen had told him that Terry and Del were getting married the following week. ('He then told me that he and Terry were not married.') Bishop asked him if he meant Auntie Gwen and Lynch replied, 'Yes, Auntie Gwen – he's a queer with a wig on.' She then asked him if he had thought to telephone Terry's place of work, and he said that she hadn't been to work, that the only work she did was on her back. 'Then he told me she was a prostitute, but I can't remember his exact words. Then he left.'

Some time after midnight Allan Lynch returned home for the first time that week. Moreover, he found himself hosting a bit of a party. Earlier that evening he'd been drinking with three acquaintances in the Victoria, Wandsworth Road. At closing time, armed with bottles of beer and spirits, they all took a taxi to Lynch's flat, where they drank and listened to the radio until 3am. His guests, Leonard Didcott, William Holman and Christopher Willgrave, stayed the night and left at about 10am on Saturday morning.

At 11am Lynch went downstairs to the Eyleses' flat. He told them he was leaving and gave Theresa Eyles 3s in small change, asking her to pay the milkman for him. She asked him if he had found Mrs Lynch. 'He said he hadn't found her and wasn't going to bother any more to look for her.'

Lynch left the house, returning a few minutes later in Gwen's van. He and Gwen carried out Linda's cot, toys and clothing to take to Amy Higgs. He gave Gwen a pair of Tailford's shoes and a cardboard box containing her clothing (most of which Gwen had given to her), with instructions to get rid of it. He gave some bedding and Tailford's grey cape coat to Mrs Clark in the ground-floor flat, and left a carrier bag of her clothes in the hall.

Later that day Lynch saw Thomas McGing, a restaurant porter and an acquaintance of Tailford's, in the Kenilworth Cafe at Victoria. Lynch asked him if he'd seen her and McGing said yes, he'd spoken to her briefly at Victoria station the previous week. She came up to him and said, 'Did you hear that I was getting married?', to which McGing replied, 'It's about time.' He assumed she meant Lynch.

But had this encounter taken place before, on or after 24 January? McGing didn't say, and Lynch didn't ask.

Lynch had collected his final wages from his temporary job in the billiard hall and he spent Saturday, Sunday and Monday getting drunk. On Monday evening Jean Bishop walked into the Victoria and saw him at the bar, drinking gin. 'There was conversation about Terry and that she hadn't returned yet. He also said he hadn't had any sleep as he had been dealing cards all night.'

In the early evening of Tuesday 4 February Lynch was having 'a few drinks' and reading the *Evening News*. He read: 'Girl In The Thames Is Identified . . . Scotland Yard fingerprint experts to-day identified the girl. She came from Northumberland, lived in a South London flat and was a frequent visitor to the West End.'

Or perhaps he just looked at the words, vacantly, hopelessly, as a drowned man looks at the water.

From the outset police treated the death of Hannah Tailford as suspicious. Accordingly a murder squad was formed, headed by Detective Chief Inspector Benjamin Devonald and based at Shepherd's Bush police station.

Devonald's first interviewee was Allan Lynch, who entered Lavender Hill police station in a highly distressed state at 10.55pm on 4 February and was immediately transported to Shepherd's Bush. His fears were confirmed as to the identity of the dead woman and he appeared genuinely upset, although drink and lack of sleep may have contributed to his mood. He denied emphatically that he had anything to do with his girlfriend's death. In interview Lynch, no doubt anxious to avoid a possible charge of poncing, adhered to the fiction that she worked in an all-night cafe in Southwark Bridge Road.

His neighbour Theresa Eyles supplied some intriguing details. She told police that every evening between 11.30 and midnight a car would pull up outside 37 Thurlby Road and Tailford would get in. ('I didn't bother to look out to see what the car was.') Friday 24 January was no exception. Eyles, who understood that she worked in a canteen in Victoria, saw her leave the house and remarked that it was a cold night to go out, 'but she said she had a man friend from Battersea pick her up, and he used to bring her back in the morning'. (She also mentioned, on this or a previous occasion, that the man also drove to Leigham Court Road 'either to pick someone up or to visit somebody'.) This exchange took place at about 11.30pm, which suggests, with reference to Lynch's chronology, that Tailford was occupied for some two and a half hours in descending the stairs.

The stairs, the stairs. Did the prostitute mount them one last time?

In the early hours of Saturday 1 February Theresa Eyles heard screams coming from the top-floor flat. 'I heard other noises – it sounded as if the furniture was being pulled about.' She couldn't say how long the screaming lasted, but these were definitely a woman's screams and they woke her daughter up: she came crying into her parents' bedroom. While she was trying to get Wendy back to sleep, 'I heard footsteps go down the stairs, and I heard the door shut.'

On the ground floor Robert Clark went to bed at 11.30pm that night. At around midnight he heard people enter the house and walk up the stairs. He also heard people coming down the stairs, and it sounded as though they were carrying something. 'I also heard people talking, and I think the radio was going.' At about 1.30am, still awake, he heard 'screaming and hysterical crying'. He too emphasized to police that this was a woman screaming; the screaming went on for about two or three minutes 'and then it stopped'. And then he went to sleep.

At 10am Lynch came down to his flat to offer him five bottles of beer. He told Clark a couple of friends had brought the beer round the previous night and that he didn't want it as he didn't drink. 'He also said that he was going to knock on the door and wake me up so as I could have a drink, but that I was not awake.' On the subject of Tailford he remarked that he hadn't found her and wasn't bothered any more; he was leaving the flat and thinking of returning to Glasgow. (Lynch in fact moved to W11.)

Allan Lynch and his guests Leonard Didcott and Christopher Willgrave (William Holman proved untraceable) denied that there was a fifth person present in his flat in the early hours of 1 February. Moreover police could find no evidence to suggest that Lynch had any contact with Tailford after she left him the previous Friday. Yet on the afternoon of 31 January he spoke as if the missing woman were within his grasp.

He and Alfred Eyles boarded the same train, the 2.53, from West Norwood station to Victoria. During the journey Eyles asked him where his wife was. Would he be seeing her? Indeed he would. He knew the pub she used in Victoria and he would be seeing her there. 'He mentioned that he didn't drink, so he would just buy a pint and wait for her.'

'Scotland Yard detectives hunting the killer of 30-year-old Hannah Tailford – the nude in the river – last night issued a picture of a diary,' Norman Lucas reported in the *Sunday Mirror* on 9 February. 'Hannah is known to have been carrying a similar diary when she was last seen alive. And the Yard are anxious to find it, because they have been told it contains a list of names, addresses and phone numbers of men with whom Hannah had secret affairs . . .'

Allan Lynch told them. He bought the diary for her from a betting shop in Twickenham and she made good use of it. 'I opened it once and started to read it, and I noticed there were entries for every day from 1 January. I did not get the chance to read it properly as Hannah snatched it away from me.'

And that was that. Still, he'd kept a few names in his head, and during the course of four long interrogations he spilled them.

Tailford used to visit a Welshman, 'Taffy' Lewis, on Wednesday afternoons at his sub-post office and newsagent's shop in Wightman Road, Haringey. She had been friendly with him for some years.

She often spoke of a Sidney Roderick Collins who resided at the White House, a block of expensive flats situated 'near the BBC building'. While searching for Tailford on the afternoon of Sunday 26 January Lynch visited this block of flats and spoke to the porter, who, having confirmed that a Mr Collins lived there, telephoned his extension and received no reply.

About a month previously Tailford had returned home one Sunday morning 'smelling strongly of drink'. She explained that she had attended an all-night party hosted by André, a Frenchman who lived in a flat at Athenaeum Court. She had known André for about two years, and told Lynch he worked at the French Embassy and owned a black Mercedes with diplomatic number plates. Last Guy Fawkes Night he had driven her and one Paul Bolton to Trafalgar Square to watch the fireworks.

'André used to live at Dolphin Square and I know that Hannah has visited him there.' Lynch hadn't met him but Thomas Trice, he said, had visited André's flat.

Sidney, André, Dr No . . . The only character detectives managed to trace was Frank Lewis, a middle-aged family man with a wife to deceive and a business to run (early closing Wednesdays).

At 1pm one Wednesday, 'I can't remember the date but it would be about the time that the girls were put off the streets', Lewis was preparing to close his shop when Hannah Tailford entered. As of late, she would sometimes come in to use the telephone kiosk. He knew she was a prostitute.

'We started talking and I pulled her leg about her business and she suggested that I could go with her for a pound. I, like a fool, agreed . . .'

That afternoon he enjoyed intercourse with her upstairs in the marital bed, but subsequent sessions took place in his car (according to Lynch, a maroon Ford Anglia), which he kept in a garage some distance from the shop. She always called just before closing time on Wednesday afternoons. They last had intercourse in early November 1963, and that was the last time he saw her. On this occasion she told the shopkeeper that she had met a young man, Carl. He was about eighteen and he worked on a coffee stall somewhere in Victoria. 'She said that every time she looked at him she wanted him. She told me she had taken him home.' She added that she would have to be careful of him as he was very jealous of other men talking to her.

What else did she tell him? 'She mentioned to me on several occasions various practices she performed with other men.' But none of these men had names.

Frank Lewis was interrogated at length regarding his relationship with the woman he knew as 'Mary Lynch', and he admitted having intercourse with her on approximately twenty occasions. He most certainly had not seen her since last November.

But Lewis may well have felt trapped, fearful, eager to minimize his own importance, for Allan Lynch appeared to regard these meetings as a weekly event.

And here's an odd thing. At 11.20am on Wednesday 29 January Charles Sutcliffe, a technical sales adviser, was driving along Green Lanes towards Wood Green in Haringey when he noticed a woman turn from Green Lanes into Endymion Road. He had often seen this woman sitting in a cafe in Wilton Road, Victoria. 'This cafe is just past the Biograph. I saw a picture of the murdered woman Hannah Tailford on television and it is the same woman I saw in Endymion Road.'

Yes, this seems most plausible. The cafe mentioned by Sutcliffe sounds like Tony's as frequented by Tailford, and moreover the fact that Endymion Road leads to Wightman Road means we can say –

'On this occasion she was wearing a red coat but nothing on her head and I would say her hair was ginger.'

Say *what*?

*

Unfortunately Allan Lynch could supply no further insights into the intriguing world he outlined, the world of foreign diplomats and all-night parties. He remained largely ignorant of whatever it was that was going on.

Wise man, eh?

By all means take the money . . .

But for Christ's sake don't open the box.

Well, perhaps Thomas Trice, having served Tailford in a dual role as unofficial chauffeur and unconventional agony aunt, might be able to help.

On 6 February Trice was brought in for interrogation. His premises in Welling, Kent, were searched and a box containing a quantity of used women's clothing was found in his workshed. Officers established that this was the box handed to him by Lynch on 1 February. This box also contained a pair of women's shoes, mud samples from which were submitted for analysis; but there was insufficient quantity for comparison with the sample taken from the Thames foreshore, where Tailford's body was found.

All the same, the sexagenarian had a confession to make.

'I usually saw Terry on a Thursday or a Friday and I was always changed into women's clothing when I visited her at Chestnut Road. I sometimes went shopping with her as a woman and Linda always knew me as "Auntie Gwen".'

Trice last saw Tailford on 23 January when, as Gwen, he drove her to the coffee stall at Charing Cross. Upon arrival he went to the lavatory (Gents? Ladies?) and when he emerged she'd disappeared.

'I never went to Dolphin Square with Terry and I wouldn't know where André lived, although Terry told me that she had visited him at Dolphin Square and that they had orgies there.'

Ah.

'Terry once gave me three Gerrard telephone numbers and said that it was the practice to ring one of the numbers and ask the man if he had the book and he would tell me where an orgy was being held.'

Where?

'I tried the numbers but the information was wrong, and when I spoke to Terry about it she said that she hadn't wanted me to get involved.'

Oh, for –

'There is a cafe in Wilton Road called Le Aperitif, and a waitress there was Terry's contact for kinky parties.'

But this waitress, who, according to Trice, was working at the cafe 'during last summer', had now left, and proved untraceable.

It was all very frustrating.

What was needed was a Mr Big.

Thomas Trice supplied a name.

'There is a Mr Hammond of 36a St James's Street, SW1, who is either an American or an Australian. I think his Christian name was Arthur. He used to run kinky parties at his flat and she used often to go there . . . He doesn't work apparently and receives an allowance.'

Mr Hammond sounded exquisite, and exquisitely pullable: a remittance man, jaded, outwardly respectable, with the wherewithal to indulge his sordid tastes . . .

But any jubilation was short-lived: 36a St James's Street, SW1, did not exist; 36 St James's Street was a branch of the Westminster Bank; and 36 James Street, W1, was a women's hairdresser's.

Yes, it was all very frustrating, and grew more so as tales of wild parties continued to reach them. The dead woman had told Jean Bishop about a party at which she got very drunk and danced on a table in her bra and knickers; she mentioned that Gwen and Del were at the party but failed to mention where the party took place. Another of Tailford's associates, a window cleaner named Frederick Townend, recalled her saying that 'she would perform with lesbians and she would say she had given exhibitions with a dildo with lesbians for money. She was dead kinky. She never gave me any indication at all of where these exhibitions were held or who the lesbians were.'

In the absence of independent corroboration of any of Tailford's titbits, it was beginning to look as if that bunk-up on the front seat of the Bentley was the highlight of her career. As we know, she met the driver, William Sales, not at an orgy but at a coffee stall, the one at Charing Cross.

Cue Frederick George, night manager, with a few strange stories of his own.

Hannah Tailford began to frequent this coffee stall in the autumn of 1963, at around the time Frederick George took Carl on as an assistant. She fancied Carl. 'After he came out the remand home she took him to her place in West Norwood and he told me that she had asked her husband to put him up.' At weekends, when Carl was on duty, she'd turn up and order two teas, one for herself and one for Jock (not Jock Lynch, another Jock, who worked on a building site in Frazier Street). Tailford and Jock were very friendly and used to talk together for a long time.

Tailford, whom George knew as 'Terry' and 'Anna', was often picked up at the stall in the early hours of the morning by a man in a dark green Morris Minor. She referred to him as 'my chauffeur' and George understood that he drove her home. 'I feel sure he was having her across.' This man was between thirty-five and forty, slim to medium build, with thinning light brown hair. He usually wore either a pullover or a brown suede sheepskin-lined jacket. He was fairly well spoken, with no trace of an accent. 'I never heard him called by any name.' There seemed a strong possibility that he was in the printing trade for often, when he turned up to collect Tailford, he would give George various newspapers with 'vouchers' stamped on them in mauve ink.

Another female customer, Joyce, also accepted a lift from him on one occasion. 'He took her home before Anna was killed, and she said she wouldn't go home with him again, but she didn't say why.'

Hannah Tailford once asked one of the regulars to give her a lift; he was 6′, about thirty, with ginger hair brushed down and parted on the side. Now he definitely was a printer – he worked for the *Daily Mirror* – and he had a name: Roy. He drove off with her in his white Ford Consul. 'I have seen them both together at the stall after that but they didn't speak again.'

This Roy was not to be confused with another Roy, who was also about thirty, but shorter, 5′ 8″. He dressed very smartly and smoked expensive-looking pipes. 'I think he was a bit of a freelance reporter.'

One night towards the end of November freelance Roy was at the stall when a girl came up and asked George for change for a £5 note. 'I went to get the change and he pulled his wallet out and gave her the change.' Roy's wallet did not pass unnoticed. 'Anna was standing near him at the time, and although they hadn't spoken before, she started talking to him and he bought her some teas.'

They discussed photography. Roy wanted to take photographs of her and Carl having intercourse together back at Roy's address in East

Putney; he would pay them £5 each for their trouble. 'Carl didn't want to know and I heard Anna rucking him later on for turning it down.'

Shortly afterwards Tailford, Carl, Roy and a Scottish boy all left together and had breakfast somewhere; Tailford then went off with Carl (presumably to Chestnut Road) and Roy and his new friend booked in at the Royal Hotel in Woburn Place. But while they were there the lad stole £8 from him; that's what Roy said when he came to the stall the following night.

Roy of the rovers . . .

One night at the beginning of January he came to the stall and met Carl, who was off that night, and his young companion, Jimmy. They met at about 9pm; two hours later Roy, who clearly fancied Jimmy, took them both home with him.

Jimmy returned to the stall at about 5am. He said to George, 'You can tell Carl I won't be seeing him any more.' He seemed a bit upset. 'I asked him what was wrong but he wouldn't tell me . . .'

That night at the stall Carl explained that he and Roy had tied Jimmy up. Roy arrived later and confirmed this, adding that Jimmy was naked. 'Carl said they had whipped him and left him tied up while Roy and him had gone to bed together. Apparently Jimmy had got himself undone – I didn't see Jimmy after this.'

Meanwhile, Carl appeared to have tired of Tailford's company, although she remained as ardent as ever. George last saw them together on the night of Sunday 26 January; Carl was asking her to ask Gwen to lend him the van for Tuesday.

But that wasn't the last time George saw her. She was there at the stall on a subsequent night (he couldn't supply a date). 'I think she was waiting for Carl but he didn't turn up.' She eventually left alone at about 5am.

He last saw Carl on 29/30 January, the night of what turned out to be Carl's final shift. 'Carl asked me some time during the night if I would get my governor to change a cheque for him.' Was it straight? Yes, it was one his father had given him. George examined the cheque: National Provincial Bank, Bath. 'It was made out to D. Witton or D. Ditton for the sum of £22 14s. The signature at the bottom of the cheque was Witton or Ditton but it looked as though Carl had written over the signature to make it thicker so that he could copy it on the back.' George asked Carl why he had written over the signature and he replied, 'All right, I'll tell you the truth – I nicked it off a queer.' George shook his head and handed it back.

At about 6am Carl departed with a youth known as 'Carol' who 'talks like a queer and always carries purple hearts'. Carl and Carol seemed quite close, and George understood that they were heading back to Carl's address in West Cromwell Road.

That was the last he saw of Carl – although, yes, there was something else. Earlier that shift, around midnight, Jock, Terry's husband, turned up at the stall with Taffy, the hot chestnut man; they were in Taffy's car. Jock was searching for his wife, and Carl looked a bit frightened because Jock seemed very annoyed with him.

Jock said, 'If I get hold of her I'll chop her fucking head off.'

Taffy said, 'Yes, he's got a hatchet in the car.'

What did Carl say?

'Carl just went red and didn't say much, and I was quite sure that Carl knew where she was and wouldn't say anything.'

The cheque for £22 14s which Carl showed to Frederick George was cashed the following month at the Southend branch of the National Provincial Bank by Peter Henning of 2a St Vincent's Road, Westcliff; it was subsequently returned to him, the bank having received orders not to pay.

Peter Henning was the licensee of the Middleton Hotel in Southend High Street. He told police that on the evening of 10 January he attended an all-male party hosted by his friend Terence Groom at his flat in St Petersburgh Place, London. Among the other guests were Carl and his companion Jimmy, both of whom appeared at that time to be homeless. 'By the time I had left Terry Groom's party I had got to know Carl well enough to have a forwarding address by which I could contact him; that was Trafalgar Square post office.'

They kept in touch and on 31 January Carl announced that he was coming down to Southend to stay with Henning's friend Clifford Stetzel, whom he'd also met at the party. ('I wasn't very impressed with him. He appeared to be scruffy and I felt that I should treat him with a certain amount of caution.' According to Stetzel, Carl invited himself to Southend.) Yet on 1 February Carl telephoned Henning to report that neither Stetzel nor Stetzel's friend and fellow bachelor

John Lynes was able to accommodate him. Consequently Henning met him at the station and drove him to York Road, where he found a room in a boarding house. 'I spent the evening with him at the cinema and also some time with him on the Sunday.'

On 3 February Peter Henning cashed the cheque for Carl, who explained that his father had sent it to him. When the bank returned it Henning confronted him at the local bowling alley. Carl reasoned that his father must have stopped the cheque because he, Carl, hadn't written to him. 'He said he would pay me back the money. I am satisfied with this arrangement and do not want to make any complaint against Carl respecting this.'

The two men continued to see each other, and enjoyed a meal together on St Valentine's Day.

On 15 February Graham Hedditch, aged twenty, was detained by request at Southend police station, and Detective Chief Inspector Devonald and Detective Inspector Reuben Ridge travelled to Essex to interview him regarding the cheque. Hedditch readily admitted the theft and was taken to Shepherd's Bush later that day.

Hedditch confirmed that on 10 January he and his friend Jimmy attended a party in St Petersburgh Place at which he met Peter Henning, Clifford Stetzel and various other guests. On 25 January Hedditch accompanied Stetzel to a party hosted by Stetzel's friend Leslie Morris at his flat in Lurline Gardens. (Stetzel told police that this was a birthday party, 'an all-male affair of about thirty persons'.) At this party he met Andrew John Fforbe-Wilton and his brother Donald ('I believe they were shopfitters'). Shortly before midnight Andrew invited him back for coffee and he was taken to a flat in Fulham. 'I don't know the address and I stopped the night.'

At about 11pm the following night Andrew Fforbe-Wilton telephoned with an invitation to supper at his flat. He collected him in his Mini Cooper and once again Hedditch stayed the night. The next morning he asked permission to try on his host's black leather jacket. 'This was in the bedroom, and after I had tried the jacket on Andrew left the room. As I was taking the jacket off some papers and three cheques fell onto the bed and floor. I picked everything up and put them back into the pockets of the jacket. I then hung the jacket on the door. It was then I noticed a folded piece of paper on the bed. I opened it up and saw it was a cheque.' At this point Fforbe-Wilton walked in, and he concealed the cheque, screwing it up in his hand until he could put it into his pocket. Fforbe-Wilton took him to Liverpool Street station and he returned home by train. 'I never saw Andrew after that.'

In Southend on 3 February he found the cheque in his jeans pocket and decided to cash it, but before presenting it to Henning he altered the signature from J. Wilton to K. Wilton and so became 'Karl Wilton', although he helpfully supplied his former London address on the back. 'I'm sorry that I did this but I was short of money.'

No one at Shepherd's Bush particularly cared how short of money or brain cells Hedditch was or, for that matter, who he did in his spare time; the real reason he was in the room, they now told him, was because his mate Hannah Tailford had been murdered.

Had he done *her*?

Hannah Tailford? He knew the woman in the photograph as Terry Lynch and Ann Lancaster. Murdered? He knew she was missing, Jock Lynch had told him, but he hadn't heard she was dead. He was living in Southend now, working as a lanesman at a bowling alley in Basildon and courting Christine, a waitress whom he hoped to marry.

He'd never gone steady with Terry. He was very friendly with her and she gave him 'the odd bob or two' and he stayed at 40 Chestnut Road occasionally, 'but I only had sexual intercourse with her on one occasion and after I'd had a lot to drink'. This was not the occasion on which Roy offered them £5 each to perform for his camera ('she was willing, but I wasn't').

Roy knew her very well and used to talk to her a lot. 'He said he used to like being in the company of people who used to use the stall as he could find out things.' But he warned Hedditch that if those people were to find things out, things about him, there'd be trouble; if Hedditch told people what he was, Hedditch would 'probably' wind up in the Thames. ('I don't know what he was apart from knowing that he was the second man in some sort of organization.') One night Roy threatened Jimmy too. 'I think Jimmy knew something about Roy.'

This Roy, who was 5′ 10″, very well dressed, with thick wavy fair hair, was not to be confused with the other Roy, who was also very well dressed but taller, 6′, with reddish hair. He drove a two-tone Consul, and he picked up the dead woman at the Charing Cross coffee stall almost every night at about 2am. 'He used to bring the *Daily Mirror* with him when he came to the stall.' Hedditch hadn't seen him at the stall since before Christmas; he had no idea where this man lived.

Graham Hedditch, bringer of light.

On 17 February he appeared at West London Magistrates' Court, where he pleaded guilty to stealing the cheque and was fined £20.

Devonald's murder squad had released him the previous day. His account of his movements during the period 24 January–1 February was checked and found to be substantially true. He insisted that he did not meet Hannah Tailford on 26 January or at any time during this period.

'I have never hit her and I am certainly not responsible for her body being found in the River Thames.'

But what about his friend Jimmy's death?

Did he feel responsible for that?

On 31 January Graham Hedditch, witness, attended the inquest into the death of James Whent, aged twenty, of 64 West Cromwell Road. At Hammersmith Coroner's Court Gavin Thurston recorded a verdict of suicide on the maintenance worker, who died from coal gas poisoning. According to the *Fulham Chronicle*, Thurston said that there was a possibility that Whent, who had pawned a camera a few days before his death, was in difficult financial circumstances and that 'it was quite clear from the evidence that this was a deliberate action on his part'.

No doubt; but not every suicide means to make a go of it.

Perhaps Jimmy was just feeling jilted.

When Clifford Stetzel, en route to Leslie Morris's party, stopped off in Piccadilly to collect Hedditch, he was greeted by Whent as well. Could he come too? Stetzel told him this would not be possible, and the two men left him in the pub. This was a bit unfair, especially as it seems to have been Whent who got Hedditch into Terence Groom's party where he made a number of contacts, including Stetzel himself.

Moreover, James Whent's roommate slept that night, and the next, at another man's flat. On the morning of 27 January he returned with a screwed-up piece of paper in his pocket to find Whent in a chair in front of the gas oven, taps on, cheque cashed.

*

At 9am on 5 February Derek Tew, aged thirty-one and a corporal in the RAF, called at Loughton police station in response to a newspaper appeal for information about Hannah Tailford. That evening, in an interview conducted at Barnes police station, he talked about the woman he called 'Cowboy'.

He was a married man, he explained, stationed at North Weald in Essex but living with his wife and four children in a flat in Wandsworth Road. His brother-in-law, George Rowley, was the proprietor of the coffee stall at Shepherd's Bush, the one outside Pritchard's the baker's. This stall was open each evening from 10.30pm to 3am, and on Friday, Saturday, Sunday and Monday evenings Tew helped out.

About two months ago a woman began to come to the stall for cups of tea. 'It was always about 1am when she arrived. We called her "Cowboy" because of the high boots she wore. She had a white pair and also a brown pair of these boots.' She was the woman whose photograph he had seen in the newspapers.

On two occasions he gave her a lift home in his van. The first time was just before Christmas when he took her somewhere in the Tulse Hill area, and the second time was about three weeks ago when he took her to Thurlby Road, West Norwood. He was friendly with her but he'd never had intercourse with her.

He last saw Cowboy at the stall two weeks ago. 'She did not come any more but I did not attach too much importance to the fact because she had told me that she was going to get a regular job in a betting shop.'

That was all, and none of it was much help really. Still, it was kind of him to give her a lift home.

And modesty was another of Tew's virtues, for as detectives began to listen to Juliana Bicknell, Jean Bishop and Thomas Trice, it dawned on them that this corporal was none other than Del, Hannah Tailford's intended, and the man who must surely hold the key to the mystery of her disappearance, and possibly even her death.

Accordingly, on 19 February Derek Tew was taken to Shepherd's Bush and interrogated at great length by Benjamin Devonald. Tew now recalled that he had taken her home on several occasions. 'I can remember taking her on about three occasions to an address in Chestnut Road, West Norwood, and on about two occasions to Thurlby Road.' The second time he drove her to Chestnut Road she invited him in, and he entered a ground-floor room containing a double bed, an easy chair, a rocking horse and a cot. 'I didn't have sexual intercourse with her but she played about with me. I have never had sexual intercourse with her but she has played about with me on about half a dozen occasions.'

Saving himself for the honeymoon, was he?

'I have never at any time discussed marrying her. I remember jokingly saying to a customer one night in her presence that I hadn't got a wife. This came about through a discussion about the number of hours I worked.'

Tew later told her that he was married with four children, but he had never claimed that his wife was living apart from him and cohabiting with a black man. He mentioned to her the fact that he had bought a radiogram, 'or I should say a big record player', not for her but for his home. They had never gone house-hunting together. He had never given her money or taken money from her. She last visited the stall about two weeks prior to his first interview, and he had not seen her anywhere since.

'I have not been to any parties with her. I have not had a night off since Christmas.'

Interview concluded.

Went the day well?

Actually, yes.

Something jumped up and bit them.

In a manner of speaking. At 5.35am on 19 February Police Sergeant John Towes in company with two constables was patrolling the Thames in King's Reach; he was navigating downriver and was approximately four yards from Festival Hall Pier when he felt the boat shudder and slow down. Realizing that some object had fouled the screw, he returned to Waterloo Pier police station and took the boat out of service. That afternoon Police Sergeant Ronald Wills cleared the screw of the remains of a woman's blue woollen coat. Since this coat appeared to fit the description of the coat worn by Hannah Tailford as circulated in the *Police Gazette* he immediately contacted Detective Inspector Ridge.

On 25 February Allan Lynch identified this coat as the one Tailford was wearing when she left home at 9pm on 24 January. 'This particular coat was one which Tom Trice had given her.'

So she left the flat, entered the Thames wearing the same coat.
In view of what follows this is almost reassuring.

24 January. When Louise Aldridge, a press operator, saw a poster showing a photograph of Hannah Tailford she remembered seeing her at Victoria station at about 9.30pm on Friday 24 January. Aldridge had decided to have a cup of tea in the station cafeteria; she sat down at a table already occupied by a woman, Tailford, and a man.

These two were talking together and seemed quite friendly. The man was between thirty and thirty-five years old, 5′ 10″, fairly slim with long dark hair and a thin pleasant-looking face. 'He appeared to have a rash or skin trouble on the right side of his face.' He was wearing a fawn raincoat, a navy-blue jacket and a blue tie with red spots. 'When I left the cafeteria they were still sitting at the table.'

If we accept Allan Lynch's assertion that Tailford left their flat at 9pm then it's possible that she was the woman Louise Aldridge saw in the cafeteria at Victoria station. But in order for her to have arrived in time she would have needed a lift, and her lift, according to Theresa Eyles, was waiting outside her home at 11.30pm as per usual.

25 January. Between 12.30am and 1am on 25 January Christopher O'Dea, a bricklayer, and his wife were returning home to Brixton from a party when, at the junction of East Lane and Wolf Road, they were approached by a woman wearing a white mac and carrying a suitcase. She was about thirty-five years old and rather scruffy with dark brown hair. She spoke with a Scottish or northern accent and she said, 'He slung me out, the bastard slung me out.' She then asked O'Dea if he knew of anywhere clean she might stay, and he pointed her towards the Elephant and Castle and told her there was a hostel in that direction. She kept on repeating, 'All he wants is money, that's all he wants.' They hailed a taxi and left her standing there.

'I have seen a photograph of the woman Tailford and it looks just like the woman I have described.'

David Bateman, a caterer, told police that Terry, whom he knew to be a prostitute, frequented a coffee stall at Grosvenor Gardens, where he had formerly worked.

'I last saw her a week ago Saturday, which was 25 January 1964, in the Kenilworth Cafe at Warwick Way, SW1. I did not speak to her on that occasion although I usually do.'

This sighting seems plausible. Thomas Trice told police that Tony's Cafe in Wilton Road had changed ownership, and that 'the majority of types who used to use Tony's, and who would know Terry, have moved to the Kenilworth Cafe'.

As previously mentioned, Frederick George saw the dead woman at his coffee stall on 26 January, and Thomas McGing spoke to her at Victoria Station on either 27, 28 or 29 January.

27 January. Shirley Woolley, unemployed, had known Terry Lynch for four years, and she last saw her on 27 January ('I am certain about the date.') at Victoria station. 'I think she was carrying a large black handbag.' She was wearing a full-length blue coat with a large collar, a floral headscarf and red Russian-style boots, and she was walking with a man. This man was about 5′ 10″, clean-shaven with a tanned complexion, and well dressed. He wore a grey Robin Hood-type hat and a light gabardine raincoat. 'I think I would know him again. I have never seen him before anywhere.'

Shirley Woolley describes Tailford as wearing a full-length blue coat with a large collar, which sounds like the coat she was wearing when she left Lynch. But how to explain the red Russian-style boots?

27 or 29 January. At about 11.10pm on 27 or 29 January Carl Holmes, the proprietor of the West Norwood service station, 76 Knights Hill, West Norwood, was closing up when he was approached by a badly dressed woman wearing a dark coat. She asked for a loan of 5s and offered to give him her name, Balham address and telephone number. Holmes declined the offer and handed her the money, along with a billhead bearing the name of his business. 'I asked her how she had run out of money and she said she had been visiting friends up Knights Hill and had run out of money.'

This woman was probably not Tailford. Granted, 76 Knights Hill was within walking distance of 37 Thurlby Road, but Tailford had left her home and as far as we know she never returned. Moreover, Hannah Tailford spoke with a strong Geordie accent, and according to Holmes, who himself hailed from Northumberland, this woman had no northern accent at all.

28 January. Robert Boyd, like Holmes, saw the photograph of Tailford on *Police 5* and recognized the dead woman. Boyd, a salesman, had known her for some five years. He last saw her at about

11pm on Tuesday 28 January, when he was at the coffee stall at Charing Cross. 'I didn't speak to her.'

Robert Boyd's sighting of Tailford at the Charing Cross coffee stall raises the puzzling question of how many visits she paid that week. Unaccountably Frederick George recalled only one visit, and this would appear to be the occasion on which she was seen by William Smith and Joyce Todd, making it 29/30 January.

On 5 February Donald Brodie, the manager of Lovibond's off-licence, Churton Street, saw a photograph of Tailford in a newspaper and recognized her as a regular customer, although he never knew her name. She came in two or three times a week for cigarettes and matches, but since the middle of January she had also been buying miniature bottles of whisky, usually Black & White. He last served her during the week ending 1 February. He could not recall the exact day but thought it was probably 27 or 28 January.

'On this occasion she bought a bottle of Lovibond's Vat 30 whisky. I remember remarking to her that she was spending extra money in a term of a joke, and she said something to the effect that it was an investment for better things. I had, of course, some time before formed the opinion that she was a prostitute.'

She was probably wearing a full-length fawn coat and a hat.

28 or 29 January. Jack Pidherney, a waiter, knew the dead woman by sight ('I have seen her about on occasions over a period of about two years') and last saw her in a red or maroon car, possibly a Vauxhall, in the late evening of 28 or 29 January. The driver was a man aged about forty with a squarish head. 'He had a white shirt. He was wearing something, possibly a suit, that was light in colour.' He drove along Gloucester Road and turned left into Lupus Street.

As previously mentioned, Charles Sutcliffe saw the deceased in Endymion Road at about 11.20am on 29 January, when she was hat-less and wearing a red coat.

29 January. At around midnight on Wednesday 29 January William Smith, a bus conductor, was on duty on a night bus travelling from New Cross to Charing Cross when, passing the coffee stall on the Embankment near Charing Cross station, he noticed a woman standing at the stall talking to some other women. He recognized her as a woman who had boarded his bus at Webber Street, Blackfriars Road, at 12.30am on 22 January and alighted at Charing Cross.

When he saw the photograph of Hannah Tailford in the *Daily Herald* he realized she was this woman.

30 January. Joyce Todd had seen the dead woman at the Charing Cross coffee stall about once a week for the past twelve months, but did not know her name and never spoke to her. At about 4am on Thursday 30 January Todd saw her leave the stall and walk off on her own towards Blackfriars.

Karl Josef Van-Lados, an unemployed boiler engineer, had known Hannah Tailford 'on and off' for several years, and last saw her on 30 January.

He saw her twice that day. The first time was at about 2pm, when he saw her standing in the small waiting room next to the first-aid room at Victoria Station. 'She looked very haggard. She wore a head-scarf. I can't remember the colour or anything about the rest of her clothing.' He said hello to her and she acknowledged him and then went to the Ladies.

The second time was at about 5.30pm, when he saw her standing by the fruit stall outside Victoria Station. They had a conversation and then went together to the station cafeteria, where he bought a cup of tea for her and an Irishman he knew as 'Paddy'. The three of them chatted for about an hour, then he and Paddy left.

Ten minutes later they returned to the cafeteria to find that she was no longer there. Van-Lados went outside to look for her and saw her on the station forecourt. She was with a man he recognized as 'John' and they were walking towards Grosvenor Gardens.

John was about fifty years old, 5' 10", and of medium build with a very fresh complexion and dark curly receding hair. He was carrying an umbrella and was wearing an expensive-looking dark Crombie-type coat, a black homburg-type hat, yellow gloves and very shiny black shoes.

Van-Lados had seen John many times before in the Victoria area and had often conversed with him. ('He is very well spoken with a cultured accent and speaks very softly . . . he is always talking about books about concentration camps.') John lived in Chelsea, somewhere near Chelsea Bridge. Van-Lados last saw him in Vauxhall Bridge Road on the night of 4 February. 'I also saw him the night before, leaning up against a barbecue window in Soho, looking at the chickens. He seemed to be drunk. I spoke to him and he told me to buzz off.'

Paddy was traced and found to be John Henderson, unemployed. Henderson stated that at about 5.45pm on 30 January he, Van-Lados and Van-Lados's girlfriend, Sheila, entered the cafeteria at Victoria Station and joined Hannah Tailford, who was sitting at a table. ('I cannot remember what clothes she was wearing.') At about 6.55pm two men walked in together. 'One was a hobo type, I didn't take much notice of him, and the other was very smartly dressed.'

This man was about forty-five years old, about 5′ 8″, with a fresh complexion and dark hair greying at the temples. He was wearing a black and white check three-quarter-length coat, a charcoal-grey suit, black handmade shoes, 'very highly polished like dancing shoes', a white shirt, a light blue tie with a 'hand-painted woman motif' and black gloves.

The 'hobo type' walked over to Tailford and said, 'You'll be all right with that guy,' and whispered in her ear. She then joined the smartly dressed man who was standing by the swing door and he said something to her and they left together. 'I have not seen either of them since.'

At about 5.20pm on 30 January Charles Sutcliffe saw Tailford for a second time. She was talking to two men outside Woolworths on the corner of Wilton Road. One of the men was aged between thirty and thirty-five, 5′ 10″, well built with a full beard and dark bushy hair; he was wearing an overcoat. 'I can't describe the other man.'

Tailford was wearing a grey/green tweed coat. 'I'm not certain of the colour because it was getting dark and I only saw her for a few seconds.'

31 January. William Burgess, a labourer, saw the dead woman frequently between 1am and 3am at the Shepherd's Bush coffee stall and he knew she was a prostitute. She was at the stall between 1am and 2am on Friday 31 January, when Burgess asked the proprietor for a 1s piece for his gas meter, and she gave it to him instead. 'That is the only time I have ever spoken to her.'

Arnold Downton, a British Rail shunter, knew the dead woman as 'Doll' and had seen her several times at the Charing Cross coffee stall. At about 6.30 pm on 31 January he and his girlfriend, Elizabeth Ritchie, saw her there, standing on her own. She was starving, so they took her to the Florence Cafe in Villiers Street and bought her a meal.

'She was miserable and had been crying. She said she was so fed up

she felt like doing away with herself and I told her not to be so daft.'
He gave her 5s and she left them. It was now almost 7pm; she said she
was going to meet someone back at the coffee stall but she didn't say
who it was.

She was wearing a dark imitation fur coat, a white blouse and a
dark blue skirt; round her neck she wore a heart-shaped medallion
and a white scarf.

Arnold Downton stated that, when he saw her, Tailford 'was starving', in which case amphetamines may have helped to suppress her
appetite. She told Downton and his girlfriend that she felt like doing
away with herself, but was it suicide she had in mind or was it a free
meal? Or was she merely coming down from the pills? She ate fried
fish, boiled potatoes and peas, followed by apple pie and custard and
a cup of coffee with milk. ('I noticed that she had put about four tea-
spoons of sugar in the coffee and I made some remark about having a
very sweet tooth.' A common feature of amphetamine/opiate
dependency.) And yet her stomach contents consisted of bacon, egg
and cheese. Once more the pharmaceutical explanation presents
itself, for if she'd been on her uppers for, say, two days or so she'd be
feeling ravenously hungry and would need to eat again during the
course of the evening.

At 7.25pm on 31 January Margaret Shepherdson, a civil servant,
boarded a bus at Queensway to travel to her home in Upper Addison
Gardens. As the bus approached the Addison Road stop she noticed a
woman sitting beside her. 'I went to get up and said, "Excuse me," and
the woman replied something like, "I'm getting off at the next stop as
well."' Both women then alighted, but Shepherdson hurried off and
didn't see which way the other went.

'Last night I saw the picture of the murdered woman on the *Police
5* programme and I think it is the woman on the bus.'

1 February. Frederick Townend, an unemployed window cleaner,
had known the deceased for about a year and saw her frequently at the
coffee stalls, cafes and clubs around the West End. He last saw her
between midnight and 2am on Saturday 1 February. She was at the
Charing Cross coffee stall and she was 'high as a kite' on amphetamines, but that was nothing unusual. 'She was always on the purple
hearts, she was always blocked up – never off them – and used to get
in the clubs for her pills.' However, on this occasion at least, she was

quite coherent; he asked her where she'd been and she said, 'Over the West.'

Townend knew she was a prostitute and had seen her pick up customers, sometimes walking off with two or even three men. One man in particular used to meet her at the Charing Cross coffee stall twice a week between midnight and 2am. This man, who always wore a navy-blue donkey jacket, was about forty-five years old, 6', fat, with receding black hair and a swarthy complexion. Townend believed he was on his way to Covent Garden when he called at the stall, as he always drove an old green lorry, sometimes loaded with vegetables and sometimes empty. 'As far as I remember I definitely haven't seen him since the time of the murder at the stall; although I did see him here a short time before she was murdered.'

So . . . Frederick Townend saw Tailford, 'blocked up to the eyeballs', some time between midnight and 2am at the Charing Cross coffee stall. The pathologist estimated that she had lain in the Thames for between two and seven days, so she most probably died very shortly after this final sighting. However, no traces of drugs or alcohol were found in her body.

Townend was certain of the date he saw her, because he'd been working in Brighton on Wednesday and Thursday and arrived back in London at midday on Friday 31 January.

Is it unreasonable to assume that he was out on Friday night blowing his wages?

Was he in a condition to judge her condition?

On 3 February a message was transmitted to all police stations requesting that records be searched in order to trace any women's clothing deposited at stations since 24 January. On 5 February police dogs searched Barnes Common, Duke's Meadows and the area surrounding the Upper Mall, but none of Tailford's garments was found. Following Allan Lynch's identification of her coat on 25 February, officers from Thames Division used creep drags to search the river bed in the region of Festival Hall Pier. The search continued for a week without result.

Enquiries were made at all lodging houses and hotels in the Victoria area, but no information was obtained as to where Tailford had been living since 24 January. Investigating the possibility that her body was thrown overboard from a rivercraft, police made enquiries at all houseboats between Chelsea and Chiswick and questioned all pier-masters from Greenwich to Kew in a vain attempt to ascertain whether any craft had been moored in these areas during the weekend commencing 31 January.

Derek Tew's flat in Wandsworth Road was searched and his blue Ford Thames van seized and examined but nothing of evidential value was found. It was established that Corporal Tew was at his unit at North Weald from 21 January to 24 January and from 28 January to 4 February. He was subsequently eliminated from the inquiry.

It proved impossible to trace any of the male companions described by witnesses who saw Tailford during the last week of her life, and the motorist who picked her up outside her home every night and the lorry driver described by Frederick Townend were never found. Neither was the printer in the dark green Morris Minor, although Joyce Todd, the woman mentioned by Frederick George, was traced and confirmed that this man had picked her up from the Charing Cross coffee stall one night in January and given her a lift home to Lambert Road. He spoke with a London accent and was in his early thirties, 5' 7", thin, with fair hair and a long thin face. He seemed normal enough; nothing unusual occurred. ('I said to him, "You had better hurry to get back to the coffee stall before your girlfriend gets there." He said, "That's all right, there's nothing in it, I just give her a lift home."') His car was a dark blue/green Ford Zephyr or Anglia.

So – no arrests then (unless Graham Hedditch counts).

Although there *could* have been an arrest.

But not by the police.

On the afternoon of 6 February Detective Sergeant Taylor and PC Varney, both attached to Devonald's murder squad, were in the Victoria area when Varney approached Karl Van-Lados, whom he knew to be an associate of prostitutes, in the station cafeteria. Van-Lados was seated at a table with two other men and seemed reluctant to discuss his knowledge of Tailford in their presence, so at PC Varney's suggestion they met in the Shakespeare pub nearby.

Here the Dutchman told the policeman of his two encounters with Tailford on 30 January. He revealed that the second time he met her she handed him a police officer's warrant card and driving licence to look after, items which he initially assumed had been stolen from one of her clients. However, she told him that she had obtained them from a man the previous night.

Later that afternoon DS Taylor took possession of a Metropolitan Police warrant card and a driving licence in the name of George Henry Chandler. It transpired that these had been lost by Detective Sergeant Chandler on 23 January 1964. He felt certain that the loss had occurred at East Croydon railway station when he was removing a ticket from his wallet.

Maybe it had. But by what means did the untraceable man acquire these desirable items? Why did he keep them for a week before handing them to Tailford? (Why trust Tailford with them anyway?) Why did Tailford give them to Van-Lados and why did Van-Lados keep them for a week? Was it out of fear – or something more sinister?

Let's face it, someone, anyone, with a gruff voice and a plausible manner could have had themselves a time . . .

The inquest into Hannah Tailford's death was opened by the coroner Gavin Thurston at Hammersmith Coroner's Court on 5 February and adjourned until 8 April, when a further adjournment was granted until 28 April.

On that day ten people were called to give evidence, among them Arnold Downton, the British Rail shunter, who, when presented with the torn blue coat previously shown to Allan Lynch, identified it as the coat Tailford had in fact been wearing when he saw her on 31 January.

The pathologist Donald Teare, when questioned by the coroner as to the possibility of Tailford's committing suicide, remarked that he knew of instances in which persons committing suicide by drowning had placed articles in their mouths to prevent themselves from screaming.

Articles, yes. But a pair of semen-stained panties? And had any of these persons eaten a substantial meal and stripped naked (in February) before jumping in?

The coroner's jury returned an open verdict, although it's hard to imagine that anyone present really believed that Hannah Tailford had killed herself, especially now that the case was altered.

Altered, yes.

For by this time another witch had entered the water.

And would you believe?

A new word had entered the language.

Scrophelia.

Fancy that.

At 2am on 18 January 1964 PC Langman and PC Barringer arrested a woman in Kensington Church Street for soliciting. When charged at Notting Hill police station she gave her name as Sandra Russell. WPC Blewett took a set of her fingerprints and compiled her antecedents.

She was born on 29 September 1938 in Gainsborough in Lincolnshire, an only child whose parents were killed during the war. She claimed to have been brought up by her grandfather and educated at Walkeringham Secondary Modern School until she was fifteen, when she worked for a year on her grandfather's farm. In 1954 she came to London and worked as a waitress in Islington for two years before leaving to live in Nottingham, where she worked as an usherette in local cinemas for twelve months. While in Nottingham she formed a relationship with a John Russell, who kept her for the next five years. The couple had a child, Stephen Colin, who was born in May 1958 and was now in care in Nottingham.

When she broke off her relationship with Russell she moved to Northampton and lived for six months with another man. She then returned to London, where she lived with Russell once more, although six months later he was arrested and charged with receiving stolen goods. He was currently in prison, serving a twelve-month sentence.

Since Russell's imprisonment she had been working as a hostess in various West End clubs, in particular the Nucleus Club in Monmouth Street, which she claimed had been her destination at the time of her arrest. She stated that exactly one month previously she moved into a furnished flat at 16 Denbigh Road, W11, for which she paid £12 10s per week, and that she had only been soliciting in the street since that time in order to pay the high rent. She did not entertain clients at this address and refused to say where she did take them. In fact she refused to say anything more.

She was taken to Hammersmith police station and detained there until her appearance at Marylebone Magistrates' Court later that day, when she was conditionally discharged for twelve months.

'Sandra Russell' was an alias, as was Barbara Norton, Barbara

Lockwood and Sandra Lockwood. The woman's real name was Irene Lockwood and her charge sheet listed fourteen previous convictions; these dated back to 1956 and included five convictions for soliciting, two for insulting behaviour and one for indecency in a public place.

It gets worse, for unfortunately the above account of Lockwood's early life, as extracted from her by WPC Blewett, is the only version we have, and should therefore be treated with caution.

We know that she was born Irene Charlotte Lockwood on 29 September 1938 in Walkeringham, Nottingham (according to her birth certificate, her mother, Minnie Lockwood, unemployed, lived at Pear Tree Farm, Walkeringham, and her father didn't exist). We know that during the period 1956 to 1960 no birth was registered in Nottingham under the name Stephen Colin Russell, Stephen Colin Lockwood, Colin Stephen Russell or Colin Stephen Lockwood, where the mother's maiden name was Russell or Lockwood, which leads us to the conclusion that the birth of her son was not recorded.

We also know that she was now pregnant again, and that this time it would have been a girl.

In December 1963 two sisters, Janet and June Taylor, aged seventeen and fifteen respectively, moved into 138 Westbourne Grove. The Taylors were runaways, up from Hounslow; their mother had died in November, they'd had a row with their father and now here they were, sharing a ground-floor room with Irene Lockwood, whom they knew as Mrs Sandra Russell, whose husband, she said, was in prison for forgery. She had bleached blonde hair and a tattoo of a tombstone on her right arm and she told them she worked in a nightclub in Leicester Square. 'She was a heavy cigarette smoker and drank whisky and vodka,' recalled June Taylor.

Cheers, girls! Welcome to West Eleven . . .

Soon it was time to go, but not very far. 'Sandra told me that she wanted to leave the house because the landlord wanted to live with her.' A few days before Christmas all three moved to 118 Ledbury Road, where they shared a flat with a young man named Jim, 'Jim Paynter or Punter. He came from Blackpool and was trumpeter in the Welsh or Scots Guards.'

When Irene Lockwood was living at 138 Westbourne Grove she received visits from a number of men. These were 'Big Mike', who was in his early twenties; 'Little Mike', who was in his late twenties, with a hook nose; 'Big Barry'; Ray, who was about thirty-five, with greased black hair and a heart-shaped face; Simon, about thirty-seven, very fat with greased dark hair, possibly unemployed; and Gerry, about forty-seven, thin, almost bald, rather scruffy.

But at Ledbury Road only Ray and Simon called on her, and Simon wanted money. June Taylor had seen her give him as much as £10, three or four times in one week. 'I got the impression that Sandra was frightened of Simon.'

On 3 January 1964 the two sisters left London for jobs at a riding stables in Surrey. The following day Irene Lockwood took a short walk round to 16 Denbigh Road to see the landlady, Mrs Pamela Edwards, who had advertised her ground-floor flat to rent at £12 10s per week.

Could Mrs Sandra Russell afford to live here?

Well?

Yes, she was employed as a barmaid at a gambling club in Gerrard Street, where she earned very good money and picked up quite a lot of tips. She worked very late hours and slept during the day. No, she couldn't supply a reference.

Convincing? Hardly. Unlike June Taylor, Pamela Edwards wasn't fifteen years old, and a single glance at Lockwood would have told her all she needed to know. At £12 10s a week only a princess or a prostitute —

Better make that two prostitutes.

Maureen Gallagher was born in 1945 in Glasgow. She left school at fifteen and for three unhappy years helped her mother run the family boarding house before escaping to London in May 1963 'for a good time before I got married'. She found a job as a chambermaid at a hotel in Russell Square and worked there until September.

'I was then involved in a car crash — a taxi I was passenger in crashed and I finished up in St Mary's Hospital, Paddington.' When she came out of hospital she discovered that she'd lost her job at the hotel. 'I felt fed up and took a bottle of codeine.' She was taken to Middlesex Hospital and thence transferred to a women's hostel in Greek Street, where she stayed for about two weeks. During this time she met some Greeks, and one of them, Jimmy, found her a job touting in the doorway of a clip joint opposite the hostel, 'but I wasn't a success'. Jimmy took her to Leicester, where she moved in with Nick, a restaurant owner, who got her pregnant. 'After that happened I started going out on the streets some nights . . . Sometimes I would see Jimmy and he would beat me up and take my money off me.'

Sick of it all, she returned to London in February 1964. 'I stayed in the Church Army hostel, Bryanston Street, W1, for about two weeks and saw an advert in a paper for a room at £1 a week. This was at 138 Westbourne Grove.' On 6 March she went round to see the landlord, but he had to go out and left her waiting in the ground-floor front room. After about an hour she got fed up and began to look around the place. She spoke to an Irish girl on the first floor who introduced her to the woman in the basement flat who knew a Sandra Russell, a business girl, who might be able to put her up, and promptly went off to fetch her.

That night Maureen Gallagher moved into 16 Denbigh Road. Lockwood's flat contained twin beds; the new girl would sleep in the one beside the handbasin, next to the window. The rent was £12 10s per week payable on Saturdays. *Oh, and by the way, two men come and hide in my kitchen every night –*

Eh?

– and you're joining them.

It was quite simple really. Lockwood, bringing a client home, would ask him to undress in the living room before he followed her into the bedroom. As soon as the bedroom door closed Ray or Simon, both of whom were hiding behind a curtain in the kitchen, would creep out and turn up the volume on the transistor radio which was playing in the living room. Upon his return the other would emerge and go through the punter's pockets. 'They would only take some of the client's money – say, if he had £10 only £2 would be taken.'

Gallagher soon settled in, and within a week she was bringing men home herself. Her flatmate advised her to charge up to £5 for a short time ('Sometimes I only got £2'). Gallagher worked Westbourne Grove as far as the Odeon and Lockwood hustled in Westbourne Grove, Bayswater Road and Queensway; their clientele consisted almost entirely of kerb crawlers. (Lockwood, unlike Gallagher, occasionally did business in cars.)

For the first few nights the girls took it in turns to bring clients back – but then someone had a brainwave. Legover turnover would increase if the keys to the flat were left in a bush outside the building; their absence would indicate that the bedroom was occupied, in which event the other woman walked her punter round the block until they reappeared.

According to Gallagher, it was straight sex only; the punters undressed (very important) but she merely removed her skirt and shoes. 'I always did business on the bed. As far as I know, Sandra was the same. There was no kinky business, although she did say twice she got it in the back way.'

As is the case with most service industries, the occasional trouble-maker presented himself. Prior to Gallagher's arrival on the scene, Lockwood had entertained a taxi driver one night, a taxi driver who discovered he was £5 short at the end of the ride. He kept coming back for his money until eventually she did business for free to pay off the debt.

And then one of Gallagher's punters, Dennis the joiner, returned and complained over the intercom that someone had stolen £5 from him; he wanted to come in. He rang the bell again and said that if they didn't open the door he would kick it in; so Ray and Simon disappeared upstairs and Lockwood let him back inside the flat. Dennis accused her of taking his money. He checked the contents of her handbag and the pockets of her coat but eventually left empty-handed. 'He left saying he was going for the police but I haven't seen him since.'

But sooner or later somebody was going to go for the police. In fact Gallagher, in her more desperate moods, felt like contacting them herself, anything to get rid of Simon and Ray – particularly Ray. When she started hustling Ray asked her to lend him some money. 'I refused and he pushed me about and said nobody was going to make a fool of him.' Notes began to disappear from her handbag. She told her flatmate that she wanted to leave.

Lockwood was now approximately three months pregnant; her condition was common knowledge. 'She said it was down to either Barry the half-caste or Jim the guardsman . . . Sandra told me she only did business with rubbers so she didn't think it was a client.' Ray brought her some tablets which he claimed would induce an abortion. Vitamin tablets: they cost him 5/9d and he charged her £4.

*

Like her flatmate, Irene Lockwood feared and detested Ray and Simon, and she talked continually about how she might get rid of them. 'She even put some paper behind the doorbell so that it didn't work.' But it didn't work – they came back night after night.

One night around the middle of March Simon told the women that Barry had told him that the police were watching the flat.

How did they take it?

Well, it was excellent news in so far as it meant that you-know-who would be staying away for a few days; and yet it also meant that the two prostitutes now faced the probability of arrest for running a brothel.

So it was heads down, legs together for the next few days. On the evening of Thursday 26 March Gallagher went out for cigarettes, but by the time she returned home she'd received a caution for soliciting. She told her flatmate that three policemen approached her client's car, that she'd given her real name. Lockwood's thoughts turned to her own conditional discharge. 'She was frightened because she said if she got caught she would get a hard sentence.'

But Lockwood couldn't help herself either. At 1am she went out to the milk machine and came back with Kenny, a client from the previous week, whom she took into the living room. 'I didn't see him. I dropped off to sleep.'

When Gallagher awoke that Good Friday morning Lockwood had already left the flat. At about 1pm she returned with 'a lot of money' and said she was going to have her hair done. Kenny had given her this money, about £5 or £6, the night before. Kenny was well off, he owned a club and a big black car. She'd explained their predicament to him and he suggested she take her clients back to one of the rooms above his club.

Gallagher viewed Kenny's offer with caution. 'I said although it sounded all right he could well be another ponce that would take money off her.' She also pointed out that Ray claimed to have discovered a gun licence while rifling through Kenny's pockets on his previous visit. But this failed to disconcert her flatmate, who perhaps hoped that he would use his gun to shoot Ray and Simon.

It all added up to a chance of escape.

And if that route failed there was another available. After saying goodnight to Kenny, Lockwood went out again and bumped into Big

Mike, and he offered to find her a business flat; although she would have to wait a few days and she wasn't to mention it to anyone.

'Sandra was really happy that day. In view of this I decided to move out.' On 29 March Gallagher telephoned Mr Andrews, 'our sugar daddy', and he agreed to let her stay the night at his flat at 118 Ledbury Road. Come bedtime, however, he took the opportunity to test her gratitude. 'I didn't want to know, so he got up and went for a walk for about an hour. Andy was like that, always nice and kind.'

On Easter Monday morning she left Andrews's flat and made her way to Paddington Station. 'I put my cases in there, they are still there.' She hung around the station for a couple of hours, and after that she just hung around. 'I just hung around until I found myself in the Comet Club, which is near Bayswater tube station. I was crying in there and I met a young chap who let me sleep in his room on Monday night.'

The next day she wandered around until she got so fed up that she bought a bottle of codeine tablets, a bottle of sherry and some razor blades. She went to the Ladies at Bayswater tube station and tried to kill herself by swallowing the tablets; but she kept being sick so she cut her wrists instead. 'The next thing is that I woke up in St Mary's Hospital, Paddington, again.'

16 Denbigh Road was a three storey semi-detached house jointly owned by Pamela Edwards and her husband, Harold, and let as furnished flats. Irene Lockwood had been made aware of the rules. 'These were, briefly, no noise after midnight, the flat must be kept clean and that there must be no complaints about her general behaviour.'

She moved into the ground-floor flat on 4 January and paid her rent regularly every Saturday up to and including 21 March. At lunchtime on Wednesday 25 March Edwards saw her at the flat and explained that because of the Easter holiday she would be collecting rents on the following Wednesday instead of Saturday. Was that all right with her? Yes.

However, on Wednesday 1 April Lockwood telephoned her to ask if instead she might pay two weeks' rent the following Saturday. Edwards agreed to this, whereupon Lockwood said she would prefer to pay one week's rent on the Saturday and one week's rent the following Monday. 'I told her that this was rather irregular and I would rather it didn't happen again, after she had told me she had spent more money than usual over the Easter.' (Visiting the property on 1 April, Edwards found a note, left on a table in the hall, in which her tenant confused the issue further, offering 'apoliges' and asking if she might pay the rent on Thursday or Friday 'as I've been away this Easter, spent rather too much & hav'nt got paid this week yet'.)

At 11.30am on Saturday 4 April Pamela Edwards and her husband arrived at the house to collect the rents. When she knocked on the door of Irene Lockwood's flat she received no reply, so she let herself in with her key – and had a good look round.

Untidy, dirty . . . the curtains were drawn, the light was on in the sitting room, so was the electric fire. The beds appeared not to have been slept in, and there were no clothes inside the wardrobe, just dirty sheets and blankets. 'Dirty crockery was left in the flat and I was of the opinion that she had run off without paying her rent.'

In the top drawer of the chest of drawers she discovered a booklet, 'Wrinkola and the care of your skin', as well as various garments including a knitted pink cardigan, a black stole, a pair of blue jeans and some dirty underwear. The contents of the flat itself consisted of some fifty miscellaneous items – a brown leather handbag, a china dog, a quantity of condoms (used and unused) – which she collected and boxed.

Pamela Edwards returned to the flat on Monday 6 April, the second of the agreed payment dates, but there was no one home. The landlady stayed and cleaned up.

At 6.30pm the following evening she was at the flat again when a man called and asked for Mrs Russell. He was about thirty-five years old, 5' 10", with dark hair, and he wore a green trilby on his head and a red slipper on his right foot. She informed him that Mrs Russell had left the flat and that, what's more, she'd left it in a filthy condition and owed her money and she was very annoyed. Had he seen her?

Yes, he'd seen her last Friday night before he went up north; he'd told her he would call round on Monday when he returned. He called on Monday evening, but got no reply.

This man told Edwards he was going to Ledbury Road to see some friends and would be back in half an hour. 'He came back and told me she wasn't there, and he telephoned from the telephone in the hall, but I don't know who he spoke to. He also told me that Mrs Russell had told him that she owed money for rent and he wanted to help her. He said he felt sorry for her.' His friends at Ledbury Road thought that Russell – who, he said, was also known as Lockwood – might be 'in jug'. Edwards telephoned Notting Hill police station but they had no knowledge of her whereabouts.

Mrs Sandra Russell, the bloody little scrubber, had done a moonlight flit . . .

But her landlady had not seen the last of her.

At 7.45am on Wednesday 8 April Police Sergeant Robert Powell was patrolling the Thames at Corney Reach, Chiswick, when he spotted the nude body of a young woman lying on the foreshore, at the foot of a sloping stone bank at a point about 300 yards above Lep Wharves. She was lying face down parallel to the bank with her head pointing upriver. He landed, and upon examining the body discovered an incised flesh wound about 6″ long above the right breast.

'The tide had commenced to flood at 7.15am and I estimated that I had about an hour or so before I would be compelled to move the body up the bank due to the rising water.'

At 8.55am the divisional surgeon, Joshua Stein, arrived to pronounce life extinct. He saw the naked body of a young woman (age estimated at twenty-five years) lying on her face on her right side. The body was cold and the face and trunk were of a rosy hue. She was turned over for examination, and he observed that her mouth was slightly open and the tongue visible. There was no froth around the nose and mouth. The hands and feet were bleached and the skin of the fingers and feet were sodden, the feet slightly less so. The incised chest wound was about 6″–8″ long, beginning on the right side below the right clavicle and extending inwards and downwards to the front of the mid-chest.

At 9.35am four photographs were taken of the body in the position found, just as the water level reached it. At 9.45am Detective Inspector Reuben Ridge attended the scene and authorized the removal of the body. At 10.30am he accompanied it to Acton mortuary and was present when Donald Teare performed the post-mortem.

The deceased was a well-nourished woman, 5′, with hair that was bleached a strawberry colour and which originally appeared to have been fairly blonde (the pubic and axillary hair was blonde). Decomposition was beginning and the body was covered with dirt. The following teeth were present: left upper 1, 2, 3, 4, 7; right upper 1, 2, 3, 6, 7; left lower 1, 2, 3, 4, 7; right lower 1, 2, 3, 4. On the right forearm was a tattoo of a cross and flower, across which a scroll bore the word 'John' and above which a second scroll bore the words 'In Memory'. There was an incised wound 6½" long on the front of the right shoulder and breast. This was a post-mortem injury; no ante-mortem injuries were recorded.

River water was present in the lungs, which showed the ballooning typical of death by drowning; there was some fine froth and fluid in the small air passages, but no unusual foreign bodies. The stomach contained a little mucus only and the bladder was empty. The uterus was enlarged to a size consistent with a pregnancy of between fourteen and eighteen weeks, and contained a female child of that period of gestation. There was no evidence of any interference with the pregnancy, and there were no marks of violence on the vagina. There was some old scarring, probably the result of a previous pregnancy. Teare gave the cause of death as drowning.

On 10 April Pamela Edwards visited Acton mortuary and formally identified the dead woman as her late tenant (who still owed her two weeks' rent).

What day is it today?

On 2 February the brothers Capon chanced upon the corpse of prostitute Hannah Tailford, naked save for a pair of suspenderless stockings, on the foreshore of the Thames at Upper Mall, Hammersmith. Nine weeks and two days later PS Powell discovered the naked corpse of prostitute Irene Lockwood about a mile upriver, on the foreshore at Corney Reach, Chiswick.

8 April.

It was estimated that Lockwood had been in the water for no longer than forty-eight hours. In his on-site examination of her body Joshua Stein found 'no signs of weeds or grasping in the fingernails', which suggested that she was unconscious when she entered the river. Upon removal of the body PS Powell made a thorough search of the surrounding shore and bank but found nothing.

Not to be confused with 1 April.

Benjamin Devonald's team of detectives were still pursuing their investigation into Hannah Tailford's death when a second murder squad, also based at Shepherd's Bush, was formed under Detective Superintendent Frank 'Jeepers' Davies (his nickname derived from his preference for suede footwear).

All Fools' Day.

Enquiries began at 16 Denbigh Road, where Pamela Edwards handed Frank Davies the contents of Lockwood's drawer and the box containing her possessions, and continued at 118 Ledbury Road, where James Panter, married but separated, shared a rented first-floor flat with his girlfriend, a secretary named Caroline Clarke.

The 26-year-old Lancashireman was a serving soldier in the Grenadier Guards and a musician with the Grenadier Guards band stationed at Wellington barracks. He was shown a photograph of the dead woman and identified her as Sandra Russell ('I also know her real name to be Lockwood'). He first met her a few days before Christmas 1963, when she was introduced to him by Simon at Lyons in Notting Hill Gate (he failed to explain how he first met Simon). He understood that she had nowhere to live so he introduced her to his landlady, Mrs Noah, as his adopted sister, and she and her two young friends Janet and June Taylor came to live with him. On 3 January 1964 the two sisters moved down to Surrey and Lockwood found a flat at 16 Denbigh Road.

'During the time she was at my flat I learned that she was a prostitute. I did not have intercourse with any of these three girls. I know the other two girls were not on the game.'

Was Mrs Sandra Russell married?

Well, she wore a thin gold ring on her wedding finger, but he didn't think she was, no. She often talked about a man named John who was 6', dark-haired and handsome. She had intended to marry him, but he got arrested and was now in prison somewhere. She also said that he was the father of her child, who had been adopted.

Who was the father this time?

Hard to say. She told him she was pregnant, but she didn't mention who was responsible. She didn't appear upset about her condition, although Simon told him that she wanted to get rid of the baby and asked if he could get some pills. Apparently she gave Simon (not Ray) £4 for pills he'd bought from a local chemist's, and later told him that they must be doing her some good because 'they were making her tummy move'.

Simon had told him that it was a toss-up whether the baby was his (Panter's) or Barry's; Simon said it couldn't be his because he'd had intercourse with her 'before she had fallen for it'. Ray said, 'It couldn't be me because I went up the other way.'

Was Barry, 'a white man with negroid features', the culprit? At a Christmas party thrown by Mrs Noah, Lockwood got drunk and went to bed with him.

Panter peeped.

'I first saw them on the bed and Barry was with Sandra, touching her up. Later I saw Barry on top of her on the bed with the counterpane over them and he was going at her hell for leather. I was worried about the two young girls, Janet and June, as I didn't want any of the men to touch them.'

Anyway, one thing was certain: the baby could not possibly be his because he'd never had intercourse with her, or either of the two sisters ('I did touch up the youngest one named June but that's as far as it went').

James Panter last saw the dead woman on 20 March. He was walking down Ledbury Road at about 11pm when he saw Ray, who was carrying two bottles and walking in the opposite direction. Ray told Panter that his girlfriend, Caroline Clarke, was at Sandra Russell's flat, and that she was drunk. 'I went to the flat, where I saw Caroline, who had just returned from a cheese and wine party held on behalf of the Liberal Party.' Lockwood and Gallagher were both present; Clarke was lying on one of the beds. Nothing unusual took place. He collected his girlfriend and left.

All the same, he knew what went on there behind closed curtains. A previous visit had opened his eyes.

Earlier that month he was walking home along Denbigh Road one night after a band engagement when he noticed a light on in Lockwood's flat and decided to pay her a call. Ray and Simon, it transpired, had had the same idea, and Maureen Gallagher made five. 'We all sat talking for a while and after half an hour the bell sounded. Ray, Simon and Maureen all made a dive for the kitchen and I went with them. I had left my trumpet by one of the chairs and Ray made a grab at it and brought it into the kitchen.'

Presently business commenced. Ray crept out from behind the curtain; and crept back again a few minutes later. He said, 'He's got no money or he has taken it in with him. I've been through all his pockets.' 'Nothing at all?' said Simon. Ray said, 'He's a big bloke.' When the client had left he told Lockwood, 'Next time pick someone with some money.' She laughed. Simon asked her how much she had got out of him. She laughed and shrugged.

'They didn't appear to discuss it much in my presence.'

That's understandable. Delicate subject, Lockwood's money. She told Caroline Clarke that Ray and Simon were always having money off her. 'She had a black diary, I gave it to her,' stated Clarke. 'That is the one you have shown me.' Clarke examined this diary some time around the end of January and saw that she had recorded the amounts owed against the two men's names. On a later occasion in Lockwood's flat Clarke witnessed a row between her and Ray and Simon. 'I think it was over money and Sandra said it was all written down in her diary.' But not any longer — several pages, including that one, had been torn out.

Caroline Clarke wasn't particularly friendly with the dead woman, although she used to talk to her. She knew that Lockwood had been forced to leave 118 Ledbury Road following Mrs Noah's Christmas party. 'Mrs Noah had said either Jim left or Sandra left.' She knew that Lockwood was pregnant because she had told her in the presence of Maureen Gallagher, adding that the father was either Jim Panter or Barry the Jamaican. ('This wasn't a shock to me as Jim had told me about a month ago that he may be the father of her child.') These announcements were made on the night of 20 March, when Clarke turned up drunk at her flat. It was the last time she saw her.

The last time she spoke to her was at about 6.30pm on Friday 3 April. Lockwood telephoned her address and when Clarke answered she asked to speak to Mr Andrews. ('He was the only client I knew she had.') But he didn't want to speak to her. The two women chatted instead and arranged that Lockwood would come round that evening at 8.30pm. 'She sounded all right and didn't say that anybody was with her.'

At 7pm Simon called round and asked Clarke for money, explaining that he had rent arrears, that he wanted to visit his wife in Birmingham and that he owed Paddy the bookmaker £300. Clarke refused to lend him any, pointing out that he already owed her £30 'and he said he must owe Sandra about as much as that too'. He left at about 8pm and Clarke waited for Lockwood to arrive. 'She didn't keep the appointment and I have not seen her since.'

Ronald Andrews, the 'sugar daddy' mentioned by Maureen Gallagher, was a ganger who rented a furnished room on the ground floor of 118 Ledbury Road. He told detectives that he'd had inter-course with the deceased on many occasions, in fact she was his only current sexual partner. However, he never paid her, and she never asked him for money. 'We used to talk a lot and she told me she knew Hannah Tailford, the other girl fished out of the river, also that she had been involved in another murder at some time, when a man had been sent to a mental home.'

Andrews last saw her at 1.30am on Tuesday 31 March, when he took her home to 16 Denbigh Road after she had spent part of the night with him. One week later he visited St Mary's Hospital, where he discovered he had gonorrhoea. That night Simon telephoned him from 16 Denbigh Road, asking if he'd seen Sandra as she'd disap-peared, owing two weeks' rent.

No; no, he hadn't seen her.

'I didn't mention to him that I'd been looking for her.'

Had she disappeared? If so, where to? Police suspected that Irene Lockwood, like Hannah Tailford before her, had alternative accom-modation in the final days of her life. And according to Maureen Gallagher, Big Mike had offered to find her a flat.

Michael Hennessey, an antiques dealer, lived at 10 Strathmore Gardens, Kensington; he shared this address, and a Humber Super Sniper, with his business partner, Ambrose 'Gerry' Fleming. Both men were gamblers frequenting spielers around west London, where they became friendly with Ray and Simon. In fact Hennessey first met the dead woman when he gave Simon a lift to her address at Westbourne Grove; he subsequently visited both this address and the address at Denbigh Road several times, but never on his own account. 'Always this has been to give lifts to either Simon or Ray, mainly Simon.'

He met her elsewhere on only one occasion. Between 1am and 2am on Friday 27 March Hennessey, accompanied by his friend John

Lloyd, drove to the launderette in Bayswater Road and saw her standing outside on her own. Hennessey asked her what she was doing at that time of night and she replied that she was just walking around. 'I knew she was a prostitute, she never disguised the fact.' She sat in the car until the two men had finished doing their laundry and then went with them to 10 Strathmore Gardens, where, over a meal prepared by Ambrose Fleming, she talked about her past.

Early in the morning Hennessey was driving her home when he picked up Derek Russell, a friend who had just finished a night shift, and all three ate breakfast at Lyons in Notting Hill Gate. Derek Russell walked home and Irene Lockwood was dropped off at the corner of Denbigh Road. That was the last time Hennessey saw her.

At no point on this occasion had he offered to find her a flat. 'She didn't ask me to get her a flat and she seemed quite satisfied with the accommodation she had at the time, except that I did try to persuade her to change her environment and friends.'

Except that some of her friends were his friends too, and something may have rubbed off.

About two weeks prior to this date Hennessey visited 16 Denbigh Road on a matter of business. He'd received a telephone call from 'Coffee', a friend who happened to be the head porter at the Rembrandt Hotel in Knightsbridge. Coffee said that one of the guests, a businessman, was lonely and wanted female company 'for the purpose of conversation only'.

Any suggestions, Mike?

Golly. Well, the only female conversationalist he could think of was Sandra Russell. 'We caught a taxi to the hotel and Sandra went in to meet the porter. I stayed with my friend Mr Fleming in the dining room of the hotel.'

What were Hennessy and Fleming up to? Were they enjoying a meal together on the house while they waited for Sandra Russell to finish her 'conversation'?

It was soon over.

'Shortly afterwards Coffee came to see me and Mr Fleming. He told me that he had given the girl a pound and sent her home. He appeared quite upset at me bringing her.'

Oh.

Oh well, at least it meant a bit of a rest for Ray and Simon.

Or should that be Simon and Ray?

I hear them.

The two of them.

Arguing over billing.

Scratching, farting, waiting in the wings for their . . .

Curtain call.

Royston Reginald Raymond, who described himself to the police as a croupier, was twenty-six years old and shared a flat at 32 Pembridge Gardens with his wife and four-year-old son. Raymond had a conviction for stealing money from a gas meter at an address in Weston-super-Mare 'about a year or so ago'. He had never owned a car and was unable to drive.

He knew the dead woman through his friend Simon, and first met her at a house in Westbourne Grove about two weeks before Christmas 1963. She was living in a ground-floor room with two teenage girls.

'We did not perform with the girls or Sandra.'

Raymond saw her on approximately fourteen occasions in all (about once a week). He and Simon visited her only twice at the Ledbury Road address, and Raymond called to see not her but his friend James Panter, with whom he'd served in the Grenadier Guards. When she moved to 16 Denbigh Road he sometimes visited her alone and sometimes with Simon. She was usually alone herself, although he had seen James Panter there sometimes, and also Ronald Andrews. But apart from these men and Simon 'I have never seen another person at the flat, either male or female.'

On one occasion, in conversation with himself and Simon, she mentioned she was pregnant but gave no details. She did not appear to be worried about her condition, and when he sold her a tin of vitamin pills for £4 he merely told her they would do her good; he did not sell them to her for the purpose of terminating her pregnancy.

Raymond last saw the dead woman on Friday 3 April. After an expensive evening at Wimbledon dog track he returned to Notting Hill and made his way through pouring rain to 16 Denbigh Road, where he had arranged to meet Simon. He arrived at the house at around 10.30pm and rang the bell, but no one answered. He was walking away down the road when he heard a voice call 'Ray!' and turned to see his friend standing outside the house. Raymond returned and joined Simon and Sandra inside the flat.

'I never went in the bedroom. This was the last time I went in this flat.'

At around 11.45pm he and Simon left to play poker at the 62 Club at 62 Pembridge Villas, but when they arrived the game hadn't started so they went to the Hot Club in Victoria Gardens, and then back to the 62 an hour later. Simon left the club at 5.30am; Raymond played on for a while before going home, where he remained with his wife for the rest of that day.

'On Sunday night I went to the Hot Club for an hour at 11pm then went home.' On Monday he stayed at home until the afternoon, when he met a friend, 'Paddy', at 3pm in the Mitre pub in Holland Park Road. The two men then visited a betting shop in Princedale Road, and from there Raymond went alone to 18 Holland Park to see a female friend, Anne Lock, with whom he spent the rest of the day, arriving home at 1.30am on Tuesday 7 April. 'I again went out as on Monday into the Mitre and the betting shop. In the evening I went racing at Wembley.'

Raymond had never argued with the dead woman; he had never caused her any harm and he could not think of anybody who would wish to do so. He had never had intercourse with her ('I don't know whether Simon has or not'); he was not poncing on her and he didn't think Simon was.

Simon Anthony Burgess, also twenty-six, lived with his wife, Muriel, and their two children in a flat at 29 Brondesbury Road, Kilburn. He too was a croupier, currently employed at the Grove Hall Court Club, Le Touquet Rooms, Hall Road, NW8. He was able to drive but had not owned a car since May 1963.

'I was convicted of intimidation of prosecution witnesses on 11 January 1963 and sentenced to four months' imprisonment, which I served in an open prison in Exeter. I was released on 29 March 1963. This is the only time I've been in court (excluding motoring offences).'

Burgess had known 'Sandra Lockwood' since about August 1963. He knew she was pregnant, and told police that he was not the father. He had intercourse with her on only one occasion and 'she and I worked out the dates and I couldn't possibly be the father'.

He first met her in the Wimpy Bar in Queensway in the early hours of the morning. She told him she was working in a club, also that she was homeless. He found her accommodation at 44 Pembridge Villas, a house owned by his 'partially coloured' friend Barry, where she shared a flat with another friend, an Irish croupier named Michael Torpey ('Little Mike'). Burgess was running a card school in the basement flat.

Torpey tolerated Lockwood for about a week; he then told Burgess she had to go. On the night she was due to leave she met and went to live with a man whom Burgess knew as 'Stan'. 'I didn't see her for about a month and then she came with Stan to a place in Ladbroke Square and said she wished to leave him.'

Burgess next saw her in December 1963; she had left Stan and was living with two other girls at 138 Westbourne Grove. 'The place was in a shocking state and I suggested to her to move as quickly as possible.' On Christmas Eve she and the two girls moved to 118 Ledbury Road, and about a fortnight later Lockwood moved to 16 Denbigh Road. He visited her frequently at this flat and on most occasions he was accompanied by his friend Royston Raymond.

On Thursday 26 March Burgess bought a pair of trousers and a pair of shoes at a shop in Notting Hill. He decided to keep them on and the assistant put his old trousers and brown suede shoes in two bags which he subsequently deposited at Raymond's flat. On Tuesday 31 March he collected these items and the two men went round to Lockwood's flat, arriving between 6pm and 7pm and departing at 11pm to go to the 62 Club, Burgess making great strides in his new footwear, leaving his old shoes and trousers behind.

Shoes were in the air, and Lockwood mentioned to Burgess that she wouldn't mind a pair herself; Kenny was coming round on Friday at 10pm to take her out and all she had to wear were her worn-to-death calf-length black leather boots. So when Burgess visited her on Friday 3 April he brought her 'something decent', a pair of blue satin court shoes which belonged to his wife. Lockwood appeared concerned about the two weeks' rent she owed; she'd also received an electricity bill for about £20. He cooked himself sausages and mash and told her not to worry.

The shoes didn't fit (too small) but it didn't really matter because Kenny stood her up anyway. Burgess understood that this man, who apparently owned a club and offered her a job, had let her down on previous occasions. He did not materialize during the five hours Burgess spent in Lockwood's flat. 'It was about 6 o'clock in the evening on Friday and we, Ray and I, stayed until about 11 o'clock, when we left and went to the 62 Club on our own.'

No, wait. That last bit wasn't true, was it, because at 7pm he was round at Caroline Clarke's flat, trying to touch her –

'I remember that on Friday evening 3 April I did go from Sandra's flat, 16 Denbigh Road, to a friend of hers, Carol Clarke, at 118 Ledbury Road. I wanted to borrow some money, £10 to help pay Sandra's rent. This was not the reason I gave to Carol, she thought it was for myself.'

Burgess now also remembered that he and his friend had not in fact arrived together at 16 Denbigh Road; Raymond turned up at about 10.30pm and Lockwood seemed reluctant to let him in. 'I rather think she wanted to be alone with me. I haven't said this before, but I also think she was a bit of a nympho.'

There was only one thing for it – his. He told Lockwood to open the front door but Raymond was now walking along the road; so he called him back and instructed him to go away again and return in fifteen minutes.

Just enough time for a quick 'conversation'. . .

Following their departure from 16 Denbigh Road, Burgess and Raymond arrived at the 62 Club shortly after 11pm, and played as partners in a game of stud poker until 5am, when Burgess left with Michael Torpey. A taxi dropped Torpey off somewhere near Shirland Road and took Burgess home, arriving at about 5.15am. He remained in bed until 1pm, and then left his flat and spent two hours in a betting shop. 'I then returned home and stayed there until midnight. I then hailed a taxi and went down to Norman's at 29 Caroline House.'

At 3am he left this club and visited the Wimpy Bar in Queensway before setting off for the Hot Club; it was closed so he caught a taxi home. Upon arrival he asked the tenant downstairs to wake him at noon in time for him to meet his wife at Paddington Station. Having collected her, he remained at home for the rest of Sunday. He spent Monday afternoon at the same betting shop as previously. 'I returned home after the last race. I stayed in the betting shop the whole time and I did not go out again until about noon on Tuesday. My wife can verify this.'

At 12.30pm on Tuesday 7 April he called round at 16 Denbigh Road, ringing Lockwood's bell several times; but she either wasn't in or wasn't answering. He called again that evening and was greeted by Lockwood's landlady, Pamela Edwards. He was wearing a red check slipper on his left foot as his new shoe had caused a large blister to develop on the heel.

They discussed her disappearance, and he hobbled round to Ledbury Road and made enquiries. 'I was rather surprised because Sandra had appeared to be reasonably happy at the flat.'

Reasonably happy, perfectly safe. When those two left her on Friday night she was, in the words of Royston Raymond, 'alive and kicking'.

Irene Lockwood rented the ground-floor flat, Flat 2, at 16 Denbigh Road. Flat 1, the basement flat, was occupied by Adele Chadwick, a laboratory assistant sharing with two secretaries and a nurse.

Chadwick and her flatmates had seen numerous men visit Flat 2. A cream and yellow Ford Zephyr or Consul was often parked outside the house, as was a taxi cab, the latter for long periods. Flat 1 was directly beneath Flat 2, and Chadwick recalled raised voices, as though a woman was arguing with men. 'This occurred with regularity until it got to such a pitch that I complained to the landlady.'

Chadwick last saw the dead woman one day shortly after Easter when she went upstairs to collect the mail. She heard one more argument, and this took place at about 10pm on Friday 3 April. A woman again, sounding distressed as she argued with a man. He told her, 'Don't be stupid' in a raised voice and shortly afterwards called 'Ray! Ray!' several times out of the window in the direction of the street. 'About an hour later the same man called out the name "Ray" a few times, as though he was calling someone sitting in a car or searching outside. I did not see anyone come into the house in response to the calling.'

All right, girl, that's enough.

'Don't be stupid', eh?

'Alive and kicking', eh?

Kicking who?

*

Somewhere inside the Corinthian clubhouse a dog begins to bark.

I'm still here.

I'm looking at the stars, but I see only mugshots — two giant mugshots spread out against the sky.

Mind you, Hannah Tailford's is more like a morgue shot . . . 'She has told me often that a geezer has had it up her arse,' recalled window cleaner Frederick Townend, and hers is a face, I suppose, that only a bugger could love.

And if Tailford is Nora Batty's understudy, Lockwood is Freddie Starr in drag.

Just look at them. You wouldn't trust these two as far as you could throw them. You wouldn't pay them either, not unless you were truly hard up.

Semen was present on both vaginal and oral swabs taken from Hannah Tailford's body, and this proved to be the case with Lockwood as well.

Lockwood was supposed to be condoms only, wasn't she? But then again a punter might offer to pay over the odds, un-protection money . . .

Refundable perhaps.

Did her murderer contract gonorrhoea?

Assuming her murderer existed.

I look behind me. The teenagers on the bench have disengaged at last and are walking away in opposite directions along the Mall. I expect they'll meet again tomorrow morning and continue where they left off. I hope so.

It's peaceful here at the moment. As I turn, my eyes register Hammersmith Bridge away to the left; and all the lights shivering on the water, as if even now — right now — men below its surface were still working on this case.

But I know they aren't.

Reaching inside my coat, I pull out the death certificates — although there's not very much light here and I'm tired, my mind's tired, I've been walking around for hours. The kids have warmed the bench for me but I can't sit down, I've got a train to catch, so I flick through the verdicts as I'm going along:

17 June 1959. Chiswick Promenade W4. Elizabeth FIGG. 21 years. Spinster daughter of James Curtis FIGG a commercial Traveller.

Asphyxia due to manual strangulation. Murder by person or persons unknown.

Found dead 8th November 1963 Barnes Council Dust Destructor Depot Townmead Road Richmond Surrey. Gwynneth REES 22 years Spinster. Causes unascertainable. Open verdict.

Dead body found Second February 1964 on foreshore of River Thames near landing stage of London Corinthian Sailing Club Upper Mall Hammersmith. Hannah TAILFORD. 30 years, of no fixed Abode. A Waitress/Spinster. Drowning. In the River Thames. Insufficient evidence of circumstances. Open verdict.

8.4.64. River Thames foreshore by Duke's Meadow Chiswick W.4. Sandra RUSSELL otherwise LOCKWOOD. 25 years. (Barmaid/Spinster). Drowning. Defendant acquitted of the charge of Murder.

I take a step back, out of the way of a cyclist's lamp.
Defendant acquitted of the charge of Murder.
Defendant?
Well, there's only one man they could mean, and that's Archibald.
Kenny Archibald.
Who could forget Kenny Archibald?
What a bloody nightmare he turned out to be.
I have always led a normal life.
The caretaker.

3
Teasers

It was the Fifties. If you can remember them you were there.

It was run-down properties in Notting Hill and North Kensington, bought cheaply and divided into highly lucrative multiple tenements crammed with, well, blacks paying very high rents indeed . . .

It was *bending the basement*, in which the landlord extracted an even higher rent for a basement flat by allowing it to be used as a brothel or drinking club . . .

It was rent collectors with Alsatian dogs, *dogs that foamed at the mouth from the Colgate on their mouths*, dogs that barked in their sleep to find themselves so famous . . .

It was the removal of all rent controls courtesy of the 1957 Rent Act, which meant that if a landlord could persuade statutory tenants – whose rent and tenure of homes were controlled by law – to leave a property, the value of even the meanest slum would be vastly increased . . .

It was *putting in the schwarzers*, moving West Indians into these properties, *bloody boatloads of them, parties all night and pissing on the landing, anything to get us out* . . .

It was no hot water, it was vermin, bedbugs, every meter rigged (*rigged by that fat cunt*) or else broken and empty and in the end –

And in the end it was Apocalypso!

It was Rottin' Hell!

From all over London vanloads of Teddy boys, armed with knives and bicycle chains, arrived; hundreds of locals searched the streets for West Indians to harm, hurling milk bottles, bricks and petrol bombs through their front windows; scores of rioters, black as well as white, were arrested; and ice-cream vans did a roaring trade touring the trouble spots, providing both music and much-needed refreshment in the shape of bricks you could lick.

Appalling housing conditions; an acute shortage of jobs and hope; sexual jealousy centring on black ponces living off white women; the street corner urgings of Sir Oswald Mosley's Union Movement to send the blacks back to where they came from . . . Some people felt that a combination of anxieties led to the Notting Hill riots of 1958.

Others believed that one big fat Jew was to blame for everything.

He was born in Poland in 1919, the son of a dentist. He fled the Nazis only to be captured by the Russians, yet he survived one of Stalin's labour camps and arrived in England in 1946 as a refugee. In 1950, at the suggestion of a prostitute named Gloria, he set up a flat-letting agency, his first venture into the property market (and one which soon worked to the benefit of Gloria and her friends). His next move was to become a landlord himself and by the end of 1956 he was in control of thirty houses in Shepherd's Bush, thirty houses in Notting Hill and twenty flats in Maida Vale. At the peak of his operations in the Fifties he owned more than 100 properties.

A short-house in built-up shoes, he waddled proudly around the nightclubs and casinos of west London (a few of which were now his). He was neckless, chinless and stateless, a squeaky-voiced eunuch-cum-sultan, with a brass on his arm and on his wrist a gold bracelet inscribed with sets of serial numbers, rumoured to be foreign bank accounts . . .

He started small and ended up in the dictionary. The *OED* entry reads: 'Rachmanism – Brit. the exploitation and intimidation of tenants by unscrupulous landlords. ORIGIN named after Peter Rachman (1919–62), a London landlord whose practices became notorious in the early 1960s.'

And yet by 1960 Rachman had disposed of his own slum properties. His new business interest was hundreds of acres of slag heaps in a valley in Staffordshire, his investment tens of thousands of borrowed pounds. The valley was reputed to be one of the world's richest in coal; Rachman also hoped to strike oil there, and to turn the millions of tons of slag and stone into building material.

The gamble never paid off, though he didn't live long enough to see the project meet its doom. On the morning of 29 November 1962 Rachman suffered a fatal heart attack at his mansion in Hampstead. He was buried on 2 December at the Jewish Cemetery in Bushey, Hertfordshire. The net total of the former slum king's estate amounted to £8,008, a figure many found hard to accept.

In the summer of 1963 Rachman's name came to the attention of the general public when it was revealed that he'd had affairs with both Christine Keeler and Mandy Rice-Davies, the two starlets of the

Profumo scandal. On the evening of 8 July 1963 the Labour MP for Paddington North, Benjamin Parkin, delivered a speech to the Commons about 'the curse of West London', the property racket, and complained that promises to investigate the 'Rachman empire' had not been fulfilled. He spoke of a house in Hereford Road which belonged to Rachman and which had been let 'at a fantastic rent, all perfectly legal, to an experienced coloured man'. This man then let the house as seven separate dwellings to seven separate girls at £3 10s per dwelling per day, payable daily at noon. 'That is £10,000 a year from one house, enough to pay the interest on the price paid for the whole road.' A house in Bryanston Mews (the house in which Rachman had installed first Keeler, then Rice-Davies, as his mistress) had been mortgaged for £30,000, and then four months later the owner had disappeared and his estate was valued at £8,000. 'Does the Right Honourable gentleman really think anybody would believe that, if investigations had ever been made?'

What Parkin said next was undoubtedly bizarre, and yet in the light of 'Profumo' it made perfect gothic sense. 'All Fleet Street is full of the idea that Rachman is not dead . . . It would be easy to switch bodies since he was "dead on arrival" at Edgware General Hospital. With an overworked houseman in charge they can only feel the body to see whether it is warm or cold. It does not require many interested witnesses – a cremation and a stateless man, and that is that.'

But if he wasn't dead, where was he?

There were several reported sightings, and yet the crafty Buddha consistently failed to materialize.

What happened to Rachman? Did he live twice? Or was he simply, as one associate believed, 'too clever to die'?

Is he still around today?

Is he still bald, brash, randy, greedy, sleazy? Is he still desperate for a British passport?

But wait. We're getting carried away here, and it's worth remembering that Rachman's biographer Shirley Green maintains her man was no monster. As slum landlords go he was one of the more attractive specimens; his methods may have been extortionate, but in a climate of 'No coloureds' and 'Europeans only' he offered West Indians somewhere to stay. One interviewee told her, '"To the West Indian he was a saviour and people still have a lot of respect for him."'

He may have slipped prostitutes into his properties, but he was more than fair to his sitting tenants. '"We found Mr Rachman quite satisfactory."' '"If we wanted any repairs, we only had to ask and we got them done."' '"I can't say other than that he was a real gentleman."' He bought many of them out, of course, 'but it is interesting to note that, despite posthumous stories of evictions and wholesale intimidation, there is little evidence to suggest that he forced them out in any way'.

Well, well, well.

Well, before we finally lay Rachman to rest, let's back up the hearse and smell the flowers.

In the Foreword to his memoirs, *Tough Guys Don't Cry*, Joe Cannon writes: 'During a lifetime of crime I have been convicted of burglary, inflicting grievous bodily harm, larceny, receiving, unlawful possession, malicious damage and armed robbery . . . I have served sentences totalling twenty years in a variety of penal institutions.'

And for six months in 1955 he worked, on and off, for Peter Rachman.

The two men would meet about once a fortnight. Rachman would sometimes try it on. 'You'd come for your money and he'd try to catch you out – change the subject then ask you: "How much did you say, Joe?"' On one occasion young Joe managed to cheat *him*:

'I went to him and said, "Look, this one's fucking hard. I've tried everything and he won't move." And he said, "Have you tried *everything*?" I said, "Yeah." But I hadn't. I'd been so busy, I hadn't even been round to the geezer. So he said, "Look, I only pay you for what you do." I said, "I've done everything." He said, "Well, I'll pay you this time . . ."'

But these were minor matters. In essence they understood each other perfectly.

Get 'em out.

Joe recalled that whenever Rachman wished to remove a sitting tenant from one of his properties his first strategy would be to send an agent round with a cash inducement to leave. In the event of a refusal he'd then send Joe and his friend to carry out 'repairs'. As 'builders' they would climb a ladder and break slates on the roof; as 'plumbers' they would turn taps on and flood the bathroom.

'One place he bought, he had ten sitting tenants in there, the whole building was sitting tenants. And we got 'em all out. Matter of a fortnight, they was gone.

'We done about fifteen houses for him altogether but the rats we only done once. First thing we said was, "Has anybody been round to see you?" "Yeah. A man came round the other day and offered me x amount to move out." "Well, you gotta move out because it's alive with rats. This whole building's alive with rats. It's condemned." So they'd say, "No, it ain't. I ain't seen no rats here." And then you'd give 'em, like, three or four days . . .'

And go off and catch some – at night, prowling round a bombed-out building in Powis Square, pulling up the floorboards. 'We found this nest of 'em in a corner, and there was little babies there. We shone a torch on 'em and they all went, like, quiet. So I said to my mate, "Come on, pick 'em up." He said, "Fuck you! You pick 'em up."' The other man held the empty parrot cage ready as Joe reached down and acquainted himself with an interesting fact of life. 'If you shine a torch on a rat it goes dead and you can pick it up, it won't try to bite you or nothing. But if there's *babies* and you try to pick it up, it goes for you, goes for your hand.'

It was a job. But there were easier ways to pay the rent, as Joe eventually discovered. In 1962, not long after his release from Dartmoor prison, he found an empty basement flat in Russell Road, Kensington, and opened an unlicensed drinking club.

Who could blame him? The after-hours racket was extremely lucrative, the start-up costs irresistibly low. All you needed was a basement flat, a makeshift bar, a few mouldy sticks of furniture – and, most important of all, a straight face for when grateful punters lined up to buy drinks from you at double the pub prices.

Of course the police might close you down at any time, but so what? The extortionate profit margin meant that every night was a bonus. 'If you opened a premises in the West End – licensed or unlicensed – within six months you'd make a bomb. You'd make a fortune. Give it six months normally, then you'd have to pull out.'

But the Basement Club surpassed all expectations, opening in 1962 and running until late 1964, when the building was sold. The club did so well that Joe considered opening another to mop up the overspill, and visited an estate agent's in Ladbroke Grove in a surreptitious search for suitable premises. He found nothing, but talked to an employee, a middle-aged northerner named Kenneth Archibald, who appeared to understand the nature of his quest.

In early 1964 these two met again, this time at the Stage and Radio Club in Spring Street. Joe Cannon's friend 'Chappy' Gibbs introduced Archibald as a man with a plan. He had left his job at the estate agent's and was now resident caretaker at the Holland Park Lawn Tennis Club. Archibald suggested that his flat in the basement of the club pavilion would make an ideal 'drinker'. This pavilion was sumptuously furnished and set in expansive grounds: the noise wouldn't travel and no one would suspect a thing.

Too good to be true? Interested yet cautious, Joe Cannon went along to see for himself. As he recorded in his memoirs: 'It was an eye opener, a large house in its own grounds with lawns and tennis courts and furnished regardless of cost . . . Even the toilets were carpeted, and the ladies' boasted a pair of bidets. I couldn't wait to get the place opened.'

Saturday 15 August 1959.

Not long now.

Soon, very soon, a giant broom would descend upon London and sweep all the women clean off their feet – and off the streets.

Saturday night would be a night to remember – the last night of the toms.

'Four of us had driven down from Northampton (where I had a job in a steelworks) because we thought sex was going to be banned. We went to some club or other and when we came out somebody said, "Look! It's twenty to twelve. We've got to find a woman." But we couldn't find one anywhere . . . and then, eventually, on our way back to the car we spotted one and I walked over to her. She wasn't bad looking actually.'

She was all nerves. She knew what to do but no longer knew where to do it. She leaned into the windows of taxis and tried to negotiate twice round the park, but nobody wanted to know, not that night, and the minutes were ticking away . . .

'While these taxi drivers were telling her to bugger off my three mates were watching from the other side of the road, jeering at us, shouting, "Get on with it!" In the end she took me to this Peabody Trust building just off Shaftesbury Avenue. We went up some concrete steps to the entrance to the flats, which was very dimly lit. Waste ground in front of us like a bomb-site, and there were these enormous bins on wheels. And we had a knee-trembler. I remember telling her – to slow her down, make it last – telling her it was my first time.

'Afterwards I produced my packet of Senior Service and I had two cigarettes left. We had one each. She pulled off the rubber (as she called it) and I squeezed the cigarette packet open and she plopped it inside. I threw it in one of the wheelie bins. She said, "You're a real gentleman. I want to use this place again." Didn't want it covered in rubbers, you see, and the tenants kicking up.'

Back at the steelworks in Northamptonshire, Alan, an ex-public school boy, was a trainee manager in the slag division. 'I took the job to satisfy my father, and then I thought, "No, I'd like to get out of this middle-class thing. I'll do tough jobs like work on a trawler or go to sea or drive trucks and . . . disappear."'

In 1960, aged nineteen, he escaped to London, where he had a succession of casual jobs such as selling caravans and working on the docks. In his spare time he hung around town in his hipster cords, waiting for something to happen.

And so one night when two attractive young women rapped at his window and brandished a bottle of wine he knew exactly what to do. 'I opened the car door and let them in. I was waiting at the traffic lights in Kensington Church Street and the bloke in front clearly didn't want to know. They said, "We've had a bit of trouble." They'd obviously rolled some poor bastard and stolen this wine. The next thing was, "Have you got a corkscrew?" I told them I had one at my flat so we drove back there.'

They liked the cream Mini (borrowed from his flatmate) and, puzzlingly, they liked the flat: a small spartan basement room dominated by a coke boiler. 'We hung a blanket in front of the boiler, but of course it still stank. Anyway these girls, Trina and Kay, kept walking round the room and saying, "This is good, this is good," and I didn't know what they meant . . .'

Business.

Two or more prostitutes operating from the same premises constituted a brothel so Trina ('very Scandinavian') and Kay ('tattooed, which I thought was quite daring') took it in turns to use the flat in Queensborough Terrace, Bayswater. On these occasions Alan was to be found at the Wimpy Bar in Queensway, sipping coffee from glass cups as he waited for the night shift to end. He became a familiar figure. 'I was sitting there one night when two guys – I'd been told they were Paddington vice squad – looked over at my table on their way out. One of them said, "Not long now, Taff," which scared me. And somehow they'd found out that I was brought up in Wales, which scared me even more.'

Disturbing words; but the arrangement continued. Alan would receive rent from the girls while his own landlord, a Pole who lived on the top floor of the house, kept conveniently out of sight, nursing a wife who was dying of cancer. But how did Alan's flatmate view the set-up?

'He spent most of his time in a van selling Mr Whippy ice cream. He didn't really care about anything so long as I kept driving the Mini around, because he was behind with the payments and he was terrified that it was going to get repossessed. Anyway, at one point he tried to get in on things himself by writing to this girl he knew in Northampton and inviting her to London to go on the game. But her father found the letter and threatened to report him to the *News of the World*.'

For Alan it was money and it was fun, and that was how Trina and Kay saw it too. In fact he was lucky to have them. The girls showed him a bunch of keys they had acquired from a friendly estate agent; they could choose from a selection of vacant properties around west London. All they needed was a mattress in a corner and a candle ('no electricity, of course') to help set the mood.

'They were wild girls, Trina and Kay. They seemed to be living on wits and air.' Immaculately turned out and toting Mary Quant shoulder bags stuffed with rubbers, tissues, Johnson's baby oil and a small travelling iron, they were equally game for a rendezvous in a smart hotel or a knee-trembler in an alleyway. At Queensborough Terrace they solicited in the street.

That wasn't all they did in the street.

'One night Trina and I had gone up to the West End to hear . . .

Georgie Fame, as I remember. Anyway, we're walking through Soho, looking very glamorous (she always wore very smart suits, long blonde hair), and I'm feeling, like, really good – and suddenly she announces, "I must have a piss," drags me down some badly lit street off one of the main arteries, hitches up her skirt (she hadn't got any knickers on as usual) and starts peeing in the gutter. While I'm standing there, holding her hand like she's a bloody dog, thinking, "This is not on." But she's rummaging in her bag with her free hand, and out comes this little paper of white powder, so as she's peeing she's snorting coke and – "Here," she says, "you have some." Well, this is 1961, and I've never seen the stuff before. She jumps up, pulling her skirt down, holds this stuff under my nose, rubs it on my gums – and off we go to the club.'

Trina and Kay soon moved on, but Alan was keen to continue subletting and this time he had someone rather special in mind, a real looker. Years before he'd worshipped her from afar at his local swimming baths in Northamptonshire; now she was in business at a flat in Monmouth Road, W2.

Alan's first visit was as a customer, his second as a hustler in love. He wanted her to know that he remembered her backstroke; he wanted to steal her heart and install her in his beautiful basement flat.

Forget it.

'I confronted her about Northampton and she denied it, said I'd got the wrong girl. She wasn't flustered or upset or anything, just laughed it off really and said, "A cup of tea?" which the maid in those places seemed to be making all the time. And so I had my cup of tea and we chatted – about the weather, I suppose . . .'

They weren't alone. Another man sat in silence beside the window, wielding a screwdriver as he peered into the depths of a suitcase.

'I didn't really take much notice of him. I thought from the look of him that he was a punter. Anyway, I didn't know what to say to her and realized the whole thing was slipping from my grasp. I just thought, "I'll drink my tea and get out." And then at this point the bloke announced that whatever he was doing was ready.'

He brought the suitcase over to the sofa and while the maid poured the tea the others looked inside.

It was ready but there was no name for it; it made no sense to Alan's misty eye.

'It seemed to be electric probes and wires . . . and a small sort of motorcycle battery. . . and a tennis ball, split. And as though it was a sort of consolation prize she said, "You can have a free go." And I said, "Well, I've no idea what you do with it." And then she explained: she'd clap it on my bollocks and I'd get a great jolt, and a great thrill. She said, "People pay good money for this, you know." Well, I wasn't having any of it – I'd never heard of such a thing . . .'

The telephone began to ring and now seemed like a good time to leave, to get the hell out of this pit of depravity while he still had a tail between his legs. Stepping out of the ground-floor flat and into the Friday afternoon sunlight, walking along pondering the fate of the tennis ball, Alan was surprised to be joined by its abuser.

I wouldn't bother trying to chat her up – you're wasting your time there. She walked out on her husband and now she's living with another man and between them they've got six kids. But she's a good grafter.

Introducing himself as Lance, he went on to rhapsodize about the flat they'd just left. *Off-street parking, separate entrance for the maid . . . never any trouble with the police, ever.* They reached Westbourne Grove; it was very hot, wasn't it? *A drink?* Lance led the way into the nearest pub, where he was straight away hailed by the actor John le Mesurier, drunkenly asking, 'How are the girls?'

Everybody seemed to know Lance and, what's more, they seemed to like him. So Alan began to relax a bit, and talk about himself. When he happened to mention that he could drive, Lance jumped up from the table. *I could use you if you could spare the time. Are you busy?*

Busy? No, he wasn't busy. He had no car to drive right now (his flatmate had taken a beating in the ice-cream wars and left London in the Mini) but he had access to a Ford Thames van.

Even better, according to Lance.

But who was this Lance?

He was a young man, not much older than Alan, it seemed, yet in appearance he belonged to the Fifties, when everyone dressed like your dad. He wore spectacles, Brylcreem, a sports jacket with leather elbows, a shirt and tie, grey flannels and – a sure sign of a square, this – lace-up shoes, highly polished.

He wasn't a punter, was he? But then again he was hardly a ponce.

So who was he?

What's my line?

Alan was about to find out.

The Holland Park Lawn Tennis Club drinking club opened for business in early 1964. Kenneth Archibald's basement flat now boasted a makeshift bar, and also a record player so that the customers, who consisted largely of villains from the Hill, might drink the night away to the songs of Frank Sinatra (the biggest crook of the lot).

Listen, it was all over in a matter of weeks.

At 3.55am on Saturday 14 March three police officers, PC Moppett, PC Summerhayes and PC Redmond, were patrolling in F2 area car when they received a call from the information room at Notting Hill police station directing them to 1 Addison Road to investigate a reported break-in at the tennis club pavilion. But their car was met en route by a Mr Andersen of Holland Park Court, who told PC Moppett that he had made the telephone call, and pointed out a man and a woman walking together along the avenue. These, he said, were two of the intruders.

Upon seeing the officers this couple split up and began walking in different directions, but they were both stopped and brought back to the car and questioned by PC Moppett about the alleged break-in. Meanwhile, PC Summerhayes called at the tennis club pavilion and discovered that a panel had been broken in the side window of the Gents at the front of the basement. He spoke to Kenneth Archibald, whose flat was situated at the rear of the basement, and Archibald explained that some people had broken into his bedroom while he was in bed and had run away when he challenged them.

In the Gents Summerhayes discovered a broken chair, a broken wall mirror and a sidepiece of a pair of men's horn-rimmed spectacles; some of the glass was bloodstained. The area was searched for other suspects without success, but the man and woman detained by PC Moppett were taken to Notting Hill police station, where they were interviewed by Detective Sergeant Franklin.

Patrick Crawford, a clerk, and Moira Fleming, unemployed, both admitted having been in the pavilion, but stated that they had been attending a party there. Neither knew the other, they had met at it. They had no idea who had organized it; both claimed to have been taken there by people they had recently met and did not know.

DS Franklin questioned Archibald about the alleged party, yet the caretaker strenuously denied that such an event had taken place or that he knew any of his intruders. Franklin then interviewed Crawford and Fleming once more. This time they were seen separately, yet each insisted that a party had taken place at the pavilion. In view of the facts that Crawford, while at the station, had been treated for cuts to his right hand and was in possession of a pair of horn-rimmed spectacles with a sidepiece missing, Franklin questioned him about the damage at the club. Crawford said that this had been caused when a fight developed between himself and three men, and that he received the cuts in self-defence. When somebody shouted out that somebody had called the police, a window was broken and the three men escaped through it. Crawford denied having caused the damage himself.

Archibald was again seen and eventually admitted that he'd given a party at the pavilion that evening. He had not admitted this before for fear of losing his job. He said that he had gone to bed and left his guests to carry on.

In the light of this information Crawford and Fleming were released without charge, while Archibald was told that the matter would be brought to the notice of the club secretary.

It was over.

Still, it was lucrative – and rich and strange – while it lasted.

Kenneth Archibald was born in Sunderland in 1910. He had served a total of seventeen years in the army when he was discharged on medical grounds in 1947. He then worked as a barman at various hotels in Sunderland, eventu-

ally joining the Merchant Navy in 1949. In 1957 he left voluntarily,
having broken his arm, and returned to London, where, middle-aged
and unskilled, he had a succession of jobs which included clerk and
rent collector for L. G. Evans & Co. Ltd, Ladbroke Grove, the estate
agent's where he first met Joe Cannon, and now resident caretaker
at the Holland Park Lawn Tennis Club, with free accommodation in
the form of a large basement flat and a wage of 30s per week. He did
odd jobs to supplement his earnings, and he also received a service
pension of £1 17s 11d and a disability pension of £2 8s 8d, both paid
weekly.

All of which was nothing much compared to the £30 he was now
receiving each week from Joe Cannon, who also agreed to a moder-
ate drinks allowance ('Only beer, I wouldn't let him have shorts.'). At
fifty-four Kenneth Archibald longed to be one of the boys, yet his
prattle irritated punters and he soon settled into the role of old maid,
fretting about the noise level as he collected bottles and emptied ashtrays, fussing needlessly and endlessly. A bit of a nuisance.

Fortunately Joe's friend Reggie Short was usually on hand to keep
the mood mellow. Short was a cab driver, a giant with a flattened nose
who was always cracking jokes and treating the drinkers to his imper-
sonations of Humphrey Bogart and Jimmy Durante. He made himself
useful, minding the door and picking up cab fares as the night progressed. He also took care of troublesome tarts. Three strikes and the
woman was outside in the grounds, where, according to Joe's memoirs, Reggie Short would 'force her to go down to him, holding her
by the hair and thrusting his erect penis as far down her throat as it
would go. The performance over, he would give her a good thumping
and tell her to fuck off.'

Prostitutes were always a tricky proposition. On the one hand they
attracted men to a club; on the other hand they encouraged them to
leave (although in the case of the tennis club punters would normally
slip out into the grounds for five minutes and re-enter to continue
spending). The females who frequented Joe's club were a mixed bag
of street-girls, call-girls and nightclub hostesses.

But one woman stood alone.

'She stank. I remember one of the other girls came over and said to
me, "She don't 'alf stink." I said, "*I know*." She said, "I can't stand it. I
can still smell it even now I'm away from her."'

No doubt it was a relief for everyone when Irene Lockwood finally had a bath.

Lockwood's body was discovered on the foreshore of the Thames opposite Duke's Meadows on 8 April. On 9 April DC Bretton and PC Spears visited Kenneth Archibald. He was shown a photograph of the dead woman but denied ever having seen her. He was also shown a card, found in Lockwood's handbag, on which was printed 'Kenny' and 'PARK 7157', the number of the call box in the passage outside his basement flat. He then admitted that he and a man named Cannon had run an after-hours drinking club in the flat. It was Cannon who had had the cards printed and Cannon who distributed them; he had never had any himself. (According to Joe Cannon, 500 were printed, of which he distributed 200, Kenneth Archibald 200 and Reggie Short 100. 'We gave them out to anybody.') He was taken to Shepherd's Bush police station where he made a statement.

On the morning of 27 April, Archibald telephoned Notting Hill police station to report a break-in at the tennis club: the storeroom had been forcibly entered and cash, spirits and cigarettes stolen. He gave permission for DC Moorehead to search his flat; no stolen property was found. (However, Archibald may have organized the raid. He appears to have been in financial straits at this time, as the club held him responsible for the damage caused on 14 March, the bill for which amounted to around £50.)

Later that morning Archibald appeared at Marlborough Street Magistrates' Court charged with theft. (On 26 September 1962 he had visited D. H. Cadman, Hearing Aids Ltd, to have his hearing aid repaired, and was loaned another while his own was being mended. This second hearing aid was valued at £66 3s. He kept it.) He pleaded guilty but the magistrate advised him to change his plea to not guilty and he was remanded to appear before another magistrate the following day.

He left court and went drinking. His friend Nancy Finnegan saw him in the Colville pub in Notting Hill. He was with his sister-in-law Elfrid and appeared depressed. When she heard about his court appearance, Finnegan told him to cheer up as the worst he could expect was a £25 fine. But Archibald grew tearful and would not be comforted. 'No, Nancy, it is much more serious than that. You don't know how serious it is.' He told her she was to have his radiogram, records and television set; his furniture would be collected from the club and sold by arrangement.

At 2.40pm Archibald announced, 'I'm going to the nick.' He walked round to Notting Hill police station and told DC Moorehead that he had come to give himself up. Asked if he was referring to the break-in at the club, he replied, 'No. I pushed the girl in the river.' Girl? 'You know, the blonde Lockwood at Chiswick.' He was taken to Shepherd's Bush, where he made a full statement.

On the evening of 7 April he finished work at the tennis club between 8.30pm and 9pm and went on a pub crawl, ending up at the Windmill in Chiswick High Road, where he got into conversation with a blonde at the bar. He bought her a gin and tonic and she asked him if he fancied a short time. He said yes and so they left the pub and she led the way to the river. They had a disagreement. 'She wanted the money first. I lost my temper and grabbed her round the throat.' He pushed her against a wall and she fell to the ground unconscious, whereupon he stripped her and rolled her down a ramp into the Thames. He took her clothes home and burned them.

He had never previously confessed to any crime, nor had he ever assaulted a woman before. He admitted that a number of women had come to his flat for intercourse who were probably prostitutes and that he had invited other women to his flat for intercourse. But he insisted that he had never met Irene Lockwood before the night of 7 April. (Contrary to appearances, Archibald was not a bachelor. He told police he had married in 1942 and that his wife left him five years later. He had no children and no knowledge of her present where-abouts.)

Archibald was at least half-drunk when this statement was taken but once sober he made no attempt to retract it. At 6.45pm on 30 April he was charged with the murder of Irene Lockwood. He was cautioned – 'I didn't hear the last bit' – and recautioned.

Kenny.

Short, fat, deaf. Fifty-four and he looked every day of it. He looked like a non-starter, and yet he was spilling facts about Lockwood – large breasts, north-country accent – that gave his interrogators pause. He maintained he'd never met her before, so how come his story sounded so convincing?

'Because he'd had her,' recalled Joe Cannon. 'Kenny Archibald would go off with anything, and he definitely had Lockwood. He used to pay her, and when she came to the club she used to always ask for Ken, that's why I let her in.'

'You didn't do it, did you?' Elfrid Archibald asked her brother-in-law this question repeatedly, growing more and more distressed, when she and her husband, John, visited him in custody the day after he was charged. The caretaker replied by asking her to dispose of all his property and bring him in a razor and shaving cream.

Did he do it? Was he a customer of Irene Lockwood's? If so, did he have an appointment with her on the night of 3 April? Was this the Kenny who had lots of money and invited her to do business at his club?

Lockwood's mutilated diary contained only two pages of entries. On the first page, in the section headed 'Notes', were the words 'Kenny came tonight March 26th Thursday.' These words were written in eyebrow pencil, as were two heavily deleted lines at the foot of the page. On the second page, also in eyebrow pencil, police read: 'Kennys coming April [deleted] 2nd or 1st. Thursday. He is young & hansome next week.'

It doesn't sound like the man with the deaf aid, does it? And yet Lockwood had drawn a line beneath these words and written: 'Kenny. Phone Park 7157.'

The recollections of Lockwood's flatmate Maureen Gallagher merely added to the confusion. She described Kenny as being in his mid-twenties, 5' 10", very slim and good-looking, and smartly dressed. He had a long face with sunken cheeks and dark hair 'like Adam Faith's'. He had offered Lockwood a flat above his club for use as a business premises and had given her his card. 'I have been shown a card and it is similar to the one Sandra showed me.' This card was left on the mantelpiece, and some time later Gallagher, who fancied Kenny for herself, copied the telephone number into a notebook. She rang this number and asked to speak to Kenny. 'A man's voice answered, it sounded like a coloured man, and he said Kenny wasn't known there. I didn't try again and I have never been to the club.'

The two Kennys seem to have merged in Maureen Gallagher's mind. (She recalled that the only client of Lockwood's who wore a deaf aid was a man of about fifty who had a box wired up to his ear.)

As for flash Kenny, he was never traced. He may have showed up at the dead woman's flat later that Friday night, after the two croupiers had left, but that in itself would not necessarily place him under suspicion of murder, for Irene Lockwood did not die on 3 April.

Marjory Connor, a clerk, saw her at about 10.15pm on Friday 3 April or Tuesday 7 April. (In view of the testimony of Lockwood's ground-floor neighbour, Adele Chadwick, Friday appears unlikely, and in view of what follows so does Tuesday, unless Lockwood changed her clothes during the course of that evening.) She was standing outside the Shepherd's Bush Hotel, Shepherd's Bush Green, and she was shouting at two men 'who I think were Irish', and she was wearing an ocelot coat. 'The reason I am not sure of the date is because I always go to a bingo club at Hammersmith on Tuesday and Fridays, and I was on my way home.'

Some time after midnight on Saturday 4 April Adrian Howe, an insurance salesman, was in the Wimpy Bar in Queensway when a blonde wearing a cheap leopard-skin coat and three-quarter-length black boots sat down beside him and asked him for a light. 'We got into conversation, during the course of which I gathered she was a prostitute.' She told him she worked from a car and took people back to her flat in Denbigh Road; she said she had to be careful. Howe was not interested in her and after finishing his coffee he left. ('I did notice that several of the same sort of girls in the coffee bar waved to her so I gathered she went there frequently.')

At about 11.20pm that day Muriel Jaruga, a friend of Kenneth Archibald's, saw Lockwood near Queensway tube station in Bayswater Road. She was standing on the side of the road and appeared to be drunk. A long blue/grey car pulled up beside her and a tall slim dark-complexioned man got out and ordered her inside. 'Both the girl and the man used bad language and they drove off towards Hyde Park.'

Early in the morning of Sunday 5 April Adrian Howe saw her again. She was wearing the same clothes as on the previous occasion; this time she was in nearby Bishop's Bridge Road, unaccompanied and obviously soliciting.

Between 10.30am and 11.00am on 5 April, 'although I wouldn't swear to that', Margaret Farmer, a pensioner, was in Kensington Church Street when she saw a young woman walking in a peculiar way, 'almost like the sideward walk of a horse', on the edge of the pavement. She was about 5' 3", slim, with large vacantly staring eyes, and she carried a bundle clutched to her bosom.

'I am positive she was the girl whose photograph appears in the papers.' She was wearing a coat similar to the check coat she wore in the photograph plus a pair of high-heeled shoes. She had something, 'I think it may have been a stole', thrown carelessly around her neck so that part of it rested on the back of her head. (A black stole was among the items found in the drawer at her flat.)

At about 3am on Monday 6 April Doreen Eden, unemployed, was sitting on the wall by the public lavatories at Charing Cross tube station (Embankment side) when she saw the deceased, whom she knew well, walking through the gardens towards her. Lockwood joined Eden and told her that she was waiting for Dickie Henderson, her ponce, with whom she'd been living for the past three years. (Eden understood that she lived near the Crown and Anchor pub in Praed Street, Paddington.) She lent Eden 10s and the two women arranged to meet in the cafeteria at Victoria Station at 3pm on Saturday 11 April, when Eden would repay her.

Five minutes later Dickie Henderson arrived in a cab and Lockwood got in. The driver asked Eden if she was going with them to the Roaring Twenties, but she explained that she was waiting for a friend.

Irene Lockwood was wearing a three-quarter-length imitation leopard-skin coat, a pale blue skirt with a pleat at the back and brown slip-on shoes with flat heels and crepe soles ('I remember these well because we were going to exchange the shoes.' Were these the brown suede shoes left at her flat by Simon Burgess?) Dickie Henderson, aged thirty-two, was Jamaican, 5' 11", and very thin; he wore a moustache.

Roy Parkinson, the proprietor of a confectionery shop in Westbourne Grove, last served Irene Lockwood, one of his regular customers, on Tuesday 7 April, 'either in the morning or the afternoon'. She usually called in to buy cheap cigarettes and appeared to be hard up. She usually looked 'a bit rough', but on this day, although she was wearing the same outfit as always – an old leopard-skin overcoat and a pair of long black boots – her hair looked 'rather nice', as if it had just been permed. (Lockwood last visited her hairdresser's,

Sonya Hair Fashions, 123 Westbourne Grove, at 2.30pm on 28 March. The appointment was made in the name of Loughan.)

John Ranklin, licensee of the Windmill, 214 Chiswick High Road, was the last person known to have seen Irene Lockwood alive. She first visited the pub about three months previously, since which time she had used it about once a week. She usually drank shorts, whisky or gin, and was usually accompanied by a white man of smart appearance. He was aged about thirty, 5′ 8″, with dark hair parted in the middle and a pencil moustache. Ranklin had not seen this man in his pub for some time.

He last saw Lockwood in his pub at about 8pm on Tuesday 7 April.

'I am almost certain it was a Tuesday; my wife is off most Tuesdays and that is why I am almost sure of the day. I was on my own that evening.'

Lockwood seemed to be waiting for someone, someone who didn't turn up. She had one drink and left ten minutes later. She had a wedding ring on as usual, and was wearing a check coat.

The case against Kenneth Archibald, predicated on his own confession, was now strengthened by the testimony of John Ranklin. However, the licensee, when presented with Archibald in person, failed to identify him as a customer. No matter. A builder named Edmund O'Neill, who used the Windmill every lunchtime and evening, recognized Lockwood from her police photograph as an irregular customer who sometimes showed up at Saturday lunchtimes accompanied by a man. He last saw these two together one Saturday lunchtime around the middle of March; they were sitting at the table by the door, and O'Neill noticed that the woman was drinking a Guinness. Her companion was aged around fifty, 5′ 4″, thick-set with receding grey hair.

'I have been shown a photograph of a man who I believe to be the one.'

Archibald remained in custody at Shepherd's Bush police station and appeared resigned to the prospect of life imprisonment. During an exercise walk in the station yard he spoke to his escorts of avocado pears, saying that he had from time to time grown them as a hobby, that he liked to watch them grow. On 28 April the divisional surgeon examined him in his cell and eventually pronounced him compos mentis.

But was he?

John Gossage, an accountant employed by the estate agent's where Archibald had previously worked, told police of his violent temper tantrums. Archibald's elder brother, John, a labourer, described Kenneth as a 'lone wolf', and mentioned that their younger brother, William, was a failed suicide who had been resident in a mental hospital in Sunderland for the past thirty years. And Mary Fox, a chemist, had an interesting story to tell.

Her acquaintance with Archibald began when she acquired an empty shop, through L. G. Evans. In March 1964 she had a row with her husband and he threw her out of their house at 38 Bard Road, as a consequence of which she began to sleep in the shop. Late on the second night she heard a tap on the door. It was Archibald. 'I opened the street door and he said, "You're a silly girl stopping here, you could be murdered." We had a few words and he said that I could go and live in his flat.' She moved in on 14 March.

She slept in the bedroom, he slept in the living room. He made no improper suggestions, yet all the same his behaviour troubled her. 'Mr Archibald insisted on me being out of the address every morning at 8am and I could not get in again until about 7.30pm in the evening.' He also drank very heavily and kept her locked up in the flat while he worked in the bar.

'One Sunday evening at about 4.30pm I was alone in his living room with his dog, Mickey. The dog prised open the door of the wardrobe and brought out a carrier bag which contained ladies' clothing. I looked in the wardrobe and saw some ladies' underslips, dresses and shoes . . . The dog also got hold of a photograph, which I took hold of, and it was a picture of a girl. I am sure it was a photograph of the girl Lockwood who has been murdered. Her hair was longer than the picture in the newspapers . . .'

This was Sunday 5 April and Irene Lockwood, according to witnesses, was still alive; but perhaps there was some explanation for the discrepancy. Certainly Fox had all the makings of a star witness, and on the morning of 2 May DC Frost visited 38 Bard Road (she had returned home on 6 April) in order to obtain a further interview. A brief one, as it turned out, for Mary Fox had begun smashing up the house and was about to be admitted to Springfield mental hospital.

*

Kenneth Archibald appeared at the Old Bailey in June, having spent almost two months in custody. At the committal proceedings at Acton Court the pathologist Donald Teare had remained firmly noncommittal: there was nothing in his findings that was inconsistent with Archibald's account of the victim's death, but there was nothing to support the account apart from the facts that she was naked and died from drowning. But by the time he reached the Old Bailey Archibald had changed his plea to not guilty and on 23 June the jury took only fifty-five minutes to acquit him of the charge of murder.

Through the doors and down the steps to freedom . . . freedom, on a summer's day.

'Phew! That's the last time I'll confess to anything – especially to a murder I never committed.' *Kenny! Over here! Look straight ahead, keep walking. Great!* 'Thank heavens I retracted my false statement in time.' *Why'd you do it?* 'Well, I was fed up, depressed, confused. I felt I had let my friends down at the tennis club, what with one thing and another. I saw myself losing my flat, my job and army pension. And somehow my imagination – yes, you can say it's a lively one – just ran away with me.' *Any plans for the future?* 'I'm turning my back on London. It's no good for me.' *One more! Over here!* 'I have always led a normal life.' *Over here!*

Yes, Kenny had amounted to nothing more than a superior sideshow. On 24 April, three days before he made his confession, a discovery took place that was to draw much of the heat away from his antics. In fact it was almost as if someone had slipped him a few quid and a few beers to go out and waste as much police time as possible . . .

You don't know how serious it is.

But you'll find out.

You'll learn.

You with the Scotch mother and the French father.

Something special . . . fancy name.

Helene.

Barthelemy.

Helene Barthelemy.

You little mystery.

You're next.

*

Tomorrow morning – don't forget.

Alan hasn't forgotten.

'Lance called round for me at about 11 o'clock and we drove to Brompton Hospital and parked the van in this big yard, in a corner of which was a pile of beds. Lance said, "It's all right. No one's going to say anything," and so we started to drive off with them. Very, very heavy iron beds – no mattress, just the frame and the springs – and they were so big and heavy that we could only take one at a time, strapped to the roof of the van. Other stuff had been dumped there as well – screens, gynaecological equipment, all in a tangle. We carted off everything, bit by bit.

'We spent most of the day going backwards and forwards. Lance liked these beds. He said they looked more professional. And there were various mechanical bits for people with broken limbs – I suppose they could be utilized.

'We took a couple of beds to a garage somewhere in north London, where they were going to be sprayed or something, and I remember we took a gynaecological inspection ramp to a girl's flat in Earls Court. It was all chipped NHS cream paint and some sort of dreadful red Rexine and it was attached to the bottom of this girl's bed. She was very excited, and she had a friend there – who jumped up on this thing, which was very high, like a throne, and put her legs into these stirrups and offered Lance and myself a free . . . a free lunch, so to speak. But I've never been turned on by redheads, and especially redheads who shave themselves. And so, like the *News of the World,* we made our excuses – and probably Lance got his money – and we left.'

Did a job like Lance's have a name?

The following Friday Lance and Alan paid a visit to the flat in Monmouth Road, and while Lance answered a call of nature the girl answered Alan's question.

'He brings me my stuff. He helps me. He's my tin soldier.'

Which has a much nobler ring to it than 'prostitute's runner', which sounds a lot less respectable than 'supplier of general sundries to the trade', which is the form of words Lance would no doubt have chosen if he'd ever sat back and discussed himself, if he'd ever had that much time on his hands.

But he had places to go, people to see – he was busy, busy, busy . . .

Lance supplied condoms, stockings, suspenders and knickers (bought by the gross from 'Knicker Norman' in the East End). He supplied screens and cheval mirrors and, in the interests of hygiene, Victorian bidets and douches. He supplied red light bulbs for bedside lamps and electric massagers ('Pifco, the name was, and they were always being advertised for back pain or shoulder pain or something') which were used to stimulate an erection in drunks. He supplied French dildoes fashioned from exotic woods and plastic vibrators. He supplied printed business cards with inscriptions such as *Secretarial Service* and *Typing* alongside the telephone numbers. He could also supply the telephones. Normally residents could expect to wait weeks, months even, to get connected, but a girl who was setting up in business required a telephone immediately. So come the weekend a moonlighting engineer would turn up with a bootful to choose from ('Lance always chose white – white Bakelite') and the problem was solved.

In short Lance supplied everything a working girl could wish for, and he liked to supply instructions as well. Upon hearing their complaints that the punters were always stealing knickers for souvenirs, he told his girls that they should be selling them, at two guineas a pair. Come to that, when the girl was performing a highly specialized service such as the golden shower (for which she required plenty of notice, and plenty of tea), then, as well as remembering to straddle the bath correctly, gripping the wall-handle supplied by Lance, she should remember to keep her knickers on and pee through them, after which she should sell them as 'deluxe'.

Lance maintained that a girl who did her job properly milked everything.

Queening was a case in point. Some of them just grabbed the headboard and faced the wall, and even when Lance explained that a girl on a face should always face the door – so enabling hand relief at £3 to blossom into *soixante-neuf* at £5 – even then they still couldn't grasp it and during most of these talks Alan was the only one who listened. He marvelled at the energy and resourcefulness of this strange man (Virgil to his Parker), this man who was so much better than he needed to be, who tore around town – Sussex Gardens, Praed Street, Lancaster Gate, Gloucester Road – lecturing his girls like a schoolma'am with a vision . . .

And he *had* a vision. While stationed in Germany during national service, Lance had been impressed by the pioneering spirit of a woman named Beate Uhse. In 1951 Uhse, a former Luftwaffe pilot, founded a mail order business in Flensburg selling various contraceptive devices. As the decade progressed her catalogue expanded to include love potions, sex aids and Parisian lingerie, and by the time she opened the world's first sex shop in Flensburg in 1962 she was a millionaire. 'Lance was full of admiration for her and her empire, as he saw it. I think he wanted to do the same thing, or something similar, over here. He was always telling the girls that they had to go kinky. That was his bloody mantra, more or less. He'd say, "That's where the money is." He saw the future, you see.'

Lance supplied sets of handcuffs, lined with velvet to prevent chafing. ('Hamley's toy shop sold them in packets with a six-inch plastic truncheon.') And on Mondays and Tuesdays, the 'dead days', as he called them, he would dress girls up as French maids and nurses and schoolgirls and take photographs to slip inside old menu covers for the punter's inspection – to get him away from the quickie, to get him spending more, and more often. They weren't the kind of photographs you'd find in *Spick* and *Span*.

'The schoolgirl scenario was a good one. Lance used to buy old hockey sticks, and he must have cut about seven inches off a broom handle, split it in half on a bandsaw and glued it round the flat handle of the hockey stick – and with a condom on it the girl could sort of simulate the frustrated schoolgirl in her uniform and her straw boater, sort of sucking her thumb and ramming a hockey stick up herself. And of course you could use it to hit people with as well.'

So who was awarded top marks?

'Well, the woman in Monmouth Road was probably Lance's favourite. He seemed to spend more time with her than with the others, normally visiting on a Friday afternoon. This was the safest time, according to Lance, because the vice squad in Paddington never did anything on a Friday afternoon; they were busy filling in their expense forms and they didn't want to get involved in overtime.

'Anyway, this woman (who seemed to work non-stop, never left the flat) would listen to him and do what he said. But she had this pressing need because of all these kids. Lance thought that if she'd come into the business sooner and under his wing she'd have been top flight.'

And who went straight to the back of the class?

'Nearly all of them, I'm afraid. They were too dopey, he said, or they were . . . madly in love with "inappropriate boyfriends" who took their money and so on – or beat them up, which was bad for business. Lance and I kept well out of all that. Trouble, trouble, trouble . . .'

Trouble was never far away. At the Old Bailey on 2 July 1963 Colin Welt Fisher, a 33-year-old engineer, was sentenced to life imprisonment for the murder of a young prostitute named Veronica Walsh, alias Vicky Pender, who was found battered and strangled at her bedsit in Finsbury Park on 21 March. Fisher told police that he and his friend Vicky Pender had gone back to her room in the early hours of 19 March. They got high on purple hearts and reefers and he had no clear recollection of the events that followed. 'As if it was something out of a dream, I seem to remember there was bubbly saliva all over her face, hair and neck, even down to the top of her body. I seem to remember touching her and my hand got all sticky . . . This saliva was like froth.' Fisher's defence argued unsuccessfully that in his drugged state he had had no criminal intent.

At 8.30pm on 19 March he met Vicky Pender's friend Irene Lockwood at the Nucleus Club (where she appears to have been working as a hostess). 'I propositioned Sandra about spending the night with me, but it was not primarily for sexual intercourse. One of the reasons I wanted to be with Sandra was because she could get better tablets.' In the clubs forty purple hearts changed hands for £1; Fisher gave Lockwood £4. She got the tablets and he booked them in as 'Mr and Mrs Welt' at Walter's Hotel in Sussex Gardens, Paddington. They took six cartons of bitter lemon upstairs to their double room and began gobbling. They also performed oral sex upon each other and he left the hotel at about 11am the following morning. 'Sandra was still in bed unconscious.'

Irene Lockwood told the court, 'I'd had a few purple hearts in the daytime – I must have had about fifty altogether.' She got into bed in her underwear and felt a bit hazy 'and I think I must have passed out then'. She was woken up at 3pm the next day by fists hammering upon the door. She was now naked and alone. She reached for her handbag (under the mattress where she'd hidden it) only to find that the ten £1 notes he'd given her had disappeared. 'I didn't see Colin again.'

That night Fisher agreed a price of £10 with another prostitute, Charlotte Megaw, whom he also took to a hotel in Sussex Gardens. They shared a pound's worth of purple hearts and had intercourse twice ('He had no difficulty'), leaving the hotel together in his Vauxhall Cresta at midday on 21 March. The car stalled and he got out and lifted the bonnet up. 'He asked me to hold a handkerchief at some place in the front of the engine. I went to do so and he drove away.' With the bonnet still up and her handbag containing £12 (which included his £10) on the seat beside him.

In the weeks leading up to his conviction, Colin Fisher was keen to capitalize on his status as chief murder suspect. He tried to sell his story to the press.

Ron Mount of the *News of the World* travelled to Fisher's council house in Hemel Hempstead to meet him and his wife.

> His powerful, 6ft. frame was draped comfortably along the settee as he chain-smoked my cigarettes and said: 'Since I came out the Army two years ago after 13 years' service I just can't seem to settle down . . .
>
> 'I started a side-line to make more money and that's brought me into contact with the seamy side of life. I'm not proud of it but I take and sell dirty pictures.'

Yes, Fisher was a hustler, but the kind of hustler that gave vice a bad name. Alan and Lance would have run a mile from a man like him.

But by 1963 Alan had left Lance behind. He'd found a proper job, working as a valet at Crockford's casino, then situated in Carlton House Terrace, overlooking the Mall. 'The club was run by two Algerian Jews and we got a lot of Jews in as customers – car dealers and bookmakers coming to launder their takings. Playing small and bringing lots of money to do it and then getting a cheque from Crockford's for giving Crockford's the money. They were all at it, and they'd bring their wives and eldest children along to watch them and for a meal because the food was free! I mean, no wonder we had Jews there.'

Valets appeared to be mere errand boys – running between the bank and the gaming rooms with money or chips, emptying ashtrays, helping the women on with their coats – but they had power. 'Valets were the only members of staff to have freedom of movement, so whoever was fiddling – the croupier, the changeur – had to cut the valet in because he was their only means of getting the money out of the club. My coat pockets were stitched up like everyone else's but I cut the lining of the tail. And I took 10 per cent.'

He bought a Volkswagen and a mohair suit and an Asprey's money-clip made of platinum.

He showed off.

'I bought my *Evening Standard*, which cost about fourpence, from a man who used to stand outside the tube at – I think it was the Haymarket. I'd give him a pound note and tell him to keep the change (that's the kind of arsehole *I* was). And he'd say, "Still playing happy families then?", referring to the casino.

'But this man was quite well known because . . . part of his face had been eaten away by syphilis.'

He enjoyed himself; and now that he was in the money he moved into Hedgegate Court.

Hedgegate Court was something more, mythically more, than just another parcel of teeming Rachman-owned slums. In seedy Powis Terrace in seedy Notting Hill, the Court was still seedy enough to set people talking. *The pipes,* they said, *the pipes are stuffed to buggery with poor little half-born bastards – and the drains are no better than they should be . . .*

But then at the beginning of the Sixties a finance company, the Elmstead Trust, bought most of Powis Terrace from Rachman and began converting the slums into smart, modern self-contained flats, at an eventual cost of £80,000 (exclusive of payments made to hundreds of West Indian tenants as financial inducements to leave). The flats in Hedgegate Court boasted G-plan furniture, fitted carpets, constant hot water, an entry-phone on every floor . . . and yet nobody was in any hurry to rent one. They were expensive, of course (£9 per week for a one bedroom-flat), but more importantly they were situated in an area notorious for vice and villainy, where race riots might re-erupt at any time.

So who were the new tenants of Hedgegate Court?

Well, they were white but they weren't the white-collar workers

that Duncan Tack, the letting agent, had hoped for. He looked on in despair as the Court steadily filled with musicians, actors, nightclub hostesses, whores, hustlers and villains – the types who felt at home in Notting Hill.

But Duncan Tack approved of Alan.

'Well, I paid the rent, didn't I? And I had a proper job. No one else really stayed there very long, they were always getting kicked out – for rent arrears, having parties, bringing clients back, that sort of thing.'

Alan's next-door neighbour, Big Donna, an Irish prostitute who took her work home with her, only lasted a few weeks. Another neighbour was Norman, a skinny young Scot who, it transpired, wasn't wearing dark glasses for the same reasons as Alan. He was a bank robber and one day he opened the door of his flat to a gang who promptly chopped a thumb off; and from then on he carried a shopping bag – rumoured to contain a gun – whenever he went out. 'We always made a joke of it when we saw him. I mean, a bloke like that didn't *go* shopping . . .'

Hedgegate Court also harboured another ex-public school boy.

'Intelligent guy, highly cultivated. A pornographer, I believe – something to do with models. I went round to his flat one afternoon and he pointed upwards and said, "What do you think of that?" There was blood all over the ceiling – which was ten feet high. Somebody trying to muscle in on his modelling game.'

Most afternoons the pornographer could be found hard at work on the *Telegraph* crossword in a nearby French restaurant, L'Escarpolette. The musician and magick-taster Graham Bond was also a regular, although he didn't eat there because they didn't serve Wimpys. ("The food of the future," Graham said – and he was right.') In the evenings, having slept, or tried to sleep, for most of the day, Alan would turn up and order French pastries and black coffee before going to work. But he never ate meals there either.

In fact the restaurant – as a restaurant – was faring badly. This was chiefly due to its location, which meant a lack of passing trade, although the proprietor did little to help matters. He looked a bit like the young John Osborne and he was very angry, in a general way.

'He was always having a go at Graham Bond, telling him that he

was rubbish, that he should pack the organ in and go back to selling fridges in Dagenham. And it wasn't just Graham. He had a go at all of us. He had a go at David Hockney as well.'

Hockney left London for New York in December 1963, but in the autumn of 1962 he had taken the lease on a first-floor flat (which doubled as his studio) at 17 Powis Terrace. 'I think it was just before he went away . . . He had some kind of drinks party there, with people on the balcony opposite. So your man, who was always going on about Hockney ("Just look at her! Who does she think she is?" sort of thing), stands in the doorway of his restaurant and shouts out, "You're nothing but a bloody poof!" And so the pornographer puts his paper down and says, "You don't know what you're talking about. That bloke's going to make a fortune." But that was him. I don't think he could help himself.'

He even had a go at Cherry. Alan's photograph captures him standing outside the restaurant, half-beard bristling, in the middle of delivering an improvised lecture on morality while Cherry, in wig-hat and smart check blouse, clutches her capacious work bag. The dark glasses indicate a woman blind to the errors of her ways; she's torn between smiling for

the camera and laughing out loud. 'He was after her, that's what it was. I don't think he was getting any from his French wife.'

Street scene.

Cherry could handle it. She'd stomached far worse – such as the long arm of the law, which apprehended her one night and forced her to fellate it beneath some flats at the bottom of Queensway. Cherry Cherry Cherry: head buried down there where the devil says goodnight; all swallowed up in the darkness of his cape; but keeping her independence.

Indeed. Walking the streets in the wake of the 1959 legislation may appear to be no more than an act of defiance but there are certain practicalities worth considering here. Some short-timers remained part-timers, out on the streets for one or two nights earning money to feed the baby or the meter and then indoors for the rest of the week. These women had no need of business flats, while a woman such as Cherry (or Trina or Kay) had no wish to commit herself to one, for by the time she'd scraped together the key money, equipped the premises, advertised an ebony chest for sale and hired a retired tart as a maid to take telephone bookings – well, by that time she'd be lumbered with all that she was desperate to escape: discipline, security, a regular job.

And along with the drudgery came the danger, for call-girls were hardly less vulnerable than street-girls to robbery and/or assault. Furthermore, once you had a centre of operations you stood a better chance of attracting a ponce. This creature (who was not necessarily a lover) would then rob you on a permanent basis and more than likely crack the odd rib into the bargain.

Pitfalls.

All the same, Cherry sometimes borrowed a flat for the odd shift: on one of the 'dead days' perhaps, or from a girl who was ill or menstruating. If she found herself without a maid on these occasions she would ask Alan to accompany her as her 'boyfriend'. He was to wear two jumpers ('I was so thin') and look 'handy'. He wasn't to take bookings if she was engaged, because a man's voice would frighten the punters; he was to leave the telephone off the hook. 'I'd be watching the telly or playing the records or something, with my back to the punter, just to show that I wasn't up to any . . . like rolling the guy or something. She'd take them into the bedroom but leave the door ajar slightly and any "funny business", as she used to say, I was to come in and sort him out. But nothing ever happened.'

Things happened in his imagination.

One night Cherry was working at a flat in Ladbroke Grove and she sent Alan out to get some milk. 'There used to be milk machines everywhere and she was always buying these little cartons. I can see her now, guzzling the damn stuff in the street . . . that was her food, I suppose.

'The night we were in Ladbroke Grove I went out two or three times to get milk. I remember, there were two guys sitting in a Hillman – which was a very bad sign then. CID car. Everybody knew that. When I saw it I thought, "Christ, they're after me." I was so jumpy, you see, with this sort of lifestyle of mine . . .'

At the end of the shift (10pm because she didn't want drunks) Cherry would pay Alan something out of her evening's earnings. He hardly needed the money; his job at Crockford's supplied him, one way and another, with as much as he could spend. He just liked the company of these women, whose hours were as irregular as his own. He liked the life.

Although he was beginning to feel like death warmed up. A single shift at Crockford's might last thirty-six hours, depending on the length of the game, and whenever he finished early he'd go straight round to Wardour Street to hear Georgie Fame or Zoot Money play at the Flamingo. ('The mc would shine a spotlight on members of the drugs squad and we'd all rush to the toilets . . .') He ate very little, chain-smoked, drank black coffee almost continuously ('I never touched pills though, only natural substances') and had precious hours of sleep disturbed by eldritch sounds of love from the opposite flat, shared by a prostitute with her lesbian ponce.

He felt worse and worse. All the kids were thin (with the exception of Graham Bond) but Alan was thinner. After eighteen months at Crockford's he consulted a doctor in Westbourne Grove who scribbled something on a notepad and pushed it towards him. 'It said: "I don't know what you do for a living but if I were you I'd give it up."'

In 1964 Alan returned to Wales and his family, leaving behind his version of London: Hedgegate Court, L'Escarpolette, Crockford's, Cherry, Norman – and Lance.

Whatever happened to Lance?

'Once I left London . . . I don't know. I never saw him again, and looking back now I realize I knew very little about him. I've no idea where he lived – he would always come round to the flat or we'd meet in town. And I can't recall ever, when we were on our rounds, seeing money change hands; though it must have done, it must have done . . . I think it was something he sorted out with the maid.

'But Lance never struck me as somebody who was in it for the money. I don't know what he was in it for – unless it gave him a thrill. He looked like a bank clerk, you know, with those grey flannels and his Marks & Spencer shirt.

'He never touched any of the girls. I know that. I asked them.'

In the end what mattered about Lance was his dedication ('He was a bit like Stephen Ward, really'), his striving for perfection in such a slap-dash world. His vision, his struggle, all those doomed grooming sessions with all his pretty ones: Lance patiently explaining the path to a flat in St John's Wood; Lance exhorting them to chat to their regulars, develop a rapport (*Accountants, lawyers – sink your hooks in*); Lance in the doorway, leaving now but still talking, still trying to whip up some –

Come on, girls, It's Motor Show week!

Don't forget.

Don't wash your hair with Persil.

Don't go to bed with your make-up on.

Don't sleep in the subway . . .

Don't bother.

Deaf ears.

Those girls!

Those girls had about as much sense in their heads as so many tailor's dummies.

I'm trying to tell you they wouldn't listen, wouldn't learn.

Helene Catherine Barthelemy was born on 9 June 1941 in Ormiston, East Lothian, the daughter of Maurice Barthelemy, a steward serving with the Free French Navy. When Helene was about four years old her Scottish mother Mary left her husband, taking the child with her. She eventually divorced him and remarried, becoming Mary Thomson and settling in Cleethorpes.

By the age of sixteen Helene was living in Blackpool, where one of her landladies, Helen Paul, remembered her as 'a gem of a girl. She used to call me Mum. She would never do anything wrong.' In October 1960 she became a mother herself, giving birth to an illegitimate son, Thomas. (Thomas's birth certificate informs us that his

father was a Kenneth Ferguson, cotton feeder. The boy was taken into care and later adopted.)

She worked as an artiste on Blackpool's Golden Mile.

That's French for 'stripper' of course, which is English for – a bit of a waste really, when you come to look at it.

Nice pair, Helene.

Slim young thing like that, capable of so much more.

On 8 October 1962 Helene Barthelemy stood in the dock at Liverpool Assizes charged with aggravated robbery and unlawful wounding. She faced these charges together with three other persons, missing and unknown.

Brian Duckworth, prosecuting, said that on Friday 27 July 1962 a man named Friend Taylor, on holiday in Blackpool, met Barthelemy and spent two hours with her at the Pleasure Beach in the afternoon. They met again at about 8pm and went to the Huntsman Hotel, and later on to the sandhills at Squires Gate. Taylor removed his coat and jacket and they lay down on the sands. A few minutes later a pebble hit him and when he got up to investigate three men jumped him from the sandhills. They slashed his face with a knife or razor, knocked him down and kicked him in the stomach and all four departed. Taylor made his way to the main road, where a passing motorist took him to hospital (his wound required approximately eighteen stitches). It transpired that a wallet containing £22 5s was missing from his jacket, which he had left on the sandhills.

Barthelemy was recognized in an identity parade as the woman concerned but pleaded not guilty to both charges. She admitted supplementing her wages with prostitution (in March she had been fined £20 at Liverpool City Magistrates' Court for assisting in the management of a brothel) but claimed that on 27 July she had visited the hairdresser's in the afternoon, and in the evening had been with another man. They had gone to see *El Cid* at the Rendezvous cinema; she had spoken to the manager as she went in. After the film she 'went on business' with three men in succession, none of whom was Taylor. She'd never met him. They hadn't gone to the sandhills. He was mistaken.

The manager of the Rendezvous remembered seeing a girl and a young man together outside the cinema, but that was on the evening of 26 July; on 27 July he was busy in his office from 6.30pm to 9.30pm and she could not have spoken to him. Moreover, a bingo stall attendant on the Golden Mile and a waiter at the Huntsman Hotel had no doubt that Barthelemy was the brunette they had seen in the company of Taylor. Taylor himself recognized one of his attackers as one of three men she had spoken to previously when he was with her, and while lying on the sand being kicked in the stomach he heard her voice: 'Leave it, Jock. He has had enough.'

On 10 October, the third and final day of the trial, Helene Barthelemy, who refused to reveal the identities of the men, was found guilty as charged and sentenced to four years' imprisonment for what the judge described as an 'absolutely appalling crime'. She gazed at him for a few seconds and then collapsed in the dock.

But the conviction didn't stand up. At the trial the victim was described as a man of complete integrity, yet later it emerged that he was an experienced housebreaker and thief who had served two prison sentences himself. On 4 February 1963 Barthelemy's conviction and sentence were quashed at the Court of Criminal Appeal in London, and she was free to hustle and thieve once more.

Not long now.

At 7.15am on Friday 24 April 1964 Clark May of 199 Boston Manor Road, Brentford, went out the back to empty the ashes and found Helene Barthelemy lying naked on the rubbish heap in the recess outside his garden gate.

Deputy Commander Ernest Millen, Detective Chief Superintendent Jack Mannings and Detective Superintendent William Baldock were among the CID officers who attended the scene that morning. A press photograph shows one man looking over a piece of sacking into the recess; the recess which has since disappeared, for

next door's garden shed is now a brick garage and it crosses the former boundary, takes up the old space.

I've arrived thirty-eight years late but now I can't seem to bring myself to leave. I wouldn't mind poking my nose into the back garden of 199, only the fence is a bit too high, and standing here I feel my shoes sinking ever deeper into the churned-up mud of tyre tracks. And so, to whoops of triumph from the adjoining playing field, I wade back the way I came.

Past garage doors sprayed with graffiti tags – and there's a mattress, a cooker . . . yes, people still dump things here. Behind me is Swyncombe Avenue, ahead of me is The Ride, another cul-de-sac, and above me is a plane on its way to Heathrow. The killer would presumably have turned off Boston Manor Road into The Ride and then driven through the alley, stopping briefly towards the end. By the time he reached Swyncombe Avenue he'd disposed of a naked corpse.

On the day of discovery Donald Teare performed the post-mortem at Acton mortuary. Barthelemy had been dead for at least twenty hours, and possibly two or three days, since rigor mortis had completely disappeared. Her body was filthy, much of its dirt accumulated after death. Hypostasis was visible on the back of the body and this indicated that she had lain on her back for some time after death. Patches of pallor traced the outlines of her knickers and bra. She had lain on her back for about eight hours before she was stripped.

The cause of death was asphyxia, due to pressure on the neck. Teare wouldn't state whether this was strangulation by manual means or ligature, but expressed an opinion that pressure had been applied probably by means of twisting the victim's clothing around her neck. Of the eight abrasions on her throat six small abrasions on the right side were apparently caused by the victim's fingernails attempting to remove the means of strangulation. There was some swelling on the left cheekbone and the bridge of the nose. She had probably been struck with a fist.

At the end of the alley I look back for a moment at the nettles, thistles and mud. I try to get this mess clear in my head.

In February '63 she was released from prison. And now in April '64 she was dead.

So what had she been up to in the meantime?

Tricks. Helene 'Teddy' Barthelemy moved to London in August 1963 and immediately took to the streets, soliciting mainly around Bayswater and Queensway but also in the West End, Shoot Up Hill and Cricklewood Broadway. She was a car-girl, directing her clients to secluded spots. She was believed to have favoured Duke's Meadows, although one regular customer would collect her in Shoot Up Hill and drive to a spot in Elstree, where Barthelemy would fellate him. (Police briefly entertained a theory that during fellatio she had bitten the penis of a client, who then lost his temper and killed her. Would a man with such injuries seek treatment? Enquiries were made at a large number of west London hospitals without result.)

She was prepared to do most things for money and felt comfortable with buggers, whom she no doubt charged extra. (She appears to have been very well used in this respect. An officer who viewed the post-mortem photographs recalled, 'When I saw her backside I thought at first that I was looking at a flesh wound.') Anal, vaginal and oral swabs were taken from her corpse with negative results.

French letters? More than likely. And yet at least one man got to ride Teddy bareback. In January 1964 an 'L. Piggott' attended St Mary's Hospital, Paddington. He had gonorrhoea and gave his contact as Helen Paul. He was Jamaican and his address, 7 Craven Hill

Gardens, matched that of Von Barrington Adams, a Jamaican man in his early twenties. Registered unemployed, he worked in the evenings as a disc jockey at jazz clubs, and for a few months during the winter of 1963/4 he conducted a casual affair with Helene Barthelemy. He told police he didn't know she was a prostitute.

Another part-time lover eager to plead ignorance was Lloyd Dehaney, a British Rail fitter who admitted having intercourse with Barthelemy on two occasions. (In August 1963 'Helen Paul' attended St Mary's for treatment for gonorrhoea, naming Dehaney as her contact.) Nathaniel Reid, her final boyfriend, was believed to have ponced on her during the last weeks of her life.

Adams, Reid and Dehaney were all black, for when she was off-duty Barthelemy preferred the company of black men.

She knew where to find them.

The Roaring Twenties, 50 Carnaby Street, was a ska club consisting of a large basement room whose air was so thick with reefer smoke you could hardly see the roach in front of your face . . .

'Down there you had a lot of black guys, mostly ponces, and a lot of iffy white women,' Alan recalled. 'The people who were smoking grass were quite relaxed. But there were guys drinking rum and others on pills, purple hearts, very edgy. And there weren't bouncers as such. Everybody was a bouncer, they all joined in the punch-ups.

'One night I was dancing with the wrong woman, and I got tapped on the shoulder. Jamaican guy – big – a lot bigger than I was. But out of . . . bravado, I suppose, I faced up to him. I even thumped him with my Coca-Cola bottle – which had no effect at all. Bloody stupid. He just smiled, took it off me, smashed it against something and drove the neck-end into my right cheekbone.'

But forget about the men. In February 1964 at Marlborough Street Magistrates' Court Diana Graves was charged with maliciously and intentionally causing bodily harm to Norma Mackie at the Roaring Twenties. The two women quarrelled in the Ladies over Mackie's black boyfriend, Shirkey, and the victim told the court that Graves had slashed her dress with a razor and inflicted cuts on her face, neck and right arm. A third hostess intervened but Graves wouldn't drop the razor and she wouldn't relinquish Mackie, so a fourth woman grabbed her by the hair and banged her head against the wall until she let go.

To Helene Barthelemy this place must have felt like home. Certainly she frequented the Twenties, and the Flamingo – and the Jazz Club, 207 Westbourne Park Road, of which Joe Cannon was a part-owner.

'It was a big big basement room. You had all these coal chutes down there, all sealed up. I think it was two rooms or two flats knocked into one. Very dark, big sound system, loud music. All the blacks and the prostitutes used to go down there. Run by a short black geezer with a bald head. We called him "African Peter".'

On her final visit to the Jazz Club Helene Barthelemy left behind a blue handbag which the Nigerian proprietor, Peter Arboro, duly handed in to the police. The bag contained her front door key, a fact which suggested this was her last night on earth.

Which was when?

As far as Arboro could recall this woman – he knew her only as Teddy or Helen – had handed the bag to him at about 2am on Thursday 23 April before leaving the nightclub. He believed she was wearing a black jumper and a green skirt. No, he wasn't aware that she was a prostitute. No, it wasn't that kind of a place at all.

African Peter was pretty hard work, yet the real slog began when detectives interviewed his clientele. It appeared that in the early hours of the morning of Thursday 23 April five members – an Irishman, a light-skinned Jamaican known as 'Indian Rudi', a black woman, a white woman and another white man – were in the Ladies sharing a reefer when Barthelemy entered and joined them.

According to Rudi, there was a knock on the lavatory door (guarded, presumably) and she entered and had a smoke with them. The white woman confirmed this, adding that everybody then returned to the dance room, where shortly afterwards Barthelemy, after having visited the bar, told them all that she wouldn't be long and left the club. She wasn't carrying a handbag and the woman didn't see her return.

But the rest of the group failed to corroborate her statement. The black woman admitted being in the lavatory with the others when a white woman entered. However, this woman said, 'You don't have to worry about me. I'm not with the police,' words which frightened her, so that she went back into the club on her own. The Irishman stated that he was in the Jazz Club on that date in the early hours but would admit nothing further. The other white man could not confirm that the smoking incident took place on the date mentioned.

Arboro's assistant manager, Lee Otty, complicated matters further when he stated that on Monday 20 April – or it might have been Tuesday 21 April – he noticed a black handbag on the shelf behind the counter. He identified the bag shown to him and said it had remained on the shelf for the rest of the week. Moreover, the last time he saw Teddy in the club was on Sunday 19 April.

But who could believe what any of this lot said? Useless, all of them, a right bunch of toerags. Where to next?

Wraggs Cafe, another of the dead woman's haunts, situated in nearby All Saints Road. A black employee named Handel Cascoe informed detectives that Teddy was a regular late-night customer and that on Tuesday 21 April she visited the cafe at about 11.30pm, drank a cup of tea and then left. She returned at about 12.30am, had another cup of tea and talked to him for about fifteen minutes. She left again, returning at about 2am, when she ate a meal of boiled rice and chicken. This time she stayed longer, leaving at 3.30am to go to the Jazz Club. At 5.20am Cascoe left the cafe and looked in at the Jazz Club and saw her there. She had borrowed £2 from him the previous weekend and she repaid the money from a red leather purse. They then walked out into the street, where Cascoe asked her if she would like to go for a drink at a friend's house. But she'd already made an arrangement to go to Ealing with a white couple who were picking her up in a car, and besides, her handbag was still in the club. Teddy went back inside and Cascoe went on his way. He never saw her again.

However, Cascoe's boss, Harold Williams, stated that the dead woman visited his cafe on Wednesday 22 April. She came in at about 12.30am and ate steak, rice and peas. Afterwards she stayed and chatted to Cascoe and Williams and finally left at around 4.15am. She had an appointment to meet a married couple at 5am in the Jazz Club, and the three of them were going to Ealing. Williams recalled that she wasn't her usual cheerful self; she seemed worried or depressed about something. She paid her bill from a black leather purse. She wasn't carrying a handbag.

Red or black, Tuesday or Wednesday, chicken or steak . . . but Barthelemy's stomach contents consisted of large chunks of potato. Whatever her final meal was, she didn't eat it here.

As for the white couple – well, a man and his wife were traced who had a casual acquaintance with the deceased, but they denied making arrangements to meet her at the Jazz Club or anywhere else.

*

What sort of a case was this turning into?

Within the space of three months three young prostitutes had been found dead in west London.

All small, all naked or almost naked.

All found within a short distance of one another and either in or in close proximity to the Thames.

All clothes missing (with the exception of Tailford's coat and stockings).

All possessions missing (with the exception of Barthelemy's handbag).

No sexual injuries.

No apparent motive.

Tailford and Lockwood had been washed clean of clues by the river. Barthelemy's was the only clear-cut case of murder, yet by now everybody – police, press, public – suspected that these deaths were linked. But nobody had the faintest idea what any of it meant. In fact the other major criminal case of the day, the 1963 Great Train Robbery, began to seem almost soothing in comparison. Yes, that was Ealing; this was Poe.

So thank God for the fingerprints, each and every one of them.

None on Teddy's body – but all over Teddy's room.

Helene Barthelemy rented a single furnished room on the ground floor of 34 Talbot Road, Harlesden; the rest of the house, in common with all the other houses in Talbot Road, was occupied by blacks. She was last seen in the house at about 8.30pm on Tuesday 21 April by another tenant, Purgy Dennis, as she was walking between her room and the communal kitchen.

Barthelemy occupied the ground-floor middle room and her neighbour was Nellie Manhertz, an auxiliary nurse who worked nights. Manhertz last saw her at 7.30pm on Monday 20 April. Later that week, either on the Wednesday or the Thursday morning, she went to Barthelemy's room and, finding the door open, looked inside. She noticed a red plastic washing-up bowl on the floor by the bed. In Barthelemy's absence Manhertz took the key, which was on the inside of the door, and locked the room.

'They had one suspect,' an officer recalled, 'and, you know, I've a gnawing suspicion he may have been black.'

Correct. He was Horace Bellafonte, one of Teddy's Jamaican friends. He lived nearby in Cricklewood and had been interviewed earlier in the inquiry after his home and work telephone numbers had been found in her diary. He stated that he last saw her on the afternoon of Wednesday 15 April in Church Road, Harlesden, when she was shopping.

'They were following him, on foot, on the Underground, for weeks and weeks.'

That's right. They knew he had no car but they kept him under twenty-four-hour observation to find out if he could drive, or had a friend who could drive, or whether he would lead them to an address or storage space where he might have hidden her body.

'In the end he sussed them . . .'

In the end he told the truth. In Barthelemy's room police had found two used cups (containing coffee dregs) and saucers, a used plate and a record player with a record on its turntable. Bellafonte's fingerprints were found on one of the cups, one of the saucers, the plate, the record player, the record's plastic cover and a clock. He admitted to Detective Superintendent Osborn, the officer in charge of this investigation, that he'd visited her in her room on the week of the murder, a week in which, it was now known, Bellafonte had not gone to work.

All of which looked highly promising, yet ultimately led nowhere. It was eventually established that this social visit, on which the pair ate fish and chips together, took place on the evening of Monday 20 April, a fact confirmed by the dead girl's landlord, who admitted having seen her return with fish and chips that evening and, on a second interrogation, reluctantly recalled a black man in her room. This appeared to indicate that the occasion on which Barthelemy received her friend was distinct from the occasion on which she had left the house without locking her room door, the obvious explanation being that she simply hadn't bothered to wash up.

'I think it was around this time, at a progress meeting in the murder room at Shepherd's Bush, that Maurice Osborn said, "If anybody's got any suggestions I'd like to hear them – and that includes you, lad (I was a police cadet, filing the indexes). Because I haven't got a clue. It could be witchcraft, voodoo, for all I know."'

Black magic began to seem more and more attractive. After all, why would a man, having murdered a low-class prostitute for no obvious reason, not leave her or conceal her in the area where she died? Why drive off with the body, store it somewhere, strip it, and keep it for a period of between one and two days before driving off with it once more and dumping it in an alley in Brentford? Why maximize the risk of getting caught?

Well, he maximized the risk but he hadn't been caught and now that Bellafonte had been eliminated from the inquiry there was no one in view who resembled a serious suspect.

Barthelemy's ex-boyfriend Von Barrington Adams underwent several interrogations. He was in bad health at the time, still suffering the effects of a car crash in March, when his white Mini went into an obelisk. Barthelemy and three other passengers all escaped pretty much unharmed, but Adams, who was driving, remained in hospital with a fractured skull and other serious injuries until 16 April. He hadn't driven since the accident and police confirmed that his vehicle was a write-off by visiting a garage to inspect it on a dump. Adams was at home with his white girlfriend on 22, 23 and 24 April. Barthelemy's final boyfriend, Nathaniel Reid, appears to have had much else to hide and could only supply an alibi for the early morning of Friday 24 April (the date of the discovery of the body), stating that he was with his white girlfriend until 4.15am. This was verified; Reid was later eliminated from the inquiry for other reasons.

Which left no one – save grave Maurice, clueless, in the murder room.

Four of Helene Barthelemy's upper front teeth had been removed. Not knocked out, since there was no bruising of her lips or gums or injury to her tongue. Not extracted by dental means, since no dentist could be traced who had treated her during the period of her disappearance. *Removed.* (And to judge by the absence of blood in her jaw sockets this had taken place some time after death. A particle of tooth the size of a pinhead was discovered at the base of her tongue.)

Witchcraft? Voodoo?

Who do? How do? Why do?

What sort of a year was this turning into?

What the bloody hell was going on?

Police believed that Helene Barthelemy was last seen alive for certain at 8.30pm on Tuesday 21 April, walking between her room and the communal kitchen at 34 Talbot Road. The clothes in her wardrobe were shown to several of her acquaintances and police concluded that when murdered she was probably wearing a black jumper with a high neck and long sleeves, a tight-fitting skirt, a brown overcoat with a black leather collar and a pair of calf-length black leather boots. She was carrying a red or black leather purse which was fitted with a clip and may have contained tickets for a Jamaican sweepstake.

At 7.15am on Friday 24 April her body was discovered in a recess in an alleyway off Swyncombe Avenue, Brentford, about forty yards from the junction with Boston Manor Road. At 10.55pm on Thursday 23 April William Reynolds of 63 Swyncombe Avenue drove his car along this alleyway and parked it in his garage. His headlights were on, the recess visible on his off-side: he saw no body.

But Alfred Harrow saw something. He wasn't a local resident, he was a farmer from Buckinghamshire, and early on Friday morning he was driving his Bedford van along the busy Boston Manor Road. As he reached the junction with Swyncombe Avenue a vehicle shot out in front of him.

'I braked and came almost to a halt to avoid a collision. This vehicle then carried on in the direction of the Bath Road, without even slowing or stopping. This vehicle was a grey shooting brake of the Hillman or Hillman Husky type. There was only one person in this vehicle, a man, but I could not identify him . . . I was unable to get any particulars of the index number of this vehicle.'

Alfred Harrow was driving to Brentford Market. It was shortly after 6am and his working day was just beginning.

The other man, it seemed, had already knocked off.

4

Frighteners

Boo!

Look out!

Here he comes!

In July 1964 at the Old Bailey Mabel Gregory, a prostitute, was sentenced to six months' imprisonment for unlawfully wounding an unemployed driller named Keith McTernan.

On the night of 9 May McTernan had encountered Gregory at a cafe in Shepherd's Bush Road and asked her to go back to his flat with him, an offer she declined because she thought he was drunk. Outside afterwards he put his hand on her shoulder and asked her again. She turned and stabbed him in the stomach with a paperknife which she stated she had been carrying for protection since the recent murders.

In August 1964 Carole Young, a machinist, appeared at Marylebone Magistrates' Court accused of demanding money with menaces from a Mr 'X'. This man alleged that after midnight on 6 August he was driving his Mini along Westbourne Park Road. He turned into Basing Street, where he saw Young walking along and spoke to her. She told him intercourse would cost £2 in the car and got in, directing him to a side street. When they got there she asked for £2 but he told her his car was too small for a short time. She instructed him to drive her back but as he was turning the car round she opened the door. Mr 'X' alleged that Young then told him, 'Give me £3 or I'll jump out of the car, tear my clothes and then run up the street and say you tried to murder me.' She said she would make a note of his registration number. 'They'll try and get you for all the other murders as well . . .'

There!

Behind you!

Mary Theresa Cuthbertson Betty was born in Clydebank, Scotland, on 16 September 1933. In 1937 her parents, Richard Betty, a coal salesman, and his wife, Helen, moved to Barrow-in-Furness, where she was educated at various Roman Catholic schools until the age of seventeen. Shortly afterwards she joined the Women's Royal Army Corps. She served as a cook until September 1952 and then as a factory hand at a steelworks until 22 August 1953, the date on which she married James Fleming at St Mary's Catholic Church, Barrow-in-Furness. She was six months pregnant.

A son, Michael, was born in November. James Fleming, a private in the Royal Army Medical Corps, returned to his unit in Germany while Mary continued to live with her parents.

But she was restless. In February 1954 she left home for a short period and went to live at the Pavilion Cafe in Biggar Bank. In October, after her mother had voiced her disapproval of the company she was keeping, Mary Fleming walked out on her parents and her baby son and never returned.

She moved to Newcastle and worked at a cannery. She met a seaman, Owen Hardie, with whom she left for London in May 1955. They lived together in Dalston for a while but by the time Fleming gave birth to her second son, Robert, in February 1956 Hardie seems to have disappeared. She was now living in Norwich, though not for long. Soon Robert was in the care of Norwich City Council and his mother was back in London.

She was in business.

In October 1956 Mary Fleming was arrested for soliciting in Commercial Road, Stepney, and was bound over on her own recognizance in £5 to be of good behaviour for six months. This sum was forfeited in November when she was again prosecuted for soliciting. In 1957 she received three court fines, two for soliciting and one for committing an act of indecency with another person.

1958 was a bit different. In August, while living in Hornsey, she stole property to the value of £65 from her landlord's room and absconded, travelling to Scotland, where she stole money from gas meters at the homes of relatives. She returned to England, where she was arrested for the London offence on 22 October, and conditionally discharged for twelve months. She wasn't tried for the other offences as the arrest warrant was only valid in Scotland.

But in 1959 her luck (such as it was) ran out. In February she was sentenced to three months' imprisonment for stealing money from a gas meter at her lodgings in the East End. The *East London Advertiser* reported that Fleming and a friend had shared a pay-out of £5 3s.

Michael Turner first met Mary Fleming in February 1959 (immediately prior to her imprisonment), when he was twenty years old and a Coldstream Guard stationed at Chelsea barracks. He was demobilized in August and in September they began to live together at a house in Pembridge Gardens W2.

Fleming was five months pregnant when arrested for soliciting in December 1961 and received twelve months' probation. In April 1962 she gave birth to a daughter, Veronica. The couple were now living at a flat in Powis Gardens, yet shortly after the birth Turner left in order to avoid possible arrest for poncing. He continued to sleep with her occasionally until February 1963, when he ended the relationship.

One evening in March 1963 he went round to Powis Gardens to visit Veronica, now almost a year old, only to discover that her mother had left her on her own in the flat. He couldn't believe his eyes. What on earth had happened? Where was Mary?

'I went to a nigger club in Westbourne Park Road and found her drunk and dancing with coloured men. I was furious and went and dragged her outside and a coloured bloke followed, a fight started between the three of us, police were called and I knocked a copper's helmet off.'

About a year after this dust-up Mary Fleming met Harry Greenwood, an unemployed painter and decorator, at Pete's, a cafe she frequented in Blenheim Crescent. Initially she talked to him about opening a drinking club; at a later meeting she confessed that she was desperate for somewhere to live as she had to leave her current address. Greenwood found a house through an estate agent and in

April 1964 Fleming and Veronica and a second child, David (born the previous year and also fathered by Turner), moved into 25 Geraldine Road, Chiswick. The other tenants were Greenwood himself, John Prendergast, a mechanical engineer, Gloria Swanson, a convicted prostitute and her partner/ponce, a black labourer named Anthony Black.

According to one of her female acquaintances, Gloria Swanson, a 35-year-old peroxide blonde, was no starlet. 'She was tall, with a big build, big thick legs, and she'd been well used and abused. She'd been on the game for years. She was wrinkled, dried-up – like a prune. She went with black men because only a black man would have her. But she loved those kiddies of Mary's because she couldn't have any of her own. She was barren.'

On 9 May Swanson, Fleming and Greenwood were present at 202 Kensington Park Road when police raided the premises and arrested Margaret Malik, a young housewife, for brothel-keeping. Four other women, their identities unknown, were also present.

It's an obscure episode. The obvious inferences are that Malik, who admitted to being a prostitute, was running the women, with Greenwood there to roll the punters. Malik specialized in, as she put it, 'corrective treatment for men', so maybe Fleming was trying her hand at fladge. Yet the facts remain that Malik was arrested and imprisoned for three months while the others escaped whipping.

Fleming and Swanson were probably too far gone, career-wise, to care a fig but Harry Greenwood got a shock that night. At the age of thirty-one he already had six convictions for theft and related offences and he didn't hang around at Geraldine Road. He saw which way the skirts were blowing and got out the following day, leaving some of his belongings behind.

Fleming herself was forced to follow suit shortly afterwards. She received notice to quit for non-payment of rent and subsequently moved to 44 Lancaster Road, W11. This was an old three-storey building whose rooms housed both black and white families. Mary Fleming occupied the ground-floor front room. Here she carried on as before, leaving home late at night and returning in the early hours to make sure the children were safe and sound.

Gloria Swanson's female acquaintance also knew Mary Fleming ('I felt sorry for her because I knew she had nothing') and visited her on one occasion. 'I'd never seen so many milk bottles in all my life – and such filth! I thought "I'm not staying here." I wouldn't breathe the air in that room. All the dirty nappies . . . it was rotten.'

It was a doss-hole. One bed, one cot and a mattress on the floor for Fleming's boyfriend, an unemployed Irishman named Patrick Craig, and whichever mate he'd brought home to sleep the drink off. No Irish? No problem. You could always get a free kip at Mary's.

While Mary was out there – somewhere – getting her own head down and adding to her charge sheet in the process.

Yet it seemed as if things might be looking up. Harry Greenwood often saw her in Pete's Cafe and remained on talking terms with her. (She had taken the remainder of his belongings with her to Lancaster Road and reminded him from time to time to collect them.) She told him she had a boyfriend who was an estate agent, and on one occasion she made her entrance wearing a new skirt and sweater which she said he had bought her.

'Another time she came in she had a wristwatch on. It was gold with a round face and a black velvet strap. She told me that this same man had given her the watch. A few days later she came in without the watch and when I asked her about it she said she had pawned it . . .'

On Saturday 4 July Fleming paid a visit to Vivian's hairdressing salon in Portobello Road. She met a girlfriend there and began to discuss the new man in her life. 'She told me she had been with a client on the previous night and he told her to strip her clothes off for £10. He wanted nothing else and only wanted to see her naked. She told me it was easy money and she was going to see him again that afternoon, that's why she was having her hair done.' This man was going to give her £50 and they were going to a hotel. He was also going to buy her some new clothes. And he was going to provide a flat (unfurnished) for her and David and Veronica and he was going to pay the rent on it. 'I asked her how the man could get a flat and she told me this man was an estate agent and she would ask him.'

However, the next time they saw each other Fleming didn't mention the flat 'but told me she had met the man and he was very nice but she did not get the £50'.

Shame. But all the same Mary Fleming was lucky to be alive. A few weeks previously a client had taken her back to his flat in Queensway late one night and tried to strangle her, but she'd fought him off with her shoe. She escaped with her clothes, got dressed on the landing and ran all the way to the Continental Cafe in Blenheim Crescent. Here she told an Irishman named Alan Martin what had happened. He saw her tears and her bleeding neck and he and a friend agreed to accompany her to the block of flats in Porchester Gardens to 'sort him out'. But when they arrived she couldn't identify his flat 'so we walked around the corner into Queensway and suddenly Mary pointed to a man who was walking past us, and he was looking at us. Mary said that was the man.'

He was in his mid-forties, tall and rather plump, with a receding hairline. He wore a smart dark suit and he carried something, a walking stick or an umbrella. When he ran back into the block of flats the men followed, lost him, knocked at a few doors, got no reply and left. ('Mary did give us a pound for our trouble.')

No wonder, then, that Mary Fleming dreamed of becoming a kept woman, with only one man to please instead of half of west London, and no rent to pay for the rest of her days – because nothing. . .

No, nothing felt quite the same any more, not now she'd been broken in.

On the morning of Tuesday 14 July 1964 George Heard, a chauffeur of 52 Berrymede Road, Chiswick, got up early.

'The reason for this being that my eldest daughter was going away to France for a day trip and I had to take her to Acton in my employer's car.'

He'd ordered a wake-up call for 4.45am.

'I received the early call and I got up, looked out of the window to see what sort of a day it was and I noticed what I thought was a tailor's dummy lying in the entrance to the garage of No. 48 Berrymede Road.'

Squatting there naked. She looked as if she were waiting for someone to come along and it might as well be George Heard. After all, he had a steady job, there could be a few bob in it if she waited till he got a bit closer, and then jumped three feet in the air and threatened to scream that he'd tried to strangle her.

Only she was –

'When I had a look I realized it was not a tailor's dummy but a body.'

This one was out of luck.

She'd been strangled.

'I came inside and phoned 999 and –'

Thank you, George Heard.

Please stand back now.

Here they come.

5.20am. Police Constables Houston and Braddock of Shepherd's Bush police station.

7am. Detective Superintendent Marchant of F Division.

Followed by Detective Superintendent Mannings of No. 1 District, Chief Superintendent Rennie of F Division and Detective Superintendent Osborn of the Murder Squad.

Followed by Detective Superintendent McCafferty and Detective Sergeant Hopgood of the Metropolitan Police Laboratory.

8.30am. Dr Donald Teare of St George's Hospital, SW1.

Donald Teare, MB, FRCP, DMJ.

There'll never be another, will there?

Let him through.

The pathologist made his preliminary examination of the body. A young woman: naked, dirty and dead. Her head and trunk were bent forward over her right knee; her left arm was lying, palm downwards, over her left thigh; her right arm was flexed at the elbow and lay with its back to the ground by the side of her head. The hypostasis visible on the back of the body – indicating that she had lain on her back for some time after death – was broken by blanching in the shape of underwear across the buttocks and small of the back, indicating that she had been stripped after death.

At 11.40am at Hammersmith mortuary he performed the post-mortem and established the cause of death as asphyxia due to strangulation. Abrasions covered an area 1¼″ × 1½″ wide on and below the chin: possibly marks left by the victim's fingernails as she scrabbled to remove the means of pressure. A series of linear abrasions ran around the front and sides of the neck, covering an area 9″ long and varying from ½″ to 1¼″ in width. The majority of these abrasions ran in horizontal and parallel rows and may have been caused by a ligature. It's possible that the victim's own clothing was twisted around her throat.

Contact with the floor of a vehicle, possibly a van, was suggested by three grease marks on the buttocks and small of the back, and the linear pattern imprinted therein indicated pressure against some closely woven type of material such as matting.

A bruise over the coccyx suggested that the victim had bumped against a protruding object, possibly while struggling with her killer. A larger bruise on the front of the left chest was consistent with a punch, directly on the heart and of stunning intensity. A swollen left eyelid with tiny abrasions was in all probability an injury too minor to have been inflicted by the killer and once again may have been the result of a struggle.

This woman was a diminutive figure, measuring 5' 1½" and weighing approximately 8 stone; nevertheless, she had begun to make her presence felt. It was time – high time – that her fingerprints were taken, and when they were . . .

Guess who?

Scotch Mary.

Aye, her.

Upon arrival at the scene William Marchant had taken charge of the investigation (headquarters was once again at Shepherd's Bush) and he organized immediate house-to-house enquiries.

48 Berrymede Road seemed like a good place to start.

This was the last house on the right at the closed end of a cul-de-sac. The occupant was one Owen Jones, a coal agent who kept his car, a black Ford Prefect, in the adjacent garage. On the night of Monday 13 July Jones went to the dog races at Wembley Stadium, returning home at about 10.30pm, when he drove his car into the garage. He neither saw nor felt a body in the driveway.

Forensic officers inspected both car and garage but found nothing to connect Jones with the murder. In fact, he couldn't really help the police any further. He'd gone to bed at about 11.30pm and he'd heard nothing, nothing at all, until they turned up outside his window.

Yet several other residents heard a vehicle in Berrymede Road between 1am and 2am that morning. Vehicles reversed down here at all times of the day and night but this one had a high-powered engine, and its revving woke people up.

Was the driver the murderer? Hearse backed up, engine running . . .

Leaking? On Tuesday morning police discovered a small pool of dirty oil in the road just outside the garage forecourt adjacent to No. 48. Some spots led off in the direction of Mary Fleming.

Getting the body on the stage.

Although there was no evidence that they were associates, both Mary Fleming and Helene Barthelemy were street-girls working the Queensway and Bayswater areas. (Like Barthelemy, Fleming contracted gonorrhoea and in June 1961 visited St Mary's. She told staff that she had received penicillin for the disease two years previously, but had failed to complete the treatment.) Each appeared to have been picked up by a kerb-crawler, strangled by whatever means and driven to a storage space (somewhere cool, since in both cases the temperature of the body when found was lower than the atmospheric temperature). Several hours after death each was stripped and laid on her back. Some time later and during the hours of darkness each was dumped at a location in west London by someone who knew west London – or parts of it – well. (Three miles separated the two sites.)

Well, there were these similarities to muse on, and there was also good news from the lab. It was known that the dirt on Barthelemy's body had consisted of fragments of coal, coke dust, red and black paint dust and particles of blue paint so minute they could only have been blown onto the body from a distance. Detective Superintendent Marchant now learned that the dirt on Fleming's body was identical.

Identical dirt.

Meant that whoever solved this one would have solved two murders. *Minimum*.

So no more talk of witchcraft or voodoo. Here you had it. Here was a solid connection. Here was something . . .

Like a rabbit's foot or a lucky tooth, here was something to hold on to.

Mary Fleming smoked heavily and drank a lot, mostly whisky and mostly at dives in Notting Hill. The Warwick Castle (whores, ponces, fights), the Kensington Park Hotel (whores, ponces, navvies, fights), the Jazz Club. . .

Mmm, she dug the Jazz Club (it was where Mick Turner found her and flew at her that night she left baby Veronica alone in the flat). But don't worry, we can leave African Peter out of this one because in the early hours of Friday 10 July Scotch Mary was not down the Jazz Club – she was at the gym.

A proper gym?

No, of course not. The establishment at 32a Powis Square merely provided a front for an unlicensed drinking club and the proprietor, a 6′ 3″ Jamaican named Roy Stewart, was less than convincing when he tried to pretend to investigating officers that the dead woman had dropped by his flat at 1am on a friendly visit. He had four convictions for selling liquor without a licence. They'd been watching his place for years.

Stewart also earned money from film and television work (he specialized in walk-on parts as a slave) and that evening one of his friends from the entertainment world was present. Raymond Cattouse, a black extra in his forties, drank and danced with Mary Fleming until about 4am, when he left the club. (He remembered she had talked about carrying a knife for protection.) Fleming left at about 5am, and by 9.30am, when her boyfriend, Pat, left the house, she was in bed at 44 Lancaster Road.

Various friends visited her during the day and at 2pm Gloria Swanson arrived to babysit, and she went shopping. At 2.30pm she was seen in a launderette in All Saints Road, and at 5.20pm she collected a child's dress from Tip Top Cleaners in Portobello Road before calling in at Pete's Cafe. According to Swanson, she returned to the house at 6pm.

Swanson often looked after the children and that day Fleming asked her if she would have her son David for good. 'I told her I could not take him on a permanent basis. She said she was going out that night for a gay time and she felt like getting drunk.' Fleming had arranged for her friend Elizabeth Heywood to call round and, as long as she could find a babysitter, the two of them would go out.

Heywood turned up at 8.30pm, by which time Swanson had left. Fleming was talking to Swanson's boyfriend, Anthony Black, who was looking for her, while the children played on the floor. After Black left, the two women had a long chat, and Fleming mentioned that she wanted to take Veronica to see her father on Friday but couldn't find a babysitter for David. 'I told her if Gloria couldn't look after him she was to bring him to me at 3pm and I would look after him.'

At 10pm she put the children to bed and changed out of the tight black trousers and black and red sweater she had been wearing since the previous night. After washing she put on a pair of lace g-string panties, and then pulled a red suspender belt up over her stretch marks and attached a pair of new dark nylon stockings, completing her underwear with a black padded bra. Over this she put on a greenish-grey cotton blouse and a matching jacket and skirt, light green with a fine check and made from a heavy woollen material. She slipped her feet into a pair of white plastic slingbacks and was finishing off her beehive when a young Irishman walked in, eating fish and chips, whom she addressed as 'William'. He agreed to babysit and the two women left the house at about 10.50pm.

It was too late to go down the pub, so they went to the Wimpy Bar in Portobello Road. They ordered a Wimpy and chips and a cup of coffee each, and they went and sat by the window. 'Terry Dawson,' Heywood recalled, 'was doing the cooking . . .'

Yes, Terry Dawson, former hot dog seller and minor miscreant in the Gwynneth Rees saga, was now managing the Wimpy Bar in Portobello Road. The meals he served the two women that night were memorable for the fact that the burgers were half-raw; returned for further cooking they came back 'just the same'.

Still, at least now the pubs had shut the place was livening up. An Irishman entered and ponced a meal off Mary Fleming; a young blonde was thrown out for causing a disturbance; and Harry Greenwood came in for his supper. He paused at their table and his former housemate reminded him for the last time to come round and collect his things. 'That was the end of the conversation . . . I was impressed by the fact that Mary was looking very smart and well dressed. I was also surprised that she hadn't had a drink, whereas at that time of night she had usually had a few drinks and was noisy.'

The two women left the Wimpy Bar some time between 11pm and 12pm and walked back towards Lancaster Road. En route Fleming pointed out three men walking along Westbourne Park Road and announced, 'There's my old man.' Heywood asked her which one it was and she replied, 'The little one with the curly hair' (presumably Pat).

'They had obviously seen her. She shouted to them by saying, "I want you —" I thought she mentioned a name but I can't remember.'

The little one in the dark suit with the dark curly hair continued walking, but another man came over and spoke briefly with Fleming before rejoining his companions. To Heywood she said, 'I told him to get out today as I was fed up with keeping him and his mates.'

Speaking of which, it was nearly time to earn some money.

Don't forget.

Always work in pairs, girls.

Sound advice from Maurice Osborn and his men, following the murder of Helene Barthelemy. Of course, to the innocent eye Fleming and Heywood *were* a pair: two grafters testing the midnight air, textbook tarts who'd look out for each other, *take down her punter's index number if you get split up* . . .

But the older woman had packed up prostitution back in 1959.

Mary Fleming worked every night alone.

They arrived at her lodgings to find William and the children asleep. Heywood also decided to call it a night and her friend saw her to the door. As she was leaving, a drunken Irishman appeared: Paul, one of Pat's mates, wanting somewhere to doss. But what of Pat himself? She said that she had seen him and he was not coming home that night, and she was worried as he would not have anywhere to sleep. Would Paul go with her to look for him?

Whether he would or he wouldn't, he didn't. The plan was quickly abandoned and instead Paul agreed to babysit (which in practice meant sleeping fully clothed on the bed, next to William) while the breadwinner went to work.

Shortly after leaving the house she stopped for ten minutes and complained to Alan Martin about Irishmen 'living' in her room. She then set off towards Talbot Road, saying she was going to work Queensway, he thought, 'or it could have been the West End'. The time was now 12.20am.

Closing at midnight, the Wimpy Bar in Portobello Road had disgorged among its customers two Greek Cypriots, Michael Zangoura, a waiter at Pete's Cafe, and his companion, George Charalambos, a builder and decorator whose car, a blue and grey Ford Zodiac, was parked in Porchester Gardens, facing Queensway. When Mary Fleming approached them from this direction the two men were seated in the front, while on the rear seat sat Maria 'Lucky' Newman, a young tart who fancied a ride. Fleming stood and talked at the window for some minutes before getting in beside her.

These two knew each other, they worked the same patch. So naturally they talked business.

'She told me that she had done all right that evening and that she would do one more client and then go home. She told me that she had an argument with Pat, her boyfriend, and she seemed anxious to get home to find out whether he was there. I remember I asked her whether she had any rubbers which I could have. She told me she only had two and she couldn't give me any.'

Most of which makes no sense at all. Between leaving Martin at 12.20am and meeting Newman at 12.30am–12.45am she would barely have had time to blow a kiss. So was Mary boasting, needling poor Lucky? Or was the other woman drunk? Blocked? Stoned? Or just a bad listener? It's impossible to square the truth of these alleged remarks with what came before, or later.

While this conversation was taking place two more prostitutes came over to the car and chatted to them, saying that they would be going to the Jazz Club later on. Fleming told them she would see them there if she could. She left the car shortly afterwards and set off towards Queensway.

At about 1.30am two young prostitutes, Mabel ('Pat') Goulding and Pamela De'ak, were window-shopping in Whiteleys department store when from the direction of Westbourne Grove a familiar figure came trooping towards them and remarked, 'Business is rotten. I wish I could get off.' She asked De'ak if she had got off, and Goulding turned round and said, 'She's gone all respectable – she's turned down a fiver already.' Mary Fleming said she wished she could get a fiver.

However, at that moment it looked as if all any of them was likely to get was arrested. 'A man was walking up and down nearby and he was clicking his teeth. Pat told him to piss off but he would not go away.' De'ak described this man as an ordinary working-class client, aged forty-five to fifty, 5′ 10″/11″ and of medium build. (According to Goulding, he was about twenty-seven, 5′ 6″ and wearing spectacles.) 'As he would not go away I said, "Have you lost your cat?" He had a cockney accent and he said, "No, I have not, love." So I said, "If you don't fuck off I will bang you one." He went away.'

De'ak, who, at the age of twenty-two, had entered semi-retirement, told Goulding that she was going home, whereupon Fleming said, 'I'm going to earn some money,' and Goulding said, 'So am I.'

The two friends moved away. Goulding walked off in the direction of Westbourne Grove and De'ak walked back past Fleming, who was now talking to another man who'd been in the vicinity all the time, although 'keeping his distance', she said. This man was aged about thirty-five, 5′ 5″/6″, of medium build, with dark hair parted on the right side and fashioned into a quiff. He was wearing an open-neck white shirt and a greyish suit. He too appeared to be working class.

'They walked away together towards Westbourne Grove down into the direction where Pat had gone. Pat was on her way back and she definitely passed them and that was the last I saw of Mary and I was pleased she had got a client . . .'

At approximately 1.45am.

Where were those two headed?

De'ak assumed that the man had a vehicle parked somewhere as Fleming would no longer venture indoors with clients. She would direct her drivers to various spots – down by the canal off Harrow Road, perhaps – and 'if they wanted to spend a fiver she would take them to the sports ground the other side of Hammersmith by the river'. Smart.

At about 2.45am PC Ferguson of the British Transport Police was patrolling along Bayswater Road towards Marble Arch when he saw the red Volkswagen ahead of him pull into the kerb, just before the junction of Leinster Terrace. The driver, 'a man of Greek appearance', leaned across the passenger seat and spoke to a woman who appeared to be a prostitute. 'I flashed my headlights as the vehicle had stopped directly in my path.' The woman looked up, stopped talking and hurried away, turning into Leinster Terrace. 'As I continued along Bayswater Road and upon passing Leinster Terrace, I glanced into the turning and saw the female walking away along the road. I now recognize this female as Mrs Mary Fleming.'

1.45am. Scotch sober, with the merest hint of raw meat on her breath and looking a good five quid's worth in her matching jacket and tight-fitting skirt, her cotton blouse that buttoned at the back, her new nylons . . .

Nothing she wore that night was ever recovered. Also missing was a black and green tartan handbag, containing a Yale key and national assistance and family allowance books in the name of Mary Turner.

Her bag may also have contained a weapon, for the knife she talked about seems to have existed. (An associate recalled a 'dirty-looking' kitchen knife, about 10″ long, with a wooden handle.) Was she shivved up on the night she disappeared? Did she make it to the brandishing stage?

And then there was the matter of pawn ticket 4282, as issued on 29 June 1964 by A. E. & D. A. Thompson Ltd of 158 Portobello Road to one of their regular customers. (The item pawned was indeed a ladies' wristwatch, as Harry Greenwood remembered, although made of yellow metal as opposed to gold. She received £2 1s 6d.) This ticket failed to surface during a search of her room and police assumed that she kept it with her.

Thompson's staff had strict instructions.

Any individual producing 4282 is to be detained on the premises.

No exit.

No redemption.

Mary Fleming's murderer stole her clothes, shoes and handbag. But did he steal any of her teeth?

Possibly. According to Mick Turner 'there was four teeth missing from her front. I can't remember whether it was the top or bottom denture.' But he belonged to an earlier phase of her history. Gloria Swanson, who knew her for the last year or so of her life, maintained that although Fleming's front teeth were missing she had never had dentures fitted. And no dental plate was recovered, from her mouth or anywhere else. Yet when wee Mary opened wide for Uncle Donald she had a total of twelve teeth missing, ten of them from her upper jaw.

If she had lost them during her lifetime she may well have found chewing difficult, although that Wimpy burger would have posed few problems had it been edible. Anyway, she ate it. The meal so lovingly prepared for her by Terry Dawson on the night of Friday 10 July lay partially digested in the dead woman's stomach. This indicates that she died some time in the early hours of Saturday morning, probably not long after leaving the man in the red Volkswagen. (But not before having sex at least once: the vaginal swab tested positive.) Three days later her murderer dumped her on the garage forecourt of 48 Berrymede Road, where she slumped naked, awaiting discovery. He'd stored her in the same place he'd stored Helene Barthelemy. But where was that?

Enquiries at boatyards, boathouses, houseboats and riverside dwellings on T, V and F Divisions failed to uncover these premises, and so an area of approximately six square miles adjacent to the Thames, from Windmill Road, W5, to Askew Road, W12, was divided into 105 sections. As the paint particles discovered on both bodies were globular – originating from a spray-gun as opposed to a brush – 105 aides to CID were searching primarily for an operation such as a small one-man paint-spraying business. But paint-spraying may take place anywhere an individual chooses to spray paint, which meant searching all lock-up garages, warehouses, outbuildings, workshops and sheds within the designated area. Around 150 premises were visited and numerous samples of dust collected, none of which matched the dust on the bodies.

Hundreds of statements were taken from prostitutes, witnesses and other associates. During all-night observations in the Queensway area officers noted the registration numbers of cars picking up prostitutes, plus time, date, place and name of woman if known, while over at Chiswick all cars frequenting Duke's Meadows had their details recorded.

All night and every night, all over the whoring grounds like a rash, officers armed with wads of pro-formas, watching, waiting for him to strike again.

Would he strike again?

This year?

Next year?

Who knew what made the killer tick?

No one.

No one, that is, apart from Ron Mount at the *News of the World*. 'Open Letter to the Nude Killer from Ron Mount, who has been on his trail' appeared in the newspaper on 19 July 1964:

This is a story that will be read by millions but I am writing it for only one man. And I know he will read it . . . You are a murderer. A multi-murderer. A modern Jack the Ripper who has caused a wave of terror among the street girls of London.

It is certain you have the deaths of two women on your hands. You

may be responsible for four. And there is even a chance that your grim
total of sex crazed killings could be as high as six, which brings you
into line with that other monster – Christie . . .

Which is harmless enough, I suppose, until:

Do you remember how you picked them up and drove them in your
car to a quiet spot? Do you remember strangling them, in exactly the
same way, by grasping the neckline of their dresses and twisting and
tightening until they were still? . . .

   What about the way you stored the bodies for two or three days,
naked, on the floor, waiting for the rigor mortis to take its 48 hours
to pass off and deciding where you were going to dump them?

   Why did you take their clothes? To satisfy another whim of your
sick mind? What about the way you wrenched four front teeth from
Helen Barthelemy's mouth just before or just after you killed her? Was
it to delay identification?

Exactly the same . . . two or three days . . . on the floor . . . four teeth . . .
You what? What's going on here? Were these details supplied by the
Yard? Or by an informant on the trail of a backhander?

   Either way, Ron Mount's rant was a love letter to potential
copycat killers and, in the wake of Kenneth Archibald, false con-
fessors.

   . . . So let me repeat my advice to you once more – give yourself up.

   Ring Det. Supt. Maurice Osborn at Shepherds Bush 1113 and get
it all over. NOW.

Stop drinking, Ron. Bill's in charge of this one.
Bill 'Lucky' Marchant.

He'd failed to find the estate agent (a Geordie, Gloria Swanson
said) who failed to come across. He'd failed to find the failed strangler
of Porchester Gardens. Interrogations, observations, searches – nothing had brought him any closer to catching the killer. He'd failed to
identify fear in a handful of dust.

   He had a longish list of possibles, together with their alibis and con-
firmations, but no real suspect.

Information, misinformation, kept on coming in – a letter suggesting 'Stephen', a transvestite taxi driver who hated prostitutes, as the killer (written by a notorious liar), a warning from an anonymous psychiatrist about a man who possessed plastic moulds of his penis – none of which filled William Marchant with blood.

Still, fingers crossed, any day now . . .

It's been a good many days now.

It's early evening in London W4. I've arrived, and to prove it, I'm here, turning my back on Quinn the builder's yard to gaze upon an empty garage drive.

So this is where she reappeared.

In deep shadow, for the nearest street lighting was forty feet away.

But I see a glow tonight. Someone's home, watching TV.

Ten minutes earlier and a bit further up the road I waited as another resident, an elderly Pole, stood by his front gate and cast his mind back. 1964? The year he and his wife moved here. The body, yes. There was a lot of fuss. Prostitute, wasn't she? No clothes! 'There must be a reason. Maybe the girl give him a disease. Revenge, maybe?'

Maybe. Or maybe not. After all, we're talking about Mary Fleming here, not Mary Kelly. That whore had her breasts cut off, her face hacked to a pulp, and her uterus and kidneys removed. But whoever killed Fleming felt no compulsion to butcher her. In fact the condition of the body – a couple of bruises and some marks on the throat, to which the victim's own scrabbling fingers possibly contributed – rather suggests a thwarted desire to simply spirit her away . . .

Wait – there it goes again. That's a curtain twitching, two doors up.

I'd better not stand here much longer. There's a story I'd like to verify – a story that this house was exorcized – but I shan't ring the bell, much as I'd like to. Three nights ago it was Hallowe'en. Why frighten people?

As I walk back up Berrymede Road towards Acton Lane, ringing the bell in my imagination, I recall with a shock the terracotta tiles, white painted brickwork and lintels in Wedgwood blue.

Who'd be seen dead outside a house like that?

*

November 1964.

Late November. Remember?

Short days, long nights.

Short arms, deep pockets.

Which might be a neat line to use down the pub but it won't work at home, not this year.

Not when every brat in England wants a Dalek suit for Christmas.

£8 12s 6d.

Go on, cough up. It's only money. It's not the end of the world, is it? It's just the way kids are.

Some of them want to exterminate.

Others make love in the park.

The car park, in Hornton Street, Kensington — behind the civil defence centre (which is to say, behind the library).

Through its unlocked gates during hours of darkness lovers enter, indulge and depart — and who is any the wiser?

Dennis Sutton, assistant civil defence officer, for one. Over the past few weeks he has noticed a deplorable increase in the litter of the gutter: used condoms, empty packets, soiled tissues . . .

Why can't boys and girls enjoy themselves at home?

Because there's nowhere —

Why don't they have a Cydrax and watch *Z Cars*?

Because homes are places to stay out of.

Now find it.

Find the lid.

The dustbin lid, that is.

The civil defence area control is situated at the rear of the car park. At the side of the entrance to the area control runs a pipe carrying a radio aerial into the building, and to protect this pipe against rain it is covered by a dustbin lid, which lid is currently missing.

Find the lid.

It'll be round the back here somewhere.

Here it is, in the corner. What's it doing over here?

Lift the lid.

A face?

A face, alive with maggots, which have devoured the eyes and nose and some of the soft tissue, rendering the features unrecognizable.

Dennis Sutton holds his dustbin lid aloft like a shield against what it's too late not to see.

He's out there in history now.

Found the lady.

On 22 July 1963 the trial of Dr Stephen Ward began in No. 1 Court at the Old Bailey. Ward, an osteopath, faced six charges: four of living on immoral earnings, one of procuring a girl under twenty-one to have sexual intercourse, and one of attempting to procure another underage girl. On 31 July the jury found the defendant guilty on two counts of living on immoral earnings, but by this time he had swallowed an overdose of barbiturates and was lying in a coma in St Stephen's Hospital, Fulham. He died in hospital on 3 August.

It was an odd trial. The police could produce no evidence to support any of the six charges and so they had coerced certain witnesses into giving false testimony against the defendant. One of these witnesses was Vickie Barrett, a prostitute (her real name was Janet Barker).

Barrett, a small pale blonde, told the court that Ward's Jaguar had picked her up in Oxford Street late one night that year, whereupon she immediately began to work for him. Soon she was visiting his flat two or three times a week to beat various men with a horsewhip and cane. How was she dressed when she performed these services? In underwear and high heels. And what would be the normal payment for such services? £1 a stroke (£5 for intercourse). But the money had been paid to Dr Ward, and he'd kept it all.

This seemed unfair. However, on day five of the trial a surprise witness materialized to cast doubt on Vickie Barrett's story. Ludovic Kennedy, who was present throughout the trial, watched as 'a small bird-like woman with a pale face and a fringe teetered down the court and into the witness box'. Her name was Frances Brown, and she gave evidence that she had known Barrett since January of that year and had been soliciting with her when she was picked up in Oxford Street by Ward. They both went back to his flat, where Barrett had intercourse with him while she watched. She was soliciting regularly with Barrett at that time and they only visited Ward's flat twice. On the second occasion they just drank coffee.

Frances Brown said that she had come to court because she had read the evidence of Vickie Barrett in the newspapers; she wished to speak in defence of Stephen Ward. She was probably sincere, and yet equally she may have felt that a cameo in the Profumo scandal was an opportunity not to be missed, a chance to hit the headlines and perhaps upgrade herself from street-girl to courtesan, exchanging mangy two-quid punters for wealthy, generous men of the world.

It was later reported that Brown, armed with flowers, had turned up at the hospital where Ward lay dying, only to be turned away. If this is true, what was her motive? Sympathy (for a man she'd met twice)? Or eagerness to get in on the act?

Probably a combination of the two. In so far as it mattered, of course. The British public soon forgot about Frances Brown and her part in the Stephen Ward affair, if her name had ever registered with them at all.

Francis Brown, a railway goods loader, married Helen McGowan, a tailor's machinist, in Glasgow in October 1942. Their daughter Frances was born there four months later on 3 January 1943.

In February 1954 at Glasgow Central Police Juvenile Court she was found guilty of theft by finding and placed on probation for two years. She left school at the age of fifteen, and worked for brief periods in various shops in the city. She wouldn't settle. 'I had a terrible time of it with her,' her mother recalled. 'She was staying out all night and I'd no idea where she was. I reported it to the police.'

In November 1958 she

made her second appearance in juvenile court. She was dealt with as a 'care and protection' case and sent to an approved school, Dr Guthrie's, in Edinburgh. She remained there until June 1960, when she was released on licence to her parents. Soon she was staying out late again and her licence was revoked. She was sent back to Dr Guthrie's at the end of August, but by this time a local man had got her pregnant (and promptly disappeared). The child, Helen, was born in April 1961.

Frances Brown was back at the approved school before the end of the month. In July the authorities finally allowed her home, where her mother continued to take care of the child. Shortly afterwards Brown left for London, unencumbered.

She seems to have taken to the streets almost immediately she arrived, for the date of her first conviction for soliciting was 21 October 1961. Many more followed. By the time she met Paul Quinn around the summer of 1962 she had a history. They both had.

Paul Quinn, a scaffolder, was born in Dublin in 1936 and had moved to England at the age of eighteen. He had numerous convictions for offences such as shopbreaking and theft and had served time in prison. He met Brown through his estranged wife, Maureen, also a Scot, who had recently moved into the same address as Brown at Westbourne Park Road. The two women became friends and were drinking in the Kensington Park Hotel one night when Quinn, on his way out, stopped to talk to them. His wife introduced him to his future girlfriend.

Quinn had lodgings in Hammersmith but soon the two of them were living together in Shepherd's Bush, and Frances Brown began to call herself 'Frances Quinn'. In September 1962, pregnant again, she appeared at Glasgow Sheriff Summary Court, where she was put on probation for two years for child neglect. She gave birth to her second baby prematurely at Queen Charlotte's Hospital, W6, in March 1963. It was a boy and she christened him Paul. After the birth she became depressed and hysterical and discharged herself from hospital the next day. (Paul stayed and was placed in the care of the authorities at Smethwick a week or so later.)

On 23 May she entered Springfield mental hospital. She wanted to leave almost immediately but was placed on a holding order for seventy-two hours under Section 30 of the Mental Heath Act. The next day she was made a compulsory patient under Section 25 of the Act, authorizing her detention for up to twenty-eight days. She told staff that she had attempted suicide by overdose during her pregnancy and by gassing after the birth. She was prescribed tranquillizers and sleeping tablets and was discharged on 5 June. (A couple of months later she reportedly travelled to St Stephen's Hospital to visit the suicide Ward, the smell of her own blood still strong in her nostrils, perhaps.)

After she left hospital Brown returned to Paul Quinn, and continued to live with him until 12 November 1963, when, at Marylebone Magistrates' Court, she was fined £10 or one month's imprisonment for attempting to steal a car. From Holloway prison she wrote to Quinn in Maidstone, where he was now working, and he paid the fine. But on her release she was rearrested and taken to Glasgow, where, on 9 December, she was sentenced to three months' imprisonment for child neglect.

Quinn followed her to Glasgow, and awaited her release. She came out in February 1964, and shortly afterwards the couple moved in with her parents.

On a previous visit Frances Brown had announced herself as Mrs Quinn. Now her mother had an opportunity to inspect the lucky man. Black curly hair, blue eyes, three or four false front teeth, cauliflower ears, a boxer's nose and tattoos on his arms and chest ('I know that one of them is a nude woman'). He told her that he was adopted, and that when he found out he ran away. He said he could never go back to Ireland 'and from that I took it that he had been in some kind of trouble'.

Helen Brown seems to have been aware – or as aware as she wished to be – that her daughter was a prostitute. She recognized her photograph in a newspaper account of the Ward trial. 'When she came to visit me I asked her about this and she said that it wasn't her and was quite indignant about it all. She said it was a girl who was quite like her and that they had often been mistaken for sisters.'

Brown signed over the custody of her daughter Helen to her parents, who had looked after the girl since birth. But what of her second child, baby Paul? In July she received a letter from Smethwick County Council to inform her that he was being adopted.

Problem solved – but for the fact that neither partner would sign the custody papers. Quinn refused because he was Catholic and the child would be brought up Church of Scotland. Brown's reasons are hard to divine. Perhaps she was just feeling cussed. But then again perhaps she was feeling a bit – what's the word? – motherly, in the wake of yet another happy event.

When Frank was born in April 1964 the couple moved out of the Browns' house in the Gallowgate but remained in Glasgow for a few more months. They returned to London in August, taking the baby with them.

The following month her parents received a letter, headed with her new address: 16a Southerton Road, W6. 'Well here I am writing to let you know that Paul and I have a great flat, 1 kitchen, 1 living room, 1 bedroom, 1 big lobby and it has a garden back and front . . .' What else was new? 'Paul got a job back with Steven & Carters. He works late nearly every night and he is always tired. Oh, Mammy we have a television and hope to get a radiogram this week.' The baby was teething and cried all the time; Paul sent his love to everyone. She signed the letter 'Frances and Paul' and closed with twenty-six kisses from 'Frankie Jnr'.

About two weeks later a colour postcard of Piccadilly Circus arrived.

Dear Mom
I received your letter ok Paul
myself & Baby are doing fine and I hope all
is the same at home
Lots of love
Frances

Helen Brown found this card a bit of a puzzle. 'Although it's signed "Frances" I don't think it's her writing. You see, when she writes to me she never puts "Scotland" on her letter and the card has "Scotland" on it.'

The postmark read: 'Hammersmith – 1 Oct 1964'. It was the month Frances Brown disappeared.

In common with Mary Fleming, Frances Brown drank at the KPH and the Warwick Castle, but she also frequented the Shepherd's Bush Hotel, Shepherd's Bush Green, and it was there, on the night of 21 October, that she and Paul Quinn made the acquaintance of a new drab in town.

'Blonde' Beryl Mahood was born Beryl Dickson in Portadown, County Armagh, in 1943. Pregnant at sixteen, she married the father, Charles Mahood, but separated from him six months later. He gained custody of their son, Stephen, and she left Ireland in 1961 and moved to Lancashire. In Blackburn she was twice convicted for larceny and in Accrington in the summer of 1964 she received a conditional discharge for fraud. That summer she met Jacqueline Atherton, eighteen and unemployed, and the two of them hitchhiked to Slough. Shortly afterwards they became homeless, a problem they solved by sleeping around.

The two girls travelled to London in the evenings, and began to use the Shepherd's Bush Hotel (possibly, in Mahood's case, for soliciting purposes). That night, shortly before closing time, they got into conversation with Brown and Quinn and Quinn's Irish friend William Kearney, and mentioned that they had nowhere to live. Brown invited them to stay with her and Quinn and the baby (who appears to have been left alone in the flat). Everyone drank up. The night was about to begin.

Quinn, Atherton and Kearney (who also had no home to go to) set off for Southerton Road while Frances Brown and her new friend went hustling in Holland Park Avenue. They worked as a pair, masturbating a motorist in his car. 'He dropped us off near a hot dog stall where Frances and I had two hot dogs.' Which must have given them an appetite, because they masturbated another motorist in his car. This man dropped them off outside the Jazz Club in Westbourne Park Road. Blonde Beryl had never been there before and didn't like it much, so they took a taxi to Southerton Road. They'd made about £9. Plus extras.

Back at the flat Paul Quinn, Jacqueline Atherton and William Kearney drank beer and played records. Quinn went to bed with Atherton while Kearney concentrated on getting drunk. In the early hours of Thursday 22 October the girls returned with two strangers' wallets. Brown produced a wallet which, upon examination, contained the first punter's driving licence, two crossed cheques and two tickets for the London Palladium, while Mahood's contained the second man's driving licence in the name of Taylor. Quinn took the first wallet and its contents, Kearney the second.

More records, more drink. At about 3am Brown changed out of her work-clothes into a jumper and jeans and left the flat with Atherton, the two of them taking a taxi to the Jazz Club. There they met two Irishmen: Peter Brady, a doorman and his friend 'Hoggy', a painter. All four left the club and Brady drove them to his basement room at 6 St Lawrence Terrace. He went to bed with Brown and Hoggy had Atherton on the couch while a stuffed fox looked on.

Having gone the whole hog, Hoggy left and Atherton decided to return to Southerton Road. Brown was staying, but she got out of bed to see her to the front gate and tell her the address.

However, when Brown arrived home a few hours later there was no sign of her. Not that anyone worried unduly; after all, she'd either got lost or got lucky. Life went on, meaning Paul Quinn went to work and Frances Brown and Beryl Mahood, flush from the night before, made for the shops.

In C&A at Marble Arch Brown left a deposit of two guineas on a green two-piece suit with a dark fur collar, and told the assistant that she would call back later in the day to pay the outstanding six guineas. The two women crossed over the road to Dolcis, where Brown bought a pair of black suede high-heeled shoes; in Oxford Street she bought a blue underskirt, a blue bra and a pair of black and pink panties. They bought a skirt and blouse for Jacqueline Atherton and identical brown plastic bracelets for themselves.

The girls returned to the flat at about lunchtime and woke up William Kearney, who was supposed to be minding the baby. At about 2pm a young black man called to see Brown (for what reason is unknown, although Kearney suspected a business connection). He stayed and chatted, and an hour later a friend, Vera Lynch, also known as 'Dublin Jackie', turned up with her friend Cecilia and her baby. Shortly afterwards Jacqueline Atherton appeared and told the story of how she got lost. (She'd taken a taxi to West Hampstead by mistake and wandered around for a while, eventually sleeping at a police station.)

By 5pm her visitors had left, and Brown awaited Paul Quinn's return from work. She told the others that Thursday was his payday and that she would go with him to C&A and he would buy her the suit. Quinn came home just after 6pm and, according to Kearney, 'did his nut. He told her to get it herself by taxi but she would not go without him.' In the end he gave in and stomped off with her in his big yellow TUF boots to spend some money. Quinn recalled that on this occasion he also paid out for a blue and white check petticoat, a white linen blouse and a light blue plastic handbag and blue gloves to match. Happy days.

Back at the flat Beryl Mahood and Jacqueline Atherton began to get ready for a night out. William Kearney looked after the baby. (Quinn, he said, had asked him to stay 'in case these two girls nicked anything'.) Some time around 8pm the women set off for the Shepherd's Bush Hotel, having left a message with the Irishman that they would meet Frances in the KPH later.

The couple returned presently, and Quinn went with Kearney to the Cambridge Arms in Glenthorne Road. At about 9pm Brown entered, wearing the new outfit which she was eager to show off to her friends. Was Paul coming with her to the KPH? No, he wasn't. 'I wouldn't go because I was still in my working clothes. I gave her a couple of quid and she went away on her own.'

But before she left she had something else off him. 'She borrowed a small gold ring I was wearing and put it on the ring finger of the left hand. It was a small gold shank with two sapphires or imitation sapphires with a little pearl in the centre. It was worth about £5.'

God rot you, my sweet . . .

Anyway, your man aside, Thursday night Frances Brown had a full house at the Kensington Park Hotel. Beryl Mahood and Jackie Atherton turned up, accompanied by Dublin Jackie, who cast a cool eye over the Scotch goods on display. ('She definitely had a blonde streak in her hair and it had not come out too well.') Peter Brady was there, drinking with an imposing figure who later described himself to police as a company director and amateur wrestler. Even Maureen Quinn – a bit icy these days – was there, somewhere. 'It was about 10.50pm . . . She was with a blonde girl. Frances was wearing a new dark green suit with a dark collar. I didn't speak to her. As she left with the blonde girl Frances called out, "Come on, Frankie, are you coming?"'

He had no choice. At closing time Francis 'Blond Frankie' Brennan, an Irish painter drunk out of his head, found himself being steered to the Jazz Club by Blonde Beryl, in company with Scotch Frances and another man, a mate, known only as 'Belfast Stan'. But when he reached the gate he confessed he was too far gone to go in.

So the two prostitutes made their descent without him, without Stan, and without Atherton either. (She'd had a row with them in the pub earlier because she refused to go hustling, and instead went home with Vera Lynch to her flat in Uxbridge Road.) But soon they were out on the pavement again, waiting for business. A motorist picked them up but they couldn't agree on a price, so he dropped them in the Bayswater Road, where they got into another car and masturbated the driver for a fiver, after which he drove them back to the Jazz Club.

By midnight they were inside again and chatting to James Corrigan, a carpenter, and his drinking pal, an interior decorator named Eamonn Hearty. They left with the two men and spent the night at Hearty's flat in Colville Terrace. Hearty went to bed with Brown while Corrigan, who'd had her before, explored the new mystery for a while, leaving at 5am to return to his girlfriend, Vickie Barrett.

Frances Brown and Beryl Mahood left Eamonn Hearty's flat at about 9am on Friday 23 October. Instead of returning to Southerton Road, they went to Pete's Cafe and killed a couple of hours eating sandwiches and talking to customers. Next stop was Woolworths in nearby Portobello Road and then it was opening time, so they went to the Warwick Castle for a drink. Belfast Stan came in and joined them.

Upon leaving the pub all three visited the Imperial Playhouse in Portobello Road and spent the rest of the afternoon watching *Destry*. Correction: 'Stan only stayed in the pictures a short while.' The other two came out at about 5pm. 'We came out and had a wash and brush up in a ladies' toilet.' Pete's next, then the Warwick. All night.

Among the faces in the pub that Friday evening were Ethel Courtney, and her sons William and Ronald. William chatted up Blonde Beryl for a while. Later on a young black man (possibly the same man who visited Brown's flat) entered the pub. He too chatted up Blonde Beryl and gave her a yellow metal locket and chain. (Ronald Courtney recalled that the girls 'were kidding me it was 22 carat gold, but it was really junk'.) She put it on. 'I was wearing a silver chain and cross which I gave to Frances and she hung this round her neck.'

Belfast Stan arrived and asked to see her outside. He wanted her to leave Brown in the pub and come with him. She refused, but promised to meet him at the Barbechick, a restaurant in Westbourne Park Road, at 1am. He left and she went back inside.

'It was then nearly closing time. I went to the bar to try and get a quarter-bottle of whisky but was told they didn't have any. The coloured man said he could get one. He left the pub and returned soon afterwards with the whisky, which Frances put in her handbag.'

She often went hustling with whisky in her handbag.

Good stuff, whisky.

Warms the cockles of your heart, and helps take your mind off the winkles to come —

Throws a mist over your eyes while you wait, night after night, for the big man to reveal himself, the man who

Will show you something different from the pavement at evening rising to meet you, who

Will not be repelled by a *small gold ring I was wearing* or a *silver chain and* —

Amulets?

Boo . . . ze.

Look out!

Here he comes!

Start slurring your prayers, girl.

Get ready.

Portobello Road.

Friday 23 October 1964.

11pm (or thereabouts).

The weekend starts here.

But will you look at her?

She's still wearing last night's finery.

She's wearing the green two-piece suit with the dark fur collar; a blue high-neck blouse with blue lace trimmings over her new blue and white check petticoat, blue bra and black and pink panties; and dark stockings with her new black suede shoes with the heels. She's also wearing blue gloves and carrying a black plastic handbag.

Her companion is wearing a grey/black mixture two-piece suit (possibly new), a red corduroy blouse and black suede shoes and carrying a black leather handbag.

Both women may also be wearing their identical 4s 6d plastic bracelets (two small balls depend from each).

What state are these toms in?

Well, if we disregard their lunchtime session, then they've been drinking for roughly five hours.

But they should be all right, so long as they stick together.

Friday night.

11pm.

Last orders inside.

First punters outside.

Upon leaving the Warwick Castle Frances Brown — *hair dark, eyes grey, left hand, middle finger deformed, right forearm and part of right hand badly scarred* — and Beryl Mahood — *well built, Liverpool/Irish accent, small sickle-shaped scar at right side of nose* — walk towards two men in separate cars waiting at the traffic lights at the junction of Portobello Road and Westbourne Park Road. As they approach, the first man waves to them to walk round the corner into Portobello Road. The men then overtake them and park nearby in a small mews, Hayden's Place.

'When Frances and I got into the alley the two men were just getting out of the cars and were walking back towards us. I was surprised at first as I had thought only one of them wanted to do business. I queried this with the smaller one and he said, "It's all right, we're both mates."'

Brown's suggestion is that the two of them should travel in one car and lead the other to a quiet spot near Chiswick Green, but the smaller man, who is the first man, persuades the girls to split up. 'I know the smaller man did ask us our names and he mentioned his and his mate's first name, but I cannot remember what they were.'

The first man is about 5′ 8″ tall and aged between thirty and thirty-five. He has dark brown hair and a full face with a clear complexion. He is wearing a white shirt beneath a light tan suede jacket with a white sheepskin or lambswool collar. 'His speech was rougher than my client and he seemed to do all the talking.' He talks Frances Brown into getting into his car, a darkish grey Ford Zephyr or Zodiac ('I don't know the index number or anything else about it'), and they're off.

Beryl Mahood gets into a fairly new light grey car with a bench front seat and a gear change on the driving column. ('I can't remember anything else about it.') Her man is about 5′ 10″ tall, of medium build, and aged between thirty and thirty-two. He has thinning light brown hair and a roundish face. He is well spoken with a London accent and he chats away as they follow the first man's car.

But what does he say?

'I know he dated me for the following Wednesday night in the Warwick Castle. He seemed to know the pub and I'm certain he and his mate had been drinking in a pub further down Lancaster Road. He must have known the area as he asked me if I only drank in the Warwick Castle.' Not unusually, her client tells her nothing about himself.

And then they lose the first car in traffic at a point just east of Shepherd's Bush Green. He turns his car round to look for it yet doesn't seem too worried. 'When we lost Frances and her bloke, the man I was with said something like, "It doesn't matter. He knows where to find me at the flat."' They have intercourse in a nearby car park – probably Barker's car park in Young Street – after which he drops her outside the Jazz Club and drives off towards Hammersmith.

The two women have only known each other for two nights, yet they already have an arrangement to meet outside the Jazz Club should they split up while on business.

Only Frances Brown isn't outside the Jazz Club. She isn't inside the Jazz Club either, and no one has seen her.

Blonde Beryl takes a taxi to the Barbechick. No sign of Belfast Stan. Brown knows about her arrangement to meet him. Did she come here instead? She describes her to the waitress, but the waitress can't help.

She takes a taxi back to the Jazz Club. It's Saturday now. Isn't it about time for a little light relief?

'I didn't go inside just then as I found a client nearby. I went with him in a side street in his car. I got £3 from him for masturbation. It was a red car – he was fairly old.'

She's just entered the club when someone tells her there's an Irishman waiting to see her outside.

It's Paul Quinn and he wants to know what's going on. Why didn't they come back last night? Where's Frances?

She explains what's happened and asks if she can go back to the flat later on in the morning 'and I would bring Frances with me when I found her'. She gives him 10s to get a taxi home.

She goes back inside and dances for a while, and sits and talks to the black man who gave her the locket in the pub. He wants her to come to his place. When she refuses he asks her for his locket back and she gives it to him.

'The little cunt hasn't come home,' Paul Quinn remarked to an acquaintance that weekend. And him with a kid to think about and pubs and work to go to! Luckily Blonde Beryl was staying on at the flat, sleeping with Paul and minding Frank when she felt like it.

Cosy? You bet, and yet nothing in west London lasts for ever. About a week later they were in the KPH when Quinn spotted his wife, Maureen, drinking on her own. He went over and explained to her what had happened and asked her to come back to him. She said she'd think about it, and left the pub. Some time around midnight she walked out on the Ghanaian with whom she was living and headed for her husband's flat. 'The blonde was there with him. He turned her out and I stayed with him at the address for about a week.' They had a row and she went back to her black man.

At 2pm on Saturday 31 October Paul Quinn entered Hammersmith police station with the baby in his arms and spoke to WPS Elizabeth Neale. He told her that the child's mother, Miss Frances Brown, who had lived with him for the past two years, left their address on Thursday 22 October and had not returned. He did not wish to report her missing as during their relationship she had frequently left him for periods of up to several weeks. According to Neale, 'Mr Quinn appeared completely at ease and he did not express any concern regarding the well-being or whereabouts of Brown. His only concern appeared to be for the child.' He had been caring for Frank since 22 October but could no longer do so as he would lose his job if he did not return to work. Moreover, the baby, having been conceived during one of the mother's absences, wasn't his. 'He emphatically denied being the child's father but stated that he had taken her back and made a home for her and the baby because he thought that with the added responsibility she would settle down.'

Was he telling the truth? Or was this just a desperate attempt to off-load? Anyway, the process began. WPS Neale examined the baby, who, suprisingly, 'appeared to be happy, healthy and well cared for', and referred Quinn to the local child welfare office on Holland Park Avenue.

On Monday morning he took the baby there and recounted his tale to a Joan Halfacree, talking her through his outgoings, such as rent and hire purchase commitments. He repeated his assertion that the child, although registered in the name of Quinn, was not his and said that Brown did not want the responsibility of the boy, that she was lazy and would not care for him. 'Quinn said that when Frances came back after a few days away he belted her. He said he would do so again if he had the chance.'

The mighty Quinn.

Why did everybody call him 'Peppy'?

I think you know very well why.

He was all hearts, he was frothing at the mouth the night he bumped into Maureen walking along Blenheim Crescent and grabbed her round the throat, saying, 'You'll hit the headlines!' Only when two policemen appeared did he release her. 'I told the policemen I was married to Paul and didn't want to charge him They let him go and I went away in a taxi.'

Maureen Quinn had a lucky escape; Frances Brown somehow got stuck with him. Every so often she disappeared, returned, took her punishment. In 1963, depressed and hysterical, she is believed to have tried another form of escape: suicide. 'She said she was very upset in her relationship with Mr Quinn,' remarked the doctor who treated her at this time, 'but he would never leave her alone, he was constantly around her. She had apparently been beaten up some time in May and this may have precipitated the crisis.'

DAILY EXPRESS

No. 20,060   FRIDAY NOVEMBER 27 1964   Weather: Sunny spells, cooler   Price 4d.

MURDERED: WARD CASE GIRL

Detectives quiz vice trial witnesses

By PERCY HOSKINS

DETECTIVES on a murder hunt were detailed last night to question people in the Stephen Ward and Christine Keeler cases.

For a tattooed girl found naked and dead in Kensington has been identified as a witness in the Ward vice trial of 1963.

Scotland Yard wants to know if other witnesses had seen her recently.

It also issued a general appeal, saying the girl was known to frequent the Kensington-Bayswater areas of Queensway, Moscow Road, and Campden Hill Road.

NAMES

Margaret McGowan was the name the police finally settled for this prostitute found on a rubbish dump near busy Kensington High Street on Wednesday.

But she had used many aliases, among them Frances Brown, which she gave in the Old Bailey witness-box at the trial of Dr. Stephen Ward.

She was called by the defence to refute evidence given by a girl named Vickie Barrett, who claimed she whipped men in Ward's flat.

Frances Brown said she and Vickie Barrett earned £9 to £15 a night soliciting.

When Ward lay dying in St. Stephen's Hospital, Fulham, from an overdose of drugs, Frances Brown called there with flowers. She was not allowed to see Ward.

In the year that followed she often talked about him and the "society vice web."

She had addresses in Kentish Town, Kensington, Hammersmith, and Paddington. She must have known prostitutes like Gwynneth Rees, Hannah Tallford, Irene Lockwood, Helen Barthelemy, and Mary Fleming.

And so, too, she must have known fear as one by one, at intervals of two to three months, these girls were found murdered.

MANIAC

The regularity suggested a maniac at work. The difference, when Margaret McGowan's turn came, was that she was hidden whereas the others were left openly.

She was last seen alive for certain two months ago in Shepherd's Bush, but it is possible that she has been dead only a few weeks.

Hence the police appeal and the search for people in the Ward and Keeler cases.

Detective Chief Superintendent Jack Manning and Detective Superintendent Bill Marchant are directing the inquiries, centred last night on Shepherd's Bush and Kensington.

Margaret McGowan, or Frances Brown—or Frances Quinn or Anne Sutherland or Susan Edwards—came from Glasgow. She was identified by tattooed flowers on her left arm.

She was 22 years old.

TRIAL WITNESS LAST YEAR—PICTURE BY EXPRESS CAMERAMAN RONALD GERELLI

Nude murder victim: Tattooed Margaret McGowan who used name Frances Brown at Ward trial

KENSINGTON BOROUGH LIBRARY

HORNTON ST.

CAR PARK

BODY FOUND HERE

NOTTING HILL GATE

Kensington

HOLLAND PARK

Gardens

TO HYDE PARK CORNER.

ST. KENSINGTON RD.

STATION

KENSINGTON

NUDE BODY FOUND HERE

Shadows amid the glare of Kensington's lights. The scene last night

Springfield, tranquillizers, back to Quinn. (Could it be that her decision to appear at Stephen Ward's trial – to briefly revisit a world where hankies might be glimpsed erect in breast pockets instead of all balled-up and salty in the kerb – represented a final bid for freedom?) Maybe she and the Irishman deserved, used, loved each other, but we can smell her fear of him on that Friday night she spent drinking with Beryl Mahood at the Warwick Castle. The reason they were drinking at the Warwick Castle and not at the KPH was that, having failed to return home the previous night, she was frightened of bumping into the man she lived with.

And now she'd cleared off and left him holding the baby – but not for long. Thanks to Joan Halfacree, Frank was soon in the hands of a foster mother in Bushey. Frank's cot and pushchair were soon in the hands of Quinn's Italian landlord, who accepted them as part payment for damage caused to his premises by some recent rowdy parties. Quinn had received notice to quit, and on 9 November he left Southerton Road.

So even if Frances Brown came back now she'd have nowhere to come back to. But he seems to have understood that she wouldn't be returning to him, that it was over. He'd already given her clothes away to Vera Lynch and told her to square it up with Frances if she saw her. He left London to work on a building site in Maidstone.

Later that month he handed in his notice. At lunchtime on Friday 27 November, his last day on the job, he and his workmates went for a drink at the White Horse at Headcorn. The conversation got round to Christine Keeler and other players in the drama of Stephen Ward, and somebody mentioned that another young prostitute had been found murdered in London. Quinn said, 'Yes, it's a woman of about forty-two, isn't it?'

No.

The landlord showed him the front page of that day's *Daily Express*.

'Weather: Sunny spells, cooler . . . MURDERED: WARD CASE GIRL . . . found naked and dead . . . maniac at work . . .'

The little cunt hasn't come home.

He stared at a photograph of a young woman with a tattooed arm lighting a cigarette, taken outside the Old Bailey during the trial of Stephen Ward. He said that he'd lived with this woman – he produced his own photograph of her – and that she had a child of two and a half which he said was his. He would go to London that day to see the police, and then he would go to see her family.

And then he bought a half bottle of whisky.

The first thing to do was get drunk.

Dennis Sutton was the assistant civil defence officer at the civil defence headquarters situated in the basement of Kensington Central Library, Phillimore Walk, just off Kensington High Street. Behind the library was a public car park, and at the rear of this car park was the civil defence control, a concrete building of which only the entrance and part of the roof stood above ground level. Behind this centre, at approximately 1.30pm on Wednesday 25 November 1964, Sutton found something he was looking for – and something he wasn't. In a corner formed by the rear structure of the entrance to the centre and the roof of the staircase leading down into the building he reclaimed his missing dustbin lid, and in so doing discovered the badly decomposed body of Frances Brown.

She was naked and lying on her back. The dustbin lid covered the top half of her body down to her breasts; the rest of her was covered by debris such as wood, concrete, leaves and dead plants, all of which appeared to have been plucked from the vicinity. Her head was twisted to the right and infested, as was the rest of her body, with maggots. Her legs were together and extended along the side of one wall. Her right arm lay across the abdomen palm downwards; her left arm extended downwards with the fingers touching the left hip. Her scalp later fell away with gentle handling.

Donald Teare's post-mortem examination took place at Hammersmith mortuary at 5pm that afternoon. The body measured 5' 1", its estimated weight 6½–7 stone. The brain was very decomposed and there was half a pint of bloodstained fluid of decomposition in the chest.

Some dense adhesions over the apex of the right lung represented old healed tuberculosis scars. A single stone in the gall bladder was attributable to bad diet and dehydration caused by heavy drinking. The kidneys bore some coarse scars which Teare believed were due to pyelonephritis, a kidney infection with a number of possible causes, among them venereal disease. (Vera Lynch recalled an incident in the Shepherd's Bush Hotel in which a woman walked in and scratched

Brown's face. 'I think this was over Frances having VD and giving it to the woman's husband.')

The skin of the neck and larynx were removed, placed in methylated spirits and examined five days later. About 1½″ below the point of the chin a series of pigmented marks had developed; these covered an area approximately 3″ × 2″ and were believed to be small haemorrhages and abrasions, indicative of an asphyxial death. Some of the marks formed a linear pattern; these were up to ⅛″ in diameter and concentrated around the larynx. The pathologist's verdict was 'Asphyxia due to pressure on the neck.'

As with Barthelemy and Fleming, the abrasions on the throat were possibly caused by the victim's fingernails, the linear marks suggestive of some form of light ligature. Examination of the larynx revealed one petechial haemorrhage, yet no fractures. In other words this was a cool professional job in which the killer exerted just the right amount of pressure: no thumbs on the windpipe, no fits. Frances Brown may not even have realized her assailant was trying to kill her. After all, she was well-used to brutal treatment and had doubtless mentally prepared herself for her next beating from Quinn. It's possible that she simply passed out, so keeping resistance to a minimum.

A linear pressure mark 5″ long and on the left side of the abdomen probably represented a blanched area of hypostasis, indicating that the body had been stripped after death and had then lain on its back for some time. Examination of dirt samples taken from the body revealed close similarities with the dirt found on the bodies of Barthelemy and Fleming. Once again the dirt contained paint globules, mainly black, red and white, with some turquoise.

There was evidence of neither sexual injury nor intercourse. Her lower jaw was missing three teeth, yet how and when they disappeared could not be determined. Anyway, the police had a more pressing concern, for her eyes, nose and half of her face were missing as well, a state of affairs which precluded conventional identification of the body.

In fact the question of her identity appears to have caused some confusion at the outset of the investigation. Who was she? Frances Brown or Margaret McGowan? Everyone who knew her knew her as Frances, and yet the press named her 'Margaret McGowan', which may have been the final alias on her charge sheet. (A special notice in the *Police Gazette* also misidentified her as Margaret McGowan, and listed her aliases as Frances Brown, Frances Quinn, Nuala Rowlands, Donna Sutherland, Anne Sutherland and Susan Edwards.)

Brown's body was initially identified by fingerprints, and within twenty-four hours of discovery her parents were contacted and interviewed by Glasgow police who, on 5 December, showed them a photograph of the tattoo on the dead woman's left forearm. This consisted of 'Helen' above three sprays of flowers and leaves, beneath which were 'Mum and Dad' and a scroll.

But Mum and Dad would not make a formal identification. Her father, Francis, recalled a tattoo on his daughter's left arm but could remember nothing of its design, save one word: 'Elvis'. Her mother told police that Frances acquired a tattoo on her left arm while staying at Dr Guthrie's: it was either 'Elsie' or 'Elvis', she couldn't be sure. Anyway, when Frances had visited her that year, 'I noticed that the tattoo was different and that "Elsie" or "Elvis" had been covered over and that "Mum and Dad" and "Helen" and leaves had been put over it.' And this masterpiece was exactly the same – only different. 'From what I remember of the tattoo, "Mum and Dad" was at the top and "Helen" was at the bottom of the arm. The rest of the design looks the same, except for the wee scroll bit at the bottom of the arm under "Mum and Dad". I don't remember this at all.'

It's hardly surprising that Brown's mother chose to reject the evidence. After all, the girl had caused her parents nothing but trouble since the day she was born. (She was probably causing trouble before she was born. Francis and Helen had to marry in a hurry and she was the reason why.) If they made a formal identification of that tattoo then they would have to face the truth – that their daughter was a prostitute who had been found naked and dead in a car park.

Scotch Frances, eh? Can you forgive her?

Now she was on offer to the Earl o' Hell . . .

She disappeared on the night of 23 October. When did the killer dump her? Dried leaves in a deep depression beneath her body indicated that it had lain there for some time.

So how long had the civil defence's dustbin lid been missing? Nobody knew. Dennis Sutton hadn't moved it for at least six weeks, 'although I don't think it was longer than that'.

The car park attendant was employed from 8am to 6pm, Monday

to Friday, and until lunchtime on Saturdays, and when he left, he left the gates open. Immediate house-to-house enquiries began in adjoining Campden Hill Road and Hornton Street (where the entrance to the car park was situated) but no resident had witnessed anything suspicious in recent weeks. It was practically impossible to see anything at all over those high walls, and besides, at night the area was in total darkness.

Meanwhile, forensic officers searched the L-shaped car park. At the side of the control they discovered a faecally stained towel and handkerchief which, although confirming the car park's status as a dumping ground, turned out to have been deposited too recently to be connected with the big drop. Elsewhere in the vicinity they found used condoms and soiled tissues . . .

All pretty much as expected. But what to make of the wad of plain paper (no sperm, sorry) found stuffed inside the dead woman's vagina?

On 27 November the front page of the *Daily Express* announced: 'Detectives on a murder hunt were detailed last night to question people in the Stephen Ward and Christine Keeler cases.'

Were they? Really? How extraordinary, that detectives should be detailed to question people in the case of a man framed by detectives.

Try swallowing that with your morning cornflakes.

Of course murder was important – front-page news in those days – but it wasn't *that* important. Nothing was.

Besides, nobody really knew the extent of the dead woman's relationship with the dead man. Vera Lynch spoke of a visitor to Brown's former address in Shepherd's Bush, a person who painted Brown's portrait. The sitter later told her this was Dr Stephen Ward.

Paint.

Well, yes, and one trial witness whom the police ought perhaps to have interviewed was the society portrait painter and sculptor Vasco Lazzolo.

Lazzolo, a married man in his late forties, had built up an impressive professional reputation, numbering the Queen and W. Somerset Maugham among his clients. But at Ward's trial Frances Brown, in addition to answering questions about the accused, alleged that she and Vickie Barrett, while grafting in Shaftesbury Avenue, had been picked up by Lazzolo and invited back to his flat, where the three of them had participated in a sex act (unspecified but possibly hand relief, which appears to have been Brown's speciality).

Now Lazzolo certainly had a name as a *bon viveur* but these allegations went way beyond the pale. He'd never felt so insulted in his life (or at least not since 1943, when the inventor Arthur Stambois denounced him in public as a pimp, a diseased pervert, a Portuguese swine and a pig). He appeared at the trial in order to refute allegations made by Vickie Barrett that he'd had intercourse with her at his studio, and that she had caned him at Ward's flat. Now here was this Scotch trollop calmly telling the world that he liked his whores two at a time!

Yes, Vasco Lazzolo might well have felt like murdering Frances Brown. Moreover, a decent period had elapsed since the trial, and now would be a good time to strike.

Yet the case for Lazzolo as the murderer is flimsy. The paint on Brown's corpse was globular and indicated that whoever killed her had killed Barthelemy and Fleming as well. And besides, if he was going to murder Brown why not murder Barrett into the bargain?

But Vickie Barrett was safe and sound – safe enough to be interviewed even, as she had retracted her trial testimony and then retracted her retraction, with the happy result that no one now trusted a word she said. She told police that she'd first met the dead woman about two years ago, when they lived in the same house in Shepherd's Bush. They worked the streets together, though of course she was in a different class. 'I don't go with clients in cars . . .'

And then – incredibly – Vickie Barrett came out with something half believable. She told them that she thought Frances's friend Beryl was a 'butch lesbian'.

If true this might explain their instant rapport. Frances Brown was a woman who gave Jimmy Corrigan the impression 'that she went with women as well as men', who may have wanted both Elsie *and* Elvis on her arm.

So there you are. The taller one gave it and the shortbread took it. The whisky, I mean. Remember?

I went to the bar to try and get a quarter-bottle of whisky but was told they didn't have any. The coloured man said he could get one. He left the pub and returned soon afterwards with the whisky which Frances put in her bag.

Or did she? She may well have done, but only if her companion wasn't lying. The black man probably paid for that whisky – he seems to have believed he was on a promise – and when he asked for his locket back at the end of the night he may have asked for his money as well. In which case Mahood may have fobbed him off with instructions to collect it from her friend.

It's feasible, and the question is important by dint of the fact that Brown's bloodstream contained a mere 71mg of alcohol per 100ml of blood, the equivalent of between two and three measures of spirits. Now the likelihood is that at 11pm, after five hours in the Warwick Castle, she was fairly drunk. And so three measures doesn't seem very much really, not if she died within an hour or so of disappearing. An alcoholic – if that's what she was – can metabolize the stuff fairly quickly, but did she continue drinking? She may have died before she had a chance to open the whisky, or she may never have had it at all.

Still, if Blonde Beryl told a lie about the whisky I don't suppose Detective Superintendent Marchant would have minded too much. He was in charge of this investigation, which was based at Kensington police station, and Beryl Mahood, well, she was his star witness. On 27 November she supplied an account of the events of 23 October along with detailed descriptions of the two motorists. Officers began to keep nocturnal observation in the vicinity of Portobello Road; their colleagues hung around in the local pubs, waiting.

William Marchant had every reason to feel confident. If the man in the tan jacket returned to the scene this entire business could be over by Christmas.

Well, well.

So the little cunt wasn't there to slap around any more.

Well, well, well.

Any other way she could pay?

Maybe.

Before Frances left me on Thursday 22 October 1964, and while we were in the pub, she borrowed a small gold ring I was wearing and put it on the ring finger of the left hand. It was a small gold shank with two sapphires or imitation sapphires with a little pearl in the centre . . .

A tattooed labourer in his workclothes down the pub . . . wearing a pearl ring?

Whatever next? A pearl necklace?

What's going on here?

. . . *It was worth about £5.*

So?

Portable property, Mr Marchant, sir.

So?

So rip it off her rotten finger, give it to me now.

Paul Quinn, eh? Can you believe him?

Even when he's wearing his new blue suit?

Daily Mirror, 30 November:

Murdered nude's lover hunts the killer

Paul Quinn, 28, put on his new blue suit yesterday and went hunting for clues to the killer of the girl he once lived with . . .

Yesterday Paul Quinn – born in Dublin, Eire, and known to friends as 'Pepe' – toured pubs and clubs, talking to prostitutes who had known Margaret McGowan . . .

A bender in other words, with the chance of a bunk-up thrown in. A bit of fun, really – like this from the *Sunday Mirror,* 29 November:

The five empty chairs

The five victims of a mad killer once sat in the empty chairs above.

The chairs are in a hair stylist's salon in Portobello-road, Kensington, London, where the five murdered women – all prostitutes – used to go.

In the salon, street girls talked of their associations with men . . . and during the past six months, their fears . . .

All five girls, with records of prostitution offences, were clients of 35-year-old Derek Walter, who has the hairdressing salon.

He said last night: 'Whenever they had the money to spare for a hair-do they came to me. They changed the colour of their hair as frequently as they changed their names.

'I shall always remember the remarks that passed between them after the first girl vanished.

'They tried to laugh it off, and thought it would never happen to them. But I could see that underneath they were scared that they might be the next.

'Every time another body was found they talked of nothing else in the salon . . .'

But on 1 December the fun stopped. The *Evening Standard* got its hands on Beryl Mahood, and she told them everything.

'I believe I saw Margaret's killer'

Evening Standard Crime Reporter

A terrified blonde girl told me today that she saw 21-year-old prostitute Margaret McGowan drive off with a man she believes to be her killer.

The girl has given detectives probing the nude murder cases one of their best leads so far.

She said Margaret was driven away in a grey Zephyr.

She has given a full description of the driver to police . . .

'I got a good view of the man and have given police his description. Now I am terrified he will try to kill me.'

She asked me to keep her name and address secret.

Last night two men in a van tried to run her down near the basement flat where she lives. She finished crying on a doorstep ringing the doorbells, then called the police. . .

Orders went out to murder squad detectives today: Find the man in the grey Zephyr – and the other man who was with him . . .

In fact orders had gone out four days previously, and the search was now severely compromised by these disclosures. Accordingly Detective Superintendent Marchant called a press conference for the following day, 2 December. This was held in the gymnasium at Kensington police station, and identikit drawings of the two motorists were handed out to representatives of the national press, the local press, BBC and ITV, in an attempt to get one or both of these men – or anyone who recognized them – to come forward.

The portraits received maximum publicity. Everywhere you looked you received those descriptions and saw those faces. See,

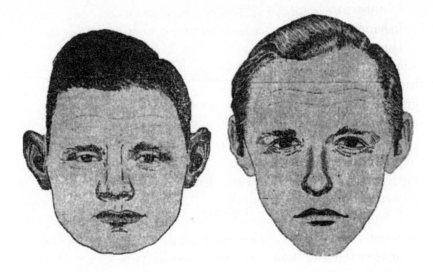

the fleshy-faced one with the bat ears and big lips, the murderer –
now he was your typical sex fiend, at the mercy of his appetites.
Whereas his mate there, in the sober suit, he was a cut above. Well
spoken, of course, upper class probably, with a bit of a drawl. He
did his best to curb the beast's excesses (*Steady on, old chap, she's
gone limp!*) but would never alert the authorities owing to a code of
honour . . .

Gruesome. Yet in the face of all imaginings the faces themselves
said nothing, thought nothing, and refused to grow legs. Police wondered whether the two men – who were in separate cars yet seemed
to know each other – were car salesmen attending the Earls Court
Motor Show. If they came forward they could perhaps be eliminated
from the inquiry. But they never came forward.

Other hopes also failed. No jeweller, pawnbroker or second-hand
clothes shop in the west London area had received any of the dead
woman's missing items. The property of prisoners coming into custody since 23 October was scrutinized, to no avail. Police requested
an identical costume to that worn by Brown with a view to making a
mock-up, only to learn that the costume, like the victim, was no
longer for sale.

Apologies from C&A:

Fashions – seasons – London etc.

Yeah.

Out there it was the Swinging Sixties.

In here it was shit.

Hundreds of telephone calls from members of the public, none of which led anywhere . . . countless toms interrogated, most of whom had bad memories . . . and as well as all this shit there was a stinking great pile of correspondence. There were letters here from every time-waster in the land.

Mrs C. V. Ward announced in her letter that she had information 'regarding the murder girl Maregate' so 'will you please send a private gentleman to 4 Wellesty place malday Rd NW5'. *Bedridden senile old woman. Nothing of use obtained.*

F. Smith, a retired police inspector, suggested a youth he arrested in about 1916 for attacking a prostitute. 'Unfortunately I cannot remember the lad's name and I guess now he would be 65.' *Too far-fetched. No further action.*

W. G. Millen recounted how late one night in the spring of 1964 he was in the Gents at Paddington station when he overheard a man in the next cubicle muttering about prostitutes. '"The Bastards they are all the same . . . They are all the same try to take you for a ride. I'll ride them."' He made so much noise that the attendant asked him to leave. 'I did not see this man's face, but I had a clear view of his back and head, the clothes he was then wearing was fairly good and clean, at this moment the Toilet attendant appeared and I remarked to him about the man's behaviour, the attendant replied, "Yes, he has been here before, he is a bloody meth drinker and a Bloody nuisance."' *Far too vague for investigation.*

Betty Huntreys of 60a Gloucester Street, Victoria, offered herself as a decoy. 'My working hours are 5–9a.m. and 5 to 7p.m. so I have all day and most part of the evening free if you need my assistance.' *Not accepted, address does not exist.*

D. A. Hargreaves suggested that one of the identikit faces, unspecified, 'looks like Chris Barbers banjoist, Eddy Smith, I am probably wrong, I hope I am'. *Man of colour, no resemblance.*

H. J. Milton, 'Supdt. Indian Police, Retd.', suggested that one of the faces, again unspecified, might be that of Captain Eugene Ivanov, the former Soviet Assistant Naval Attaché in London and a key player in the Profumo affair. Ivanov had not publicly resurfaced since leaving England in 1963. 'It would not be difficult for the Russian Govt. to get him back into England as a member of the Russian Civilian Embassy.' *No further action.*

J. J. Tallanti, a widower, offered Vickie Barrett free accommodation in return for some light housework. 'I had only been out of the Infirmary two days when my wife died. I was Due for a Final operation But Cannot Have it just yet . . . I Carry a Drainage tube from my stomach attached to a rubber Bag Down the Side of my Leg.' *No further action.*

On 6 December the front page of the *News of the World* offered a side view of 'Beryl, a buxom blonde', sitting on a bed in her slingbacks, face hidden, legs crossed, ready for business (*How much am I getting?*). She talked for the second time that week about the two men, the grey Zephyr and the last time she saw her friend alive.

The following Sunday the newspaper revealed that Beryl had been attacked as she left a west London jazz club. 'In a dingy basement the frightened blonde said: "The man kicked me and told me to mind my own business and keep my trap shut . . ."'

Maybe it was time to leave the stage.

Another friend, Vera Lynch, the one who ended up with the dead woman's clothes (most of which she gave to a charity shop) . . . She also had a story to tell. She told it to the police as it was told to her by Frances Brown in October, the month of no return.

Brown told her friend that she had had a bad scare while out on the street the previous night. A man in a small van had stopped her and she got in. He asked her how much she charged, but before she could answer he produced a small black card which bore the words 'Metropolitan Police' in gold lettering. He said he was CID. 'She said to the man that he could not nick her as he was on his own and the man said he had his mate up the road and could easily do it.' The man told her she had a laughing face and discussed the maniac who was murdering the prostitutes. She asked him how the women were murdered and he explained that the murderer 'pulled the coat down over the shoulders locking the arms and screwed whatever they were wearing underneath around their neck and strangled them'.

Frances Brown couldn't work this man out so, feeling frightened, she left him. ('He did give her a pound but it was not for intercourse or anything like that.') She offered her friend no description of the driver and no detailed description of his van, remarking simply that it was grey, and that in the back 'there was a lot of rubbish like clothes'.

5

Rubout
(revisited)

25.7.65

To C.D.   *From* Russell Square.
                                                   Ambulance H.Q.

We have just brought in a dead male to the Middlesex
Hospital from Charing Cross Road. Suspected suicide. Can
you please send an officer.

R.S.T. One will be sent.

Time of origin 1.55am.

                                          25th July, 1965.

To D.I. Walton.   *From* D.S. Dennis.
(At Home).   C.I.D. (CD).

Freddy Mills has just been found shot dead at Goslett Yard
W.1.
His body is now at Middlesex Hospital.

<u>R.S.T.</u> I will come direct to the hospital.

Time of origin: 2.20am.

25th July, 1965.

To D. C. Bowne.   *From* D.S. Dennis.
M.11 "Q" Car.   C.I.D. (CD).

Freddy Mills, the well known boxer, has just been found shot
dead at Goslett Yard, W.1. His body is now at Middlesex
Hospital. Will you please go to 142, Court Lane, Dulwich,
and see his stepson, Mr Don McCorquindale. Obtain from
him a statement giving any details of history which might
assist the enquiry. Mrs Mills, wife of deceased, is also at this
address. She knows something has happened to her husband
but may not know that he is dead. If her condition permits,
please obtain a statement from her. When complete, please
bring all information to me at Middlesex Hospital.

Time of origin 3.00am.

25th July, 1965.

To Det Supt. Walker.   *From*: C.I.D. (CD 2)
(At Home).   D.I. Walton.

Freddy Mills has been found shot dead at Goslett Yard, W.1.
His body is now at the Middlesex Hospital. He was found in
his car with a rifle, I am almost certain it will resolve itself as
suicide but there are one or two things to clear up first.
    It seems a bit like the suicide we had quite recently.

R.S.T. Inform Ch. Insp. Virgo who will take charge but should any-
       thing develop to indicate foul play contact me again.

Time of origin 3.40am.

25th July, 1965.

To D.I. Walton   *From*: P.C. 194 'D' Hall.
                                   Coroners Officer,
                                   Marylebone.

I understand you have a dead body. What action do you wish
me to take.

<u>R.S.T.</u> This is being treated as a murder inquiry. What arrangements
         can you make for a Pathologist to carry out a post-mortem.
<u>R.S.T.</u> I will make arrangements and inform you later.

Time of origin 4.00am

Just what is it that makes yesterday's suicides so different, so appeal-
ing?

*Those old enough still remember Freddie Mills with affection as a great boxer
and entertainer, but for Chrissie Mills and their daughter Susan fond memory
is complicated by the enigma of his death in 1965 — some say at his own
hands, others as a victim of murder.*

I'm at home tonight (though not to visitors) and I'm watching a
video of *The Freddie Mills Story*, an hour-long documentary broadcast
on BBC2 in 1985.

Reporter James Hogg faces the camera lens, his back to the beach
at Bournemouth, birthplace of the boxer.

It stands for everything that's genteel, decorous and non-violent.

Freddie's sister Cissie reminisces; his friend Peter McInnes reminisces. When I return from a visit to the bathroom it's 1942 and
Freddie Mills is boxing Len Harvey, British light heavyweight champion, in an open-air ring at Tottenham Hotspur football ground. He's
flooring him. He's punching him through the ropes. He's won.

*By now Freddie had joined one of the best-known managers in the country,
Ted Broadribb. Broadribb's daughter Chrissie, later to become Mrs Freddie
Mills, was then married to another fighter, Don McCorkindale. Chrissie
already had a young son, Donny, long before she even knew the man who was
to become her second husband.*

She became Mrs Freddie Mills on 30 September 1948 at the Methodist Church, Half Moon Lane, Herne Hill. He was twenty-nine, she was thirty-three.

Why marry a divorcee? Why choose second-hand goods?

Was it his manager's idea? Broadribb wanting to keep the money in the family?

Or perhaps he thought it about time Mills, the clean-shaven cruiserweight, was supplied with a permanent beard.

Back on screen it's 1946 and Mills's temples are taking an historic pounding from world light heavyweight champion Gus Lesnevitch. This is, Peter McInnes is telling us, *the first major promotion after the war, promoted by the great Jack Solomons, the late great Jack Solomons, at Harringay Arena.*

Jack 'No comps' Solomons, the fat promoter who believed he was as big a draw as his fighters, and whose intense greed for money led him to stage mismatches such as 'Freddie Mills v Bruce Woodcock' and 'Freddie Mills v Joe Baksi'. Mills was a light heavyweight, whereas Woodcock was the British heavyweight champion. Baksi, an American heavyweight, outweighed his opponent by almost four stone.

Woodcock defeated Mills.

Baksi defeated Mills.

1946 wasn't his year. 1948 – the year he fought Lesnevitch for the second time – and won – and became the new world light heavyweight champion – that was his year.

Paving the way for the time when he could no longer fight, Freddie put his money into a Chinese restaurant in the Charing Cross Road in London.

The Freddie Mills Chinese Restaurant had opened the previous year in the basement of 143 Charing Cross Road. Mills's partners were Andrew Chin Guan Ho, the manager, George Riley, a purveyor of pet meat, and Charles Luck.

Charles Luck, the restaurant's licensee, was a partner in Scudamore and Luck, a civil engineering firm based in Northamptonshire. In 1951 Peter Hill joined the firm as company secretary.

'I stayed for the next twenty years. Mr Luck was a big man, 6′, and a big boxing fan. (His friend George Ribey was a big man too. He wore a green trilby and looked the spitting image of Fred Elliott, that butcher on *Coronation Street*.) He had a Purdy, I think, and he loved shooting. He was always shooting rabbits. I remember they were put (unskinned) into hundredweight sacks addressed to the Freddie Mills Chinese Restaurant, and I put them on the goods train. Of course rationing was still on, and I expect these rabbits were sold as chicken.

'The firm did a lot of tarmacking, and whenever the men were in town on a job I'd go up at weekends to help out, and to bring them things from their wives. And if Mr Luck was up there as well he'd take us all – as a treat – to the restaurant at the end of the night.

'We thought, "Well, if it's Freddie Mills's restaurant it's going to be like Buckingham Palace." But it was just a cellar really. Very basic, dingy, two or three Chinese waiters. We'd eat sausage and mash, something like that. At first we thought we'd see Freddie there, but we never did, and after a while we stopped expecting it.'

On one occasion the job took place in the restaurant itself. There was damp in the basement and Charles Luck's son Philip and his men were working through the night, tearing up the woodblock floor and replacing it with asphalt. One of the workers went into the kitchen to make a cup of tea. He opened a cupboard and showed Philip Luck what he found.

'The 4' Chinese chef asleep on the shelf. I think he was on the premises as some kind of nightwatchman, he was supposed to be keeping an eye.'

Wakey wakey!

Now it's nearly the end. Mills has had three of his front teeth removed between rounds, painful proof of the venom in Maxim's cunning. Now he's swallowing blood all the time. Breathing is difficult – every blow on the mouth is sheer agony.

I'm seeing footage of Mills attempting to defend his world light heavyweight title against the American Joey Maxim.

Earls Court, 24 January 1950.

This will be the final match of his career.

It's carnage.

It's brain damage in black and white.

The teeth may have needed fixing but the personality was as scintillating as ever, and Freddie began his transformation from boxer pure and simple to popular entertainer. He enlivened the drabness of post-war Britain with exhibition matches and his irresistible gift for clowning.

Fooling as an Arab on the beach at Broadstairs.

Jiving in a drapecoat on *Six-Five Special*.

Punching his way out of a giant paper bag.

And now here's Chrissie on Freddie: 'He was a very, very sincere person, and if he liked somebody he really liked them. He loved Alfred Marks and Paddy. Paddy used to say, "He's bloody starstruck, that one."'

Starstrucker. In 1964 Freddie Mills – proposed by Andy Ho and seconded by musician Judd Solo – was initiated as an apprentice in Freemasonry at Chelsea Lodge (no. 3098), an entertainers' lodge established in 1905. The ceremony took place at Great Queen Street on 20 November, an occasion on which comedian Reg 'Confidentially Yours' Dixon was also initiated, and Bob Monkhouse was elevated to the Degree of Master Mason. Boxer Ted 'Kid' Lewis, singer Issy Bonn and actor Ken Barnes were among those present.

But meanwhile he had changed the Chinese restaurant he owned in Soho into a nightclub.

By this time Charles Luck had died and George Ribey had allowed himself to be bought out by Mills and Ho. The Freddie Mills Nite Spot opened for business on 9 May 1963. On 5 July 1964 the *People* newspaper published a detailed report on its attractions.

> Last week at least four customers there were introduced to hostesses whom, they were told, they could 'take home with them' after the club closed at 3am.
>
> All the girls offered immoral services to the customers – at a price.
>
> The introductions were made by the manager of the club, a 'Mr Toni'.

Mr Toni interviewed a female reporter for a job as a hostess, telling her she would receive no wages, and no commission on food and drink bought by customers (although he expected her to drink at least two bottles of champagne every night). She would make her money from tips ('"We expect our hostesses to tell the men at their table that they expect £5 or £6"') and from sexual services, for which she should charge about £15. It was perfectly safe for a girl to leave the club with a customer. '"How can the police prove she is not a girlfriend?"'

The police couldn't but the *People* could. Two male reporters investigated the club on separate nights and the racket was duly exposed. The newspaper refused to believe that Freddie had sanctioned it but a headline warned: 'It's time you cleaned up your club, Mr Mills'.

Norman, the youngest of Andy Ho's three sons, visited the club several times as a teenager.

'There were some steps which led down to the basement . . . I seem to recall a corridor with an office and a cloakroom, and then you entered the club itself. There was a dance floor, a cabaret, a three-piece band. Looking back, it was all pretty ordinary, really. I don't recall any sense of menace.

'Freddie Mills would sit and talk to me sometimes. I got the impression he was just a really nice man. He wasn't there very much, but neither was my father. He had small parts in films as a sort of token Chinaman, and he would sometimes be away for days, even weeks at a time. He was a pretty useless actor – he could never remember his lines or anything. He saw it all as a game.

'Even when he was supposed to be at the club you would often find him playing cards or snooker at a snooker club around the corner. I think, in the early days, when the restaurant was starting up, he worked quite hard, but by that time I don't think he was really bothered. He and Freddie Mills were babes in arms as far as the club business was concerned. My father was one of life's great innocents.'

On 6 May 1965 the Nite Spot was in the news again. The *Daily Sketch* reported that Mills had given evidence on behalf of the club at Westminster County Court the previous day. He was speaking in support of a claim for £27 10s against two customers, Peter and Patrick Bateman. The judge heard that after spending several hours at the club the brothers were presented with a bill for £33 10s, of which they paid only £6. By then one of the Batemans had drunk a bottle of whisky, the other had drunk three-quarters of a bottle of vodka, and two hostesses sitting with them had drunk a bottle of champagne apiece.

The Batemans brought a counter-claim for assault, alleging that they had been attacked and thrown out of the club by four 'muscular' members of staff. This was denied and their claim was dismissed by the judge, who told them, 'To go into such a place with only about £8 and order freely was as near to being fraudulent as I can imagine.'

What was Freddie Mills near to being? Here he was, a national hero, presiding over a clip joint. And he wasn't cleaning up either. Business was bad.

On screen Andy Ho is explaining why.

'Well, in club business you have spasms, you see. You have one period where you could be very busy, and then sometime you could get – ah – terribly slack. And with heavy overheads you've got to be – ah – really have financial reserves. And overheads were so heavy we had no financial reserves.'

What did these overheads consist of? Angela Deacon, widow of Robert Deacon, the club's doorman, offers a clue.

'I don't think Freddie Mills was aware of a lot of what was going on. Robert told me how Andy Ho was conning both the taxman and Freddie, and bringing wads of money home from the club and hiding it in the loft at his house in Bushey.

'Robert also told me about the trick of putting four champagne corks in the bucket when the customer had only drunk two bottles, and then charging them for four. Another trick, one that the hostesses played, was, at the end of the evening, to tell a customer to meet them behind "that door over there" in five minutes – and the customer would find himself walking into a broom cupboard. Robert and I would laugh about that.'

This is a .22 repeater –

James Hogg is back, stony-faced. He's sitting in an old car and waving a rifle about.

— *fairground rifle, identical to the kind that killed Freddie Mills. Now according to the family they found him in the back seat . . .*

I close my eyes, curl up on the sofa, and listen once again to the voice of Andy Ho, Andy Ho the bit-part actor (*Satan Never Sleeps, The World of Suzie Wong*), telling me things about Freddie Mills's last night, things he somehow never got round to telling the police, saying, 'I said, "What's wrong, Freddie?" He just goes like this — wince his face and he didn't say anything, you know,' and it strikes me I could stop this tragedy this minute if I chose to and so I reach for the remote control which happens to be resting against my right leg and —

Stop.

Stand back, Charlie Chan.

Stand back, all of you.

No ghouls, no cameras.

It's not a sideshow, there's nothing to see.

And I'll take over now.

'Recently there was another court case when the club was prosecuted as a result of a police raid,' Chrissie Mills told police. 'This also worried my husband considerably, who, at the time that the summonses were served, was ill in bed with pneumonia . . . On Friday 23 July 1965, or it may have been the day before, the case against the club was heard at Marylebone Court. My husband went and when he come home he told me that he and Mr Ho had each been fined £68. In telling me this, he said to me that whatever he tried he could not win. I told him that no doubt in September things would brighten up.'

Freddie and Chrissie Mills lived with their daughters, Susan, aged thirteen, and Amanda, aged seven, at Joggi Villa, 186 Denmark Hill, Camberwell. Chrissie's son, Donald McCorkindale, an actor, left this address at 2.30pm on Saturday 24 July 1965. 'My stepfather was there with my mother. He was in a mood, but not one that was peculiar. He seemed quite happy.'

At 4pm Mills, who was still recovering from his bout of pneumonia, went to bed while his wife was out shopping. He resurfaced at 7.30pm to eat his dinner and then told Chrissie he was going back to bed as he had a headache. 'I knew that he had had difficulty in sleeping over the last few weeks. He was only in bed for a very short time and then came down again and had a coffee.' The Beatles were on television, and he and his wife watched Susan and Amanda do the twist in the kitchen.

Mills went upstairs to change into a suit and came down again at about 9.45pm. 'I was surprised that he was going to the club as I did not think he was well enough to go.' He knew his wife, who came to the club on alternate Saturdays, would be joining him for supper later. He left home in his silver-grey Citroën and headed for the Nite Spot in Charing Cross Road.

At 10.30pm Robert Deacon, the doorman, and Henry Grant, the head waiter, were standing at the front door of the club when a stranger approached them.

'A man, who I have never seen before, came up to us and said that Freddie was down the mews and wanted to see Bob. The man was aged about fifty years, about 6 feet, with long grey hair, wearing a raincoat. I think I would know him again.'

Deacon found Mills sitting at the wheel of his car at the entrance to Goslett Yard, a mews at the rear of the club. 'He told me that he had had a few drinks and that he didn't want to go into the club and that he was going to sleep it off in the mews. He told me to wake him up in half an hour.' (A post-mortem test showed that Mills's blood alcohol level was 50mg per 100ml, the approximate equivalent of one pint of beer or two measures of spirits.)

At about 11.10pm Deacon returned to the Citroën, which was now parked at the end of Goslett Yard. He said, 'You told me to wake you up.' Mills, who was still in the driving seat, replied, 'No, come back in half an hour.' At about 11.15pm Andy Ho arrived at the club, and Deacon informed him that Mr Mills was having a nap in his car in Goslett Yard and that he, Deacon, had been instructed to wake him in time for the cabaret, which usually began some time after midnight. Ho said OK and entered the club. According to his statement, he himself had no contact with Mills that night.

At about 11.45pm Robert Deacon again walked round to Goslett Yard. Mills's car was in the same position but Mills wasn't. 'He was sitting upright with his head slumped forward. He was sitting on the nearside rear seat. The offside rear window was wound down . . .'

The doorman called out 'Mr Mills!' several times through the window and banged on the car door. Mills failed to respond, and so Deacon opened the offside rear door and leaned in. He pushed Mills's right shoulder and patted his right cheek. 'He still didn't respond. There was what appeared to me to be saliva round his mouth and nostrils. I felt uneasy but I didn't think that anything was wrong as he had told me that he had had a few drinks.' Deacon closed the car door and went back to work.

An hour passed. It was almost time for the cabaret but the host had yet to show his face. At around 1am Henry Grant decided to go and wake him. He found Mills, apparently asleep, still sitting in the near-side rear seat of the Citroën. He opened the nearside rear door and spoke to him, and shook him vigorously by his left shoulder. He slapped his boss's face several times and then noticed what looked like saliva coming from his nose and mouth. 'I thought he was ill.' He went back inside the club and reported his fears to Andy Ho. What did Ho do?

'I phoned Mr Mills's wife immediately, but on getting through I was told that she was on her way to the club and should arrive at any minute.' Donald McCorkindale was driving both his wife and his mother in Chrissie's blue Mini, and they arrived at the club shortly after 1am. Ho approached the car and, taking Chrissie Mills by the arm, led her into Goslett Yard.

'The offside rear window was down and he was sitting on the back seat on the other side. I went to the open window and called him but he did not answer. I got in the back seat next to him and put my arm round him. I did see some discoloration on my jacket and saw something black on the floor which looked like a starting handle. When I moved I saw that it was a gun.'

McCorkindale pulled his mother, crying, out of the car, and by the flame of his cigarette lighter saw a rifle propped up against Mills's leg, muzzle up. 'I picked the gun up, looked at it and put it back again more or less in the same position.' He asked Andy Ho to telephone for an ambulance. Meanwhile, he sat in the car 'to keep people away'. He produced his lighter again and noticed a wound in Mills's right eye.

At 1.34am on 25 July Leslie Rowe, ambulance attendant, received a call informing him of a casualty in Goslett Yard, at the rear of the Freddie Mills Nite Spot. 'Originally this call went to "Echo 1", but as we were nearer I accepted it.' The ambulance arrived in Goslett Yard at 1.39am. At the end of the yard four men were standing by the Citroën. 'I think it was the little fat Chinese man who spoke to me. He said, "Quick, quick, he's in there."'

Rowe went up to the car and opened the nearside rear door. Thomas Spalding, the ambulance driver, fetched a torch and shone it on Mills's body in the nearside rear seat. His head was upright and his hands were in his lap. Congealed blood was hanging from his nose and from his right eye. The waistband of his trousers was soaked in blood and there was blood on his shirt. 'I felt the pulse and I thought that it was beating,' Rowe told the police. 'His hands and wrist were warm.' Rowe fetched a stretcher, and Spalding opened the nearside rear door and half dragged the body out.

These two men also took charge of the rifle. The weapon was leaning against the offside rear seat in an upright position, between 6″ and 8″ from the offside rear door. The butt rested on the floor, and the trigger guard pointed towards the front of the car. Spalding stated that after dealing with Mills he returned to the car, opened the offside rear door and removed the rifle and placed it in the ambulance. 'I did this as there were no police on the scene at that stage.'

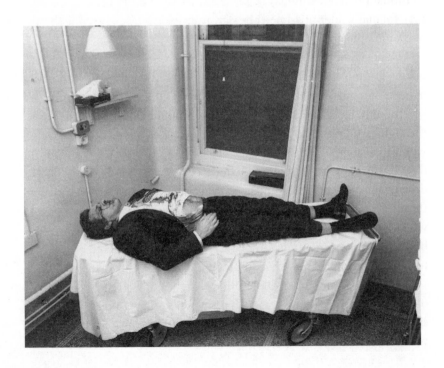

At 1.55am Mills was certified dead on arrival at Middlesex Hospital. At 2am Detective Sergeant Raymond Dennis went to the hospital and spoke to Spalding and Rowe. They showed him the body ('I recognized the man as Frederick Mills, whom I knew personally'), and Rowe handed him the rifle. At about 3.20am Detective Inspector Harold Walton arrived, took possession of the rifle and saw the body. He saw that Mills had an injury to his right eye. He saw that there was blood on his face and on the front of his clothing.

Anyone could see that –

This is being treated as a murder inquiry.

So why wasn't it?

At 4.45am Harold Walton showed up at sealed-off Goslett Yard, in the north-east corner of which stood Freddie Mills's Citroën. He examined the vehicle and noticed blood on the rear seat towards the nearside. He also noticed a spent cartridge case on the floor on the rear nearside. 'The light was bad so I decided to examine the vehicle in more detail in daylight.'

Later that morning he and DS Dennis attended the post-mortem examination at Westminster mortuary. At 6am Freddie Mills's body was formally identified by his stepson Donald McCorkindale. At 6.10am pathologist Keith Simpson began his examination.

The deceased was a very well-built male, aged forty-six and measuring 5' 10". There was no disease, and there was athlete's hypertrophy of the heart. There was some ballooning of the lungs.

The only injury was a single firearm wound at the inner angle of the right eye. Simpson's report specifies a 'contact, or near contact, wound causing slight splitting around the 3–4mm entry hole, and directed straight back through the centre of the head, angled slightly downwards and inwards'. The main course of the trajectory was through the bony sphenoid of the skull base back past the brain stem – which suffered irreversible damage – into the left hind lobe of the brain. There was no exit wound: the bullet had shattered and scattered around the course of its passage through skull and brain.

'There is nothing from the medical examination of this wound or of the body generally to give cause for suspicion of foul play. In the site of election (if a little unusual) and the direction of discharge the wound shows nothing out of keeping with deliberate self-infliction.'

By 8am DI Walton was back in Goslett Yard. He re-examined the
Citroën and noticed bullet holes through both the inner and outer
surfaces of the lower part of the nearside front door. The hole in the
exterior of the door was an exit hole, indicating that a shot had passed
from the interior of the car to the exterior.

'A straight line through the two holes ran approximately from a
point on the ground about one foot from the car to about shoulder
level when sitting in the driver's seat.'

Walton collected the spent cartridge case, and found a second one
on the floor in front of the front passenger seat. These cases plus the
rifle itself and a metallic substance found in the vicinity of the car
were submitted for analysis, together with samples of Mills's blood
and metal fragments retrieved from his head. The scene at Goslett
Yard and the rear interior of the car were photographed by Detective
Sergeant David Adams, and the vehicle was deposited at Tottenham
Court Road police station to await testing for fingerprints.

The inquest into Freddie Mills's death was held at Westminster
Coroner's Court on 2 August 1965. Much was made of the fact that
Mills parked his car in Goslett Yard that night. 'He might quite likely
sleep in the car behind the club,' his widow told the coroner, Gavin
Thurston. But Robert Deacon and Henry Grant both contradicted
this, claiming that Mills usually parked at the front of the club in
Charing Cross Road. On the final page of his notes Thurston wrote:
'DEACON Car in mews – not in C + Rd' and beneath this, 'TO BE
LEFT ALONE'.

Thurston, who sat without a jury, delivered a verdict of suicide. He
found the additional rifle shot difficult to explain, although Mills, he
believed, could have been testing a weapon with which he was unfa-
miliar.

The deceased, then, had fired one shot from the driver's seat which
went through the nearside front door, before getting out and entering
the back of the car, where he sat in the nearside rear seat and fired
another shot which went through his right eye.

But how did the dead man contrive to eject the second cartridge?

It was all a little unusual, as suicides go.

But as suicides go, he went.

What did any of it matter now?

*

He left no suicide note, but the explanation appeared to be that he had shot himself in a fit of depression at the state of the Nite Spot's finances.

Although a rumour was beginning to circulate around London, a dark rumour about Freddie Mills and his activities.

Some people still believe it.

The *Observer*, 4 November 2001, 'News' section (Tony Thompson reporting):

Freddie Mills 'murdered eight women'

For 20 years Freddie Mills was one of the best-loved figures in British sport. Even after hanging up his gloves to become a club-owner and promoter, he remained a darling of the media and a hero to millions.

But, according to a new book to be published next year, Mills took terrible secrets to his grave. It claims he was a vicious serial killer, responsible for the brutal deaths of at least eight young women whose naked bodies were found in or around the River Thames between 1959 and 1965 . . .

Reformed south London gangster Jimmy Tippet . . . believes he has uncovered the truth about the former champion . . .

'In those days the members of the boxing fraternity were like a Masonic circle,' says Tippet. 'A lot of people who were close to him, including my father, are still unwilling to talk about exactly what was said during those times and those who are won't say anything on the record. But I have been told that Freddie feared the police were closing in on him and decided to take his own life rather than face trial . . .'

Tippet's book (no title given) should make interesting reading (should it ever appear).

Decided to take his own life . . .

What more is there to say?

Take his own life . . .

Well, of course he did. The alternative explanation (murder, cover-up, conspiracy to pervert the course of justice) hardly bears thinking about.

*

The bald, bird-like gentleman who bent over Freddie Mills's corpse that morning in Westminster mortuary was one of the most distinguished pathologists of his day. Professor Keith Simpson, CBE, as he introduces himself on the title-page of his autobiography, *Forty Years of Murder*, had, by this stage of his career, worked on several well-publicized murder cases, such as that of Neville Heath ('"If you find that whip you've found your man," I told the police') and that of John George Haigh, the 'acid bath' murderer ('It was lucky for us that Mrs Durand-Deacon was stout, for the preservation of our exhibits was due to the protective action of a film of fat'). In 1962 Simpson was appointed Professor and Head of Department of Forensic Medicine to the University of London (at Guy's Hospital Medical School). He was the author of *Forensic Medicine* (1947), *Modern Trends in Forensic Science* (1953) and *A Doctor's Guide to Court* (1962), and the editor of the twelfth edition of *Taylor's Principles and Practice of Medical Jurisprudence* (1965).

We may therefore assume that Cedric Keith Simpson knew his job. He certainly knew what he was doing when he prepared his report on Freddie Mills.

He was doing something wrong.

Jack Crane, State Pathologist for Northern Ireland and Professor of Forensic Medicine at the Queen's University of Belfast, has studied the report and offers several devastating criticisms, criticisms that force us to reconsider the dead man's final moments.

Professor Simpson describes a single firearm wound 'at the inner angle of the R eye, a contact, or near contact, wound causing slight splitting around the 3–4mm entry hole'.

Professor Crane observes:

Contact or near contact wounds to the head may be associated with splitting of the margins of the wound due to the blow-back effect of the discharge gases. Such wounds would also be expected to show scorching and blackening of the margins of the wound and of the tissues within it. The scorching is caused by the effect of flame and is usually seen at contact or near contact range (i.e. within an inch or so). The blackening is caused by sooty material in the discharge gases and is seen up to about six inches. Punctate discharge abrasion is not usually seen at contact or near contact range. At contact and near contact range one would expect to see a mark caused by the imprint from the muzzle of the weapon in contact with the skin. Although the splitting of the wound margins may be a feature of a close range discharge it may also be seen at much greater distances, particularly if the skin is thin and delicate and closely applied to underlying bone, which if thin and delicate, is likely to fragment and thereby tear the skin around the wound margin. If Professor Simpson is relying solely on the splitting to indicate a contact or near contact wound then he is in error. Furthermore, since he fails to describe any blackening or burning of the wound then I would be very hesitant to reach such a conclusion as to a contact discharge. In addition, the site of the entrance wound is atypical – I have never seen a deliberate self-inflicted gunshot wound to the eye. This should raise the suspicion that a third party was involved.

In conclusion, there is nothing in the description of the entrance wound to confirm that this was a close range wound which had been self-inflicted . . .

The post-mortem on the post-mortem.
Each time I finish reading it I feel I need to read it again.
I'll read it again.
Contact or near contact wounds to the head . . . would also be expected to show scorching and blackening of the margins of the wound and of the tissues within it.

Two mortuary photographs, both facial, were taken by Detective Sergeant Adams. In the second of these the wound has been cleansed and there are no signs of scorching and blackening around its margins. In fact the absence of these features was noted by Dr Wingate, the resident medical officer at Middlesex Hospital who examined Mills upon arrival in his bloodstained condition. On the dead man's admittance card Wingate wrote: 'No sign of powder and scorching on face.'

Moreover, examination of this photograph reveals that Keith Simpson has misdescribed the entrance wound itself. According to Professor Crane, 'It is apparent that the entrance wound is through the upper eyelid of the right eye.'

The blackening is caused by sooty material in the discharge gases and is seen up to about six inches.

Having learned that the bullet was not fired at contact or near con-

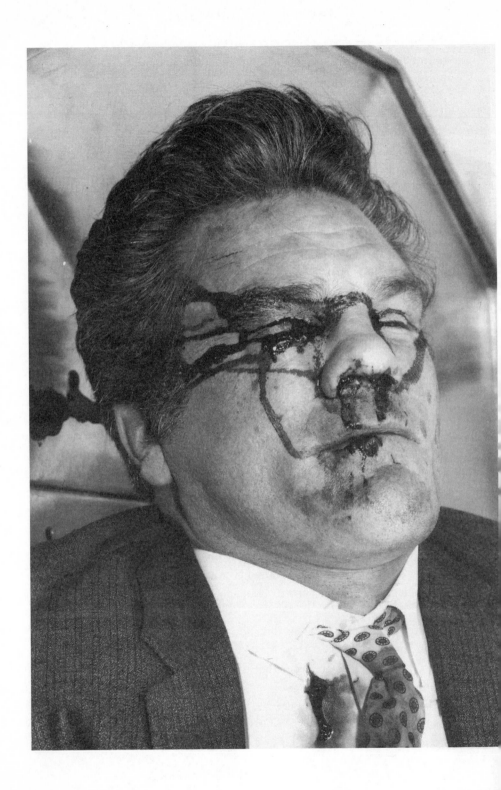

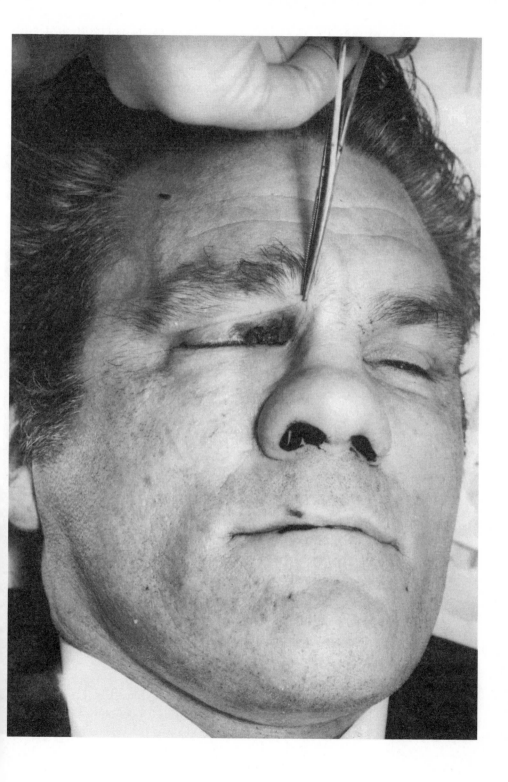

tact range we now discover that it was fired at a distance of more than six inches.

At contact and near contact range one would expect to see a mark caused by the imprint from the muzzle of the weapon in contact with the skin.

Among Simpson's verbal findings we find: 'Expressed the opinion that the rifle muzzle may have been applied to the middle of the forehead and slipped at the last moment into the corner of the eye.' Yet if we look again at the second photograph no imprint is visible.

Although the splitting of the wound margins may be a feature of a close range discharge it may also be seen at much greater distances, particularly if the skin is thin and delicate . . .

Well, the eyelid is certainly thin and delicate (extra delicate, perhaps, in the case of Mills, an ex-boxer).

If Professor Simpson is relying solely on the splitting to indicate a contact or near contact wound then he is in error.

He is in error.

In addition, the site of the entrance wound is atypical . . .

As was the angle of the bullet, 'slightly downwards and inwards', as described by Simpson.

I have never seen a deliberate self-inflicted gunshot wound to the eye.

The commonest sites of election are the temple (revolvers, pistols), the mouth (rifles, shotguns) and under the chin (shotguns). The centre of the forehead (rifles) is relatively uncommon.

In conclusion, there is nothing in the description of the entrance wound to confirm that this was a close range wound which had been self-inflicted.

Nothing whatsoever.

You know what?

Somebody murdered Freddie Mills, and Keith Simpson was covering it up.

Four days after Mills's death Scotland Yard received an anonymous note informing them that he had been murdered.

'It was set up to look as if he did himself. The word went round the clubs within minutes. A protection mob got him because he wouldn't pay Protection money.'

The Kray twins ran a protection gang, collecting from East End and West End pubs and nightclubs. Did Freddie Mills try conclusions with them? Was he killed to encourage the others?

A key member of the Firm was an Irishman named Albert Donoghue. Early in 1965 the twins entrusted him with the Friday 'milk round'. He was to go up West, then back East, then return to the Colonel with the envelopes.

'Freddie Mills? No instructions whatsoever. The Nite Spot never came into it, and if anybody else had been collecting I would have known. Straight away. We knew everybody's movements in the West End. We knew where Fraser's firm was, we knew where Nash's firm was.

'If there was anyone milking that club it was the Chinaman. The Chinese, whatever they can pull out of a place – twenty-five, fifty per cent – they'll pull it out.'

Chrissie Mills, interviewed for *The Freddie Mills Story*, recalled seeing the twins at her husband's club on several occasions. They always chose the same table on the edge of the dance floor, and Mills would go and talk to them. One night she called him over and asked him, 'Do you know these two fellows, Freddie?' 'Yes,' he replied, 'they used to be boxers at the Solomons boys club.' 'Well, Nick has just told me that they are the head of everything that's rotten in London.' 'Oh Mum, don't be so silly – they're lovely boys!'

Mills returned to stand at the twins' table, and addressed them while facing his wife. 'And I was absolutely horrified to see him say to them, "What do you think my missus has just told me? That you two are the heads of everything rotten in London." And I nearly died. I was so frightened.' But there was no cause for concern. 'Came back, threw his head back, screaming laughing, said, "Here you are, Mummy, I told you. They said, "You, Fred? Never. Wouldn't hurt you."'

And yet if any friendship, true or false, existed between Mills and the twins, Albert Donoghue remained unaware of it.

'They didn't nurse him. There was just no conversation about him. They might have been invited to the opening night of his club but he's never been invited to any of their clubs: Double R, Kentucky, Esmeralda's. I've never seen him in.

'After he went the twins were expecting a pull, but it didn't happen. The water didn't ripple.'

The water rippled, albeit very gently, three years later when Detective Superintendent Leonard 'Nipper' Read and his team, exultant at having arrested the Kray twins for the murders of George

Cornell and Jack McVitie, conducted a reinvestigation into the death of Freddie Mills.

Mills's death occurred a few months after an Old Bailey trial at which the twins and their associate 'Mad' Teddy Smith were acquitted of demanding money with menaces from Hugh ('Hew') McCowan, part-owner of The Hideaway, a Soho nightclub. McCowan had convictions for sodomy and gross indecency (with another man) and his reliability as chief witness was called into question. The case collapsed and the three men, who had been held in custody for ninety days, returned home in triumph to an East End welcome. They felt untouchable. They felt they could get away with anything. Murder, perhaps? Certainly Read now hoped to add the shooting of Freddie Mills to the existing charges.

But in this he was disappointed. The official report, dated 9 October 1968 and prepared by one of his sergeants, states:

> I have discussed the matter with Detective Superintendent Virgo, the Officer who dealt with the matter and during the course of his investigations he could find no evidence that the Krays or any other person was demanding protection money from Mills, respecting his club known as Freddie Mills Nite Spot, 143 Charing Cross Road, W.C.2. The Kray twins and some of their hangers on had visited the club and had in fact been photographed with Mills, but it is a well known fact that the Krays delighted in having their photographs taken with well known personalities and particularly with persons connected with boxing.

No, the twins didn't kill him. In fact the good news was that nobody killed him. Police had questioned Mills's business partner, Andrew Chin Guan Ho, 'a man who was probably closer to Mills than anybody', and Ho insisted that no protection money was being paid by either Mills or himself. He confirmed that for some time before his death Mills was depressed over his financial position and the failure of their business. The two-page report concludes: 'From the remarks made by Dr Keith Simpson, Pathologist, who conducted the Post Mortem examination, and the findings of the Coroner's Court held at Westminster on 2nd August 1965, there is nothing further to suggest that this was anything but suicide in which Mills took his own life as a result of a self inflicted firearm wound.'

Leonard Read supplies a handwritten postscript in which he describes the original inquiry as 'painstaking & thorough'. He has interviewed the widow, he says, and 'I am satisfied that she has an ulterior motive in having the coroner's verdict set aside.'

Shortly before his death from cancer in October 2000 Reg Kray was interviewed for a BBC1 documentary, *Reggie Kray: The Final Word*. The interviewer, having covered George Cornell, Jack 'the Hat' McVitie and Frank 'Mad Axeman' Mitchell, asked him if there were any more killings.

'One,' he replied. 'One'. He didn't enlarge.

Why didn't he enlarge? Why keep quiet?

Image?

If the victim was Freddie Mills, if the fans learned that Ron and Reg murdered sporting heroes as well as criminal lowlifes – well, it would tarnish the image. And the image was everything.

He was a vexation to the spirit.

No, he wasn't, he was loved by millions. Anyway, let's forget for a moment about who may have killed whom. Let's celebrate happier times.

Joe Cannon ('It was either me or one of the others') took a photograph of the champ and a few of the chaps one night, possibly the opening night, at the Nite Spot. Extreme right is little Sam Lieberman alias Lederman, theatrical agent. (Is he in the picture without permission?) He's a small-time old-time villain, and a runner for the twins. Next to him is Dickie Morgan, the twins' old friend and mentor; and there's Ron, blinking or sleeping or something, and there's his brother, catching him up. And then three more of their associates: John Davies (strong-arm man, likes guns) and Mickey Fawcett (collects protection money) and one

One

'Mad' Teddy Smith.

Gangster without Portfolio.

Missing, presumed swimming.

Edward Richard Smith was born in Islington in 1932, the son of a painter's labourer. According to Albert Donoghue, Smith joined the circus early.

'He was there before me, he was always there. He was a floater.

'I remember once (and this was before I was ever involved with the twins), I had a silly pub fight in the East End and a guy got hurt, badly hurt, and I disappeared. Now the woman who used to run the Black Swan in Bow had recently bought an inn in Ashford in Kent. So Ronnie arranged that I go there – and Ted Smith was the driver. This would be '59, '60, something like that.'

Teddy Smith was on the Firm, and yet he wasn't really of the Firm. His pseudo-Western ways tended to set him apart.

'You'd recognize him immediately as a West End woofter. The way he used to hold his glass. And the rest of us wore East End suits – three-piece normally, dark, wide shoulders, drapes, turn-ups – and he would wear figure-hugging Chelsea-type West End suits.' Queen? 'Fairy, yeah.' One of Ron's back numbers? 'Teddy Smith was too old for Ronnie. Ronnie liked them young, fresh. He liked young fighters. I think he did have a connection with Teddy Smith, but grew out of it. He'd quickly . . . like, divorce and marry again, that sort of thing. Probably he had some of Teddy Smith's seconds, and vice versa.'

Smith had no clearly defined role within the Firm, yet he gave good value. He was a mimic, a performer, a bit of a turn. 'He used to like that Shakespearean shit, and when he'd had a couple of drinks he could do a good impression. He'd go to the Astor and he'd sit on the stage and sing like Al Jolson.

'Baby face, about 5′ 8″, well built, with dark brown shortish curly hair, well controlled. He was always immaculately dressed, and he could swan in anywhere and go, "Oh, good evening, wonderful to meet you, absolutely enchanted to meet you," etc. That would go for a session, and then we'd all piss off somewhere else. Stork, Astor, Embassy, Churchill's . . .'

We're talking proper clubs here, proper West End clubs, clubs that put Mills's operation to shame.

'You'd be in a club, two-handed. As soon as you sat down two girls'd come. They'd go, "Hellooo" and you'd go, "Turn it in."

'If you were known that was different. Like we'd go in and sit down and no one would come near us. But you'd watch . . .

'Most of these clubs a bird used to come round in fishnet stockings, little skirt. "Would you like some cigarettes, sir? Cigars? Bunny rabbit for the lady?" Or a cuddly little teddy bear or a box of chocolates wrapped with a ribbon (no chocolates in it). It was a token, that's all. She'd hand it in and get . . . whatever.

'When you ordered your drinks the waiter would give you the bottle, and it had a tape measure running down it. You might say, "I drink gin, he drinks whisky and he drinks rum," and they'd give you the three bottles, inched off.

'And it's all dim-lit, so when it's time for the bill the waiter comes over, gets out his lighter and tells you how many measures you've had. They'd say to us, "£147, sir." Well, it's a load of shit, isn't it? You could buy a house for that. So we'd say, "Cut it in half and we might pay it." And he'd scuttle off, and come back and get a tenner. "That's it. Fuck off." But once they knew who we were they wouldn't try it on.'

Hugh McCowan didn't know who they were. They'd heard about him, though, and towards the end of 1964 Ron and Reg Kray began to take a close interest in his business affairs. McCowan, the son of a Scottish baronet, was about to open a nightclub, The Hideaway, at 16 Gerrard Street, Soho, and the twins initiated talks with the wealthy socialite and his agent, Sidney Vaughan. In return for a percentage of the takings they promised to introduce to The Hideaway visiting stars such as Nat King Cole and Frank Sinatra. Furthermore, they would install two doormen who would keep out the villains; and in order to guarantee the success of this new enterprise they would, on slack nights, fill the club with their friends. But first they needed to agree a figure. Ron Kray said, 'We want fifty per cent straight away as soon as you open.' Sidney Vaughan told him, 'You're a cunt.'

McCowan, for his part, appears to have found these meetings sexually arousing. Nevertheless, by the time The Hideaway opened on 16 December negotiations between the two parties had broken down. The twins now decided to deploy their secret weapon: Teddy Smith.

At about 2.30am on Saturday 19 December the doorman at The Hideaway told Sidney Vaughan that there was a drunk outside, demanding entry.

'The doorman said he knew him as a tearaway and I said, "Refuse him permission and put the crash bars down."'

But as a couple were leaving Teddy Smith forced an entry. He pointed at Vaughan, sitting at a table with a woman, and said, 'Look at Flash Harry.' He swore at McCowan and shouted that he would come back with a gang to wreck the place. When Vaughan went behind the reception desk to sound the police alarm, Smith flew at him, kicking and punching, and in the ensuing struggle a telephone and two small neon signs were broken. Waiters eventually managed to restrain Smith and eject him from the club. 'This isn't the last you'll hear of me,' he warned. 'You know who I am and who my friends are.' He caused another scene outside, but disappeared before the police arrived.

On 5 January 1965 the Kray twins were arrested in the basement bar of the Glenrae Hotel, Seven Sisters Road, which establishment they had taken over by dint of terrorizing the landlady and her common-law husband. Smith remained at large until 14 January, when he was traced to 151 Dartmouth Park Hill, the address of a relative, and taken to City Road police station. Here, in the presence of Detective Chief Superintendent Gerrard and Detective Inspector Read, he admitted causing the fracas at The Hideaway, but dismissed it as a drunken brawl. 'I haven't been with the Krays . . . I managed a few singers for them, but I haven't been having anything to do with them.' (Smith at that time numbered among his clients Lennie Peters, the blind pianist who later achieved success through his appearances on *Opportunity Knocks* with singer Diane Lee.) Gerrard said, 'But you were known to have been living with one of them.' 'That's right,' Smith replied, 'in Cedra Court, but I've got a lovely little place in Queen's Drive now.'

Fabulosa, Mr Read! Finsbury Park — with a heavenly view of the abyss . . .

'Teddy Smith was a woman,' recalls Albert Donoghue. 'It was like talking to a woman. Now and again he'd try and be tough. There was that Hideaway shit where he was sent in, but there was no one there to be worried about. There was no minders, stuff like that. An exhibition. Exhibitionist. Just smash the place up.'

Yes, well, The Hideaway may have been a pushover, but let's not underestimate Teddy Smith. His charge sheet lists a conviction for assaulting a police officer, and another for robbery armed with a revolver.

Bad enough perhaps; and yet Smith claimed to have a far more serious weapon at his disposal. When arrested each of the twins gave his occupation as company director, but Teddy Smith announced, 'I'm a writer.'

Was he?

Really?

We know he held a pen on at least one occasion. When the twins engineered Frank Mitchell's escape from Dartmoor prison, Smith ghosted several letters for the Axeman (including one to Smith's sometime boyfriend, the Labour MP Tom Driberg) in which he humbly requested a release date.

But what else did the writer write?

Donoghue recalls mention of a radio play. 'Apparently he won a competition. That's what he's telling me. But he was definitely *in* a play, because I watched it. Television play, black and white. He's playing a hard man, and he's just got to go into a room and grab this guy. There's two hard men, one on each arm. Anyway, I'm watching this and he goes in the room and grins straight at the camera. He's out of the game! He's never gonna act again.'

Never gonna corpse again.

Stick to the writing, Smithy.

The Top Bunk, a play by Ted Smith for *Thirty Minute Theatre*, was broadcast, in colour, on BBC2 on 30 October 1967. 'Write about what you know,' the experts advise, and Teddy Smith certainly knew about prison.

'Big' Bill Bishop, a dull-witted quick-tempered prisoner (petty larceny, six months) is both mocked and feared by his cellmate Bonkey Stone (shopbreaking, nine months), who concedes him the top bunk. The introduction of a third man, timid, bespectacled James Smithers, into this three-bunk cell causes fresh conflict. 'Here, you one of those public school geezers?' Bill Bishop asks him. He is, and he assumes he will be sleeping in the top bunk – until the big man sets him straight. 'This is my bunk. Got it? My bunk! Yer don't git on it. Yer don't touch it. Yer don't even look at it! Understand?' The two men then proceed to bully Smithers, who is told he will be sleeping in the bottom bunk. However, during the course of the evening Smithers explains that he is in prison for murder. He stabbed a man who was bullying him. He enjoyed the experience tremendously ('Oh, what fabulous rapture beyond compare!') and he admits, when pressed, that he would be prepared to kill again. All this has the desired effect upon his cellmates, although in fact Smithers has killed no one. 'Come in tonight, doing eighteen months for fraud,' remarks one warder to another during lights out. Meanwhile, inside the cell the new man is top dog, and sleeping in the top bunk.

The Top Bunk was the first television drama to be produced in colour. *The Top Bunk* by Ted Smith. Would that be our Ted Smith? The Ted Smith who, long before the date of transmission, had managed to disappear?

On 12 December 1966 Teddy Smith drove Albert Donoghue to Dartmoor, where the two of them picked up escaped prisoner Frank Mitchell and returned with him to London. Some time later that month, some time between Mitchell's escape and his violent death in the back of a van on Christmas Eve, Smith went missing.

The Regency was an upmarket nightclub in Stoke Newington, run by two brothers, John and Anthony Barry, and frequented by members of the Firm. According to Albert Donoghue, Teddy Smith was in the Regency late one night, extremely drunk and bragging about his part in Frank Mitchell's escape.

'The Regency was split in three. You went in, you had a ground floor bar, and an upstairs bar for private do's, functions, and the Dungeon, it had double doors, padded. That was for after hours, and that was where we found him.

'One of the Barrys had phoned Reggie and said, "Teddy Smith's here mouthing off about Mitchell." Reggie phoned me and said, "Go and get the cunt out of there." So I pulled . . . I can't tell you exactly . . . it was probably Scotch Jack and Ronnie Bender, but I wouldn't swear to that. But it was three-handed, I was leader of the pack. And I went in and Teddy Smith was talking to a couple of girls, which was unusual. I just looked at him and I said, "Come on," and he walked out with us.

'We got him in the car, we got him up the Balls Pond Road, we're going east to Vallance Road. We know what's gonna happen. He's either gonna get a fucking good spanking or he's gonna get a bullet. See, I knew how they worked. The fact that they phoned me . . . they're elsewhere, preparing an alibi.

'Teddy Smith says, "I want to go for a piss," so we dropped him for a piss. We never thought about it. Anyway, he's fucking bolted, ain't he? It was, like, a derelict site, and he just went missing. So we went back and said, "He's bolted," and they went apeshit.

'We had a quick look for him. We weren't really fussed. We knew what the guy was in for and, like, fucking good luck if he gets away. And he was no mug. He knew the twins, as I say, from the Fifties. He knew the whole shit, he knew the scene. And he's got three fucking well-known hooligans taking him east in a car. . . "Bollocks. I ain't having none of this." That's what I'd think as well. He bolted. He went for a piss and he bolted. We chased him. Gone. No one ever see him again.'

Correction. 'A copper said to me: "I seen Teddy Smith." This was from the arrest to the trial, which took about a year. '68, '69, something like that. They was pumping me to find out what I knew. So I said, "Teddy Smith. I ain't seen him since . . ." And he said, "Well, I see him, the other week." West End somewhere. I said, "Oh good, he's still hopping about," you know. And then he switched to something else, another line of questions. I think he just stuck it in to find out if I knew something. If I'd have gone, "Fucking liar!" . . . he was watching my reaction. But I went, "Good. You see him? He's all right," and the copper went, "Uhh."'

It's Teddy, not Freddie, who is popularly believed to be the 'one' to whom Reg Kray alluded on his deathbed. But once again, why keep quiet about it? After all, writers, unlike boxers, are better off dead anyway.

The possibility remains that Reg was lying, joking even (ha croak ha) – that he had no one specific in mind.

In which case whatever happened to Teddy Smith?

'Nipper Read's convinced that Teddy Smith went. I'm pretty convinced because Teddy Smith was . . . he was loud, he was a drunkard, he was a . . . exhibitionist type. You couldn't have missed him, he'd have come to light somewhere. I'm sure he's killed.

'But let me know if you find him. I'd like to see him again.'

On 26 July 1965 Detective Chief Inspector Virgo, the officer in charge of the Mills inquiry, and Detective Sergeant Harris visited 316 Queenstown Road, the home of Mrs May Gladys Ronaldson, a 65-year-old woman who owned an amusement arcade at Battersea funfair. She, it now emerged, had lent the fatal weapon to Freddie Mills, whom she knew well and looked upon as one of the family. 'I have known Freddie Mills since about 1933–34, and met him travelling the West Country and he was in the boxing show.'

On the morning of Tuesday 20 July Mills called round unexpectedly. 'I didn't answer the door at first as my daughter and I were not dressed.' So Mills went away. When he returned shortly afterwards he declined her offer of a cup of tea. He was in a hurry, he told her, as he had had trouble with the windscreen wipers on his car. He then said, 'I'll tell you what I've come for. Have you got an old gun I can have? It's only for a gag. I am going to open a fete at Esher tomorrow.' 'What do you want a gun for then?' she asked. 'I am going to dress up as a cowboy,' Mills explained. 'It's just a gag, and I must have a gun to have my picture taken.'

She believed him, and handed over a .22 FN automatic rifle of the type used in her amusement arcade. 'I had an old one in the house, it was four years old and it was faulty. By this I mean it would sometimes misfire and because of this it was unreliable and could not be used on a range and I kept it at home. Knowing Freddie appeared on TV and charity shows I regarded this as a prop and allowed him to have the rifle. He had no ammunition from me at all.'

On the morning of Thursday 22 July Mills returned the gun. He said, 'The fete has been cancelled because of the weather and no one there.' She checked that the rifle was empty and placed it in the corner under the stairs. Mills thanked her and left saying he was having the brakes fixed on his car.

The following morning he called again. They went into the

kitchen, and this time he had a cup of tea. He said, 'The fete is on Saturday and I have to go then. Can I borrow your gun again?' She handed him the same rifle as before, and he jumped up, saying he had 'so much on', and prepared to leave. She wanted to know when he intended returning the gun. He said, 'I'll bring it back Sunday at three o'clock without fail,' and left.

On Sunday 25 July her son telephoned her, having read in a news-paper that Freddie Mills had been shot dead. 'I said, "Oh my God, how could he be shot." I then remembered my son had brought five shots back on Thursday together with two duds.' She rushed to the kitchen and looked at the shots on the mantelpiece, only to discover that three were missing. Nobody in her family had touched them. She could only assume Mills took them. 'On realising this I immediately telephoned Sergeant Harris of the Flying Squad who I know as a police officer.'

Ronaldson handed Virgo a bullet from the same packet as those she had left on the mantelpiece. She told the officer she knew of no reason why Freddie Mills should want to commit suicide. In an additional statement she told him, 'I should say that the .22 bullets used on my range are special bullets with no lead and they disintegrate on contact with a hard surface.'

Both statements were taken, read over and witnessed by Detective Chief Inspector Virgo, who interviewed no one else during his inquiry. Statements were normally taken down by sergeants or con-stables: it was a little unusual for a senior officer to take them himself. But Virgo no doubt realized the importance here of getting the right story, and of getting the story right. After all, he was calling the shots.

At the police laboratory, Michael Isaacs, a senior scientific officer, examined the rifle, empty cases and control sample bullet. He certi-fied he found one live round in the breech of the rifle, and that this round was of identical manufacture with the two empty cases found in Mills's car and also with the control round. He carried out tests and certified that comparison of the firing pin and breech face impressions on the cartridge fired in the laboratory with the two spent cartridge cases found in the car showed that the two bullets fired in the Citroën had been fired from May Ronaldson's rifle. These were lead bullets which would shatter on hitting hard materials. (Isaacs also examined the metallic substance found in the vicinity of the car, and reported that this was not lead but a clinker-like substance.)

May Ronaldson had stated that hers were special bullets which contained no lead. By the time they got to that bit, she would have been scared out of her wits.

There are different kinds of fear, aren't there?

This wasn't like the dodgems or the ghost train or the Wall of Death.

This was these two on her doorstep on a Monday afternoon.

Harris and Virgo.

Famous master tailors.

Coming to stitch her up.

On 23 November 1969 Detective Sergeant Gordon Harris made the front page of *The Times*: 'Tapes reveal planted evidence. London policemen in bribe allegations.'

A south London thief had provided two journalists with incriminating tape recordings of conversations with Harris and with two other officers, Sergeant John Symonds and Detective Inspector Bernard Robson. These three were all members of a team attempting to capture several gangs who were raiding shops and stores with the aid of skeleton or duplicate keys. The tapes revealed that they routinely planted evidence on suspects and then demanded substantial bribes in order to drop the charges.

Symonds fled the country, but Robson and Harris were eventually prosecuted. Harris received a six-year sentence for offences which included conspiracy to demand money with menaces and conspiracy to pervert the course of justice.

In March 1977 ex-Commander Wallace Harold Virgo, QPM (he retired from the force in 1973), stood trial at the Old Bailey in company with five other officers. The six men were charged with conspiring to take money and other considerations from pornographers operating illegally in the West End during the period 1964–72. Each man was charged on twenty-seven specimen counts of bribery and corruption, involving £87,485. Mr Justice Mars-Jones spoke of corruption 'on a scale which beggars description'. (Virgo alone, it was alleged, had received £60,000 in bribes.) All six were found guilty, and Virgo, as one of the chief culprits, was sentenced to twelve years' imprisonment.

Men that money could buy.

Virgo, who had previously served as a detective inspector in the Flying Squad, certainly knew Harris, and Ronaldson, in view of her occupation, was probably one of Harris's informants. She now found herself in trouble, and she looked to Harris for help.

Serious trouble, as Virgo no doubt reminded her. She had supplied a firearm to an individual who was not in possession of a firearms licence. As set out in the 1920 Firearms Act this offence carried a maximum penalty of three months' imprisonment plus a fine of £20. It was now up to Uncle Wally to supply her with an old wife's tale.

First things first. She was a good friend of Freddie's, wasn't she?

'I looked upon Freddie as one of the family . . . I used to see him fairly regularly since 1951, and accepted him in my home.'

That's right, a good friend, the kind of friend he could call on unannounced for a cup of tea and a faulty rifle. The rifle was faulty, wasn't it?

'I had an old one in the house, it was four years old and it was faulty. By this I mean it would sometimes misfire and because of this it was unreliable and could not be used on a range and I kept it at home.'

Not much of a rifle at all then, more of a toy really . . .

'Knowing Freddie appeared on TV and charity shows I regarded this as a prop and allowed him to have the rifle. He had no ammunition from me at all.'

No, no, of course not. So how did he obtain the three rounds?

'I can only assume he took them.'

But they weren't really bullets at all, were they?

'I should say that the .22 bullets used on my range are special bullets with no lead and they disintegrate on contact with a hard surface.'

Toy bullets?

No, not toy bullets. Ronaldson's appended statement was a transparent lie. Bullets used on rifle ranges were made of lead, as was the bullet handed to Virgo from her original stock and subsequently test-fired by Michael Isaacs. However, Virgo had no doubt warned her that she faced the possibility of an additional or concurrent three-month sentence for supplying Mills with live ammunition.

How do we know that she supplied him with the ammunition? Well, Mills presumably borrowed that rifle for self-defence. (Chrissie Mills told police that although her husband had never owned a rifle,

'I had seen him at the amusement place at Battersea use one and he was a good shot.') A man as powerfully built as Mills was clearly expecting his assailant(s) to come armed. He therefore needed to fully prepare himself, and that meant bullets – and bullets, it turned out, meant death.

So she said what she said, or rather she signed what Virgo wrote, and he brought no charges against her. DCI Virgo was making good progress with his inquiry. Simpson yesterday, Ronaldson today.

Keith Simpson.

A safe pair of eyes.

Safe as corpses, Keith.

And yet his post-mortem report betrays a certain anxiety: a desire, perhaps, to be found out.

'Reach 34in.–35in.'

A dead man's reach can never be accurately measured, yet in lending Mills the reach of a chimpanzee Simpson is surely attempting to explain away the absence of blackening around the wound, blackening which may be seen at a distance of up to about 6 inches. Why is he bothering?

'Time since death. Some 4–5 hrs.'

Here again Simpson, who examined Mills at 6.10am, overcompensates by recording a time which roughly coincides with the arrival of the ambulance in Goslett Yard. Even though at 11.45pm, almost two hours earlier, Robert Deacon found Mills sitting upright in his car, head slumped forward, dead to the world. Concerned, Deacon told Grant, who took no action until 1am, when he himself went to rouse Mills and subsequently informed Ho that he was ill. Ho then telephoned Mills's home and was told that Mrs Mills was on her way to the club. But who told him? Susan (thirteen)? Amanda (seven)? A mystery babysitter?

It's possible that Ho was lying, that he never made the call. It's certain that Deacon was lying, for at 2.15am, shortly after Mills's admittance to Middlesex Hospital, Dr Wingate took the dead man's temperature for the admittance card. He recorded: 'Oral temperature at 2.15am was 89.4°F (assuming normal temperature of 98.4° and average fall of 2½°F per hour in fully dressed condition).' He concluded: '?? time of death was 3–4 hours earlier.'

In other words Deacon probably never saw Mills alive at all that night. He was shot dead almost as soon as he arrived at the club, and his car would have reeked of cordite.

Forget about 11.45pm ('He was sitting upright with his head slumped forward').

Forget about 11.10pm ('He said, "No, come back in half an hour"').

What really happened at 10.30pm?

Robert Deacon, twenty-one, and Henry Grant, forty-six, were standing at the front entrance to the club.

'My duties are to show people to the reception and find taxis for people who want them,' Deacon explained to the coroner. He was studying law at University College and had obtained this summer job through his friendship with Andy Ho's son Anthony. He had been working at the Nite Spot for just three weeks, which indicates, with reference to Angela Deacon's remarks, that the hostess racket was continuing at the time of Mills's death.

Grant, on the other hand, had been at the club for sixteen months and was almost certainly the 'Mr Toni' referred to by the *People* reporter, who urged Mills to get rid of him. But Mills hadn't got rid of him. There he was.

There he was, standing with Deacon at the front entrance to the club, when a stranger approached and told them Freddie was in his car in the mews and wanted to speak to – whom? According to Grant it was 'Bob', but according to Bob it was 'one of us'. Anyway, what did the message really mean? Job done?

Grant stated that the messenger was about fifty years old, about 6′, with long grey hair, and was wearing a raincoat. 'I think I would know him again,' he added helpfully. Deacon supplied police with a more detailed description – grey hair, long at the sides, slim build, fawn raincoat – but his statement ended, 'I doubt if I would know him again.'

Were the law student's words weighted with the knowledge that he was now an accessory to murder?

The man in the fawn raincoat wasn't traced, wasn't looked for, wasn't even mentioned at the inquest. But he may well have had some connection with Mills's murder.

So how was Freddie Mills killed?

Well, let's assume that he arrived at the club armed in expectation
of a meeting, and let's assume that he was the victim rather than the
aggressor. Now the police photograph of Goslett Yard shows the
Citroën with its offside rear window wound down; the car is parked
in such a way as to enable Mills, sitting in the nearside rear seat where
he was found, to cover the side exit of the club with his borrowed
rifle. (According to Deacon, the club had six or seven customers that
night – none of whom was interviewed.)

Let's assume that a man emerges from this exit to find Mills pointing a gun at him. Whereupon this man shows Mills he is unarmed,
and persuades him – *That's not fair, Freddie, is it?* – to put the rifle
down, before joining him in the back of the car for a chat. But of
course he doesn't like it in the back, he'd prefer to sit in the front –
Is that all right? – so, all right, he goes and sits in the driver's seat. And
pulls a pistol (where did that come from?) on the man in the back,
forcing him to hand over his weapon.

Is this a real one, Freddie? Is it even loaded? He answers his own question by firing a test shot through the nearside front door. But don't

forget, he's upset the former light heavyweight champion of the world, whom he must cover with his pistol while firing the rifle. Firing the rifle one-handed is a possibility, but reloading? It wouldn't be easy, could prove fatal.

Let's go back to the beginning of the end. Let's assume that *two* men pass through the side door and into the yard, two perfectly harmless individuals who together persuade Mills to put down the rifle before they commence their chat. The first man sits in the driver's seat; the second man sits with Mills. But the second man – a big man, say – presently complains about the shortage of leg-room: he pleads cramp, steps outside, massages his leg. And, availing himself of the open window, pulls a pistol on the man in the back, forcing him to hand over his weapon to the man in the front. This man then fires and reloads at leisure before killing Mills. (Is he given a drink before dying?)

He shoots Mills through the upper right eyelid. Has Mills been instructed to close his eyes? Is he preparing himself for death? Or merely blinking?

Anyway, having now adopted, naturally or unnaturally, a natural sitting position, Mills is in no position to create further difficulties. The murderer leans across and places the rifle –

Where exactly *did* he place it? When Chrissie Mills discovered the gun (the gun which neither Deacon nor Grant, amid all their shakings and slappings, had managed to spot) it was 'on the floor'. On the floor as opposed to on the seat? Donald McCorkindale, the next person to see the rifle, noticed it was propped against Mills's leg, muzzle up. He picked it up, looked at it and put it back 'more or less' in the same position. When the ambulance men arrived the rifle was leaning against the offside rear seat in an upright position, between 6″ and 8″ from the offside rear door. 'The rifle was out of his reach,' Leslie Rowe told the coroner. 'Nobody gave any indication that the gun had been moved.' In the absence of police, Rowe, the man who suspected a pulse in a corpse three hours old, handed the rifle to his colleague, who removed the offensive weapon from the scene.

The rifle was not tested for any remaining fingerprints. As for the car, well, the car was certainly *preserved* for fingerprints . . . a police photograph taken at Tottenham Court Road station shows the nearside front door of the car, and fingerprint powder on the nearside front and rear window and front windscreen. But if the tests were actually carried out the results were not recorded.

Who killed Freddie Mills?

It's the title of a book by a man named Tony Van den Bergh.

He doesn't know the answer either.

Who paid Wally Virgo?

Who paid him all that money to go to all that trouble to cover this murder up?

Or was it an inside job?

Should anyone want me tonight I'm here, in my bedroom, looking down into the yard, listening.

'I know. I'll work it out myself. I'll deduce it. I'll be Johnny Oxford.'

Listening to Tony Hancock. He's sitting up late reading a library novel, *Lady Don't Fall Backwards* by D'arcy Sarto. It's a murder mystery with a very nasty twist at the end: the last page is missing.

I used to enjoy *Hancock's Half Hour*. Mind you, I haven't listened to it since – when? where?

I was here, I was in this room, that's right, I was in bed.

I had company, didn't I?

'Freda Wolkinski was asleep in her pull-down bed, when somebody pressed the button, and she flew up into the wall and suffocated.'

Yes.

Yes, we'd lie there together and laugh at this stuff . . . in another life.

'Now that must have been somebody who knew her bed was a pull-down one –'

I turn it off, and go to bed, and wait for other voices to find me.

The voice of Detective Chief Inspector Arthur Phillips (retired):

I remember once, when I was a DC at Paddington in the Fifties, I had a call to go to Paddington Station. Someone had found a dead baby in the toilet – in the cistern.

Francis Camps (he was the pathologist) turned up. He used to smoke all the time, and he always had a cigarette in his mouth when he was cutting people open. He'd give you his packet of Player's before a post-mortem, and when he finished one he'd spit it out and nod, and you had to light another one and put it in his mouth.

He turned up and he said, 'Do you know whose it is?' I said, 'I've no idea.' So he said, 'What do you want? Stillborn or murder?' 'Well, I didn't want a murder — all that bloody paperwork, and we'd never find them. Anyway, it turned out he was just having a joke. He tore the lungs out and stamped on them and gave them to me and said, 'There you are.'

The voice of Albert Donoghue:

There's a guy I used to knock around with in the late Fifties. Norman Winters (he's dead now). He lived in Bromley Hall Street, between Bow and the Blackwall Tunnel. We worked together.

His wife was very strict, very uptight, near-Methodist. And she thought he was a roof felter. That was his official job, but he was a wheel man, a getaway man. We used to take a few security bags. We'd come in covered with cuts and bruises and tell lies, say we'd been in an accident, and she'd believe him.

Norman Winters had this little dark-haired Welsh bird, pretty little thing she was. She used to live in his van, in his pick-up. It was a pick-up with a canvas hood on the back, you know, like a flat-back. It had a bed in there. He used to buy her fish and chips. He'd buy her a new coat, dress, shoes — send her to the hairdresser's. And she would come out with us, in the pub and stuff like that. His wife didn't know about her.

She used to use a coffee bar in the West End, and when we didn't need her, when we didn't want her around us, like, she would go to the coffee bar and pull a customer. Sometimes you wouldn't see her for a couple of days. When they found her body he just said, 'Oh shit.' He's worried, in case they track it back to him. And I suppose, in these days of DNA, they would have tracked it back to him.

She was a fierce little girl: most of them girls are. But you could sit there and talk to her. Conversational. I used to mix with these girls and listen to their stories. I rescued one girl from a Maltese gaff in Brick Lane. Three weeks later she was back. What can you do?

The voice of Inspector Ron Turner (retired):

You say this woman Tailford had a gag in her mouth? Well, I worked on Thames Division 1955–77, and with suicides you normally had a neat pile of clothes on the bank, with shoes. I never encountered a suicide with a gag in the mouth in twenty-two years. Was she dead before she hit the water? Did she die in a bath full of river water? You only need a cupful of water to drown.

February . . . you see, if it's a slack part of the water a body will stay put until degeneration causes it to lift. The water was colder, which meant less deterioration, and if she was last seen on Friday night . . . Saturday, Sunday, well, that body didn't move much, if at all. It was found more or less where it entered the water.

She was found at Hammersmith? And her coat was found by Festival Hall Pier? Well, a wool coat would have buoyancy, but no coat would drift that far without sinking. And it would have drifted to the pier, not away from the pier.

Yes, yes . . . I'm thrashing around like a hunchback cutting a rug . . .yes, they all came out from beneath Tailford's overcoat – Lockwood, Barthelemy, Fleming, Brown . . . Barthelemy in Blackpool (a pound of raw liver in the Palace of Strange Girls) . . . Brown in that van with that man with the CID card, the man who explained to her how the murders were done and had a lot of rubbish in the back like clothes . . .

Did the coat enter the water before she did? It could have been dropped from Hungerford Bridge: a nice quiet pedestrian bridge. Or if she was last seen alive at Charing Cross, well, Festival Hall Pier is just opposite. . .

Drowners are different, they're not like the others.

I wouldn't want to swap places.

Post-mortem wound 1½" long on the back of the right calf . . . it's only a small tear, isn't it? I would say that was probably caused by sliding the body over a stone wall – a wharf-front, perhaps.

Maybe I deserve it.

I still don't deserve it.

No.

I wouldn't want my life to flash past me when I'm dying.

I wouldn't want to have to watch the things that I've done.

In April 1970 New Scotland Yard received a letter from Irene N. Cox (Mrs) of Saltdean, Sussex. Describing herself as a spiritual healer and medium, she reported that she'd recently had a sudden feeling that Freddie Mills was murdered:

> Would you be good enough to find out from the Pathologist in charge
> of the case at the time to see if he considered the possibility of Freddie
> Mills having been the victim of an Indian or other nationality's indi-
> vidual having killed him by the KARATI METHOD . . .

Shortly afterwards she sent another letter.

May I Please have an intelligent answer to my intelligent question in my letter of April 29th regarding the probability of Freddie Mills having been 'Karati-d' or shot through the temple with a gun fitted with a 'silencer' and then carried out to his car and the gun placed in one of his hands to make it look like suicide, particularly as Freddie Mills was being blackmailed by a gang extorting, or trying to extort what I have since learned is called 'protection money' from those who have or are running whatever establishments they call 'Clubs.'

Later that year she sent another.

. . . surely dear old Agatha Christie must have taught the pathologists something about how these vile specimens of excuses for human beings have been murdering innocent victims. . .

In May 1972 a letter was received from a Peter Neale of Balham. Freddie Mills did not commit suicide, he wrote, but was killed for refusing to pay protection money to racketeers. Neale also suggested that Mills was responsible for the nude murders.

In July police interviewed Neale, a freelance journalist, at Vine Street police station. He explained that he'd heard from several people that Freddie Mills had two bullet holes in his head, and that he'd suggested to a chief inspector that Mills's body be exhumed for verification purposes.

'This same chief inspector, who is a good friend of mine, also told me in confidence that Freddie Mills killed the nude prostitutes in west London, Shepherd's Bush area. This was also common knowledge in the West End. Many people would say, "Oh, Freddie did them in . . ."'

But Neale could produce no evidence to support this allegation.

In July 1979 R. N. Sheppard, public relations manager for Bournemouth Town Hall, sent a letter to the Commissioner:

This morning my Department received an anonymous telephone call relating to the late Freddie Mills (Boxer). We here in Bournemouth are proposing to set up a memorial to Mr Mills in our Lower Gardens in the form of four Public seats and a plaque. The caller told us that we would be wrong to set up such a memorial as Freddie Mills committed suicide shortly before he was to be arrested for murder.

The Assistant Commissioner replied:

As regards the suggestion made to you that Mills's suicide occurred shortly before he was to be arrested for murder there is no evidence known to this Force which would substantiate such a theory.

Mediums . . . Indians . . . karate chops . . . 'protection money' . . . nude murders . . . memorial seats . . .
What do *you* think?
Why not drop us a line?

Freddie Mills's funeral, organized by Jack Solomons, took place on 30 July 1965. Almost a thousand people packed the parish church of St Giles, Camberwell, for the service, and as many more lined the streets outside in the rain. Stars from the worlds of both boxing and show business turned up to pay their respects. (But where was Freddie's manager, Ted Broadribb? And where was his old pal Norman Wisdom?) Bruce Forsyth gave the funeral address, and was

one of the pallbearers led by Solomons to the private burial service in Camberwell New Cemetery. 'The catafalque itself was surrounded with wreaths,' the *Daily Sketch* reported. 'On top lay a heart in red roses with the word "Broken" on a printed card from his wife.'

All that summer they went mad, his public: they could not, would not desert him. They brought sandwiches, and transistor radios (in the hope, perhaps, of waking the dead); they stripped the grave of flowers. The Reverend Stewart Carne-Ross told the *People:* 'It is appalling what has been happening. Parents bring their children here for a day out. They come here to have picnics and poke morbidly round the grave.'

No peace.

In June 1966, as the result of an objection raised by the British Board of Boxing Control, Mills's remains were exhumed and reburied in a more accessible part of the cemetery. A headstone was erected in November of that year.

This headstone: what is it? black granite? marble?

1919–1965

In

Loving Memory Of

Freddie

A Husband And Father

Who Was

Loved And Adored.

Whatever it is, it wasn't cheap. I step back to admire an engraving of the deceased in action. He's in the ring, gloves on, ready to do battle with whoever it was that boxed him. There's also a giant F, finished off with a lion couchant (no one ever said he wasn't brave).

There's also bird shit smearing both sides of the headstone, and weeds surrounding the receptacle at its base. This contains a fistful of plastic flowers, mainly bluebells, colourless.

Chrissie

Mills

25.2.13–4.11.94

Forever

In Our Hearts.

I recall the words of Terry in the office. 'I've worked here for twenty-eight years, and the only time I've seen her up here was when they made that film.' And she's not up here now. 'The wife wasn't buried with him. Cremated, maybe? I don't know.'

I reach forward to touch the white marble boxing glove.

Broken.

Removing it from its plinth, I leave the graveside and walk across to the hedgerow, and a bench. I lay the glove down beside me and unscrew the top off my flask, and listen to a man talking on the other side of the hedge.

'If people come up here and say, "That looks nice," I shall tell them, "I done that," and I'll say, "It's about time you did something. Don't just look after your own, look at the one next to you. If there's leaves in it, take the fucking things out . . ."'

Murder, post-mortem; burial, reburial, investigation, reinvestigation. Why did Keith Simpson Camp it up? How many other murders did he hex? ('Michael Gregston was dead and Hanratty was dead, but the ghost of the A6 murder has lingered on . . . But no one engaged in the case, as I was, and entirely disinterested in the innocence or guilt of the accused, as every pathologist should be – and I certainly am – could fail to be impressed by the weight of the evidence.') Why did Leonard Read, one of the most rigorous and scrupulous detectives in the history of the Met, declare himself satisfied with Virgo's inquiry? (Did Wally warn him off?) What did he mean when he wrote that the widow had 'an ulterior motive in having the coroner's verdict set aside'? Was this a reference to life insurance? But her husband had no policy, as Read could have seen at a glance. Coroner's officer's report, page two.

'These buggers, they really piss me off. I'm going to clean that bird shit off that poor fucker over there. All right mate, see you in a bit.'

I pick the glove up and take it to the office. As I circle the main building I notice an impressive black cross, flowers and everything, and read:

Also of my dear husband
George Cornell

6

Taste in Mouth

On 12 February 1965 Thelma Schwartz was late for work. She was a cleaner at Zonal Film Facilities Ltd on Acton's Heron Trading Estate. Mrs Tyson, the head cleaner, normally picked her up at Western Circus and gave her a lift. But sometimes Thelma Schwartz missed her lift and had to make her own way in, as on this quiet windless Friday morning. It was 5.45am and she was already half an hour late as she crossed the bridge to the industrial estate. Halfway across she heard a noise coming from the direction of the sheds which backed on to the railway embankment to her right. She thought at first that it was birds, 'but it was too noisy for birds and I realised it was someone rustling leaves or some other dead vegetation'.

She crossed the bridge and walked along Westfields Road in complete darkness. She crossed over into Alliance Road. Still the noise continued. She turned right, into the passageway between Union Cold Storage and Carrier's engineering works, and the noise stopped.

Although the leaf-rustler would have stood little chance of twigging her in her rubber-soled boots she became very frightened and, without looking back, ran until she reached the Zonal factory.

'I didn't mention the incident to anyone at work that morning. This was because I was behind with my work, and the supervisor doesn't allow talking.'

At about 10.30am on Tuesday 16 February Leonard Beauchamp, another worker on the estate, walked across to a stores shed at the side of his firm's factory next to the railway embankment. Beauchamp worked for Surgical Equipment Supplies Ltd as an electrical fitter and all-round odd-job man, and he had just discovered, while changing the hand towels in the Gents, that the liquid-soap dispenser was empty.

He unlocked the shed and, having filled a small jug with liquid soap, placed it on the floor. He then left the shed – unlocked, because he wanted to have a look round the back first to see if he could find anything worth taking. 'This sounds a bit funny but I have seen wireless posts, old cabinets and other property abandoned there on previous occasions. It seems to be used by many people as a dump.'

He saw nothing he fancied behind his or the adjacent shed, so decided to venture further afield. He walked across to have a look behind the third one.

Something poked out through the undergrowth.

Something he couldn't take home with him.

'I first noticed a pair of feet and I could see them up to the ankles. My first reaction was that I was looking at a dummy.'

He looked again and noticed that the toenails were painted. It wasn't a body, was it?

The third and final stores shed was the main one, so he went inside and spoke to Maurice Chester, the storeman. 'I told him there was a woman's body behind the stores. I was half joking. We had a laugh and a joke about it with a Mr John Cheese, who was also in the stores.'

Chester went with Beauchamp to have a look. Beauchamp stood back as the storeman peered into the undergrowth. Presently he announced that he could see the feet, but could not be sure if this was a body or a dummy; and besides, he never interfered with anything behind the stores.

Beauchamp went to the office and reported what he had seen to Gerald Marshall, the production manager, and his colleague Kenneth Watts, and the two men accompanied him to the spot. 'Mr Marshall had a look and said it looked like wax, but told us not to touch anything and he would contact Acton police station.'

Bridget alias Bridie Moore was born in Dublin on 2 March 1937, the daughter of Matthew Moore, a plasterer, and his wife, Mary. The sixth child in a Roman Catholic family, she attended school in Dublin until the age of fourteen, and spent the next four years working in hospital cleaning and factory jobs in Ireland.

At the beginning of 1954 she left for England, where she took up similar work, living in Acton with an older sister. This woman returned to Dublin a year later, and Bridget Moore then lived with a Margaret McEvoy on Gloucester Terrace, W2. But not for long.

'Bridget started staying out all night,' her brother William recalled, 'and I heard about it from Margaret McEvoy.' At this time William and Matthew were working in London; William told his father, who tried to persuade Bridget to return to Dublin, without success. 'My father went to the police at Acton about it, but they said there was nothing they could do.' Matthew took her to live with her stepsister in Hackney, but she soon disappeared. Two years later William learned that she was living with a labourer named Michael O'Hara in Shepherd's Bush.

'At about this time Mick got three years for robbery and on the Sunday after he got sentenced on the Thursday, that would be Easter 1958, I saw my sister drunk at Shepherd's Bush. She had been arrested, and another brother and I tried to help her and we got arrested as well. At court I learned that my sister had convictions for prostitution. That was the first time I knew she was a prostitute.'

Bridget Moore was nineteen when she picked up the first of eleven convictions for soliciting. She was last arrested in 1958, and when she failed to appear at Marylebone Magistrates' Court a warrant was issued for her arrest. This warrant was never executed and was withdrawn in August 1963. Meanwhile, she went about her business on the streets of Bayswater, Notting Hill, Holland Park and Shepherd's Bush. She and O'Hara lived together as man and wife at a succession of west London addresses. They wanted to start a family.

In March 1962 'Bridget O'Hara' was admitted to Hammersmith Hospital following a miscarriage at her home. The miscarriage was a normal one and not the result of an abortion. She was allowed to leave hospital the following day.

Bridget Moore married Michael O'Hara on 17 September 1962 in Dublin, and later that year the couple moved into their final home together, a rented flat — one room with a communal bathroom and kitchen facilities — on the upper floor of 41 Agate Road, W6.

On 14 February 1964 Bridget O'Hara attended the antenatal clinic at Hammersmith Hospital and underwent a fertility test. The test proved positive, and an appointment was later made for both parties to attend, though neither did.

On 27 February she attended the hospital's casualty department and complained that her husband had assaulted her. She was treated for small lacerations on the back of her head and allowed to go home.

1964 ended badly. 'On New Year's Eve we both went to the Swately pub and had a lot to drink,' Michael O'Hara remembered. 'We were with friends but I can't recall who they were.' When the couple arrived home they had a row, breaking windows and crockery in the process. At about 1.30am Bridget left the flat.

Her friend Mrs Jean Lovelock lived nearby, and shortly after 2.30am O'Hara paid a call on her. She was wearing a white coat stained with blood, and she was carrying a bloodstained bricklayer's trowel. 'It was obvious to me she had been in a fight.'

The blood on the trowel, it transpired, belonged to Bobby Brown, the Irishman who entered the flat with her. He now had a wash and the two of them laughed it off. She'd also had a fight with Mick earlier on 'and had left him and had gone and got Brown from somewhere, she did not say where'. They had both been drinking, together or separately, and they wished to continue. O'Hara produced a small bottle of whisky and all three sat in the kitchen and talked. 'They drank the whisky and I had a brown ale which I had in the house.' By 5.30am Jean Lovelock had grown tired, and told them to leave. She lent O'Hara one of her daughter's coats in exchange for her own soiled garment.

Later that morning O'Hara called round again to return the borrowed coat. ('The white coat that Bridie had bloodstains on we still have and my Pat has had it cleaned.') They had a cup of tea and a chat, and Lovelock asked her if she'd been home but she said no, she hadn't. She told her friend she'd arranged to meet Bobby Brown at the Brook Green Hotel, Shepherd's Bush Road, around noon. 'I told her that I would see her there as well.'

But when Jean Lovelock turned up at around 1pm she saw O'Hara standing on the steps on her own. They went inside and ordered two tomato juices, and O'Hara cursed Brown for standing her up. Soon Lovelock wanted to leave, and suggested the British Prince in Goldhawk Road. On the way she looked in at the Railway Tavern and saw Michael O'Hara. He offered to buy her a drink, and she told him his wife was outside. 'He did not pass any comment about Bridie.'

In the Prince, O'Hara talked about their fight the night before. She had thrown things at him, she said, and the flat was in a mess and the landlord was due back that evening and Mick had the keys. Jean Lovelock agreed to help her clean up, and later called in at the Railway Tavern to pick up the keys.

'Their room was in a terrible state.' Two windowpanes had been broken and the glass was all over the floor, together with broken bits of crockery and spilt milk. 'There were chips on the floor as well. Bridie did say that prior to the fight they had had a good time and she was cooking a meal in the room on their return and a row was started which ended in a fight.' The two women cleaned up, and when Lovelock left the flat at about 5pm they arranged that O'Hara would call on her later.

Lovelock went home and cooked her two teenage children their tea, and shortly afterwards Michael O'Hara and another Irishman, Eddie Fenlon, turned up at her door. Both men were extremely drunk and explained that they'd just come from a club in Earls Court. Mick wanted to know where Bridie was. Lovelock told him she was at home. 'He didn't believe me and wanted to search my place for her, but I did not let them in.'

They came back while she was out, though, and her daughter Pat let them in; and this time the prostitute was with them. Pat told her mother that when they arrived Mick picked up 'a knife or a fork' and threatened Bridie with it, but Eddie Fenlon had prevented any trouble. The men left presently, but a few minutes later Mick was back again. Lovelock told him his wife, who was hiding upstairs in the bathroom, had already left. 'He insisted on being allowed to search my downstairs rooms and I let him search under the beds and I threatened to call the police if he did not go. Eventually he left.'

At 8pm Jean Lovelock and her friend went out for a drink at a local pub, the Eagle, and stayed until closing time. (Where did O'Hara sleep that night? She did not go home with Lovelock, nor did she return to her flat.)

At 2pm the following day Lovelock was drinking in the British Prince when O'Hara entered and joined her; they drank together until closing time at 3pm. 'I did ask Bridie if she had seen Mick and she said no.' And then, as they left the pub, they saw him crossing Goldhawk Road towards them. He thanked Jean Lovelock for helping his wife to clean up the flat and apologized to her for any inconvenience he had caused the previous day. He seemed very sorry for himself. All three went for a meal at a nearby cafe, and he began to cry; he begged Bridie to come back to him. ('Although he had been drinking, I think he was genuine in his request.') She promised to meet him at the flat at 5pm to talk things over, and he left the cafe. The two women left shortly afterwards, O'Hara setting off, so she said, to borrow money from friends.

The last time Jean Lovelock saw Bridget O'Hara was on the evening of Friday 8 January. She was in the British Prince with her sister Betty and her husband, and some time after 9pm the O'Haras walked in and joined them. They all drank together until closing time ('Bridie and Mick were both in good spirits'), when Betty and her husband drove the others back to Jean Lovelock's flat in Brook Green.

Lovelock made the three of them a cup of tea, and added the remains of a bottle of gin. Mick wanted to drain the bottle, but Bridie told him he'd had enough; they fought over the dregs. 'And to think I sold my fucking cunt for you today!' she shouted at him. She took her shoes off to hit him, but he hit her instead. 'They were still fighting and shouting when they left me at about 12.30am.'

But the rest of the weekend passed peacefully. Bridie did some shopping, and the pair of them stayed out of the pubs. On Monday 11 January Mick, who'd been unemployed for some weeks, began a job on a building site at London Airport. He arrived home at about 6.30pm to find that his wife had cooked a casserole. After the meal they sat and watched television.

And then she went out. They had approximately 11s between

them, and at about 9pm she left to borrow some money from Jean Lovelock.

Bridget O'Hara was wearing a loose-fitting grey herringbone tweed coat, attached to which was a black-fringed scarf of the same material, and beneath which she wore a fawn cardigan over a red and black speckled-pattern blouse. She was wearing a black skirt and black calf-length boots, and she was carrying a small black plastic purse. She wasn't wearing earrings, but she was wearing an octagonal gold wedding ring and a white metal eternity ring. She had a dental plate for six teeth that were missing from her upper jaw. 'She always wore her dentures even when in bed and only took them out to clean them. She was wearing them the night I last saw her.'

Some time after 1pm on 16 February pathologist Dr David Bowen arrived at the premises of Surgical Equipment Supplies Ltd, Westfields Road, Acton, and met Detective Superintendent William Baldock, the investigating officer. Bowen was directed to a narrow area of ground between the rear of a stores shed and a chain-link fence.

There he saw the naked corpse of a young woman, her torso almost covered by dried grass and thistles. She lay on her back but her head was turned to the right so that her face rested on her right shoulder, the left shoulder lying partly against the base of the fence. The body showed no evidence of rigor mortis. Some greenish discoloration due to post-mortem changes was seen on the abdomen. The undergrowth appeared to have been placed so as to cover this, and had caused minor abrasions on the trunk. The head and legs were not covered. Bloodstained material was present around the mouth and this had dried along the front of the chin. Once the undergrowth was removed Bowen saw that her left hand, the skin of which was white and soggy, lay tucked beneath her left upper thigh, and that a fine white mould decorated the back of the right, dry congested arm, while a mass of moist grass adhered to her back. On the left forearm a tattoo of a heart enclosed the word 'Mick' or 'Nick'.

Every Monday night a twenty-year-old Dubliner named Joseph Kelly met and had a drink with his elder brother, Edward, in the Shepherd's Bush Hotel; except for Monday 4 January, when Joseph was sick.

Back to normal the following Monday? Not quite. Both brothers managed to turn up, but they had had an argument and were not on speaking terms; they both drank in the lounge bar that evening, but neither man would acknowledge the other.

Neither brother could recall who arrived first, but by 9.30pm Joseph was seated with his back to Edward, who was drinking alone at the table behind. Joseph was chatting to a drinker whom he knew as 'Jock', a slim, short, smartly dressed Scotsman in his late twenties. 'I had met him twice previously in that pub but didn't know him very well . . . We spoke about the band that was playing and the fact that the place was fairly empty.'

At about 10.15pm Bridget O'Hara's head appeared round the door. She spotted Joseph's table and beckoned.

Joseph and his brother knew Bridie O'Hara as a friend of a widow of a friend. Joseph had met her on numerous occasions, and he rose in the belief that she was beckoning him.

Was she beckoning him?

'I think she's calling you,' Joseph said.

'Who the fuck's that?' Jock asked, and walked over to the door. He went outside with her and a minute or two later returned alone to his table. He knew who she was now, he told Joseph. 'He said something about having had it away with her the other night.' He went off and ordered a vodka and orange.

At this point Bridie O'Hara entered the bar and joined Joseph. She said, 'I didn't think you knew him.' He said, 'I didn't think you knew him either.' She laughed, and her drink arrived.

She called out a request to the band and they played it, while she sat and drank with Jock and Joseph, who continued to ignore Eddie. But

O'Hara had two words for him, and she was soon seated at the next table. Eddie asked her who her new boyfriend was. 'Just a friend,' she said, and left him. 'The last time I saw Bridie she was wearing the outfit she was wearing in the pictures published on television and in the *Evening News*. I remember the tight black skirt because when she sat down beside me I could see well above her knees.'

At closing time Eddie wisely called it a night, leaving the pub on his own at about 11.05pm. But Joseph felt lucky. He could see that O'Hara was fond of Jock, putting her hand on his knee and so on, but he had the impression that your man wasn't keen, and he began to wonder if a bunk-up was beckoning him. He decided to stick around.

They finished their drinks. Jock visited the Gents, and O'Hara walked through some swing doors which led out to a corridor. As Joseph left by the front door he saw her standing in this corridor, apparently waiting for Jock. 'I then stood by the entrance to the front door in Goldhawk Road on my own. I hung about, waiting for Bridie to see if she was coming down my way, which was the direction she lived.'

She failed to appear, and he walked away slowly up Goldhawk Road. He looked back but could see no one. Presently he stopped, turned and looked again. He saw her leaving the pub with a man. Outside the pub they stood and spoke briefly before walking together towards Shepherd's Bush Green. They stopped at the traffic lights on the corner.

Joseph had seen enough. He walked home and didn't bother looking back again. 'This man was Jock. I will swear my life on it.'

At 4pm on 16 February David Bowen performed the post-mortem at Acton mortuary.

The deceased was a young woman of average build, measuring 5' 1" and weighing approximately 9 stone. She had light brown eyes, short dark hair and a small nose. On the right side of the body, 3" above the crest of the hip and just behind the lower rib margin, was an oval depressed scar 1½" long, in the centre of which the skin had thickened, indicating an old wound or chronic infection.

The pericardial sac was healthy. A single haemorrhage was seen at the base of the heart on the left side, and this contained dark fluid blood, without abnormality of the muscle. There was no valvular disease, and the condition of the aorta was indicative of a poor diet and an excess of alcohol.

There were congestive changes around the epiglottis, but no actual bruising. The small air passages were discoloured and contained a little fluid, and the lung surfaces showed petechial haemorrhages on the left side, very few on the right. The substance was dark and discoloured mainly due to congestive changes, but partly due to post-mortem change.

The liver appeared normal in size. The stomach contained a few ounces of food debris which included fragments of meat and vegetable.

Examination of the uro-genital system showed that the uterus was perfectly normal in size; there was no pregnancy, and no injuries to the vagina. However, purulent material was found around the cervix due to chronic infection.

The face showed dark reddish-brown abrasions, and these covered the nose and ran down across the left side of the mouth and lips on to the chin. There were scattered punctate abrasions and old scars on the left cheek. The skin on the right side of the cheek and neck which had rested on the top of the right shoulder was not decomposed or injured. Dried abrasions were present on the forehead, specifically on each side of the midline with slight underlying bruising. There were parchment-like patches of abrasion at the sides of each eye.

The ears were small; the right one was pierced but the tip of the left lobe was missing, as if it had been pierced and torn off some time ago. In the upper jaw only the two back molars remained, together with the slightly protruding stump of the right lateral incisor (her dental plate was missing). The lower jaw contained the nine front teeth with a single back molar on the right side, nothing on the left.

There were no marks of injury on the right side of the neck, or across the back of the neck. On the left side of the neck there were four small oval patches of altered skin. There was also an oval, slightly brownish discoloured area 1″ to the left of the mouth, and a second similar oval patch 3″ down from the corner of the mouth. The skin of the neck muscle, layer by layer, showed no evidence of damage.

Purplish hypostasis was present along the back of the body, and on the left side. Both arms and the back showed some sogginess and peeling of the superficial skin layers, to which grass debris had adhered, after the body was left in its final position. On the right side of the chest, between the breast and the costal margin, were four small areas of abrasion, corresponding to pressure of grass material after death. Hypostasis was seen along the back of the trunk, and there was a patch of bruising about 2″ across to the left of the upper mid-dorsal spine. Greenish discoloration extended from the costal margins to the pubis, as rigor mortis had passed.

The legs were rather pale, and there was an oval parchment-like abrasion on the front of the right knee. An old scar was seen on the inside of the left knee, and a small abrasion on the lower right kneecap. The back of each leg was covered with grass and the upper layers of skin were soggy.

There was a large pressure mark on the front of the left thigh, indicating that the deceased had been lying in a semi-prone position after death. There were pressure marks of clothing on top of both shoulders: a V-shaped area ran across the right shoulder, fading away at the edge of the shoulder blade, and on the left shoulder a single vertical mark ran in a similar position. Pressure streaking was prominent on the left side of the chest onto the breast and also on the right side, across the inferior margin of the right breast. The deceased had been wearing a bra while lying after death. Stockings and suspenders also, for between the umbilicus and the pubis areas of pressure blanching were interrupted by congestive changes in the skin, and similar pressure marks ran down the front of the legs.

David Bowen gave the cause of death as asphyxia due to pressure on the face and neck. He noted that there were many tiny petechial haemorrhages present in the upper conjunctival sac and on adjacent sclera, but none on the lower eyelids. There was a fine sprinkling of haemorrhage on the right eyelid. There was marked congestion throughout the mouth, with small haemorrhages towards the rear, where the tip of the tongue had been held between the lower teeth and upper jaw. There were many scattered petechial haemorrhages over the surface of the left lung, but only a few in the fissures on the right side. There was a single epicardial haemorrhage at the base of the heart.

Bowen, concluding his report, stated that he could find no natural disease. There were signs of asphyxia in the mucus membranes of the face and eyes, and on the lungs, and two of the abrasions on the left side of the neck could also have been caused by pressure. But there was no injury to the larynx or neck tissues, and subsequent X-ray examination showed no fractures.

He found it very difficult to estimate the time of death. The areas of lividity interrupted by clothing pressure marks on the chest, abdomen and legs indicated that the deceased was partly dressed at the time of death, and that subsequently she lay in a prone or semi-prone position for some hours at least.

The killer had later removed her clothing and placed her body in the supine position in which it was found. Post-mortem decomposition was absent on the legs and on the right side of the neck, which suggested that it was unlikely that the woman had been dead for many weeks, unless she had been stored somewhere cold. Changes on the back of the body together with adherent grass and slightly soggy skin suggested that she had lain at the back of the shed for up to a week, and that death had occurred two to three weeks previously.

On the evening of 16 February Michael O'Hara and William Moore identified the dead woman as Bridget O'Hara, née Moore.

They tried him drunk and they tried him sober. They tried locking him up until he sobered up, but when he eventually began to make sense they didn't believe him.

He maintained that on the night of 11 January his wife, Bridget O'Hara, left their home between 9.30pm and 10.00pm with the intention of visiting her friend Jean Lovelock to borrow money. But Lovelock and her children were out between 9pm and 10pm that night and by about 10.15pm O'Hara had arrived at the Shepherd's Bush Hotel.

And to think I sold my fucking cunt for

Michael Joseph O'Hara who, at twenty-eight, had racked up eleven convictions for offences such as theft, shopbreaking, robbery and assault. And in his spare time he ponced on his wife.

'She has never given me any money that she has received from any man, and as far as I know hasn't made a regular habit of prostituting recently. I have never encouraged her or told her to do any prostitution. In fact we have had rows about it.'

Rows can make a marriage worthwhile. No doubt they would have enjoyed a spectacular row over the fact that she went out and never

came back, only she never came back. Three weeks later he took the
initiative and reported her disappearance to Hammersmith police,
who recorded the information in their occurrence book as a simple
matter of a prostitute leaving her ponce.

On several previous occasions, when he was in prison or when he
wasn't looking, she had left him for other men.

Such as?

Bobby Brown, Belfast man, self-employed roofer, now working in
Leeds. 'I don't know his address or anything else about him.'

Andy Ross, Scotsman, killed in a car accident.

Geoff Matthews, divorcee, lived in Acton. 'I don't know this man
and have never seen him.'

A man named Frank. 'I only saw Frank on one occasion but I had
no conversation with him. Bridget had pointed him out to me in the
street.'

Not everybody had a name. A few months ago she informed him
she had a sugar daddy, a motorist she'd solicited in Holland Road.
'Apparently he had a large modern car . . . I got the impression he
worked with cars, but I can't be sure about this.' She went to pubs
with him and he gave her money. All he enjoyed was the pleasure of
her company; he didn't want business.

But he must have meant business, because she told her husband he
wanted to marry her. When he asked her what this man was like she
said he was thirty-six, about 5' 2" and skinny.

'I didn't raise any objection about her going with this man because
there was nothing wrong between them and every time she met him
she was getting £8 or £10 from him, but I never had any of the money.
I've already said I never met any of the men she went with.'

Can I have a drink now?

Shortly after closing time Joseph Kelly was walking slowly (drunkenly?) along Goldhawk Road in the direction of his lodgings. When
he'd put some fifty yards between himself and the pub he turned and
looked back.

That's when he saw them, the two of them, leaving the pub
together, walking together towards Shepherd's Bush Green.

Stop your tickling, Jock.

William 'Jock' Kelly, a Scottish labourer in his late twenties, was traced and brought to Shepherd's Bush police station on 20 February. He was married but separated from his wife, and he rented a furnished room in Hammersmith. He worked nights, and in the evenings frequented the local pubs, favouring the Shepherd's Bush Hotel and the Wellington in Uxbridge Road. 'The first time I knew that the girl I met on 11 January 1965 was Bridie O'Hara, the murdered girl, was when I was shown the photograph by police this evening.' He'd only met her twice.

One evening just before Christmas he was drinking alone at a table in the Bush Hotel when a Scots girl he knew as 'Flo' entered, accompanied by another woman. They approached his table and the other woman asked him if the spare seats were taken. ('There were no other empty seats in the bar at that time.') She asked him to save them, and ten minutes later the two women returned with three men.

'Flo' was Flora Forbes, a barmaid and casual friend of O'Hara, with whom she'd been drinking at the nearby Beaumont pub. 'When we arrived I met a Welsh boy I knew as "Taffy" and he bought Bridie and me a drink. We then sat down with him and his Welsh brother and a middle-aged man. This was the first time I had met Taffy's brother but I had seen the other man in the Wellington pub some time before.' Forbes suggested they all move on to the Shepherd's Bush Hotel and listen to the new band, and so some time after 10pm this group joined the Scotsman's table.

William Kelly talked to them but could recall little of the conversation. He did not speak to O'Hara: all he could remember of her was a pair of spectacles and a black eye. O'Hara danced with the two Welsh brothers; the older man danced with Forbes. Kelly left them shortly before closing time to begin his shift.

According to Forbes they all went on to Coco's Club after the pub had shut. O'Hara danced with all three men; Forbes danced with the two Welshmen 'and eventually they had an argument and the younger one left'. This was Taffy's brother, who was walking up the road towards Shepherd's Bush Green when the other four left the club together at about 2am. Behind him the older man walked slowly ahead; and then turned into Sulgrave Road, and waited. 'I went with Taffy and I saw Bridie go to the older man in Sulgrave Road and they both walked down the road together.'

On 11 January William Kelly entered the Shepherd's Bush Hotel at about 8.15pm and sat drinking alone at a table. Shortly after 9pm an Irishman he now knew as Joe Kelly entered and joined him, and the two men sat drinking and listening to the band. At about 10.30pm the Irishman stood up and looked towards the doorway, where Bridie O'Hara stood, beckoning. 'It's you she wants', he decided, and William Kelly went to investigate.

He did not recognize her at first as she wasn't wearing her spectacles. Out in the corridor she asked him if he'd seen Flo. No, he said. Did she want a drink? No, she said. 'Go on, have one.' 'All right, I'll have a vodka and orange. To tell the truth I'm skint.'

He re-entered the lounge bar and told his companion, 'I remember her now.' While he was ordering her drink she came in and joined Joseph Kelly, and the three of them drank together for the remainder of the evening. 'I cannot remember if Bridie got up for any reason, but I may have been mistaken.' Nobody spoke much because they were listening to the band but he recalled asking O'Hara why she wasn't wearing her spectacles, and she replied that she only wore them sometimes (she was long-sighted with a slight squint in her left eye). 'I noticed that there was still a trace of her black eye. There was a slight bruise at the bottom.'

At closing time she told him, 'I need to go to the toilet, Jock. I'll see you in a minute.' She left the table and walked out of the door leading to the corridor. He visited the Gents in the same corridor a few minutes later and left the pub via the street door. He waited outside for between five and ten minutes. 'I did not see Bridie.' (Neither did he see Joseph Kelly, who also claimed to have been in the vicinity.)

He then noticed a couple standing on the corner of Shepherd's Bush Green, the corner by the telephone kiosks. The woman held on to the man's arm as they waited to cross to Kelly's side of the road. But she let go while crossing and as a bus came towards them the man grabbed her by the arm and pulled her onto a centre island. When the bus had passed she laughed and took his arm again and they crossed over to the pavement outside the pub. 'I got the impression she knew the man well as she was holding his arm tightly. As the couple reached the pavement near me I saw the woman was Bridie.'

She was walking on the outside; she did not look in his direction and he made no attempt to speak to her. Her mood, he thought, had changed. 'When we were sitting in the bar Bridie had been quite serious but when I saw her with this man she looked very happy.' As they passed him the man looked towards her and appeared to be talking. The pair continued up Goldhawk Road in the direction of Goldhawk tube station. 'After they had gone about 10 or 20 yards up Goldhawk Road I crossed the road and went into the Wimpy Bar and had some coffee. I did not see Bridie again.'

O'Hara was wearing a grey check coat which she kept buttoned up all evening. Her companion was neatly dressed in a three-quarter-length suede jacket, dark brown with a fleecy collar, and grey flannel trousers. He had a full round face and fresh complexion beneath a green or brown trilby, and Kelly noticed thick brown hair at the back of his head, 'I think dark with grey coming through.' He was about 5' 6", heavily built with broad shoulders. 'He was close enough for me to have touched him if I had wanted to.'

Did Bridie O'Hara know this man or was she just pleased to have picked up a punter? Did she leave her home that evening with the intention of soliciting? Police disbelieved Michael O'Hara's statement that she had left to borrow money from Jean Lovelock, but Lovelock confirmed that she and Bridie lent each other money on occasions. O'Hara may have called at Lovelock's flat in vain; she seems to have visited the Bush Hotel in the hope of borrowing money from Flora Forbes.

But then she saw William Kelly, and one man led to another.

I need to go to the toilet, Jock. I'll see you in a minute.

Why didn't she leave the pub with him?

Joseph Kelly insisted that she did leave the pub with him, that she waited for him outside the Gents.

But if this man wasn't William Kelly, as William Kelly said he wasn't, who was he?

During his second interrogation, when his original story was being tested, the Scotsman stated that this man could have been the third man in O'Hara's party on the previous occasion. 'The reason why I say this is because of the height and the man's hair, which I can recall on the first occasion as being darkish brown, long and brushed back.' Both men looked about forty.

But Joseph Kelly was not convinced. On the evening of Monday 22 February the two drinkers renewed their acquaintance in the Gents at the Shepherd's Bush Hotel. William opened the exchange by asking if it was Joseph who had been down the police station. Joseph said, 'I hope you don't get the impression that I was putting the finger on you, but I had to tell them who the last person was I saw with Bridie.' 'No, that wasn't me,' said William. 'What, that wasn't you?' 'It was another Scotsman. He was dressed in a brown suede jacket with a fur collar.' 'The bloke who walked out of the door with Bridie didn't have a suede jacket on.' 'Well, it wasn't me. When I came out of the lavatory she was gone. She must have gone out through the saloon bar door.' 'I saw her come out of the Goldhawk Road entrance with you.' 'No, it wasn't me. The last I saw of her she was going off with a bloke dressed in a suede jacket.' Joseph asked him if he knew the man and he replied, 'I have seen the man in the suede jacket with Bridie, another girl and two Welsh blokes, just before Christmas. I would know him if I saw him again. I heard he had an argument with a woman and had tried to throttle her, either in Acton or Chiswick. He put his hands round her neck and the woman had kicked the man who ran off.' Joseph remarked that if it was a Scotsman he would be back up in Scotland now. 'Yes, he probably would be. The police want me to look at some photographs.'

In addition to which the police talked to him about this conversation. He confirmed that the encounter took place and that Joe Kelly's was a true account 'except that part about a Scotsman. I said they are looking for a Scotsman.' What about the woman at Acton or Chiswick? 'The story I told him about a woman being throttled at Acton I had heard somewhere.'

William Kelly's address was thoroughly searched but nothing was found which could connect him with any of the murders, and it was established that he neither owned nor drove a motor vehicle. Moreover Flora Forbes's description of the man she met in the Beaumont — forty, well built, brown hair, straight and brushed back, fawn overcoat — accorded roughly with the details supplied by Kelly. An identikit picture of the suspect was duly assembled, but it was a poor thing and the police never released it to the press. In fact they were on the point of dispensing with it altogether — but then they took a squint at a face that seemed to fit.

On 9 December 1964, during the inquiry into the murder of Frances Brown, a prostitute named Janet Quinn came forward with information regarding a possible suspect.

The previous evening, while looking for her friend Kay Ryan, she'd visited the coffee stall at Shepherd's Bush, 'and I walked up to Royal Crescent and a little bloke who calls himself Cyril came over to me'. He asked her where her mate was as he had a couple of men lined up who liked young girls. He said, 'It's business, you know.' What sort of business? 'It's photographs and things like that, there's quite a bit of money in it.'

She told him she didn't know whether her friend would be interested; and at that moment two men aged between thirty and forty walked up together and joined him. They looked a bit drunk and a bit high; they also looked a bit like the recently released identikit pictures of the two men wanted for questioning.

The first man was about 5' 9", thin build, with fair thinning hair brushed back. He was wearing dungarees and a white shirt beneath a dark grey shortie coat. 'He called himself Bert Roberts and said he was in the CID from Scotland Yard.' He resembled the picture of the motorist who had intercourse with Beryl Mahood.

The second man, who introduced himself as 'Ken', was sturdily built with dark crinkly hair brushed straight back; he had a round face, protruding ears and a pointed chin. He was wearing a black barathea suit, a white shirt and a chocolate-brown tie with red and yellow stripes. He resembled the picture of the motorist who drove off with Frances Brown.

These two had a cream van, and they drove Janet Quinn and Cyril to a garage in a mews off Shepherd's Bush Road. Someone switched a light on, and she was taken into a small office. 'They asked me if I wanted a smoke; I said no. One of them was playing with a massager and was rubbing it on his skin. They asked me to strip off and said we would have some fun.'

But Cyril said that they were not doing anything until he had some money, and a row started which ended with Cyril receiving a bunch of fives for his trouble. It was at this point that she left them. 'I've come straight down here to tell you.'

Quite right too, yes, and beautifully told. Hell's bells, what a story: drugs, violence, kinky fun, garages . . .

Murder?

Investigation soon revealed 'Bert Roberts' of Scotland Yard to be William Chissell, thirty-three, proprietor of Wimpey Autos, 1a Barb

Mews, Hammersmith. He stated that at 1am, that morning, after 'a couple of drinks', he and his friends Cyril and Jim found themselves by the coffee stall in Shepherd's Bush Green. 'We saw a young lady on the corner; we went over to her, she said she was on business.' She initially wanted £2 from each of them but settled for £1; she got into a van which Chissell was driving and they all set off for Wimpey Autos.

The proprietor presumably pulled rank for he was masturbated first. 'When I left the office I left Cyril in there with her and then Jim went in after Cyril.' All four left the premises together; the woman walked away.

This was the first time he had taken a woman back to his garage, and he did not have intercourse with her ('nor do I think she had intercourse with any of the others'). He admitted that he kept a 'vibro-massager' in his office. James McCarthy ('Ken'), a car dealer, and Cecil Spurgeon, a car mechanic who worked at Wimpey Autos, were both interviewed and corroborated Chissell's account: first time in that garage; masturbation only; no parking.

Nevertheless this inquiry continued into the New Year. On 12 February 1965 an officer visited Wimpey Autos and obtained a dust-and-paint sample from the garage doors.

Four days later Bridget O'Hara's nude body was discovered, and forensically examined. Coal dust and minute particles of paint were found which followed a pattern set by deposits on the previous three corpses, both colour-wise and proportionately. In O'Hara's case the main colours present were once again black, red and white; trace colours were pearl, turquoise, yellow, orange, brown, green, blue and grey. As before, the paint appeared to be cellulose and the colour black greatly predominated. As before, these droplets, being globular in form (10 x 50 microns in size), had issued from a spray gun. Was the man in the mask awake to the corpse in his vicinity? Were the sprayer and the killer one and the same?

On 18 February officers attended a hastily called conference at the Met laboratory, where Thomas Jones, the chief scientific officer, informed them of an important development regarding the sample taken from William Chissell's garage. Although his examination was as yet incomplete, this sample was found to be similar to the samples taken from the bodies of the murdered women; out of the many

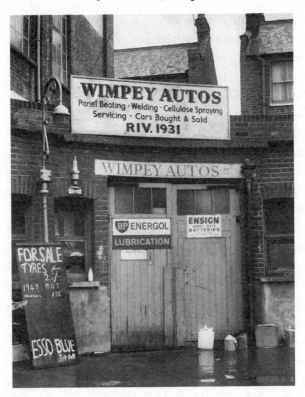

hundreds of previous samples none had shown such striking similarities.

That evening at Shepherd's Bush police station Cecil Arthur Spurgeon, thirty-four, of Riverside Gardens, Hammersmith, was asked whether he often picked up prostitutes. 'I occasionally go with a prostitute for a bunk-up,' he replied, 'but always round the back streets for a stand-up bunk-up. The last time I went with one was about four or five weeks ago . . . I think it was on a Wednesday or a Thursday night.' He could not remember what he was doing on the night of Monday 11 January but most Monday nights he drank in the Railway Tavern in Goldhawk Road, 'and I was probably there that night'.

Spurgeon admitted knowing a Mick O'Hara but had never met his wife; he had not met any of the murdered prostitutes, and neither had his boss, Bill Chissell, 'as far as I know'. In fact Chissell, apart from that one occasion, never seemed to go with prostitutes at all.

Did Spurgeon possess a key to the garage? No. Who, apart from Chissell, had a key to the garage? No one. Had Chissell ever brought a woman back to the garage? No, not as far as he knew (apart from that one occasion). 'I am quite certain that he could not have hidden a dead body anywhere in the garage without me knowing.'

James McCarthy, thirty-seven, of Binden Road, was shown photographs of Bridget O'Hara and the other murdered women, none of whom he recognized. Interviewed regarding his relationship with William Chissell, he explained that he became acquainted with him one night in September 1964. The two men got talking in a pub in Shepherd's Bush, and McCarthy learned that his companion was in the motor trade; 'it came out in conversation that I sometimes obtained tyres, and from then on every time I had tyres I took them to Chissell's.'

Yes, Chissell always had a car; he'd recently replaced his little black Morris Minor van with an old black Vauxhall Velox or Wyvern ('I have seen this vehicle at the top of the mews with a £35 ticket on it').

He and Chissell sometimes drank together socially in the Railway Arms, or the Mail Coach, near Shepherd's Bush Green; Chissell never talked about prostitutes and apart from one occasion 'which you already know about' he had never seen him with a woman, 'not even his wife'.

Spurgeon and McCarthy were released pending further enquiries but Chissell, protesting his innocence, was detained overnight. Chissell, of course, was the key-holder, the dust-owner. He was also, it emerged, an associate of one Anthony John Holland. Detectives understood from an informant that this man consorted with street-girls; furthermore, he'd recently been in possession of two Luger pistols and, thus armed, had sworn he would kill the next police officer who tried to arrest him.

Holland was a car dealer and a frequent visitor to Wimpey Autos. He dropped by on Saturday 20 February and saw them – searching, snapping, seizing . . . crawling all over that garage like blowflies at breakfast.

Later that day it was his turn. They travelled to Trumper's Way in Hanwell, where they descended on Atwell's Motors, the garage run by Holland in partnership with his brother William; and then they turned over his Hammersmith flat. Not at work, not at home. 'Nude

Murder Hunt: Yard Seeks Man's Help' ran the front-page headline of that weekend's *Sunday Mirror*. 'Detective Superintendent William Baldock, one of the senior officers in the case, said, "We would like to trace Anthony John Holland, who recently lived in Hammersmith, as he may be able to assist inquiries into the deaths of women found in the nude."'

It was around this time that police took one last despairing look at their unreleased identikit picture. . . and a fresh imaginative look at short, stockily built Cecil Spurgeon.

Could it be?

He knew the husband, used the pubs, poked the toms – and in the interview room on the morning of 21 February he once again failed to remember what he was doing on the night of 11 January; 'but I'm sure I wasn't with a woman and I'm quite sure I wasn't with the woman named O'Hara outside the Shepherd's Bush Hotel'. He hadn't had a drink there for years and years, not since the old Empire closed down. 'I don't like the type of people that use the pub.'

Later that morning Spurgeon took part in an identity parade at the station, but William Kelly failed to identify him.

Meanwhile, in response to Scotland Yard's press and television appeal, Anthony Holland's solicitor, John Wood, had made contact with the news that his client was available for interview.

The interview took place at Shepherd's Bush on the afternoon of 21 February in the presence of Wood and his clerk. William Baldock attended, but the man asking the questions was Detective Superintendent John du Rose.

'We are making enquiries into the deaths of these nude women and our enquiries have led us to Wimpey Autos, a garage, and your address at 182a Hammersmith Grove, and to some premises of yours at Hanwell. You will appreciate these addresses cover all the areas where these girls have been found . . .

'It is my desire to ask a few questions on all these matters. We have good reason for asking and we consider any ordinary person would not have the least trouble in answering.'

Was he married?

'Never been married.'

Did he own a car?

'I own an Alpine.'

Registration number?

'You've got me there. It's at Leamington Garage near the railway gates in Acton.'

Did he know William Chissell?

'Yes.'

Business associate?

'I would not say that.'

Did he know Cecil Spurgeon?

'Yes.'

As a car dealer, did he ever involve himself in the spraying of cars?

'No, my brother does, if there is anything to do like that.'

Had he ever had any cars sprayed at Wimpey Autos?

'I should say approximately two years ago.'

But he was a frequent visitor?

'I go for a cup of tea.'

Purely social visitor?

'Yes.'

When did he last visit the garage?

'I was in yesterday morning when your men were there.'

Yesterday?

'I asked where was the proprietor to a woman. She said he was at West London Magistrates' Court.'

Had he been in the garage when prostitutes were present?

'Never.'

Did he know any prostitutes himself?

'No.'

There were, of course, many hundreds of them in the area. Was he still saying he didn't know any?

'None at all.'

Had he ever been in the Shepherd's Bush Hotel?

'No, not for years.'

Did he know Agate Road?

'I know a bit.'

Did he know any people living there? Did he recognize this photograph of Bridie O'Hara?

'No.'

Ever met her?

'No.'

Quite sure about that?

'Yes.'

It emerged during the course of the interview that Holland was no longer resident at 182a Hammersmith Grove, and had not lived there since October. Could he remember where he was living at Christmas time?

'Yes.'

Where?

'If you want to know where you can go with my solicitor – he can tell you my address, I can take you there. I don't want police putting anything in my place and that is the reason for not telling you. If you do come up I shall move again.'

The interview ended with du Rose informing Holland that other officers wished to interview him regarding another matter, 'something which is not my concern'.

Something to do with a gun?

On the afternoon of 19 February William Chissell was about to be released from custody when detectives discovered a Luger pistol and a magazine containing four rounds of 9mm ammunition in a bag concealed in the space between the ceiling and the roof of his garage.

When presented with these items he disclaimed all knowledge of them, but agreed that only he had the keys to the lock-up. The following morning he appeared at West London Magistrates' Court charged with receiving stolen property and with possessing a weapon and ammunition without a firearms certificate.

Well, it wasn't much of a news story – but was it a nudes story?

'When garage owner William Edward Chissell appeared in court yesterday,' the *Sunday Express* reported, 'a police witness was asked if further inquiries were connected with a murder inquiry. Detective Inspector Edward Crabb answered: "I cannot answer that question."

'The magistrate at West London refused a request that the man's name should not be published.'

Chissell was refused bail and remanded in custody until 26 February, when the receiving charge was dismissed, the magistrate declaring that he could see no evidence of the circumstances in which the items were received. In respect of the remaining charge Chissell was remanded on bail of £50 until 6 March; on this date the charge was dismissed and he was awarded twenty guineas from public funds towards his legal costs.

Spurgeon, McCarthy and, finally, Chissell were all eliminated from the inquiry, as was Anthony Holland, who, it transpired, was in custody in Brixton prison from early June to late August 1964, when Mary Fleming was murdered. (But whether the Luger discovered in the garage belonged to Holland, whether it was planted there with the proprietor's knowledge, nobody could ascertain, or, at any rate, prove; Holland's second interview did not take place and the matter was dropped.)

Twenty guineas.

He'd had his name blackened, his lock-up turned over, his freedom taken away . . . Twenty guineas to forget all about it and go back to selling Esso Blue. Chissell instructed his solicitors to begin proceedings against the police for false imprisonment and malicious prosecution.

'When Pauline the Headmistress gives you a taste of her cane she means business and makes you take it and you then know you've had it. Cruel but a lovely headmistress. I suppose you have booked me a dozen extra for this script. Well until Thursday at 9.45. Slave B.'

Be quiet.

Bend over.

Keep still.

Take that! And that! And that!

And this.

Pauline Cudmore, a young mother who accepted lifts from men in cars, accepted a lift one night in January 1965 from a middle-aged man calling himself 'Bob' who drove her down to Duke's Meadows and began to talk kinky. 'He asked me if I liked whipping and all that sort of thing and I said no. We then had an argument about whipping and money.'

In some woods in Orpington the following Tuesday she gave him six strokes of the cane on his bare bottom and received £2. On Thursday he picked her up again and took her back to his house in Tunbridge Wells, smuggling her in via the garage ('so the neighbours wouldn't see me'). Inside he instructed her in the art of flagellation, playing her tape recordings of performances by other girls, some of whom he'd picked up at Shepherd's Bush. He made her strip off and put on black underwear and nylons, and she caned him again for another £2.

Thereafter she thrashed him soundly at his home once a week. But he could be pretty cruel too. He gave her typewritten lines to learn, recording her efforts and playing the tapes back to her so he could point out the mistakes. Yes, he was a sadist all right.

On 22 February Cudmore reported her client to Shepherd's Bush police as a possible suspect regarding the nude murders. He was about 5' 6", she said, and about fifty but looked younger; he had a chubby face and thinning light brown hair. He lived at 32 Front Road and his full name was Bob Bourne ('I found his name on a football coupon in his house').

His full name was Lionel Hugh Oswald Bourne; he was a retired electrical engineer, living with his wife. He had never had intercourse with Pauline Cudmore. He had met her on about four occasions, and on one of these occasions she had visited his home. Other girls had also visited his home. But he denied all knowledge of the murdered women and further enquiries proved fruitless; no action was taken against the middle-aged whipping boy.

No fresh leads had materialized, and the case against Chissell was turning to dust. So, in the absence of any new faces, the Yard brought back an old favourite. On 27 February, at one of the twice-daily press conferences now held at Shepherd's Bush, William Baldock announced that police still wished to interview a man who was driving a light grey car in the area of Notting Hill on the night of 23 October 1964. This man met Margaret McGowan, another girl and another man near the junction of Westbourne Park Road and Portobello Road. The other man drove away with McGowan, who was not seen alive again.

'The man who accompanied our witness may be embarrassed by this association or the circumstances in which the meeting took place. It is of importance that we interview this man as we believe he has information that is vital to our inquiries into the nude murders.' Detectives were willing to meet him anywhere, at any time, and he could rest assured that his confidence would be respected and his anonymity preserved.

The man was aged between thirty and thirty-two, 5′ 10″, medium build with a clean-shaven oval face and thinning light brown hair parted on the left side; he was well spoken with a London accent, and was wearing a light grey two-piece suit and a white shirt. His car was in fairly new condition and had a front bench seat with the gear change on the driving column.

And so the newspaper-reading public, eager for fresh titbits, found themselves pondering a reissued identikit picture of a man who knew a man who might have murdered Frances Brown.

Still chasing last year's werewolves . . .

There was more old news, but it was more interesting. A workman, William Kirwan, came forward to report an incident that took place back in the summer of 1964, yet whose possible significance had only lately occurred to him.

In the early hours of Tuesday 14 July Kirwan and his colleagues John Boyle and Patrick Beads were painting the interior of the ABC restaurant in Chiswick High Road. They were on the ground floor working on the staff room, situated at the rear of the building and overlooking the car park. At about 2.20am Kirwan, painting the inside of the windowpanes, was looking out towards Acton Lane, 'when I saw a vehicle . . . drive up the service road and reverse towards the pedestrian passageway, stopping after reversing for about eight or 10 feet'. A vehicle with no lights on and 'no writing on the side as far as I could see'. He felt sure it was a small van.

By this time he had called Boyle over. It was a clear night and the two men gazed out through the open top part of a lighted window. They watched as a man got out of the driver's seat and walked all round the vehicle before stopping at the back door. The man was between twenty-five and thirty-five, 5' 10", medium build. He was clean-shaven, wore a suit with no topcoat, and Kirwan gained the impression that he was an 'office type'. He decided to have some fun.

'Whilst the man was walking round the vehicle he was looking all around him as if looking to see if the coast was clear before doing something. That is what made me shout at him. I shouted to him, "Who dat out dere?", more as a joke than anything else.'

But whoever he was, he was in no mood for jokes. He saw the faces at the window, jumped back into the van and drove off quickly, turning right from the car park in Acton Lane.

2.20am? This was around the time that revving noises woke up residents in Berrymede Road, less than ten minutes' drive away. Police strongly suspected that the man in the car park was the killer, and that he'd intended to dump Mary Fleming there. Instead, the presence of the workmen had panicked him into unloading her at the nearest convenient spot, the closed end of a cul-de-sac where in all likelihood no one would discover her until dawn.

Neither Kirwan nor Boyle could put a name to the vehicle or supply police with a registration number, but the information they gave recalled the farmer Alfred Harrow's description of the vehicle he almost collided with as it sped out of Swyncombe Avenue early on the morning of the discovery of Helene Barthelemy's corpse. Harrow saw a grey Hillman Husky-type vehicle; Kirwan and Boyle saw a small grey van with no rear windows visible. Kirwan recalled a vehicle 'dark in colour, definitely not a light grey'. He was looking out from a lighted window into (presumably) total darkness, so his recollection suggests an undercoat, the matt grey of primer.

The Rootes Group began to manufacture the Hillman Husky in 1954. 1958 saw the production of the Husky in Series 1 form; certain design changes meant that the car was smoother, faster and more compact than previous models. On 24 February 1958 the *Motor*

THE DOUBLE DUTY **HILLMAN HUSKY**

A ROOTES PRODUCT

Smarter appearance
greater comfort
more space
higher performance

PLUS real economy

reported that 'this new version retains the old "go anywhere, do anything" character in full', but now the car was compact enough to provide 'extra ease of parking or turning round in confined spaces' and behaved 'in reassuringly viceless fashion on the road'. Most importantly, perhaps, the maximum interior depth had increased by 5½″ to 4′ 6½″ so that 'when the rear seat is folded forward out of harm's way it becomes a two-seater van which can carry a very substantial amount of goods'.

Excellent news. Scrub the Minx and stow the hussy in a Husky! But a word of warning:

A tall driver may find that the knees of a passenger behind him contact his spine through the seat backrest, and the folding rear seat back is not held positively upright so that heavy luggage slid forwards by emergency braking can tilt it forwards, but this lengthened Husky now rates as a very comfortable saloon. Folding the rear seat away to extend the luggage space is the work of a moment, but the metal luggage floor needs a covering of rubber . . .

Alternatively, with a maximum interior width of 4′ 6½″, why not remove the rear seat altogether, and behind the front two fit a false floor of plywood or, even better, sheet metal, beneath which the naked corpse of a petite street-girl might fit safely and snugly without subjecting the motorist to annoying distractions during his journey.

It was a mark of this estate car's versatility that it could be transformed, with a little effort, into a miniature hearse. And the Comma Cob light van, cousin to the Husky, also offered generous body space, with a maximum interior depth of 4' 4½" in 1956, its first year of production, 4' 9½" in 1958/9, and 4' 8½" from 1960 to 1964. The Comma Cob was supplied in grey primer for painting to individual requirements.

Did the killer get a Cob on the job?

A team of six women police constables began to check motor taxation records held by Middlesex County Council and London County Council in an attempt to trace all registered owners and/or drivers of Cob and Husky vehicles in use during the period April–July 1964. Middlesex held approximately 600,000 motor record files and London held more than a million. (The birth of the GLC in April 1965 complicated matters, for these two sets of records were amalgamated with those of other councils and authorities.) As the registration authorities did not index the makes of vehicles separately, the officers had to examine each file in order to obtain the relevant information, from which they compiled lists containing the names and addresses of the registered owners, together with the colour of their Husky or Cob; from these lists action lists were prepared at Shepherd's Bush and distributed to detectives who visited each address and collected a dust sample on Sellotape from the boot and interior of the vehicle. They also collected details of the vehicle and its use in the west London area between the hours of midnight and 7am, as well as information about its garage (was paintspraying carried out in or near where the vehicle was kept?) and the full name, date of birth and home circumstances of the owner/driver.

The six women (later increased to eleven) who checked the files became known as the 'Husky Squad'. Theirs was an enormous task and it was never completed.

*

The search for the killer was by now the biggest police manhunt in British criminal history.

On 8 March three teams of officers began to conduct daytime house-to-house enquiries throughout parts of Kensington and the whole of Paddington, Hammersmith, Fulham, Ealing and Hounslow. They had instructions to call at every residence and building, occupied or empty, and examine any space such as a shed or garage where a body could be stored; any suspicious property found was to be the subject of special enquiry. (Suspicious, that is, in so far as it related to the investigation. 'We'd give advance warning of which street we were visiting,' recalls team member Brian Smith, 'and so there was probably a lot of bent stuff being removed.') Samples of dust and debris were obtained from lock-up garages (or any other premises where paint-spraying took place) and submitted for laboratory analysis.

When the daytime enquiries ended, the night shift clocked on. A night patrol squad was formed, its core a team of fifty-eight aides to CID, paired off and authorized to use their own cars. They toured an area of London stretching from Marble Arch westwards to Hounslow and north to south from Harrow Road to Bayswater Road, an area of approximately twenty-four square miles which covered both the (presumed) pick-up points and dump sites of all six victims. These men were supplied with pro-formas on which they recorded details of all vehicles seen on major roads, side roads and secluded spots between the hours of midnight and 8am: registration number, date, time, place and where possible description of occupant(s). If a vehicle was seen more than once its details were recorded separately, its route followed and its owner's garage subsequently visited by detectives seeking a dust sample.

'I was part of the investigation,' recalls John Sorfleet, 'patrolling Shepherd's Bush, Notting Hill, Duke's Meadows in early '65. We were plain clothes but they all knew who we were. It was a long, freezing winter and the inside of my Mini Cooper used to ice up.

'We were working 14-hour shifts, from 6.00 pm to 8.00 am. We'd pick up a wodge of forms at Shepherd's Bush and one of us would do the driving, while the other filled in the forms attached to a clipboard. We'd be told which area to cover when we clocked on and we'd hand the forms in the next morning. We were told, "Don't do more than

80 or 100 miles a night." I can't remember how much we got per mile but we made a lot on expenses.'

Light relief came at a later stage of the investigation in the form of walkie-talkies. 'Big bulky crackling things that hardly ever worked, but we thought all this was exciting. We used to shout, "Stingray to base!" over the radio.' A transmitter was installed at Shepherd's Bush and in view of the large area covered three radio vans with wireless operators were stationed at strategic points in the area.

The Thames from Hammersmith Bridge to Chiswick Bridge was also under observation, with Duke's Meadows receiving special attention. In addition to the night patrol squad, fixed points of observation were set up in the 'busy' areas of Notting Hill, Bayswater, Kensington and Shepherd's Bush.

Roger Crowhurst spent his nights on Ealing Common. 'I was a temporary detective constable, seconded from Notting Hill, and I sat with a civilian driver in a big baker's van. This van had concealed slits along the sides and I had to squint through the slits. We parked up by some trees. It was freezing cold, I remember snow on the ground. We brought our own blankets, and our flasks of porridge and stew.

'We did 12-hour shifts, continuous night-duty. The job was to watch the girls, clock them on and off duty. The girls knew the drill, they reported to the van and I booked them on and off. If there was a new face I'd sit with her in the van and get details for the pro forma. I was also checking the index numbers of the vehicles, seeing which county they came from. You'd use a Glass's Guide; this showed which number came from which area, and if it came from outside the area, from Cornwall, say, or Ireland, it might arouse suspicion. We actually got incidental arrests that way.

'Inside the van there was a small light you could sit and read by, an ancient stationary radio in the back. We had a tiny transistor radio with a pink earplug, and we'd take it in turns to listen to Kenny Everett on Radio Caroline.

'There was a steel seat which spun round, a bit like an office seat. The other seat was a biscuit tin with a cushion on it. We had to pee in another biscuit tin — and shit as well. The only way to get rid of the smell was with a little electronically operated fan in the roof.'

*

The scent had grown cold, no question. Baker's vans, unmarked cars, river police . . . a nightly cordon was thrown around those twenty-four square miles, with every con-
ceivable avenue of entry and exit covered — but the weeks passed and the killer remained at large. On 27 February Scotland Yard reissued their identikit drawing of Beryl Mahood's punter in a plea for this man to come forward. On 17 March the Assistant Commissioner, Ranulph Bacon, made a television appeal for information about the murderer. On 3 May the *Daily Express* published 'A Tough Week Ahead', in which reporter Jeremy Hornsby inter-
viewed Detective Chief Superintendent John du Rose,
head of Scotland Yard's murder squad.

The day O'Hara's body was discovered John du Rose arrived in St Mary's Bay, Kent, on holiday with his wife, Constance. He received orders to return and take charge of the investigation at Shepherd's Bush. 'They called him "Four Day Johnny" because of his knack of solving crimes in double quick time. This time it's different.' You bet. He'd been working on this case for almost three months. O'Hara had been dead for approximately four months so, in view of the fact that from Barthelemy on the killer had claimed his victims at three-monthly intervals, the next murder was about a month overdue.

What news?

'"It's a question of going over the ground again and again and checking and re-checking. There are hundreds of police involved in this inquiry . . . more than on any inquiry ever before."'

Confident?

'"We'll get him. Oh yes. We'll get him. You can be sure of that."'

Bit like a detective novel?

"'I don't read detective novels, you know. I haven't seen a play for years and I don't think I've read a piece of fiction for 25 years. But I do know that real life detection is far more exciting than any fiction could be.'"

And yet he fell back on fiction in the end. Didn't he just?

Painted ladies.

Ready and waiting.

Forget all your scruples, forget all your cares and go . . .

Nighttown.

It was a numbers game.

BYT 332B

was the number of a beige Austin Mini van used by window cleaner Edward Kelly of Uxbridge Road, Shepherd's Bush. *The* Edward Kelly, the Irishman who sat apart from his brother Joseph in the lounge bar of the Shepherd's Bush Hotel on the night of 11 January. Edward had the use of the van from November 1964 until 29 March 1965, when he was working for the Kensington All British Window Cleaning Company. 'I have been told that the van was seen picking up prostitutes on 15 and 19 March late at night. It certainly wasn't me who was driving. It could have been my brother Joseph.'

Paint-sprayer Joseph Kelly denied using the van on 15 March, but admitted borrowing it on 19 March to drive around west London. 'I did not pick up any prostitutes or women that night or any other night. I have not driven since.'

GYG 807

was the number of a Bentley seen in Kensington Church Street at 12.15am on 30 April. This car belonged to antiques dealer John Brocklebank, who was driving home to Campden Hill Road. He refused to give his age or answer 'impertinent' questions about his marital status. He was a member of the National Council for Civil Liberties.

H362 PL

was the number of a grey Ford Zodiac seen – twice.

'I am told by police that my Zodiac car was seen between 12.35 am to 1.30 am at Notting Hill Gate on 2 March 1965 and again at Holland Park Avenue on 29 April 1965.'

Alistair William Berwick, thirty-four, of Upper Richmond Road, was a dental surgeon with a practice on Harley Street and a Justice of the Peace at Chelsea Juvenile Court. He was also a married man living with his wife and their two young sons. So what was he doing kerb-crawling around west London in the middle of the night?

'My father is the registered owner . . .'

Answer the question.

'I do not go out looking for prostitutes and I never go with prostitutes. It is true that I sometimes go up to town for various reasons in connection with my professional and political interests and do drive home down the Bayswater Road.'

Why wasn't Berwick believed? Well, on 22 March John du Rose's night patrol operation underwent a refinement, one guaranteed to make playtime even less fun. A special decoy squad of twelve female officers went on patrol from 11pm to 2.30am each night, working in pairs under observation at Queensway, Westbourne Grove, Pembridge Road, Kensington Church Street, Holland Park and Shepherd's Bush Green areas. They dressed like tarts and hung around the streets, surreptitiously scribbling down the registration numbers of the kerb-crawlers who formed a constant queue. These law whores seemed to haggle for all eternity over the price of a short time and never entered their prospective clients' cars; they wished to know where a man liked to take a girl – hotel, flat, nice quiet spot? They had to hide any embarrassment at hearing *how* a man liked to take a girl, yet whenever the banter grew too bullying, a male officer or 'ponce' would step in to save them from the base attentions, the baroque hand-gestures, the foam-flecked faces of . . . barristers, solicitors, doctors, vicars, company directors.

Dentists. JPs.

During interrogation at Shepherd's Bush by Detective Sergeant Hall, William Berwick denied importuning a police decoy on Holland Park Avenue during the early hours of 29 April. He was allowed to return home, although police subsequently discovered that he was the registered owner of a Rolls-Royce, registration no. 660 HLA, which had been seen in the same area in similar circumstances on a number of occasions between 6 March and 22 April.

Berwick, perhaps understandably, had not volunteered this information to David Hall, and on 13 July he was brought in for further interrogation, this time by John du Rose, who found it hard to accept that Berwick was merely driving home on these occasions. He explained that on certain dates his vehicle had been seen several times during the course of a single evening, and that while this was not a moral issue, it would appear that he was in the area for the purpose of picking up prostitutes. Berwick replied that if his car was seen by the police he would not deny that it was in the area but could go no further than that. Du Rose asked him if he had any connections, business or otherwise, in the Acton area. No, he hardly knew the area, and the only time he remembered visiting it was roughly two years ago when he was driven there by his secretary to collect a previous Rolls-Royce that he owned. Did he purchase any dental equipment from this area? No, he dealt through an agent and all the equipment was German. Did he have any dealings of any description at the Heron Trading Estate? No. Did he own any boats? Yes, he owned two motor launches, a twelve-footer, *Suki*, and a ninety-foot single screw, *Herga*; both boats were berthed at Sunbury.

'You will realise that after being seen by Detective Sergeant Hall and then these other dates coming to light, it was necessary to see you again, particularly as you are a dentist and you also have connections with the river. Both these have a great significance in this inquiry . . .'

Dentistry; the river. The river, yes, at least in respect of Hannah Tailford and Irene Lockwood. Dentistry, perhaps, in respect of Helene Barthelemy, who appeared to have had four of her front teeth removed after death. But the preoccupation of the police with mouths and teeth went far deeper (and dirtier) than that.

Cause of death: asphyxia. The sets of linear marks around the throats of the previous three corpses suggested strangulation with a ligature, possibly the victim's clothes; but what happened to Bridget O'Hara? Her body bore no such marks. She was the odd one out.

William Kelly, the last person to see her alive, observed that she looked happy on the arm of the man in the suede jacket. This man appeared protective towards her, pulling her out of the path of a bus (she might have been killed).

It was estimated that she died within an hour or two of Kelly's sighting, no later than around 1am. Her stomach contained fragments of meat, onion, carrot, cabbage – the undigested remains of the casserole she shared with her husband on the night of her disappearance –

and citrus fruit, most likely derived from the orange juice she consumed with her vodka at the Shepherd's Bush Hotel. Her blood contained 78mg of alcohol per 100ml, the equivalent of three or four measures of spirits, a concentration low enough to suggest that her final drink was consumed on those premises.

So she wasn't drunk when Kelly saw her, and she looked 'very happy', perhaps at the prospect of money changing hands. She walked off out of sight along Goldhawk Road, and at some point within the next two hours entered a vehicle. Her pathologist noted an abrasion on each of her knees, so she was probably in a kneeling position when the attack took place. She could kneel on the front or back seat of a car, but a car would provide insufficient space for her attacker to position himself appropriately. She probably entered the back of a van.

Why was she kneeling? So that she could take it like a bitch? Or had she negotiated extra for buggery?

There is not the merest suggestion, forensically speaking, that Barthelemy, Fleming or Brown adopted this position prior to death. They struggled, he strangled, they died, and there is nothing to indicate that this sequence of events did not take place in the front of his vehicle. But somehow he and O'Hara found themselves in the back of the van. It could be that the other three victims were not known to him, or it could be that this one alone was not known to him, that he felt obliged to allay her suspicions. (Did he have intercourse with her? Why were the standard semen tests not taken?) Or it could be that something went wrong for him.

Something certainly went wrong for her, as is clear from the dried abrasions present on either side of her forehead. There were no marks on the top or back of her head, so he didn't strike her from behind. He may have pulled her legs out from under her, causing her to bump her forehead against the rear seat, or he may have bumped it for her, to shut her up. Although these injuries may belong to a slightly later stage in the proceedings, as she thrashed around, gasping for air, on the floor of the van. The patch of bruising in the region of her left shoulder blade suggests that her killer shoved his knee into her back, the four small patches of altered skin on the left side of her neck corresponding to fingerprints as he steadied her head with the heel of his left hand. She would have been pinned thrashing; struggling for leverage, struggling for air, held down mainly on her left side, as indicated

by the mass of petechial haemorrhages on the surface of the left lung
and the reddish-brown abrasions on the left side of her face. That face
could have come into contact with anything that was lying around.
Any solid object might account for the two oval patches of altered skin
on the left side near the mouth. The end of a tool? Fingers? His or
hers?

Struggling, still struggling. Engine running for noise and warmth;
windows misted up, iced up, blacked out – take your pick; and some
kind of mat on the floor, or a bit of filthy carpeting . . . or clothes.

It's as far as we can go. We cannot reconstruct the final moments
of Bridget O'Hara's life, we can only string together whatever possibilities the forensic evidence suggests to us. But the police went
further, or rather they went in a different direction – completely.

Discounting the sets of linear abrasions present around the throats
of Helene Barthelemy, Mary Fleming and Frances Brown, they concentrated on the throat-marks they perceived – probably correctly –
to be scratches left by the victims' fingernails as they scrabbled to
remove the means of pressure. But the means of pressure, they concluded, was not a ligature, but rather the killer's penis. That's right,
the penis itself was the killer, choking these women as they fellated
this man. In his investigating officer's report William Baldock states
that the marks on their faces seemed consistent with 'the slight bruising such as would be caused by the face being pressed, from the back
of the head, into a man's lap or on his knees', and this obstruction
prevented them from reaching the obstruction in their throats.
According to Baldock, lack of teeth, allied to the difficulties experienced in manipulating the jaw 'when the mouth or throat is fully
occupied', would have prevented the victims from biting the murder
weapon.

Was it strictly speaking a *murder* weapon? The police were uncer-
tain in this respect. They believed they were looking for a sexual
pervert, a creature in the grip of ultra-kinky compulsions – the man
with the velvet gun. He could no more stop killing than stop breathing, and sooner rather than later he would attempt to strike again.

Where did Bridget O'Hara fit into this picture?

She didn't, but they decided she did.

'Oral masturbation when leaning over a man sitting in a car, as
the cause of death, has been put to Dr Bowen, who carried out the

examination on O'Hara. He wholeheartedly agreed that all the signs he found would be consistent with a death in this way. When asked if he had previous experience of a person dying by this means he said he had not, but had examined a number of bodies which showed certain similar signs to those in O'Hara's death.

'He had in mind the cases of mental defectives who, from some basic instinct, push large objects, such as a whole apple, into their mouth and attempt to swallow it. The result, quite often, is almost <u>instant asphyxiation. Such deaths show distinct features. These fea-</u> <u>tures he recognised in the examination of O'Hara.</u> In his opinion five or six seconds would suffice to cause death.'

Apples, whole apples.

Plums. Bananas.

Figs to fill your mouth.

Tadpoles from the south.

Being the True and Awful story of Jack the Stripper.

A mythical figure – the old Jack repackaged – a terror – a monster – suck it and see. Why did the police try to soothe themselves with this fairy story? What were they fending off? After all, the forensic evidence pointed not to animal lust and abandonment but to impressive self-control and a calculating mind. Here was a man who on each occasion used no more force than was necessary in order to dispatch his victims. If he was having fun, well, it was the kind of fun that beat oral sex hands down.

Remember William Berwick, our dentist on the job? Dust samples were taken from his cars and boats, and a vegetation sample was taken from the vicinity of his home. It was ascertained that he had never performed surgery on any of the dead women (in fact, according to records only two of the victims, Barthelemy and O'Hara, had ever visited a dentist at all). No evidence was found to connect him with the murders.

Heron Trading Estate.

Thirty-five factories of varying sizes, segregated by a sports ground, service roads and open spaces of waste ground. All the factories south of Western Avenue to the railway embankment where Bridget O'Hara was found. Some 6,000 employees. Unrestricted public access twenty-four hours a day.

In May 1965 police decided to interview all staff (including management) past and present plus visitors to the estate; their vehicle registration numbers were recorded and checked against the car index. Nobody objected to being interviewed, but nobody volunteered any information either. It was not until thirteen weeks after the discovery of the dead woman that cleaner Thelma Schwartz was traced and detectives learned of the rustling noises she had heard on her way to work on the morning of 12 February. Schwartz indicated that the sounds came from the general direction of the store sheds. The rustler was very probably the killer, in which case the corpse was dumped just four days prior to discovery. As with his previous victim, Frances Brown, the killer had attempted to conceal the body with whatever lay to hand, in this case undergrowth from the immediate vicinity. Had he begun to panic, or had he chosen merely to prolong the fun?

His treatment of O'Hara was somewhat different from his treatment of Brown. When Dennis Sutton discovered Brown on 25 November 1964 she was rotten with maggots; she had disappeared on 23 October and had probably been stored for no more than a few days prior to disposal. O'Hara disappeared on 11 January 1965 and was probably dumped on 12 February; the state of the undergrowth beneath the body and the excellent condition of the body itself certainly lent weight to that date. It looked as if the killer had stored her, and stored her in a cool place, for just over a month.

The police, in their unresting search for reassurance, suspected he was scared to let her go.

On the evening of 21 December 1961 Charles Albert Turner, sixty-seven, picked up a parcel that had been left on his doorstep that afternoon. A label on top was addressed to 'Mr Chas. A. Turner'; there were three other labels – 'Scotch Whisky', 'Dubonnet', 'Spanish Graves' – indicating that the package contained wines and spirits. He left it in the porch and he and his wife, Margaret, went out for the evening. Charles Turner was a company director and his company, Diamond (H) Switches Ltd, was having its Christmas party, so the couple travelled from their home in Kings Langley, Hemel Hempstead, to the firm's premises in Gunnersbury Road, Chiswick.

They arrived home at 1.30am, Margaret Turner carrying flowers, which she put in water before going upstairs to switch the fire on in the bedroom. While upstairs she heard a hissing noise which grew steadily louder. The landing filled with gas. She opened two windows and ran downstairs and found her husband in the garden. She said, 'Who sent you this parcel?' He said, 'I don't know, I don't know.' He was now on fire.

Margaret removed his burning jacket and rushed back indoors. He telephoned for an ambulance himself and was admitted to West Herts Hospital with severe burns to his face and chest.

'Letter enclosed', the address label promised, but there was no trace of any letter. The bomb consisted of a well-made switch gearbox 14″ high and 8″ square; a T-shaped piece of metal was screwed to the lid, the screws holding down a set of springs which released six twelve-bore cartridges when the box was opened.

The heat from the explosion was so intense that it fused the glass in the victim's spectacles, but this saved him from being blinded. Moreover, the maker of the bomb had miscalculated, for the screws holding the springs down were too strong, as a result of which Charles Turner survived.

All the same, when he returned home on 6 January 1962 he was a changed man, apprehensive and nervous of visitors. He appeared to be wondering who wanted to kill him.

On the morning of 14 January he was found dead in his garage. He was lying in a corner with a shotgun partly under his body; a piece of his skull lay immediately inside the door. In a note left in his jacket pocket he explained his action, saying he feared that not only his own life but the lives of his wife and family (he had two sons) were in danger, and he would rather die in his own way than see a murder committed.

The following day Detective Superintendent Leonard Elwell, head of Hertfordshire CID, told reporters that his men were intensifying their search for the bomb-maker. He emphasized that Diamond (H) Switches had never made this sort of gear, and that the recipient genuinely believed he had no enemies. Most of his business associates and former employees had been cleared, and 200 current employees had been interviewed. 'It must have been a man with not only a mechanical but a very precise mind who contrived this. There is nothing in it, apart from the design, which could not have been done on the home bench.' Press and television publicity had prompted a flood of anonymous letters which were being investigated, and experts were working on the handwriting on the label. 'We are far from licked,' he said.

However, the mystery of Chas Turner's Christmas box was not solved. The years passed, and the public forgot; it wasn't quite a murder after all, and therein lay the seeds of its mortality. But John du Rose's team had occasion to recall it in the summer of 1965.

During their checks on workers on the estate they became interested in a maintenance scheduler named George Charles Atwell. They discovered that Atwell, who now worked for Ultra Electronics, Western Avenue, was a former employee of Diamond (H) Switches, and had been a suspect in the parcel bomb inquiry. It was believed that Atwell, a skilled engineer, was capable of making the bomb, although nothing was proved against him.

But the nude murders team thought outside the box. They'd learned from the security officer at Ultra that Atwell regularly deposited cardboard cartons by the firm's dustbins, and that these cardboard cartons contained particles of burnt material and soil. What was he up to? They began to keep an eye.

Atwell left home each weekday morning at 6.55am and his grey Morris Traveller arrived at Ultra Electronics at about 7.10am. (*Hadn't Mr Christie worked at Ultra during the war?*) Upon arrival he read his newspaper until the factory opened at 7.30am. (*Hadn't he met his second victim there?*) After clocking on he usually took a carton from his car and deposited it by the dustbins. Over a period of two weeks he deposited nine of these cartons, each of which was seized and sent off for analysis.

He drove home at lunchtime, and he drove home after work. He never re-emerged in the evenings.

And he always set off early in the mornings. Why? O'Hara's body was dumped early in the morning. Was that why? Was another dead tom now cooling her heels at his home?

George Atwell lived at 8 Burlington Road, Gunnersbury, with his wife and teenage daughter. On 25 June the house was searched but nothing was found which could connect Atwell with the murders. The following month police took a statement from him in which he explained that his cardboard cartons contained bonfire residue which he had accumulated in his garden and which consisted of wood ash, for example, and earth and grass and weeds – and bits of glass. 'Some of this glass would have come from some fluorescent tubes which had been broken when they were blown over during a recent gale. The reason why I did not dispose of the burnt rubbish on the garden was that I believed it contained particles of glass which would have made it dangerous for anyone doing the garden in the future.' He'd tried disposing of this material in his dustbin but the dustmen had complained about the weight. So . . .

So laboratory examination revealed no materials relevant to the murdered prostitutes, and enquiries revealed that Atwell was not known to associate with prostitutes. A comprehensive search of his work premises also proved fruitless. His attendance records for January 1965 showed no absences, while two periods of absence in 1964 did not coincide with the relevant dates. In his statement Atwell told police that he did not recognize any of the women whose photographs were shown to him, and that he only ever ventured out in the evening on lodge nights, which fell on the second Thursday of certain months. He had not done any night work or overtime at Ultra for five years.

George Atwell.

A perfect illustration of the naked desperation of the nudes team.

George Atwell and his cardboard cartons.

Ultra-unlikely.

And what of his suspected connection with the 1961 parcel bomb incident? Well, not only had Atwell ceased working at Diamond (H) Switches some three years before the explosion occurred, but an eyewitness description of a man seen delivering the bomb that December afternoon can hardly have fitted him. A neighbour recalled that the man, who delivered the parcel at around 4pm, was thick-set with light bushy hair; he was 5′ 5″ and thirty-five to forty. Atwell was then fifty-nine.

He was now sixty-three, and he became so distressed during his interview that at times he was unable to speak.

Still, no harm done, eh? Let us leave George Atwell to cultivate his garden (no more bonfires, mind) as we try to come to terms with the fact that this manhunt was now burning up more than £5,000 per week.

'I worked briefly as a DC on the case towards the end,' recalls

David Cant. 'Now at that time CID officers were paid £17 or £18 per month detective duty allowance plus a plain clothes allowance of a couple of pounds. Now this was averaged out over the whole of the Met, and it never varied, so no matter how much overtime you did that's all you got.

'And then John du Rose declared this to be a "special occasion" and everything suddenly changed. You were working 14, 15, 16 hours a day and you could earn a fortune, or what seemed like a fortune then. Mick Strapp, who worked as a DC for about a year on the case, he made enough to buy a brand new Austin Morris 1100 – two-tone as well, which was more expensive. I can tell you how much it cost as well: £435. All of us were talking about it. We were in awe.'

Nothing's good or bad but earning makes it so. Yes, a breakthrough, you might feel, was well overdue. But the police had already had their breakthrough, which only made matters better – or worse.

The breakdown.

Particles occurring in the dust on the four bodies were mounted on aluminium blocks and examined by electron probe analysis in Manchester. The black paint globules, it transpired, were only partially paint and mainly carbonaceous material, which meant that red, not black, was the predominant paint colour. Particles of brass, aluminium, rust, cement, possibly plaster, and mineral grit were identified in the remaining material.

The breakthrough.

Approximately 2,000 samples were taken from cars and their garages, out of which only 300 had red paint globules present, and of these only five showed a degree of similarity to the globules on the bodies.

Of the 290 samples taken from the vehicles of individuals under investigation, only one showed an approximate similarity but here the paint globules showed a difference in chemical constituents.

Approximately 1,300 samples were taken from factory premises. Samples from premises where spraying was taking place showed that the dust present consisted almost entirely of paint globules. Only one sample showed a degree of similarity. But it was a high degree of similarity, and it offered tantalizing glimpses of a brave nude world.

*

On 6 May Thomas Jones of the Met laboratory broke the news. He had examined dust from vegetation at the locations where the four bodies were found. In the cases of Barthelemy, Fleming and Brown this dust was completely dissimilar to the dust on their bodies. However, O'Hara's case was different.

Initially samples of vegetation were submitted from four points approximately one mile from where she was found. The dust on these samples contained very few paint globules and the rest of the dust showed very little similarity to that on the bodies.

But then vegetation samples were taken from sixty-eight points within half a mile of the spot, and from these samples 136 dust slides were prepared. The slides revealed that out of these sixty-eight points ten were completely negative, twenty-four showed traces of similar material and thirty-four showed varying degrees of similarity. The greatest amount of similarity was in samples from a disused aircraft factory in Mansfield Road, W3.

This factory was rented by Napier Aero Engines, who began to shut it down at the beginning of 1963. All the staff had been made redundant by August, yet the building itself (which belonged to the estate) remained open, and unsecured. Staff from neighbouring factories began to use it as a short cut to a cafe in Westfields Road. At night the factory attracted courting couples, who also parked elsewhere on the estate, including the unmade road where O'Hara's body was found.

The eastern side of the Napier factory comprised a number of male lavatories, an outbuilding housing transformers, another male lavatory, a locked switch-room and a boiler-house.

'Abandon hope all who enter here': these disquieting words were written in chalk on the wall of the disused boiler-house. The boiler-house would have made an ideal hiding place for the bodies, but dust samples proved negative, and other samples from the switch-room, factory floor and lavatories did not show the same degree of similarity as samples taken in and around the transformer shed.

Positive dust samples were taken from a lamp glass which was attached to the outside wall at the south-east end of the factory. Approximately fifteen feet away, at ground level in a southerly direction, positive samples were taken from a metal pipeline, and yet more were found in the transformer shed about forty feet from the lamp glass. Access to this shed could be gained through any of its many unfastenable windows or a large double communication door, secured only by two sliding bolts.

The buildings on the eastern side of the Napier factory ran parallel with a large building on Western Avenue occupied by Shaw and Kilburn Ltd. The two factories were separated by a distance of some forty-five feet.

Shaw and Kilburn, motor engineers and coach builders.

Here be spray shops.

Extractor fans.

And *adjacent* to the Napier factory were premises rented by Westland Aircraft, in which the company carried out precision casting, a process which created considerable quantities of dust. This dust left the Westland factory via extractor fans, and was bagged for disposal at the rear of the building.

The Westland dust contained an abundance of brass, aluminium, rust and other particles which formed part of the materials found on the women's bodies, while the Shaw and Kilburn dust contained an abundance of the carbonaceous materials and particles of paint (a mixture of cellulose and acrylic) which made up the remainder. These were the dusts that entered the transformer shed.

Entered and exited through wire-mesh openings: two of them, one on each side of the shed.

What were they there for?

Cooling purposes.

Detectives reflected upon Bridget O'Hara's excellent state of preservation, indeed, on the partial mummification of her left hand and arm, and the parchment-like quality of certain abrasions. Her body was stored in winter: it was now early summer and the temperature inside the shed was decidedly cool. The prevailing south-west winds striking the south-eastern corner of the Napier factory would sweep up into the transformer shed through one wire-mesh opening and out through the other (each measured $6' \times 3''$), and a great deal of airborne dust would settle inside.

Dust had settled on O'Hara, and on Barthelemy, Fleming and Brown. Their storage periods varied, yet on each body the head hair had caught the majority of the material, a feature consistent with a current of cold air passing over the corpse.

The transformer shed stood approximately 150 yards from the spot where O'Hara's body was dumped. They had finally found the hiding place. The estate inquiry now intensified. Was the murderer an on-site employee? (Enter George Atwell.) Or was he an ex-employee who'd recently severed his connection with the estate? That would make sense, wouldn't it?

Certainly it would, but other theories, not entertained, also made sense. The theory that the killer was equally likely to be a member of the public, that same public that had twenty-four-hour access to all parts of the estate. The theory that he dumped her body in the vicinity of the transformer shed because, all things considered, he'd decided to call it a day.

But back to the big one, the theory that Napier's transformer shed housed the bodies. Initially police understood that the Napier factory was emptied of all its machinery by May 1964, yet further enquiries revealed that in January 1965 the estate hired a firm of cable jointers to remove one of two 750 VKA transformers which remained in the shed. Workmen carried out the removal between 25 and 30 January, a time when O'Hara's body was supposedly stored there.

Rather worrying, this. Were these British workmen? If so, what were they up to? Why weren't they nosing around, why weren't they on the scrounge like Len Beauchamp when he discovered O'Hara's body behind the Surgical Equipment Supplies store shed? Why didn't they discover her body inside the Napier transformer shed?

The nude murders squad traced and interviewed these workmen, and other workmen who had legitimate access to the factory. They also interviewed ex-Napier employees, and they took dust samples from anyone who owned a vehicle. They got nowhere, they learned nothing, and yet they couldn't get it out of their heads.

The shed, the shed, the shed.

It was where their search had led them.

It was all that was the case.

Inside Swansea station I hurry past posters: one advertising a new detective novel ('The brilliance of *Cracker*. The suspense of *Prime Suspect*. The complexity of *Rebus*'), another advertising Swansea itself (Dylan Thomas lounging in the ether, great with mild).

Outside Swansea station. There's a black man out cold in the cul-de-sac where the taxis line up. He's lying semi-prone in the recovery position; a policeman stands astride him while two colleagues work their way up the rank, interviewing drivers.

'I didn't really see anything, not really, no . . .' says my driver out of his window, his Peugeot pulling out as the uniforms approach. He's seen it all of course ('Those drunks back there were trying to take something off him') but who cares? He's got a fare. Let's go.

And now we're out of danger I tell him where I want. I hand him my sheet of paper. '£190 I got yesterday for a wait-and-return. Transporting blood, I was.' He taps the tiny screen by the dashboard. 'They track us with that, our routes. So they know where we are all the time. But after midnight I turn it off and they think I've gone home. But I'm still here, see, and that's when we make our money.' He nods reflectively at a nearly finished stadium on our left ('We've got a chance next year') before looking down and frowning. 'I won't get a return fare from here.'

He goes quiet and stays quiet as we speed through the Swansea valley, past any number of villages, each with its own abandoned mine. We arrive at Upper Cwmtrwch, and he hands me a receipt for £23, and I begin to drag my bag up the hill in search of the Stickler inn.

The body of Bridget O'Hara was buried on 16 June 1965 in a private grave at Hammersmith New Cemetery, Mortlake. The inquest into her death was held on 9 February 1966 at Hammersmith Coroner's Court, where evidence was heard from Michael O'Hara, David Bowen, Leonard Beauchamp and Detective Superintendent Baldock. After a brief summing-up by Harold Broadridge, the coroner, the jury returned a verdict of murder by person or persons unknown, and the inquest was closed.

On 3 July 1965, owing to shortage of staff, the large-scale night observations in west London ceased. Most of the officers concerned returned immediately to their divisions, although a team of seven men continued in their duties until the week ending 15 January 1966 (which marked the first anniversary of O'Hara's disappearance).

On 28 August 1965 the Husky squad was disbanded and the estate inquiry ceased. Also on this date the house-to-house enquiries ceased: 648 streets had been visited and approximately 120,000 people seen, yet owing to shortage of staff the work was left incomplete; only half of the designated area of twenty-four square miles had been covered.

On 10 October the *People* newspaper reported: 'Scotland Yard murder hunter Chief Det.-Supt. John du Rose, the man who for months has led the vast search for the London "nudes killer", returns to his office tomorrow – his expensive bid to catch the murderer a failure.' The cordon, the car index. . . he'd staked everything on the killer striking again – and lost.

Yet according to the *News of the World* on 21 November, 'this brilliant detective' would never rest until justice was done. He liked to wander through the pages of a red diary filled with names, the names of outwardly respectable men who led a sordid double life, haunting by night the seamy vice spots of west London. 'Most of the men listed in the diary are frightened that their guilty secret will be uncovered . . .

'But it is a groundless fear. Their secret is safe. Chief Supt. du Rose, a man noted for his discretion, will only ever disclose one name in the diary – and only if it can be proved that the man is the Nudes Killer.'

Was the Nudes Killer still killing? The discovery of a naked female torso in the Thames at Wapping in February 1966 provoked much speculation in the press, although this crime, a curious blend of Ripper and Stripper, was not linked by the police to the previous murders.

Years passed without any news, and then on 2 November 1969 the *People* published this report:

The day the murders stopped

Officially the file is still open but . . . SCOTLAND YARD BELIEVES IT KNOWS THE SECRET OF THE NUDES' KILLER

Here, exclusively, MICHAEL WELLS reveals the astonishing story of the suspect who will never be charged . . .

In the murder files of New Scotland Yard, eight unspeakably bestial killings will remain unsolved – for ever. The case of the nude murders, the most fearsome series of sex crimes since Jack the Ripper terrorised London in Victorian times, will never be closed – officially.

Today, however, I can disclose for the first time that the search for the killer is over. Though they can never declare it officially, some of Scotland Yard's top brass believe they know the identity of the sex maniac, who, between 1959 and 1965, murdered at least eight London prostitutes and kept their nude bodies for days or weeks in his secret hideout before dumping them.

It seems now that 'Jack the Stripper', as the killer became known in Soho viceland, will never be brought to trial.

He is dead. He committed suicide just a few hours before detectives, having finally secured the evidence they wanted, were to swoop on his home to arrest him.

Why have Scotland Yard allowed the world to assume that they failed in their search? Why have they never taken the credit for one of the most painstaking and inexorably efficient investigations in criminal history?

Because of a remarkable act of fairness and humanity that perhaps could only happen in this country.

THE SECRET

Jack the Stripper was just John, a quiet 'respectable' family man in his forties, living in a quiet 'respectable' London suburb.

To this day his wife and several children do not know the secret of their loving, devoted father. They believe that his suicide was caused by worry and over-work.

The police have accepted the role of 'failures' rather than allow that family to suspect that for years they were living with the most insanely perverted sex-killer of this century.

That this man, who spent long nights in the company of his victims' nude corpses, was their husband and father.

Detectives, who quietly built up their evidence against John 'X' after his death, pretended they were merely making routine inquiries on a suicide.

In the fairness of British justice they can never accuse a man who cannot now defend himself.

But that evidence, as we shall see, is overwhelming.

THE EVIDENCE

Forensic examination of the bodies had revealed certain important clues. On all the victims were traces of acetate used in paint-spraying. On some bodies police scientists found minute particles of a certain type of paint flake, and traces of coal, iron filing and oil.

In a house-to-house search over a 24-mile square area of London, detectives found *all* these substances on the floor of a garage where a local man kept his car.

That man was John 'X'.

And, dramatically, John 'X' became Suspect No. One. Police built up further evidence against him:

(1)   His car's registration number was among those noted by police in the area where the murderer picked up his victims.

(2)   His face and general description fitted the description the police had of a man seen around the area during the times of the killings.

(3)   Discreet preliminary inquiries showed that he was in London during *all* the periods when the murders were committed.

Significantly, during the times he was known to be out of town, no killings occurred.

(4)   Scientists finally established that at least two of the bodies were kept in a factory which used paint for its products.

John 'X' had access to that factory – alone and undisturbed. He worked there.

THE PATTERN

John 'X' must have known the net was closing when he learned that detectives had made a minute inspection of the garage where he kept his car. He did not wait for them to come for him. He killed himself. And the nude murders came to an end.

Northern childhood . . . gloomy household . . . extreme Puritanism . . . frequent beatings . . . war service . . . drinking . . . brawls with prostitutes . . . civvy street . . . marriage . . . job as a clerk . . . quiet existence . . . more drinking . . . more prostitutes . . . self-disgust . . . sadistic urges . . . murder.

And finally he'd committed suicide. *Killer dead.* It was official; or rather it was unofficial, which somehow made it even more official, even more like the truth.

The newspaper's source soon revealed himself in a television exclusive. On 2 April 1970 Tom Mangold interviewed John du Rose on the subject of the nude murders for the BBC current affairs programme *24 Hours*.

The mystery so far:

'When, on February 8 1965, Detective Chief Superintendent John du Rose took charge of the case, the press was getting a little hysterical, the police were baffled and the public (in London anyway) was frightened. And then suddenly, eight weeks after du Rose took the case, the file on the west London nudes' murderer was closed. No arrest was ever made, no suspect was ever charged. The huge police squad handling the inquiries dispersed. . . The murders stopped. There was plenty of speculation but no official explanation has been given from that day to this. Now the man who stopped the inquiry is free to say what happened.'

Deputy Assistant Commissioner John du Rose, fifty-eight, had retired from the Met a mere two days previously. Six weeks prior to his retirement du Rose, now a widower, married WPC Merle Taylor. (Taylor, a much younger woman, was popular in the force, and had been first to volunteer as a decoy prostitute during the 1965 night observations.) The newlywed was interviewed at his home in Great Yarmouth. Sitting in an armchair, smoking a cheroot, he was now free to say what happened.

'As time went on, of course, we, um, realized that the suspect, whoever he was, must be reading the news of what was going on, the activities of the police and so on. And so we got the press and the radio and the television on our side, and we fed them stories every day, this was our one way of communication with the murderer. And we hoped by this means to start him up, to get him frightened, to make him run – to do something which would point the finger towards his guilt.

'And I think eventually . . . it didn't have the effect that we actually desired, but he obviously became so frightened he took his own life. And this was within a matter of weeks of this inquiry starting by me in February 1965.'

So the answer at last to the riddle of the nude murders was that – the murderer killed himself?

'I think he did, and time has really shown that my opinion at that time was correct. We've not had a nudes murder since that day.'

Was this man already a suspect?

He was.

How did this work? Was there a shortlist?

'Well, the list started off with, I think, twenty . . . It came down to sixteen, to twelve, to six, to three eventually. And it was at this time that the man died.'

One of the three?

'One of the three. Now we couldn't talk to him – he was dead. We couldn't ask any questions, we could only make enquiries about him: check his employment, check his activities, his movements, where he associated and so on. And when you bear in mind that there were six takings of the women, and six droppings of the body, we had twelve occasions on which to check an individual out. A wonderful set of circumstances, really, to pinpoint an individual. Not just one murder, with one mad killing and away, but twelve occasions this man could have been available to have committed all these murders.

'And even now I'm not in a position to name this man. He has relatives who are still alive, it would reflect on them. It would be utterly wrong, and we don't do that sort of thing.'

Killer dead. But within twenty-four hours of *24 Hours* Scotland Yard had publicly dissociated itself from du Rose's remarks, maintaining that the case remained open.

By way of response, du Rose leaked further information to journalist Peter Deeley, and a detailed feature on the investigation appeared in the *Observer* magazine on 3 May. Readers learned that the deceased suspect was a 45-year-old night patrolman who drove a van for a 'now defunct' security company. He visited factories and offices in Shepherd's Bush, Holland Park and Acton to check for intruders or fires. His working hours, 10pm to 6am, accommodated the relevant times, for the women were disappearing between 11pm and 1am, and reappearing between 5am and 6am. His duty rota included a factory where spraying with cellulose paint took place. 'This factory used large sheets of tarpaulin to protect areas against the "spreading" effect of the spray guns. It seemed likely that the bodies had in fact been wrapped inside tarpaulin and in that way they had come into contact with the paint flakes.'

John du Rose, of course, had the dead man's number – but only *after* he died. The suspect came to light during a routine check on recent suicides in the capital. This man left a note saying that he was 'unable to stand the strain any longer'.

'Outwardly there still seemed no trace of a connection but du Rose asked one of his men to check the suicide's background. Slowly facts emerged which began to suggest he had had "exclusive opportunity" to commit the crimes.'

Michael Wells in the *People* had previously reported that police found evidence on the floor of the deceased's garage which linked him to the murders, whereas Peter Deeley now stressed that the case against the security guard was purely circumstantial. It was all becoming rather confusing.

Re-enter the guv'nor. On 17 May serialization began in the *Sunday Mirror* of John du Rose's autobiography, *Murder Was My Business*: 'Beginning the inside story on crime, from the casebook of the world's top investigator.' In Part One he provided readers with a lengthy yet easy-to-follow account of how he solved the nude murders. This version mercifully accorded with his on-screen utterances, and also included some shocking revelations which – be warned – may sound familiar.

I was convinced that the killer was a man in his forties with extremely strong sexual urges which, because of his age, were no longer satisfied in a normal way . . . *He wanted a different type of sex.*

The facial injuries the victims suffered and the displacement of their teeth could have been caused by pressure from the killer's hands on the back of their heads. Their faces were forced into his lap while in an utter frenzy he fought to reach the peak of a sexual act.

The cause of death – by asphyxiation – can best be compared with some insane people who have died because they tried to swallow a whole apple . . .

In my view, the sheer weight of our investigation and the fact that we have made inquiries about him, led the killer to take his life.

And yet, because he was never arrested and never stood trial, he must be considered innocent, and will therefore never be named.

The Stickler, room 4. I'm sitting on a twin bed examining something I found at the back of a shelf in the wardrobe. Rope of some description, a foot long or thereabouts. Stripy and silky – like dressing-gown cord, only thicker. I turn it over and over beneath my bedside lamp. It's knotted towards one end.

I put the thing back where I found it. Time to freshen up.

What was it Malcolm the landlord had said in the bar downstairs?

'Good luck for tonight.'

Good luck.

I bloody need it, don't I?

I spit mouthwash down the plughole of the cracked china basin and try to get in the mood. After all, I'm lucky to be here tonight, lucky to have found her.

Katy.

She's my lily of the valley.

She does the faces.

She does the voices.

She's preparing herself right now.

In February 1972 Owen Summers re-examined the nude murders case in a series of articles for the *Sun*. He began by questioning the theory that a dead security guard was the murderer. The theory was plausible, he allowed, in so far as this man had the means and opportunity to commit the crimes, only 'later, it was found that the man had been working in Scotland at times when at least one of the killings occurred'. In fact the police uncovered no evidence, either at his home or at premises he visited, to link him to any of the murdered women. Neither his suicide nor his suicide note ('I cannot go on . . .') constituted evidence of guilt. The killings ceased, but they would have ceased anyway, wouldn't they? Du Rose had set up an ambush involving hundreds of officers. 'It would surely have trapped the killer had he made another move.'

No, 'Four Day Johnny', a brilliant detective, could be wrong on this occasion. The killer could still be alive, and could strike again. 'My view is shared by certain senior police officers who were engaged in the massive inquiry seven years ago.'

And now Summers went further. The murders, he observed, were committed by a man with an unusually intimate knowledge of the west London area. This man 'may well have been a policeman, perhaps retired'; he could have been in touch all along with the progress of the murder hunt.

> This theory, which no one wished to believe, grew in the calculations of many officers tracking the unknown killer.
>
> A chilling fact emerged at this time. Each of the women was dumped in a different police subdivision – invisible boundaries which very few members of the public would know.
>
> *Was it a coincidence? Or was the killer to trying to hamper the investigations of his own colleagues?*

This new theory sounded disturbing. Scotland? Subdivisions? Still alive? Summers was clearly in possession of highly privileged information. But who was his source?

'Certain senior police officers'.

Such as . . .

The investigating officer?

Detective Superintendent William Baldock (retired)?

According to some of his ex-colleagues, Baldock at this time was wont to express contempt for du Rose and his claim to have solved the case. In the opinion of one officer, du Rose was 'what these days you would call a bullshitter. He never solved the bloody nude murders. Bill was very angry about all of that, I remember him telling me. Upset as well. See, Bill was convinced he knew who killed those women, and when he told me it all seemed to fit.'

Du Rose died in 1980, but Baldock is still with us. He's eighty-nine and living in Finchley – and he's still a bit angry.

'John du Rose should never have been called in. He hindered more than he helped. "Four Day Johnny!" And if he couldn't solve it in four days he wasn't interested.

'But I'm enjoying my retirement. I don't want to get drawn into all of this . . .'

I'm lying on the bed with the *Guardian*, sipping tea and reading the obituary page when I hear a thump on the door and Malcolm's voice telling me, 'The lady in the village has just rung to say, will the two gentlemen please hurry up as she's ready and waiting'; and my elbow tilts and the tea spills, a hot dark stain spreading across the page, soaking part of a large photograph of the New York Dolls. I'm about to clean up when I notice that Brian McConnell has died.

John Brian McConnell, journalist, 1928–2004. The obituarist describes him as an 'heroic drinker' whose conversations often 'bordered on the surreal'; but he is also remembered as a 'competent, hard-working and diligent reporter'.

Competent? Diligent? I consider the author of *Found Naked and Dead* as I make my way down the hill towards the village, and almost immediately recall this sentence: 'Margaret McGowan died leaving the problem of her name a mystery.' I telephoned him to say I'd solved it. 'Frances Brown? That was the alias she used at the Bailey.' I ordered Brown's death certificate and posted him a copy. 'Well, I never. Well, it seems they misled me at Somerset House.' Surreal, heroic . . . 'Cut to the chaser' McConnell.

Now I must look out for the fork in the road – there – and the bus shelter – there.

There – a Seventies homestead, bungalow ranch-style.

I pause in the twilight by the mock five-bar gates, grinding my teeth at the wind chimes in the cypresses that line the driveway.

The lady in the village says, will the two gentlemen please hurry up. . .

Well, I asked Katy if I might bring a friend. Yes, she said, but only if my friend and I were in complete harmony. 'We're like Simon and Garfunkel,' I told her.

And now he's cried off.

Who'd have thought it, eh?

Don't you think it.

I pass through the gates, following the curve of the drive.

Don't think about
Betty and Tina and Hannah and Sandra . . .
Old whores in new brothels.
Will they lift their skirts for me tonight?

The man who 'will therefore never be named' was a 45-year-old Scot named Mungo Ireland of 132 Tildesley Road, Putney. On 3 March 1965 he was found dead in his car in his lock-up garage on Solna Avenue, Putney. The petrol tank was empty and the ignition switched on; Ireland had committed suicide by inhaling the exhaust fumes.

He left a note to his wife:

I can't stick it any longer. It may be my fault but not all of it. I'm sorry
Harry is a burden to you. Give my love to the kid.
Farewell,
Jock.
P.S. To save you and the police looking for me I'll be in the garage.

The dead man came under suspicion during the Heron estate inquiry, which began, as we know, in May 1965. He was employed as a patrolman by Night Security, Paradise Walk, from 6 October until 25 October 1964 (when he resigned) and his patrol included various factories on the estate.

He drank heavily and had been drinking on the night of 17 October, when he was found in the vicinity of the Renault factory on the estate and admitted to Middlesex Hospital with minor head injuries. He claimed that just before midnight he had been attacked by two unknown men, but was thought to have caused his injuries by falling. He returned to work but was off on 23 October, the date of Frances Brown's disappearance.

On leaving Night Security, Ireland found a job as a factory cleaner with the New Century Cleaning Company in Harlesden. He began work on 13 November, and on 28 November accepted the position of foreman cleaner on contract at Jute Industries in Dundee, the city of his birth.

While in Dundee he stayed with relatives; he declined the opportunity to spend holidays with his wife and family in London. His contract was ended on 8 February 1965, and he arrived back in London on 11 February, the day before the murderer, it was believed, deposited O'Hara's body on the estate.

He left his job five days before he committed suicide.

Why did he commit suicide?

I can't stick it any longer. This would appear to refer to emotional/domestic pressures. His wife, Elizabeth, stated that they had been on bad terms for some time. *It may be my fault but not all of it.* Was some of it hers? *I'm sorry Harry is a burden to you.* Harry was Mungo Ireland's brother. Drunkard? Invalid? *P.S. To save you and the police looking for me I'll be in the garage.* Aside from the obvious meaning, this may refer to the fact that on the morning of his death Ireland was due to appear at Acton Magistrates' Court to answer a summons for failing to stop his car, registration no. YUL 333 (not recorded in the car index).

Police found no evidence of any description to link this man to the murdered women, and the fact that Ireland was in Scotland on 11 January, the date of O'Hara's disappearance, served to eliminate him from the inquiry. He 'will therefore never be named' because he was framed, his suicide exploited for gain and glory by

John du Rose.

John Valentine Ralph du Rose.

By any other name he'd stink as sweet.

'Take your shoes off, please.'

You what?

What?

'Shoes.' She means what she says, and what's more there's a good 20 stone of her beneath that velour jogging suit.

I leave them by the welcome mat and follow her into the dining room. Music is playing; another woman awaits me at a table by the window. A bit younger, I would say (sixties, perhaps?), and more conventionally dressed. She is smiling.

'This is Mareth, who will be helping me. Mareth is Welsh.'

I smile back at Mareth, and shift my new weight from foot to foot. What do I do? Where can I go without my shoes?

Katy switches off the music (which had something in common with Bach's 'Air on a G String'). 'Do you like it?' she asks. 'It's classical music, with the jolty bits taken out. Sit down.'

Katy joins me at the table; reaching past the teapot and the oil burner, she proffers a small plate of gypsy tarts, and watches intently as I eat. She plants her hands on her knees and leans forward and stares, at me and at the space around me.

I turn uneasily to Mareth, who turns and smiles out into the night.

'He liked his pussy, didn't he?'

Mareth's face twitches in the glass. I wonder momentarily if she has thrown her voice.

'Yes, he certainly liked his pussy!'

It's Katy.

She nods at me, inviting me to speak.

I can't speak; I splutter cake into my lap, and the next minute the plate's on the carpet. Mareth retrieves it, and as she straightens her hand finds mine. 'The murderer,' she breathes.

Katy lights a Dorchester and a look passes between them, between her dark blue eyes and Mareth's pale blue eyes.

I've got green eyes.

Who am I, Katy?

'. . . pussy, yes, we both picked up on that . . .'

I am the customer.

I'm here to talk about death.

I ask her if she has studied the images I sent her. I tell her I realize she can hardly guarantee to summon the spirit of the murdered boxer Freddie Mills or any of the eight murdered women; that even if summoned any or all may refuse to speak to me through her; that tonight I shall be witness to an experiment and an experiment is defined by the possibility of failure.

'Nevertheless,' I add, rising from the table, 'nevertheless . . .'

It's my money.

Katy grunts, and exchanges another glance with Mareth before stubbing out her cigarette. 'Come on then.'

'Because he may well have been a policeman, perhaps retired, who knew the area better than most men . . .'

Owen Summers here cautiously alludes to a genuine suspect in the investigation. But this man did not retire from the police force; he was thrown out.

He was born in Middlesex in 1936, the son of a post office worker.

He had a grammar school education, and for his national service served as a corporal with the Royal Mechanical and Electrical Engineers. He joined the Met in October 1956, and in February 1957 was posted to B Division, where he served at Fulham and Notting Hill. In March 1961 he was appointed to the CID as a detective constable, and transferred to F Division. He served first at Kensington police station, and his former sergeant remembers him well.

'Well dressed, always spotless. Thick dark hair and a pale, podgy sort of face; full lips, a kind of sensuous look about his mouth. The eyes looked like a spaniel dog's; they bulged a bit, watery.

'He had no pals that I remember. Normally in the CID you'd pal up with somebody, but nobody seemed to be his pal.

'He was creepy, a creepy type of bloke, you know. He always seemed to be hanging around, and he always seemed to be bloody listening to other people's conversations. When I look back now I think, "How the bloody hell did he get in the CID?" That's what puzzles me.'

Strange days . . .

'At Kensington one of the detective sergeants had been out for a drink. He was what we used to call a first class sergeant; he was in charge of the office. He came in about midnight and smelled burning in the corridor. And he went into the Gents and it was full of smoke, and he found a lot of papers, burning, smouldering down in the bowl.

'They were my court papers! I had to take them with me to court the next morning, and somebody had taken them out of my tray.

'And then the crime book went missing. Now the crime book was like the bloody Bible; it looked like the Bible. And it went missing and we didn't know where it had gone.

'It turned up in Edward Square, just lying there, open, on the pavement. A passer-by picked it up and handed it in.

'After these two incidents we thought, "What the bloody hell's going on in the office?" We couldn't work it out. Now nobody said, "It must be him"; it wasn't like that. But eventually the finger started pointing at him.'

In January 1962 he sat and failed his detective sergeant's examination. In February he was transferred to Hammersmith police station for closer supervision.

'And then at Hammersmith this WPC's handbag was stolen. They saw this bloke running down the corridor, and she chased him, and two or three people chased him, but he ran up Shepherd's Bush Road, toward Shepherd's Bush Green, and they lost him.

'But I think somebody recognised him and the story came back: "It's him."'

In June he was transferred to T Division, where he served at Acton and Brentford police stations; but on 17 September 1962 he was suspended from duty and charged with five counts of office breaking.

At his trial he pleaded guilty to breaking and entering the office of Sycamore Ltd, Commerce Road, Brentford, and stealing nine paintbrushes and twelve files on 13 September; breaking and entering the office of Permutit, Commerce Road, and stealing a spanner and £11 on the same day; attempting to break into the office of the Admiralty Oil research laboratory, Great West Road, Brentford, with intent to steal on 16 September; breaking and entering the store of Coley Thermometers, London Road, Isleworth, between 15 and 18 September and stealing a quantity of tobacco. He pleaded not guilty to breaking and entering the factory of Julius Sax, Commerce Road, with intent to steal on 13 September, and his plea was accepted. He was sentenced to twelve months' imprisonment, and dismissed from the force.

The court heard that at 11am on 16 September Arthur Cox, a security officer at the Admiralty laboratory, saw a man on the roof with a green chisel. The man went down the fire escape and rode off on a moped. Cox managed to note down the registration number of the vehicle, which, it turned out, belonged to the officer in question.

When the attempted breaking and entering was reported to Brentford police, this man was the only CID officer on duty at the station and he took down the details. A uniform officer made a note on a pad of the number of the moped; this note was later found in pieces in the wastepaper basket.

As a result of enquiries the accused was told he would be placed on an identification parade, at which point he confessed to the offences. He did not know what made him do these foolish things, he said, but he had not been feeling too well lately. He spoke of a bump on the head.

This had occurred while he was studying at home during the

Hendon CID course. He became distracted by a noise in the street and went over to the sash window, pushing the bottom part up as far as it would go. As he leaned out, the window crashed down on the back of his head, rendering him unconscious. 'When I came to I felt a severe bump rising on the top of my head and this was very painful.'

Four days later the bump had disappeared, but an unbearable headache had begun. He sought treatment at St Stephen's Hospital, where a senior doctor expressed the opinion that he had picked up a bug of some kind. Four days later he was allowed to return home.

He completed the course and was posted to Kensington. 'I got on quite well at Kensington at first but after a bit I got the impression that my every move was being watched by other CID officers with whom I was working. This played on my nerves and I was very unhappy.' Yes, he stole the crime book. 'I found I was doing stupid things and then developing a technique whereby I convinced myself I had not done these things.'

He was transferred to Hammersmith, where he felt accepted and settled down happily. 'This happiness was marred by an incident in March or April 1962 whereby I felt I was being blamed and I felt how unjust it was.'

He was transferred to T Division, but at Brentford he felt the eyes of his colleagues upon him once again. One officer had the audacity to accuse him of theft. 'It was not true and I felt awful about it and my feeling was that I would never be left alone to work happily. After that incident I decided to show them and I have done things that I recognise now are utterly stupid. My feeling, wrong as it was, was that if they thought so strongly that I was a black sheep I will show them and be a black sheep.'

Detective Superintendent Maurice Osborn told the court that he had transferred the officer from Kensington to Hammersmith because 'I felt he was not mixing with his colleagues as he ought to do and in his work he was inclined to be rather careless.

'In June there was a complaint against him and he was dealt with for gross negligence and transferred to Brentford. Meanwhile he had applied to join the Surrey constabulary and was due to be transferred a few days after this matter arose.'

Maurice Osborn was to lead the investigation into the murder of

Helene Barthelemy in 1964, although it appears that the ex-officer did not come to William Baldock's attention until the following year. His report states that the man 'became a strong suspect about 14 days after the O'Hara murder on information received that he may have committed the murders and that he was a car salesman for an unknown firm in west London'.

The identity of the informant is not known, and it's possible that Baldock, who would almost certainly have been acquainted with the man's history, felt a hunch coming on. For he was beginning to discern something rather odd when he studied the wall map at Shepherd's Bush; something a bit, well, embarrassing.

Something which might just change everything.

Now Baldock believed, as did du Rose, that the deaths of Hannah Tailford and Irene Lockwood were cases of murder, and that these murders opened the series; yet he did not entirely reject the possibility that the six deaths which occurred in 1964–5 were linked to the death of Elizabeth Figg in 1959. Figg was found a mere 500 yards upstream from the spot where Lockwood surfaced, and, as proved to be the case with all the victims bar Tailford, none of her possessions was ever recovered. Figg had been interfered with; someone had inserted a finger (?) into her anus. But then someone had inserted a wad of paper into Frances Brown's vagina.

However, Figg had been *manually* strangled, and there was no evidence that she was stripped after death, only that she was redressed. Moreover, there was a gap of some four and a half years between her death and Tailford's.

No, he couldn't make up his mind about Elizabeth Figg. But he makes no mention of Gwynneth Rees in his report, having no doubt accepted that she probably died as a result of an abortion.

So Baldock settled for the final six, and tried once more to figure out why they were killed, and why their bodies were dumped in those particular spots.

A line on the map linking the six corpses formed a crude crescent radiating two to five miles from Shepherd's Bush.

So what?

What else?

Could it be that —

Each of the women was dumped in a different police subdivision — invisi-

ble boundaries which very few members of the public would know . . .

Hannah Tailford was found on FD subdivision (Hammersmith, divisional headquarters); Helene Barthelemy was found on TB sub-division (Brentford); Mary Fleming and Bridget O'Hara were both found on TA subdivision (Acton); and Frances Brown was found on FK subdivision (Kensington).

The man in question had served on each of these subdivisions during his six years in the Met.

The odd one out here was Irene Lockwood, whose body was found on the Thames foreshore on FC subdivision (Chiswick). But was she dumped there or did she merely drift there? Or was it her murderer's intention to throw her in at, say, Hammersmith, only to find himself panicked into off-loading at Chiswick? (Such a disaster may have sup-plied the spur to find a hiding place for the bodies.) Certainly from that point on the murderer chose to put his trust in land rather than water: no more open verdicts, no more mistakes.

Subtract Lockwood and that left:

Four subdivisions.

Five bodies.

Two fingers?

'I would like to point out again that when I broke into the premises I have mentioned I did not set out to steal but rather to have the sat-isfaction of doing something which I knew my colleagues would have to work on but get nowhere. I now strongly regret what I have done . . .'

Could this be the individual responsible? Could revenge supply the motive for the nude murders, a seemingly motiveless series of crimes?

It was necessary to find the man and find out.

He married in 1959, and at the time of his trial was living with his wife and baby boy in police married quarters, East Acton Lane (less than half a mile from the estate where O'Hara's body was found). Upon his release from Ford prison in June 1963 they went to live at an address in Leigh-on-Sea, Essex. The suspect was employed as a travelling salesman for a local battery firm until February 1964, when he left to work as a car salesman at the Hadleigh branch of Brew Brothers, a firm based in Old Brompton Road.

He was dismissed for inefficiency at the end of July but immediately obtained a similar position at Continental Cars, Leigh-on-Sea. He was working for this firm in February 1965, when investigations began. Essex police, working on behalf of the nude murders squad, kept observations on the suspect, recording the make and registration number of the cars he drove (none of which, it transpired, was recorded in the car index), searching any premises where he may have hidden bodies or clothing, and interviewing his associates.

In March he resigned his job and in June he changed his address, taking great care to keep his whereabouts to himself. Eventually he was traced to another address in Leigh-on-Sea, and on 4 August Baldock and du Rose called to interview him. He showed no surprise at their visit, and both he and his wife appeared unconcerned. He readily admitted that he was aware enquiries were being made about him and told his wife, 'They have come about what I mentioned the other month.' She made some reference to Brew Brothers. 'Not that,' he said, 'the other business which we joked about.' 'Oh, not the nude murders!' she exclaimed, and laughed. He denied any involvement in them.

The two officers learned that he resigned his job at Continental Cars on 30 March and was now working as a car salesman for Bright and Marshall of Hadleigh.

'I have avoided going to London owing to my previous trouble. I bear no animosity to the police force because I felt I'd let them down on the job and they may have felt bitter towards me.

'When I speak of London and west London I include the Notting Hill, Shepherd's Bush and Brentford areas . . .'

Since leaving prison he had spent the evening in London on just three occasions, all of them work-related. He put in two separate days at the 1964 Earls Court Motor Show, 'when I was employed . . . on the Volvo stand in the daytime and the Saab stand in the evening'. On these two occasions he had finished work at about 9pm and come home by tube and train, arriving at Leigh-on-Sea between 10.30pm and 11.15pm. ('I will have claimed my travelling expenses from my firm.') On the third occasion he attended a one-day Volvo sales course at the Washington Hotel, Curzon Street, in February 1965. Here he met an Essex business associate, a garage proprietor with whom he left the hotel. They had a cup of coffee in Shaftesbury Avenue and took a taxi to Liverpool Street Station, where the associate caught a train to Chelmsford and the suspect caught a train as far as Rayleigh, travelling the rest of the way by taxi and arriving home between 10.30pm and 11pm.

This associate was subsequently interviewed by PC Boon of the Essex police. He confirmed that he met the suspect, a business acquaintance, at a Volvo sales course at the Washington Hotel but stated that this course was held on 25 January. He corroborated the suspect's version of events, although he did not actually see him catch his train. In a letter dated 11 August PC Boon informs Detective Superintendent Baldock that the interviewee 'is well known to the police in this area, and has been very helpful to us on a number of occasions . . . He describes [the suspect] as a very "smooth" type of person, who he would not trust too far, and who he understands had a nervous breakdown in the not too distant past, although details of this are not known.' (Was this how he explained away his time in prison?)

Alexander Bowie, the managing director of Continental Cars, also confirmed that the suspect attended the sales course on 25 January: 'He travelled by train.' Bowie described him as a very good salesman who seemed to have a way with people, particularly women ('Women have described him to me as being very pleasant and charming'). He drove a company car, a white Saab saloon, and was allowed five gallons of petrol per week for demonstration purposes 'but he did in fact exceed this'. Bowie had a word with him about his heavy petrol consumption. 'I had no check for his actual mileage, it being very easy to disconnect the milometer.'

All car repairs and spraying for the company were carried out by Kent Elms Coach Company, Southend, although Bowie recalled his employee recommending M and B Repairs, Canvey, for cheaper panel repairs; 'but I never took this up with him'. (Dust and paint samples were obtained from the Canvey firm's premises, and from many other garages in the county with which the suspect may have had contact, with negative results.)

The suspect represented Continental Cars on two separate days at the 1964 Earls Court Motor Show. On 23 and 30 October he was employed on the Volvo stand from 10am to 5.30pm and on the Saab stand from 5.30pm to 9pm.

About 130 representatives were employed on each stand, and

according to Bowie the suspect could have left at any time, and for any length of time, without attracting notice; he might, say, have taken a prospective client to lunch, although he appeared to have stayed put, to judge by his expenses sheet. He claimed a total of £3 5s for both days. 'This would in fact show that this is his own expense, and that he had not entertained anyone to lunch during the course of the show.' On the other hand Bowie, who did not attend himself, had only this expenses sheet to show that his man turned up at all.

Further enquiries were made. A Mr Burn, managing director of Saab (Great Britain) Ltd, recalled seeing the suspect on the stand on both days.

But where did he go at 9pm on 23 October, the night Frances Brown disappeared?

Alexander Bowie corroborated his statement that he travelled to the motor show by train. 'As far as I am aware he went alone. He certainly did not go to the motor show with anyone from my firm.'

He knows where to find me at the flat. Two men, known to each other, driving round west London in separate cars on the night of 23 October . . . these facts certainly suggested salesmen from the motor show. Indeed the suspect bore a resemblance to the identikit drawing of the man who drove off with Frances Brown. Unfortunately Brown's companion Beryl Mahood, who helped police to prepare the drawing, failed to pick him out from their photograph album.

She got in the van and the man asked her how much she charged and before she could say what price she charged the man produced a small black card with the words 'Metropolitan Police' written in gold lettering on the outside. He said he was a CID man. Who was this man? In Vera Lynch's account he drove a small grey van, in the back of which was 'a lot of rubbish like clothes', and he supplied Frances Brown with what appears to have been an accurate description of the way in which the victims were murdered. He gave her a pound and a bit of a scare and shortly afterwards she was murdered as well.

Was this man the suspect? Did he seek her out to secure her silence? If he was the CID man, then it's highly unlikely that he was the man Brown was last seen with, for, as we know, *she* accosted *him*.

In the end William Baldock failed to build a case against the suspect. He couldn't place him in west London, or any part of London, at the relevant times, and he couldn't connect him in any way with the murdered women. All he had was a theory, concerning Metropolitan police subdivisions and a misfit's revenge.

It's an intriguing theory, and Baldock seems not to have considered its ramifications. In his report he writes that this man 'cannot be eliminated from the enquiry and it is felt that he is still a strong possible suspect. The circumstances surrounding his mental history, knowledge of the area and background are ideal in every respect for his being the murderer. If he is the man responsible he will certainly kill again in the absence of any precautions.'

Not necessarily, Bill, not . . . necessarily.

If – and it's a big if – this man were the murderer and revenge his motive, then he would have had good reason to stop when he did.

1 April 1965, the date of the formation of the GLC, saw the introduction of new Metropolitan Police boundaries. This reorganization of divisions and subdivisions, the first since the early Thirties, was designed to relate police boundaries to the new local authority boundaries created by the 1963 London Government Act.

And so from 1 April the suspect's elaborate taunts would have lost their significance. Bridget O'Hara's body may have been discovered on the TA subdivision, but a mere six weeks later TA became XA – and he hadn't worked on XA, had he? So where was the fun in it now?

Well, bad things, like good things, must come to an end. That's life, I suppose, and it doesn't mean you have to kill yourself. So let's just say:

The suspect did not kill himself.

He is not dead.

I hadn't realized Mareth would be joining us in the dark room, but here she is, slipping into the seat beside me, smoothing her dress out, all smiles.

I look where Mareth looks, and I look around me at the psychic drawings hanging in frames upon the walls. My eyes, never good, discern almost nothing. I face the front once more, and a sketch of a black vicar, weakly illuminated by infrared light, that hangs on the wall above Katy; and Katy.

Eyes shut, she lolls hugely before us in a high-backed chair, filling the room with her sighs. Ebb-tide sighs; beached-whale sighs, profound.

Five minutes more by my non-existent watch, and she returns to us. Yawns.

Speaks.

'Good evening. Tonight we have a . . . special evening . . . an unusual request. And we have brought forward some of our helpers to answer any questions that you may have.' Her eyes remain closed as she continues, 'I believe you are the one that would want to ask these questions, David. Have you anything specific you would like an answer to?'

Yes. Who killed Freddie Mills?

'The precise one was an officer . . . and I believe he is dead now, because he is on our side of life. He did not want . . . um . . . certain blackmail issues to come forward.

'There were quite a few — I'm looking at four people who worked with Freddie to . . . um . . . how would you say? . . . It was to gain . . . um . . . information . . . but Freddie Mills wanted them to stop having money and because . . . they still . . . wanted money . . . they . . . they had quite a . . . an argument.

'It's too late to go back now to that incident. Just know there was a big cover-up in the police force.'

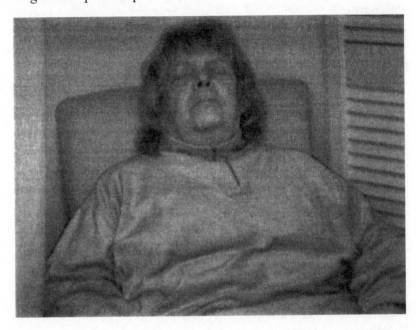

Who were the four?

'One of them ran a gymnasium . . . he was the one who owned the gymnasium. Was he Joe? It's a . . . name beginning with a J . . . it sounds a little bit foreign, but I am not being given the precise name.

'Why am I getting . . . drugs and undercover work? Mills knew unsavoury characters within the boxing world, and because he knew them he was being used by the police to find out more. They were looking into becoming involved for money and there were primarily two policemen who were involved in this.'

What were their names?

'One was a detective . . . an Ian came to mind. Ian . . . an . . . Ian . . . and . . . an Irish name . . .

'I am not being given this information. It has to be a closed book.'

How much did the Chinaman know and where does he fit into this?

'He did not see it. He knew there was more to it than was opened up at that time, but he could not change . . . anything, because he had no proof. I believe . . . um . . . he was involved with Freddie as the foreign gentleman.'

But he didn't own a gymnasium.

'No, he's not the owner of the gymnasium. That was somebody different.

'Why am I getting a connection to Cairo for some reason? I don't think it is to do with Mills. There was an Egyptian link but it is not the man you are looking for.

'I am going to step out and hopefully somebody else will come through, and bring something else forward.'

And with that she recedes into the gloom of her chair, and the sighing recommences.

But I don't have to wait very long: before I can turn and get Mareth's attention, Katy's back with us, sitting forward and nodding away. She opens her mouth (but not her eyes) and tilts her head doggy-style, as if listening to someone on the left of her. 'You have nice colours,' she says; pauses, and addresses me.

'I believe that you would like information. I'm sorry we cannot bring the actual people forward for you to talk to. They would have *all* the answers . . . but they are not . . . capable of this form of communication . . . and it is very difficult to get the truth out of a stone.

'What would you like to ask me?'

Was there more than one murderer?

'I believe that there were . . . two murderers. The majority, the bulk, were of one killer. Does that help?'

Could you be more specific?

'It's like . . . the first two were a different killer.'

But the first two were killed by the same man?

'Yes, and the last . . . this was . . . um . . . the name, it comes in and goes out. You'll have to wait until it comes in properly . . .'

How and where was the last one killed?

'She was taken to a quiet street . . . I'm getting . . . um . . . hands round her neck . . . a scarf or a . . . something pulled tight round her neck.

'She knew . . . a little bit too much and could not be left. Did this . . . um . . . she was found in a room . . . but she was killed in a car.'

It was definitely a car?

'Well, a vehicle on wheels.'

And she was found in a room?

'Or was this the plan, to put her in a room?'

What kind of room?

'Why am I getting the old-fashioned cars? There are people who are . . . he's no longer alive. He must have been in his fifties, sixties, when this all happened. He did not like women to ply themselves to men . . .'

It's only money.

'He was . . . um . . . he had pneumonia but he had something else before he got . . . he died with pneumonia but there was something else to cause that. I'm not being given this.'

It's my money.

'He died . . . not that long ago – not that long ago but he stopped. It's like something happened . . . happened to him, and it stopped him.'

It would have spent, anyway.

'The police did not get the evidence they wanted. They heard, and they followed up leads all over.

'Nothing seems to be precise. Nothing seems to be concrete.'

I suppose.

A car reverses in the distance.

Katy continues to talk ('I am only the spokesperson for a group of souls around here, and they are feeding me little pieces') but my attention begins to wander, as it always used to when I was a boy, in church on Sunday mornings, and I'd squirm and I'd groan and I'd dynamite the old place in my head.

Cannon, Joe, *Tough Guys Don't Cry* (Magnus Books, 1983)

Cox, Barry, Shirley, John and Short, Martin, *The Fall of Scotland Yard* (Penguin, 1977)

Du Rose, John, *Murder Was My Business* (W. H. Allen, 1971)

Galton, Ray and Simpson, Alan, *The Best of Hancock* (Robson Books, 1986; 1993)

Green, Shirley, *Rachman* (Michael Joseph, 1979)

Kennedy, Ludovic, *The Trial of Stephen Ward* (Gollancz, 1964; Penguin, 1965)

McConnell, Brian, *Found Naked and Dead* (New English Library, 1974)

Simpson, Keith, *Forty Years of Murder* (Harrap, 1978; Grafton Books, 1980)

24 Hours BBC1 2 April 1970

The Freddie Mills Story BBC1 27 December 1985

Reggie Kray: The Final Word BBC1 29 March 2001

I have benefited enormously from the kindness of the Metropolitan Police, who granted me access to all the available police files relating to the nude murders: MEPO 2/9895, MEPO 2/10292–10301, MEPO 2/10303–10318 and CR/201/72/60. These files are closed to public inspection; David Capus of Metropolitan Police Records Management informs me that they will remain closed for '100 years from the date of the last active minute'. I would like to thank Mr Capus and his colleagues Andrew Brown and Alan Oakley for their assistance in making the files available to me, and for the patience and courtesy with which they dealt with my many queries.

I have also made extensive use of MEPO 2/10756, on the police investigation into the death of Freddie Mills, and MEPO 2/10763, on Teddy Smith and the Kray twins, and have consulted CRIM 1/4136, on Colin Welt Fisher. All three files are housed at the National Archives in Kew.

I would like to thank the staff of the following institutions: Jeff Walden at the BBC Written Archives Centre; Blackpool Public Library; British Newspaper Library at Colindale; Caroline Hammond at Chiswick Public Library; Corinthian Sailing Club; Canterbury Public Library; Diane Clements at the Library and Museum of Freemasonry; Hammersmith and Fulham Archives and Local History Centre; House of Commons Library; Hazel Cook and Peter Grimwood at Kensington Central Library; Joanna Pateman at Maidstone Public Library; Nick Henwood at Margate Public Library; Metropolitan Police Museum; Metropolitan Police River Museum; National Archives; National Motor Museum; Richmond Public Library; Terri Hardy at South East Arts; Edda Tasiemka at the Tasiemka Archive; Westminster Coroner's Court.

I would also like to thank the following individuals: Leslie Bolland; David Cant; John Coulthart; Roger Crowhurst; Angela Deacon; George Geare; Norman Hamilton; Gareth Hancock; Roy Herridge; Peter Hill; Philip Luck; Bryan Martin; David Medina; John Medlock; Rod Pittam; John Salfleet; Keith Skues; Brian Smith; James Smith; Ron Turner; Anthony Woodgate; Stephen Wright; several others who prefer to remain anonymous.

Special thanks to: Alan, for sharing his reminiscences of the early Sixties with me, and for permission to reproduce three photographs he took in 1964; Joe Cannon for discussing his early career with me and for permission to reproduce his photograph of Freddie Mills and company; Jack Crane; Albert Donoghue; Frederike Gausling; Deborah Jones for her researches on my behalf; Paul Knapman for permission to inspect the inquest papers on Freddie Mills; Fred Lambert for his advice on matters Metropolitan; Gail Lynch and my editor George Miller for their support and enthusiasm; Arthur Phillips for his recollections of the Figg investigation, and for much else besides; Nigel and Eden Pittam; Steve Taylor for assistance far beyond the call of duty; Rebecca Wilson.

It is a final pleasure to record my immense gratitude to David Foulser and Anthony Frewin, without whom this book could not have been written.